THE EVOLUTION OF JAZZ IN BRITAIN, 1880–1935

The Evolution of Jazz in Britain, 1880–1935

CATHERINE PARSONAGE
Leeds College of Music, UK

ASHGATE

Published by
Ashgate Publishing Limited
Gower House
Croft Road
Aldershot
Hampshire GU11 3HR
England

Ashgate Publishing Company
Suite 420
101 Cherry Street
Burlington, VT 05401-4405
USA

Ashgate website: http://www.ashgate.com

British Library Cataloguing in Publication Data
Paronage, Catherine, 1976–
   The evolution of jazz in Britain, 1800–1935. – (Ashgate
   popular and folk music series)
   1. Jazz – Great Britain – History and criticism
   I. Title
   781.6'52'0941

Library of Congress Cataloging-in-Publication Data
Parsonage, Catherine, 1976–
      The evolution of jazz in Britain, 1800–1935 / Catherine Parsonage.
         p. cm.—(Ashgate popular and folk music series)
      Includes bibliographical references and index.
      ISBN 0-7546-5076-6 (alk. paper)
      1. Jazz—Great Britain—History and criticism. I. Title. II. Series.

      ML3509.G7P37 2005
      781.65'2'0941—dc22

2005005940

ISBN-10: 0 7546 5076 6

Printed and bound in Great Britain by MPG Books Ltd, Bodmin, Cornwall

Contents

Contents

List of Illustrations

Preface

'Jazz. Made in America. Enjoyed Worldwide.'

The slogan for the annual Jazz Appreciation Month organized by the Smithsonian Institution's National Museum of American History undoubtedly illustrates one aspect of the relationship between jazz as American music and the rest of the world.[1] Certainly, as jazz spread to Britain in the early twentieth century through the visits of musicians, American recordings and transatlantic radio broadcasts it was widely enjoyed as a new and vibrant form of popular music. However, the slogan characterizes America as the place where jazz is actively created and the outside world as where it is received relatively passively, whereas this book will show that the evolution of jazz in Britain was (and is) a more dynamic, passionate and reciprocal process. This evolution is unique to Britain and demonstrably more complex than a simple replication or reflection of developments in America. Moreover, the perceptions of, responses to and modes of engagement with jazz, which are a particular focus throughout this book, were often extremely diverse and fluctuated over time. Indeed, the enjoyment of jazz was frequently matched by attitudes of abhorrence in Britain.

The subject of the presence of jazz in countries other than America has been receiving increasing academic attention, as part of the growth of critical scholarship in jazz epitomized in Gabbard's seminal anthology *Jazz Among the Discourses* (1995). Gabbard's introduction, entitled 'The Jazz Canon and its Consequences' demands that the canonization of jazz, that was inherent in its incorporation within the academy as serious art, is countered by critical writing which is more aware of the processes and implications of canon formation. The consistency of the canon of 'great' jazz performers and masterpieces has led to a typified, linear history of the genre that has essentially served to strengthen and perpetuate the notion of jazz as 'America's classical music' (Gabbard, 1995:1-2). Subsequently, as E. Taylor Atkins, the editor of publication *Jazz Planet* (2003), has identified, the study of jazz outside its native America actively contributes to the reconsideration of the 'popular and rarely contested notion' of jazz as 'the product and reflection of a uniquely American national experience', epitomized in the Jazz Appreciation Month slogan and Ken Burn's recent documentary *Jazz* (Atkins, 2003:xxvii; Stanbridge, 2004).

Although detailed scholarly studies of jazz in countries including Germany, France and Japan have been produced in recent years, Britain has not been examined specifically or even included in Atkins's anthology. This is surprising considering the acknowledgement of the role of the country as a gateway for jazz to be disseminated in European countries such as Sweden (Fornas in Atkins,

---

[1] The JAM slogan was subtly altered in 2005 and now reads 'Jazz. Born in America. Enjoyed worldwide'.

2003:207) and Germany (Kater, 1992:7). However, there have been earlier publications on the subject of jazz in Britain, which have provided historical foundations for my own work. In particular, two authors have attempted a wider survey of jazz in Britain, Boulton (1959) and Godbolt, whose two volumes of *A History of Jazz in Britain* (1986 and 1989) have become the standard and largely unchallenged texts on the subject. In addition, Howard Rye's chapter 'Fearsome Means of Discord: Early Encounters with Black Jazz' in Oliver's *Black Music in Britain* (1990) presents a succinct overview of the area. Rye has also undertaken valuable work in establishing the movements of American musicians and groups in Britain in the 'Visiting Firemen' series published in *Storyville*. Brian Rust's discographies and John Chilton's *Who's Who of British Jazz* (1997) represent useful reference works.

In this book, I have attempted to take a critical view of the history of jazz in Britain in order to offer explanations of why the music evolved and developed in the way that it did, rather than documenting its presence. This has necessitated an approach in which the scope of consideration is widened, rather than focused by means of imposing a spurious definition of jazz. The wide scope has been absolutely vital in achieving insight into the reception of the music, and most fundamentally, this has involved abandoning modern received notions about what constitutes jazz. In attempting to understand what jazz meant to people in the early twentieth century in Britain, I have taken my lead instead from historical voices as much as possible, who repeatedly express that jazz was understood unequivocally as more than just a style of music. Indeed, the idea of jazz was represented in contemporary art, culture and society before its musical basis had been clearly articulated. The 'arrival' of jazz in Britain, which tends to be dated with reference to concrete musical manifestations of what may be appreciated in modern terms as in some way constituting jazz, can therefore be regarded as a retrospectively manufactured event, as the image of jazz had clearly pre-dated aural experiences of the music.

Commensurate with the wide consideration of 'jazz' is the variety of source material used in this study. Conventional musicological sources, where these even exist, can present particular problems for the study of jazz, in that sheet music of jazz compositions does not generally indicate performance practice, unlike recordings, but these too may not always be representative of the repertoire and style of live performances at a time when the technology was still developing and could limit recorded performances. However, cross-referencing recordings with contemporary comment can permit both the nature of these historical performances and their reception to be contextualized. Reviews from national, local and trade press have been utilized extensively as a way of assessing contemporary reaction to performances. Whilst it is recognized that these reviews represent a limited spread of opinion, they were also influential on the perceptions of a wider population of readers, especially when they were not able to experience these performances for themselves. The views of musicians are increasingly represented in the trade press over the period, but it is interesting to note that these can be at odds with the prevailing public opinion. Biography and oral history are also incorporated, with recognition of the possible differences between contemporary reactions and retrospective recollections.

In pursuance of assessing contemporary perceptions of jazz in Britain, the extensive theoretical writing that emanated from the country in the 1920s and 1930s is often used in favour of the more sophisticated modern texts. Although this early writing is frequently fresh and insightful, the inconsistencies, flaws, misunderstandings and prejudices, when evaluated in context, also provide rich sources of historical opinion. In particular, my work has been inspired by *The Appeal of Jazz* by R.W.S. Mendl, published in 1927, which the author claimed 'is the first book about jazz to be published in Great Britain' (1927:v). Mendl was educated at Harrow and University College, Oxford, obtaining his BA on 21 October 1915 (first class honours in Classical Moderations in 1913 and second class honours in *Literae Humaniores*).[2] He wrote several books on musical aesthetics and one on Shakespeare. Even in 1927, Mendl recognized the importance of jazz that had 'secured and still retains a more widespread vogue among its contemporary listeners than any other form of music ever known' (1927:80). Moreover, the book is exceptional, certainly for the period, in that the author sets out to evaluate the place of jazz in society and in the history of art.

There is a sense that no art, no matter how apparently radical and different, can be viewed and evaluated in complete isolation from everything that has gone before and the circumstances that surround it, and audiences will naturally bring their own experiences to bear when confronted with something new. The changing circumstances of life in Britain from Victorian times to the Depression of the 1930s provide the broad context within which jazz is evaluated. More specifically, the attitudes to America and particularly African-Americans in British society, which remained inherently linked with the images presented in black and blackface entertainment, profoundly influenced the reception of jazz in the twentieth century. Minstrelsy is one example of popular culture that would not be conventionally identified as jazz but was vital in shaping the future development of the music, which is the case for many of the musicians and most of the music under consideration in this book. Similarly, styles such as 'dance music' and 'symphonic syncopation', frequently written off as inauthentic white imitations, were responses to what the contemporary public believed to be jazz, thereby rendering them of fundamental importance in this study.

In recent years, the place of jazz within the academy has become arguably more assured, and it is recognized that jazz has relevance and status as popular and art music. However, jazz has often remained a specific and marginalized area within musicology, and it seems timely for jazz to become implicit in both contemporary and popular musicology, having been excluded from the former due to its popular status and the latter as a result of the emphasis on artistic qualities that ensure its legitimacy as a field of study. Jazz has played an integral and influential part in the evolution of music in the modern world, particularly multifarious popular forms. This study of the evolution of jazz re-establishes fundamental relationships that exist between different genres of popular music. This provides the necessary

---

[2] Information courtesy of Oxford University Archives.

foundation for the understanding of later developments in popular music in Britain.

Although this book is essentially historical in nature, rather than presenting a chronological narrative, certain aspects are examined in much greater depth. As such, it is by no means comprehensive in that not every musician, band, venue or circumstance that might be deemed relevant is included. Rather, a series of case studies are presented in Part II, each of which consists of a detailed investigation of a particular group, period or idea. This book is not particularly concerned with establishing historical facts as a means to an end, although this process is often inherent. Salient analysis of the available information has enabled a comprehensive understanding of these individual cases and their role in the holistic evolutionary processes, and these studies are used in series to formulate conclusions and hypotheses about trends and their causes.

In addition, in order to be able to research in sufficient detail to reach meaningful conclusions, some limitations have necessarily been imposed on the parameters of this book. Firstly, the study is centred on London, principally in order to limit the wealth of material to be taken into account. It is recognized that the situation in London was not always replicated consistently throughout the country, and it is hoped that this book will encourage detailed studies of jazz in other areas that will surely yield interesting results. Secondly, this book focuses on the period 1880-1935. Although this time span is not rigidly enforced and reference is made to events outside this range, these dates were not chosen arbitrarily. It was in the 1880s that an important American musical craze, the banjo and its music, hit Britain as the culmination of the nineteenth century popularity of minstrel shows of which this instrument was a significant part. American banjo players performed, recorded, passed on their skills and were accepted into the highest society in Britain. Conversely, the increasing opposition to American musicians in Britain resulted in the imposition of official governmental restrictions in 1935 that remained in place for the next twenty years.

The Evolution of Jazz in Britain thus encompasses the antecedents of jazz, the processes through which jazz evolved, and subsequent developments in the genre in Britain. In Part I, *Historical and Theoretical Perspectives*, Chapter 1 establishes the context of popular music and society in Britain in the nineteenth and early twentieth centuries, and investigates the presence of American entertainment in Britain that provided the cultural and musical antecedents for jazz. In particular, the popularity of the minstrel show is examined to assess the development of racial attitudes and musical expectations. The visits of minstrel troupes also established the movement of theatrical productions from New York to London and *visa versa* that was essential to the later importation of jazz. Chapter 2 examines the image of jazz that evolved in Britain before jazz bands themselves became commonplace. The rapid formation and wide dissemination of the idea of jazz through sheet music of songs demonstrates the importance of the consideration of manifestations of the genre other than live performance. Finally in this part, Chapter 3 is concerned with the historical and theoretical background of the reactions to jazz in Britain in the extended 'jazz age' of the 1920s and early 1930s. The idea of jazz as the music representative of the changing spirit of the age is explored with reference to the social context of the period and contemporary theoretical writing by Mendl,

Lambert, Nelson and Adorno that was the earliest extensive jazz criticism in Britain. The influence of the broadcasting and recording 'culture industries' and the changing attitudes to race on the reception and perceptions of jazz are of particular interest. Chapter 3 concludes with an examination of the growth of popular criticism in the late 1920s alongside electrical recording, which together led to a deeper understanding of jazz, prompting new modes of engagement with the music.

In Part II, *The Evolving Presence of Jazz in Britain*, six specific areas are the subjects of detailed analysis. Chapter 4 is a consideration of the content and reception of the American production of *In Dahomey* that was performed in London in 1903. This show was significant as the first all-black production on Broadway, and is also notable for the quality of Will Marion Cook's music. *In Dahomey* was very successful in London, and provokes interesting comparisons with the reception of nineteenth century minstrel shows. Chapter 5 focuses on the music and symbolism of the banjo, an instrument that had a continuous presence in American music in Britain throughout the period under consideration. In particular, the black banjo bands that visited Britain during the second decade of the twentieth century are evaluated as the immediate precursors of jazz. Chapter 6 examines the visits of the two American ensembles widely cited as the beginning of jazz in Britain: the Original Dixieland Jazz Band and the Southern Syncopated Orchestra. The former often and the latter occasionally are mentioned in the available literature on jazz, but extensive comparisons of their respective performances and reception have not been made, although the consideration of the situation of one white and one black group of American musicians performing contemporaneously in London is extremely informative. Accounts of popular music and jazz in Britain in the 1920s have tended to focus on the dance orchestras that performed in upper-class hotels and on the early BBC radio service. Chapter 7 offers a detailed analysis of the bands associated with the Savoy Hotel that formed the backbone of the BBC's popular music output in the 1920s as a response to the image of jazz that had been established in Britain in the preceding years. However, there was also a continued presence of American musicians in Britain that is considered in this chapter. British dance bands were influenced by the 'symphonic syncopation' introduced Paul Whiteman and George Gershwin and perpetuated by other white American groups, but black musicians mainly visited within the context of 'plantation revues' which continued to present the familiar minstrel stereotypes. Significantly, performances by American musicians and especially black American musicians became increasingly restricted during the decade and jazz was increasingly forced into the underworld of London. Chapter 8 considers the incorporation of hot jazz into British popular music as a result of direct contact and recordings of American musicians in the late 1920s. The reactions of Jack Hylton, Bert Firman and Fred Elizalde to hot jazz will be examined through analysis of the circumstances of their live performances and the legacy of their recordings. This period was fundamentally important in the development of jazz performance and criticism in Britain, particularly as the input of American musicians was already becoming increasingly restricted. Finally, Chapter 9 contextualizes the visits that Louis Armstrong and Duke Ellington made to Britain in the early 1930s. These musicians, unlike some earlier American visitors, were already known to a limited extent in Britain through their recordings, which were being imitated by British musicians before their arrival. This chapter centres on comparative analysis of the reception of Armstrong and Ellington's first performances in Britain. The debates that surrounded these appearances provoked extensive comment and reassessment of the criteria for evaluating jazz. However, contemporaneously with the recognition of the importance of the black American contribution to jazz, restrictions on American musicians in Britain were being formulated and finally imposed in 1935.

This book not only sheds new light on the history of jazz in Britain, but also contributes to the critical development of the de-canonization and re-canonization of jazz proposed by Gabbard. Consideration of jazz in Britain brings figures from the periphery of the American canon to the fore because of the influence that they exerted in Britain. It also offers an entire alternative canon of 'local heroes', that is, musicians, composers and critics that may have been 'innovative but influenced noone' (Atkins, 2003:xxii). Although jazz was increasingly recognized in Britain as primarily American music, there is evidence throughout the period that jazz was also adopted and developed in ways that were appropriate to the social and musical situations in which it was performed in Britain. As a result, by 1935 not only 'jazz in Britain' but also 'British jazz' can be identified.

General Editor's Preface

The upheaval that occurred in musicology during the last two decades of the twentieth century has created a new urgency for the study of popular music alongside the development of new critical and theoretical models. A relativistic outlook has replaced the universal perspective of modernism (the international ambitions of the 12-note style); the grand narrative of the evolution and dissolution of tonality has been challenged, and emphasis has shifted to cultural context, reception and subject position. Together, these have conspired to eat away at the status of canonical composers and categories of high and low in music. A need has arisen, also, to recognize and address the emergence of crossovers, mixed and new genres, to engage in debates concerning the vexed problem of what constitutes authenticity in music and to offer a critique of musical practice as the product of free, individual expression.

Popular musicology is now a vital and exciting area of scholarship, and the *Ashgate Popular and Folk Music Series* aims to present the best research in the field. Authors will be concerned with locating musical practices, values and meanings in cultural context, and may draw upon methodologies and theories developed in cultural studies, semiotics, poststructuralism, psychology and sociology. The series will focus on popular musics of the twentieth and twenty-first centuries. It is designed to embrace the world's popular musics from Acid Jazz to Zydeco, whether high tech or low tech, commercial or non-commercial, contemporary or traditional.

Professor Derek B. Scott
Chair of Music
University of Salford

Acknowledgements

During the years that I have been researching jazz in Britain I have been extremely fortunate in the help and support I have received from many individuals and institutions. Above all, I wish to express my gratitude to the late Gerry Farrell, who supervised my PhD at City University. Gerry was an inspirational and dedicated educator and a warm and generous person, and I feel privileged to have benefited from his knowledge and insight.

The Arts and Humanities Research Board supported my doctoral research and provided a travel grant to enable me to undertake a study visit to the USA in 2001. Leeds College of Music has contributed to the costs of my postdoctoral research. I would also like to thank my colleagues at LCM for their practical and emotional support, in particular Tony Whyton, whose vigorous approach to academic debate has been much appreciated. Krin Gabbard and Barry Kernfeld very kindly read and commented on drafts of this book. Dave Webber provided useful feedback on the Ellington and Armstrong material. I also express my appreciation of Derek Scott's consistent support of my work.

Some of the material in this book has been previously published as 'A Critical Reassessment of the Reception of Early Jazz in Britain' in *Popular Music* Volume 22 (3): 315-36 and is reprinted here with the permission of Cambridge University Press and as 'Jazz in Britain in the 1920s' in the *International Association for Jazz Education: Jazz Research Proceedings Yearbook 2003* edited by Larry Fisher and reprinted with the permission of the IAJE.

I have made use of many archives, libraries and museums in my research. I would like to thank the staff at the Barbican Library, British Film Institute, British Library (especially Rare Books and Music and Humanities 2 Reading Rooms), City University Library, Newspaper Library at Colindale, Public Records Office at Kew and Westminster Music Library. I would particularly like to thank the following for taking the time to assist me with specific enquiries: Jeff Walden, BBC Written Archive; Edward Lamberti, British Board of Film Classification; Jacqueline Cox, University of Cambridge Archives; Suzan Griffiths, St Catharine's College, Cambridge; John McCusker, leader of the 'Cradle of Jazz Tour' in New Orleans; Liz Fawcett, Jack Hylton Archive at Lancaster University; David Nathan, National Jazz Archive; Andrew Simons, National Sound Archive; Alice Blackford, Oxford University Archives; Robin Rodger, Perth Museum and Art Gallery; Pamela Clark, Royal Archives, Windsor; Mark Pomeroy and Laura Valentine, Royal Academy of Arts Archive; Susan Scott, Savoy Group Archive and Dr Robin Darwall-Smith at University College, Oxford. Nick Jones at the Max Jones Archive provided many of the wonderful photographs that illustrate the book and Pete March and Ned Newitt were generous in lending their personal collections of Bert Firman material.

During my visit to America, I was privileged to access a wealth of archival information with the guidance of Vincent Pelote and Dan Morgenstern at the Institute of Jazz Studies, Rutgers University, Newark, New Jersey, Charles Chamberlain and Bruce Boyd Raeburn at the William Ransom Hogan Archive of New Orleans Jazz, Tulane University, New Orleans, Louisiana and Deborah Gillaspie at the Chicago Jazz Archive. I thank them for their hospitality and willingness to answer my questions. Exhibitions in the following museums were of great help and interest: the Calbido (Louisiana State Museum), New Orleans, Tate Britain, Theatre Museum, Museum of London, New Orleans Jazz Museum in the Old Mint, New Orleans and the Victoria and Albert Museum.

Finally, I would like to thank Will Michael, a truly inspirational educator who first introduced me to the fascinating world of jazz, my travelling companions, Alison and Heather, and my former housemate and drinking partner Lippy. Dan has been a constant source of love and support and I am most grateful for his computational excellence.

List of Abbreviations

BBCWAC   British Broadcasting Corporation Written Archives Centre, Caversham Park, Reading

HJA   William Ransom Hogan Archive of New Orleans Jazz, Tulane University, New Orleans, Louisiana

IJS   Institute of Jazz Studies, Rutgers University, Newark, New Jersey

NJA   National Jazz Archive, Loughton Public Library, Loughton, Essex

ODJB   Original Dixieland Jazz Band

TNA: PRO   The National Archives: Public Records Office, Kew, London

SSO   Southern Syncopated Orchestra

PART I
HISTORICAL AND THEORETICAL PERSPECTIVES

Chapter 1

The Cultural and Musical Antecedents of Jazz in Britain

The established view of the history of jazz in Britain is that it began in 1919 with the arrival of the Original Dixieland Jazz Band and Will Marion Cook's Southern Syncopated Orchestra. Although these visits were undoubtedly important events, as these were the first bands that came from America to specifically perform jazz music, this premise is clearly an over-simplification for a number of reasons. Firstly, sheet music of jazz compositions, including those of the Original Dixieland Jazz Band, had been published in Britain since at least 1917 and was widely available.[1] Recordings made by this band may also have been heard in Britain prior to their 1919 visit. Secondly, the *Dancing Times* had reported as early as January 1918: 'A fearsome thing called "Jazz music" has reached us from the other side of the Atlantic: it has been described as "syncopation runs riot". What its effect will be, time alone can show.' (January 1918:126). The word 'jazz', then, was in general use in Britain before 1919, albeit in various contexts and layers of meaning, but this in itself illuminates the wider picture of the development of the genre in this country, which will be considered in Chapter 2.

Most significantly, to examine the evolution of jazz in Britain beginning in 1919 fails to take into account the cultural and musical antecedents of the genre, including the complex evolutionary pattern of events in the history of American culture and music in Britain, which fundamentally influenced the way in which jazz itself was perceived and received. Many black and blackface performers came to Britain from America during the nineteenth century, beginning with individual performers who took their place on the music hall bills alongside native artists, and later complete minstrel troupes of sixty or more entertainers (Pickering, 1986:72). Although the music performed by these groups was not necessarily musically related to jazz, the importance of their performances as both antecedents to jazz as an American music and as part of popular culture in Britain should not be under-estimated. In addition, consideration of popular culture in Britain in the pre-jazz period provides a framework for analyzing the encounters and reactions of the British public to earlier forms of American syncopated music. Therefore, the 1919 visits described above should be examined as part of a well-established pattern of visiting American musicians and entertainers touring in Britain and Europe. The

---

[1] The British Library Collection contains three compositions by the Original Dixieland Jazz Band published in Britain in 1917; *Ostrich Walk: Jazz Foxtrot*; *Sensation: Jazz One-step*; and *Tiger Rag: One Step* (contained in h3828.yy). The first songs in the collection published in London and containing the word 'jazz' in the title are also from this year.

various responses to jazz can then be understood within the historical and social, as well as musical, context of Britain in the early twentieth century.

The Victorian period was particularly rich in musical entertainment and there is evidence that the Victorian middle- and working-class population was actively involved in music in a number of ways. The period has been described by Ronald Pearsall as 'the age of both the large choir and the small piano' (1973:12). Amateur choirs and brass bands were prolific, the former gained in popularity due to the teaching of tonic sol-fah from the 1840s. Choirs also formed an important part of the popular political movement, with musical performance becoming a metaphor for socialist fellowship ('the act of performing and its social context mattered more than the music performed' [Russell, 1987:55]) as well as a way of communicating political messages. The competitive music festival movement also began at this time. Pianos and pianolas were to be frequently found in homes and became central to domestic music making. Musical activities were encouraged by the developments in printing which made a huge amount of sheet music available to the general public, including music hall and minstrel songs.

In addition, Victorian upper-class philanthropists organized concerts for the ordinary people in an 'attempt to broaden popular cultural horizons'. This even went as far as presenting orchestral performances in the streets, which were known as 'court and alley' concerts (Russell, 1987:35). There is evidence of the popularity of serious concerts and of operas staged by touring companies during the Victorian period among the lower classes (Russell, 1987:69). Popular opera melodies were also the staple repertoire of other musical entertainment including music hall, and arranged for brass band and even heard on barrel organs on street corners. As a result, 'not that many Victorians drew a sharp distinction between serious and popular music' and 'middle class tastes ranged easily from religious arias to popular tunes' (Read, 1979:84). This meant that most people were familiar with a wide range of music whatever their social class, and this mix of musical styles also characterized the music hall, which was 'the most highly organized sector of the entertainment industry' at that time and as such, significant, as a 'prefiguration of the mass entertainment business of the twentieth century' (Russell, 1987:72).

The music hall evolved throughout the Victorian period from 'song and supper rooms' and 'pubs which had been extended to include a singing saloon' (Kift, 1996:2). Derek Scott has pointed out that:

> The tavern concert room, with its lower-middle-class patrons and professional or semi-professional entertainment, has a more direct link to the music hall than do the song and supper rooms around Covent Garden and the Strand, which were frequented by the aristocracy and wealthy middle class. (2001:216)

Purpose built halls began to exist from the 1850s in the suburbs and spread steadily during this decade into the city centres. London experienced a music hall boom in the early 1860s 'with the help of a new law which allowed the setting-up of limited companies' (Kift, 1996:21). The music hall was firmly established as a national institution from the 1870s through syndicates that set up halls in smaller provincial communities, and enabled acts to tour throughout the country (Russell, 1987:77).

Contemporary writers on music hall have not always made explicit the links between this flourishing tradition and the large numbers of visiting black and blackface American performers in Britain in the nineteenth century, but it seems likely that they often performed within the established shows, and certainly at the same venues. The blackface performer, T. 'Daddy' Rice, famous for his Negro impersonation and song 'Jump Jim Crow', was an early visitor to Britain in 1836. Blackface minstrel troupes such as the Virginia Minstrels, the Ethiopian Serenaders and Christy's Minstrels arrived from the 1840s, followed by black minstrel troupes such as Hague's, Callender's and Haverley's in the second half of the century. As individual members often remained behind after the troupes had departed, black performers must have been well represented on the British music hall stages and 'the 'nigger' minstrel remained a ubiquitous entertainer in Britain until the end of the [nineteenth] century' (Pickering, 1997:181). Heindel states that 'by 1905 one-third of the music-hall performers were Americans' (1940:330) and 'a great deal of American music was known in England' at this time (Mackerness, 1964:222).

Whilst 'the history of Negroes in Britain in the nineteenth century [has been] largely a matter of conjecture' (Field and Haikin, 1971:1), recent research has challenged the previously held assumption that 'all black people in Britain during the era of slavery were enslaved, and that they were all household "servants"', and has illuminated the variety of occupations in which black people were employed (Sherwood, 2003; Fryer, 1984). Walvin suggests that the black population of Britain had been in gradual decline from 1800 (1973:202) and 'by the end of the century the majority of them seem to have been absorbed in the population' (Field and Haikin, 1971:1), as there is evidence that they intermarried with white Britons (Sherwood, 2003). When discussing the response of white South Americans to black culture, Christopher Small states that 'white people have always viewed black culture with a mixture of fascination, fear and even envy' (1987:141). These emotions must have been even more concentrated in nineteenth century Britain, where the 'absence of any significant black population meant that minstrelsy appealed ... for different reasons than in the United States' (Pickering, 1986:81). British audiences were fascinated with the exoticism of the Negro character and culture, and minstrels developed a great novelty value as entertainers. Indeed, despite 'a few isolated grumbles from snobbish gentlefolk about its stage inanities or street disturbances, minstrelsy was subject to very little ideological censure' (Pickering, 1997:183). Among the lower classes, black performers may have been regarded 'as much with a self-regarding sympathy as with a self-appeasing pity' (Pickering, 1986:84). Thus, black music and entertainment had already begun to develop 'the power to seize the imaginations of so many different kinds of people ... a phenomenon which still lacks a satisfactory "official" explanation' (Small, 1987:11). Similar widespread appeal amongst people of different classes was to be a feature of the reception of jazz in Britain.

Black people would certainly have been familiar in Britain as subjects of artistic and literary caricature since the eighteenth century (Walvin, 1973:159), and contemporaneously, plays were beginning to use slave life as a subject (Nathan, 1962:13). The dominance of whites in blackface in early minstrel shows, who presented 'essentially grotesque imitations of black plantation life in the South', established certain features that were expected in the performances of later black minstrel troupes, that also blacked up and presented 'an imitation of an imitation of plantation life of Southern blacks' (Sampson, 1980:1). This included exaggerated physical characteristics, psychological traits including music making, dancing and stealing, and standardized, romanticized images of plantation life (Pickering, 1986:85). Blackface stereotypes could easily become established as permanent truisms in the mind of the British public who had limited acquaintance with black people. The early blackface performances established expectations that not only influenced the reception of black minstrels, but, aided by the latter's perpetuations, established criteria against which black performance continued to be evaluated in the twentieth century.

Two specific and important factors emerge in the British reception of minstrelsy that can also be observed in reactions to jazz, and exemplify Small's idea of 'fascination, fear and even envy' in the white reception of black culture. Firstly, the idea of the Negro as 'primitive' influenced the positive reception of black entertainers in Britain as representative of a culture that was fascinatingly 'other' in its simplicity. Specifically, an innate musicality was considered to be one of the characteristics of the otherwise 'primitive' Negro, an idea that was confirmed through the centrality of music in the minstrel show. The banjo became the instrument most closely associated with black music due to the minstrel show, and developed a clear musical and symbolic identity. This had important long-term effects on British perception and reception of African-American music that will be examined in Chapter 5. At the same time, the 'primitivism' of the Negro could engender an attitude that black culture was fundamentally inferior in an extension of 'scientific racism'. This imagery was also used in support of colonialism, particularly in British Exhibitions in the late nineteenth and early twentieth centuries (Sherwood, 2003). In the 1920s, the lingering assumption that all black culture was 'primitive' and therefore needed to be injected with a healthy dose of 'civilized' white culture was to influence the value judgements which were made by white Britons about jazz. Yet, jazz also had appeal as an exotic music at this time, which like minstrelsy, whose protagonists opposed 'the dominant moral and institutional order' of the Victorians, offered escapism to British audiences by providing an 'inverted image of society' (Pickering, 1986:88-89).

Secondly, although the popularity of minstrel shows demonstrates that 'there was need in white culture for what black culture had to offer' (Sidran, 1981:32), black entertainment that was understood to be founded on realism was less popular than versions presented by whites in blackface. The apparently threatening nature of the 'realistic' portrayals of black culture to the British public is shown by problems encountered by Sam Hague, who brought an all-black troupe to Britain in 1866. In the end, Hague had to replace most of the troupe with white, blacked-up performers 'as the public seemed to prefer the imitation nigger' (Reynolds, 1927:165). Likewise 'the Haverley Coloured Minstrels [visiting in 1881] did not meet with the same amount of success as the Haverley Mastodon [white] Minstrels in 1880' (Reynolds, 1927:207). The resulting competition between black and blackface minstrel shows would have increased the pressure for black minstrels to conform to white stereotypes for their survival. The threat of 'genuine' black minstrel performers was clearly being felt in Britain as late as 1912, as one writer commented:

> When the nigger-minstrel can wash his race off after office hours he is harmless; but the true negro singer is often a dangerous fellow to be let loose in a hall - we dare not be so familiar with him. (Titterton, 1912:213)

Similarly fearful responses to black performances can be observed in the reception of jazz. In particular, the perceived threat of the overtly sexual nature of black people, which Walvin suggests was taken for granted by the English by the early nineteenth century (1973:163), recurs as a principal reason for the opposition to black culture in Britain in the twentieth century.

Minstrelsy was introduced to Britain against a background of vigorous debates over slavery. The abolitionist movement was extremely strong in Britain in the early nineteenth century, and public meetings and appeals on behalf of the cause continued even after British participation in the slave trade had ended and the Emancipation Act had been passed. It had become fashionable for 'idle ladies' and rich philanthropists to patronize emancipation societies (Little, 1948:206-207). The movement was fuelled by the publication of abolitionist literature and the visit of Martin Delany in 1860 (Fryer, 1984:275). The pro-slavery movement also gained in strength through the economic arguments of Thomas Carlyle in his *Occasional Discourse on the Negro Question* published in 1849 and 'pseudo-scientific' racism, which also provided justification for the expansion of the empire: 'The golden age of British empire was the golden age of British racism too' (Fryer, 1984:165).

Although generally 'minstrels thrived upon an appeal to the anti-slavery sentiments of their audiences' (Lorimer, 1975:40), minstrelsy was in a way as much of a yoke to black people as slavery, as in order to ensure their success, minstrels had to present entertainment that adhered to blackface stereotypes and was 'a reflection of the prevailing attitudes of the day' (Small, 1987:149). Minstrel shows included elements that could be used in support of both sides of the slavery debate; on one side sufficient anti-slavery sentiment, and on the other, the acknowledgment of the improving influence of whites. This was typical of the inherently paradoxical nature of the presentation of black characteristics in minstrel shows, including 'faithful servant/indolent laborer, Christian/sinner, patient slave/lustful, vengeful savage' (Pickering, 1986:85). As a result, 'whenever the Victorians considered the position of a black man, they could conjure up an image of a patient suffering slave, a comic minstrel or a cruel lustful savage to fit the particular situation' (Lorimer, 1975:45). Walvin shows that an understanding of the Negro as being 'sexual, musical, stupid, indolent, untrustworthy and violent', characteristics that could be observed in minstrel performances, could be used to justify slavery (1973:160). Blackface Negro characters could be easily imitated, and thus further exaggerated and disseminated, by British street performers and amateurs. Certainly, just as 'long after the material conditions that originally gave rise to racist ideology had disappeared, these dead ideas went on gripping the minds of the living' (Fryer, 1984:190), the widespread dissemination of the peculiar mixture of black characteristics in the minstrel show amongst different classes of people and throughout Britain via the established national chains of venues was significant in forming the basis of both positive and negative reactions to black culture.

The legacy of minstrelsy and slavery can be observed with reference to the Fisk Jubilee Singers, a choir of young African-American students who were attempting to obtain funding for university buildings on a visit to Britain in the early 1870s. The group was fortunate enough to secure the admiration of the Earl of Shaftesbury who organized a concert that was attended by many influential people. Subsequently the Singers were invited by the Duke and Duchess of Arygll to perform at Arygll House in the presence of the Queen who 'listened with manifest pleasure' (Marsh, 1902:50). Royal patronage was extremely important for visiting black musicians, as it exerted influence on the general public as well as providing the artists with all-important publicity. Stimulating philanthropic interest was essential to the fundraising of groups such as the Jubilee Singers and the Jenkins Orphanage Band. Many subsequent visiting artists gave command performances that ensured their success in Britain, for example the *In Dahomey* company in 1903. On one hand, the Singers' performances demonstrated direct opposition to minstrelsy in that their presentation demanded serious attention. The strength of the abolitionist feeling in Britain meant that the group was received with considerable sympathy and enthusiasm as their performances evoked memories of slavery and offered redemption and 'moral rectitude' for their 'liberal patrons' through the religious messages of their songs (Gilroy, 1993/R2002:90). Conversely, the success of the Singers could also support the idea that slavery was beneficial to Africans as they could be converted to Christianity and thus 'improved' (Walvin, 1973:170). Even as late as 1927, Mendl commented that spirituals 'are filled with a pathos and a nobility and a devotional fervour which were the spontaneous outcome of a people torn from their homes and who found their solace in the great religion of the oppressed, Christianity' (1927:30). Paul Gilroy has pointed out that the Jubilee Singers were frequently assessed with direct reference to minstrelsy, as critics struggled to find suitable criteria with which to evaluate their performances. This demonstrates that minstrelsy had become synonymous with black culture, and indicates that there were difficulties in reconciling these black people with the familiar and expected minstrel stereotypes (Gilroy, 1993/R2002:88-9).

Minstrelsy was so influential upon British perceptions due to its success within the evolving popular culture in Britain in the nineteenth century, and hence became 'one of the most prominent forms of entertainment in the nineteenth century, both inside and outside the music hall' (Pickering, 1986:70). The minstrel show provided a culturally interesting novelty for the Victorian public, fuelling the 'keen appetite for new forms of popular entertainment in the newly industrialized towns and expanding metropolis' (Pickering, 1997:191). Initially at least, minstrelsy was probably seen as an extension of the caricature, clowning, melodrama and sentimentality already existent in the British music hall, but with an extra dash of exoticism due to the racial characteristics, imitative or otherwise, of the performers, who emphasized these for maximum effect on their white audiences. In addition, Pickering suggests that visiting performers made adaptations to ensure their success in Britain, such as including an orchestra and musical director, and drew particularly upon sentimental and comic aspects that were already inherent in contemporary British popular culture (Pickering, 1986:76). The flexibility of the minstrel show format, particularly within the 'olio' section in the centre of the show, allowed the introduction of 'new and spectacular elements', prefiguring the twentieth century variety show (1986:75).

Minstrels appealed equally to the philanthropic upper class as to the empathetic lower class; groups that increasingly played their parts in the formation of late-nineteenth century music hall and variety show audiences. The wide repertoire of music presented in music halls (for example, performances often included an operatic overture) led to them being regarded by Victorian philanthropists as a source of musical education for the lower classes (Russell, 1987:88). In this context, it seems likely that minstrelsy could be considered to be a musically and culturally educative experience, as it had 'quickly established a reputation for respectability and propriety that was long maintained' (Pickering, 1986:73). The continuing concern of the abolitionists, together with natural curiosity about Negro life and culture which fitted in well with the philanthropic desire to use the music hall for the education of the masses, meant that minstrelsy was novel but yet respectable family entertainment. In addition, widespread belief in the 'primitive' myth advocated that minstrel shows presented 'authentic' Negro culture that was basic, simple and even spiritual. Thus, minstrel performances continued to be appropriate within the increasingly civilized late nineteenth century British popular culture.

The rise and fall of minstrelsy in Britain is closely allied to that of the music hall. Whereas early music hall was 'financed by the sale of alcohol, and in many cases, the entertainment on offer did not correspond with what was regarded as socially acceptable' (Kift, 1996:2) over time, the music hall lost its vulgar associations. From the 1870s, proprietors 'not only moved sales of alcohol and drink completely out of the auditorium, but also replaced the rows of tables by fixed rows of seating. The internal architecture of halls increasingly came to resemble that in the theatres' (Kift, 1996:22) and the entertainment became increasingly respectable (Scott, 2001:216). These new standards ensured that eventually smaller informal institutions were wiped out and music halls became more respectable and began to appeal directly to the middle and upper classes.

The addition of new social classes to the music hall audiences in the late nineteenth century meant that theatre managers now had to pay more careful attention to the tastes of their clientele, and 'by conceding to middle-class tastes the halls had become detached from their popular roots and lost a considerable amount of vitality' (Kift, 1996:25). In particular, 'performers no longer had any great say in shaping the programme along with the audience and were overwhelmingly restricted to conforming to a set time-table' (Kift, 1996:61). Theatre managers in the Edwardian period were increasingly concerned with commercial success rather than the educative potential of their shows, continuing a trend in the development of music hall entertainment. Kift suggests that even 'by the 1860s educational components had almost completely disappeared from the music-hall programme' (1996:58). Access to art music, formerly integrated within the music hall or street entertainment, was often provided separately by cheap concerts at venues such as the People's Palace and the coffee music hall at the Old Vic (Scott, 2001:121) from the 1880s. Proprietors of central London music halls in the late nineteenth century had to provide a diverse programme of 'respectable' and novel entertainment to entice an audience drawn from various social classes (Kift, 1996:62), and therefore popular music began to develop a specific function as an alternative to highbrow art music.

Just as traditional music hall developed into civilized variety theatre, the standardized minstrel show format had become increasingly outdated and also began to dissolve (Pickering, 1986:77). However, nineteenth century minstrelsy had established strong links between British theatrical promoters and African-American performers which laid a firm foundation for subsequent visits in the twentieth century, and thus helped to pave the way for the presentation of jazz in Britain. In the late nineteenth and early twentieth centuries, most American musicians were brought to Britain through these pre-existent theatrical channels. Although it seems unlikely that any large minstrel troupes visited Britain after the 1880s, undoubtedly individual performers continued to be featured on the West End variety stage. The flexibility of the variety show format allowed foreign acts to be included within British popular culture and to be disseminated widely through the national networks of venues. Although the traditional minstrel show was not as popular as it had been, many of the American musicians who visited Britain in the late nineteenth and early twentieth centuries were directly linked to and actively built upon the popularity of minstrelsy in Britain. These include, for example, the large numbers of solo banjo players that visited Britain to record and perform, and all-black groups such as the Memphis Students, who were presented as a novelty act on the variety stage, as well as Will Marion Cook's show, *In Dahomey*. Members of these two groups were later founder members of the Clef Club, an organization that was established in New York in 1910 to promote black musicians. The exploitation of the long-standing contacts between Broadway and the West End by the Clef Club was instrumental in the visits of three important black pre-jazz ensembles and later the Southern Syncopated Orchestra.

Novelty and variety remained fundamental to popular entertainment, and for these reasons cinematograph and bioscope presentations were initially easily incorporated into music hall and variety theatre. The rise of the cinema is important when considering musical life in the early twentieth century, as the silent films all required musical accompaniment that ranged from a solo pianist or organist to a full orchestra and was therefore an important source of work for musicians. The first cinema opened in 1907 and became popular with young members of the working-class who became 'a brand-new public for mass entertainment' (Read, 1979:421). There is evidence of use of new American music to accompany films, 'imported by a ship's musician on the Atlantic run' (Ehrlich, 1985:199) may well have been the first exposure of the young audience to the new 'syncopated dance music'.

Musical comedy became a central form of popular theatrical entertainment at the turn of the century, as is shown by the popularity of selections from the shows for brass band (Russell, 1987:71). Musical comedies of the period were 'self-consciously modern', often including the latest fashionable clothes and commenting on contemporary life (for example, *In Town* of 1892 was based on life in London (Pearsall, 1975:19)). Other shows reflected the contemporary trend for the exotic, such as *The Geisha* (1896) and *A Chinese Honeymoon* (1901) (Pearsall, 1975:21). In 1903, the African-American composer Will Marion Cook presented *In Dahomey*, which was an early example of a new type of black musical entertainment that aimed to elevate black culture away from minstrelsy. This show was very successful in Britain, as it reflected the vogue for exoticism (due to the whole company being black) and light-hearted musical comedy at this time.

The establishment of routes from the theatrical communities of America, specifically New York, to London, were exploited not only by African-American musicians but also by the producers of revue shows that were responsible for introducing the latest trends from across the Atlantic. This included ragtime and later, jazz, both in terms of the presentation of the actual music and also the attendant symbolism and metaphor. Extensive transferring of shows between London's West End and Broadway in New York began as early as 1898 with the presentation in London of the musical comedy *The Belle of New York*. All things American became fashionable in pre-War Britain, and in his book *London in my Time*, Burke states that:

> The first quarter of this century, indeed, may be known to history as London's American phase, since the major part of the many and rapid changes it has suffered may be traced to America ... . The bulk of our entertainment is American in quality and largely in personnel. (1934:35)

Albert De Courville, a producer and impresario, was a particularly important figure in the development of the American-style revue in London. As a journalist, De Courville had travelled widely, and had seen American revue shows in New York (De Courville, 1928:52). De Courville was employed by Sir Edward Moss to secure the necessary attractions to 'make the [London] Hippodrome pay' (De Courville, 1928:77), and he immediately began to import foreign acts and then to commission new musical comedies for the theatre (De Courville, 1928:92). Eventually, to reduce costs, he began to write and produce his own material, influenced by American ragtime revues, of which he wrote: 'The new rhythm fascinated me. It seemed to fit into the atmosphere of revue marvellously, as its tempo was suitable for chorus work.' (De Courville, 1928:97). De Courville continued to import American performers, and was responsible for booking African-American musicians such as Joe Jordan's Syncopated Orchestra for the revue *Push and Go*, Louis Mitchell for *Joyland*, (both in 1915) and Dan Kildare and Harvey White for *Hullo America* (1918). After the War, De Courville was responsible for importing the Original Dixieland Jazz Band for another Hippodrome revue, *Joy Bells*.

Hullo Ragtime, the first in the series of American-style revues presented by De Courville at the Hippodrome, and was apparently seen by 400,000 people (Pearsall, 1975:185), defined and popularized ragtime in Britain in 1912. The revue included

American artists such as Shirley Kellogg and Ethel Levy and was a huge success, as De Courville recalled:

> I do not think I am exaggerating if I say it was one of the biggest successes that has ever been put on in London. We were sold out for weeks ahead, and the show ran nearly a year, playing twice daily to figures which I had never dreamed of at the Hippodrome. (De Courville, 1928:108).

De Courville's description of the orchestral rehearsals for *Hullo Ragtime* shows that ragtime was unfamiliar to the musicians at the Hippodrome:

> Syncopated music had to be played in a certain way ... . I used to insist on the American melodies I had brought over being played in a certain way, with a proper sense of rhythm and syncopation. I met with all sorts of protests when trying to achieve this object. They told me it was not music. To keep the balance I had brought over a trap drummer and a cornet-and-trombone player from America. Jones [the leader of the orchestra] told me that their playing was something quite new and against all principles of music, but nevertheless he agreed with me that the syncopated rhythm was effective. (De Courville, 1928:105)

American revues established orchestrated ragtime songs rather than solo piano ragtime as the standard manifestation of the genre in Britain. As piano ragtime was hardly represented at all, this helped to ensure that the banjo-based bands remained central to performances of pre-jazz syncopated music in Britain and perpetuated minstrel imagery. This will be discussed further in Chapter 5.

Minstrel shows and revues not only brought American performers to Britain but also provided a direct insight into American life, albeit in exaggerated form. It was through revue shows that the British public was initiated into the latest pre-jazz dances and music, either directly through watching the show or indirectly through the various sheet music publications. The publication, wide dissemination and subsequent domestic performance of songs from American revues followed the same pattern as earlier music hall songs, and numbers such as Irving Berlin's *Alexander's Ragtime Band* could make 'traditional popular music out of date almost overnight' (Pearsall, 1976:10). The resulting vogue for American culture led to the replication of dances and music in the most fashionable London clubs and increased the demand for the latest styles. Therefore, it was as theatrical entertainment and as accompaniment for dancing that the first jazz songs and bands were brought to Britain.

Chapter 2

The Evolving Image of Jazz in Britain in Sheet Music

Music theatre, and in particular the revues produced by Albert De Courville at the Hippodrome in the period 1912-1919 (detailed in Seeley and Bunnett, 1989), was fundamental in introducing American fashions of all kinds to Britain. The popularity of ragtime reached its peak in Britain through the revue *Hullo Ragtime* (1912) and the earliest 'jazz' song contained in the British Library sheet music collection was included in *Box o' Tricks* (1918). However, it was not the music of these shows that defined either ragtime or jazz as musical styles, as most of the songs, including those that specifically referred to these genres, used a standardized musical idiom that was related to the music hall song and often included some syncopation. Rather, it was the verbal and visual imagery associated with these musical styles, presented in the song lyrics and dances of the revues, which provided the earliest clear descriptions of these genres. The popularity of these shows led to the importing of American sheet music and the publication of songs in Britain. As this sheet music could easily be disseminated outside London, it was very important in establishing the image of ragtime and jazz throughout the country.

The growth of the sheet music industry ran in parallel with the evolution of jazz in Britain and, before the widespread use of recording and broadcast technology, this was the main way in which music of all types was disseminated. There was certainly a great demand for sheet music around the turn of the century, and popular hits could sell as many as 200,000 copies (Ehrlich, 1989:5). The popularity of sheet music is shown by the widespread piracy where 'material was hawked on the street of London and provincial cities, in vast quantities and at a fraction of its legitimate price' (Ehrlich, 1989:8). The sheer scale of the music publishing industry is extremely significant, especially when considered in conjunction with the estimate that 'by 1910 there were some two to four million pianos in Britain – say one instrument for every ten to twenty people'. Therefore, ownership of pianos, and hence sheet music, was 'by no means confined to the middle classes' (Ehrlich, 1990:91). In addition to the publication of songs from American revues, trends of all types were reflected in contemporary song in Britain, a feature inherent in the music hall tradition of humorous, satirical parody of public figures, fashions and events. This led to the composition and publication of British songs, influenced by American models, that described jazz as it became the latest fashion. Therefore, many people would have experienced jazz initially, or even exclusively, particularly outside the main cities, through domestic music-making rather than live professional performances that tended to take place in socially exclusive venues.

The importance of printed music in forming a public perception of jazz cannot be underestimated, and it is informative to examine the evolving image of jazz in the proliferation of sheet music available from the period. This chapter will investigate these perceptions through a socio-cultural examination of the image of jazz created in songs from contemporary shows that were published in London, as it can be assumed that these would be known in Britain.[1] Songs published in America were also available in this country, but it is also clear that only a few of the songs published in London were also published in America[2] or written by known American composers and lyricists. This confirms the presence of a group of British composers and lyricists writing songs in an American style for the British public.

The *Dancing Times* reported in 1919: 'The Jazz was always primarily a word. It was a word which to some suggested the acme of poetical motion, while to others it conveyed conceptions of the lowest depths of immorality and degradation.' (September 1919:544). The analysis in this chapter will focus primarily on lyrics and title page illustrations,[3] rather than an extensive musicological evaluation of the jazz elements used.[4] In many cases the song accompaniments are simple and chordal, which may indicate that they were being aimed at the domestic market. Some songs incorporate elements such as complex syncopation, dotted rhythms, 'breaks', triplet patterns, and repeated rhythmic and melodic motifs that show the influence of the syncopated banjo music that was the prominent popular and dance music in early twentieth century Britain and can be seen to prefigure jazz. Although these elements became part of a style that was by no means unique to songs with lyrics concerned specifically with syncopated genres, it is noticeable that the accompaniments of some later songs, especially those that describe a 'jazz band', make greater use of these features. This suggests that by 1920, jazz had begun to develop some kind of musical as well as symbolic identity, which will be discussed later. However, more often it seems that the writers of these often topical and era-specific songs were under pressure to produce

---

[1] These songs will be referenced in the text using the British Library volume number. A full list of songs consulted with detailed information is contained in Appendix 1.

[2] Through comparison with the songs contained in the online sheet music database of Duke University in the USA, it can be assumed that very few of the composers of songs published in London were American. (http://scriptorium.lib.duke.edu/sheetmusic/)

[3] Unfortunately, very few of the songs considered here have title page illustrations. Derek Scott has suggested (in a seminar given at the Institute of Historical Research for the Music in Britain Seminar Group entitled 'Music Hall Cockney: Flesh and blood or replicant?' on 14 February 2000) that the lack of illustration on the covers of songs in the nineteenth century implied that the song was aiming to be more upmarket. However, in the case of the latter part of the period 1900-1919 it is more likely that economising due to the effects of war was responsible for less lavish publications.

[4] A similar aim is expressed by Leppert in relation to his study of the depiction of music in art in the eighteenth century: he aims to examine 'not just 'how it looked' but 'how it was made to look in art'' (1988:4).

new compositions that reflected ever-changing fashions and trends, including music and dance, but also extending to matters such as politics, celebrities and dress, and necessarily worked at speed. For this reason, many of the songs considered here are stylistically very similar and often formulaic in structure, as Stanley Nelson observed: 'Occasionally one is struck by the melodic or harmonic aspect of a particular number, which raises it above the mass but this is rare, and a regular harmonic and melodic routine is usually followed' (Nelson, 1934:29). Although songs have limited use as a resource for investigating the *musicological evolution* of jazz, the retrospective examination of the lyrics gives a clear idea of the *image* of jazz that was presented to the British public.

It is easy to see the popularity of jazz in Britain as simply a result of the increasing American influence on many aspects of British life and culture. However, retrospective analysis of contemporary song lyrics illuminates jazz as a replacement for the previous ragtime craze, which was rejected for various reasons by a surprising number of songs, almost all written as early as 1912-1913. Songs mention as one reason for this the age of the music and the craze associated with it, for example in *Goodbye Mr Ragtime!* [h3989.d(5)]: 'Ragtime really has to go, its getting old and tottering with age', suggesting that the replacement dance will be the tango. Similar ideas about the tango are evident in the media from this point onwards, illustrating the ability of songs to accurately reflect the trends of fashionable society.[5] More importantly, this establishes that ragtime was regarded primarily as dance music in Britain and would probably be encountered in performances by the banjo bands that played for dancing rather than solo pianists. This was an important factor with regard to the way in which jazz was to evolve in Britain.

Two songs reject not only ragtime, but also the whole idea of dance crazes. One song is entitled *Don't Sing in Ragtime!* [h3994.hh(10)] and suggests that 'To abstain from all these crazes for a time will do us good' and the song *There ain't going to be any ragtime* [h3994.cc(24)] continues:

> There ain't going to be any dancing
> No not even the old cakewalk
> But just for once we're all going to all sit round
> And have a nice quiet talk.

In *Don't Drive Me Crazy with Your Ragtime Song* [h3996.e(26)] and *I Don't Want a Ragtime Coon* [h3994.jj(48)], the rejection of ragtime is linked with race:

---

[5] The revue *Hullo Tango* was presented at the Hippodrome in 1913. Josephine Bradley, a leading dancer and dance instructor in Britain at this time, described how the craze for the tango was 'interrupted' when war broke out in 1914 (1947:9). It was then that the foxtrot began to evolve and there was a move away from set dance patterns towards dancing that was more improvisational in character.

> I don't want a ragtime coon
> I don't like his ragtime tune
> His syncopating and his hesitating
> Won't set my heart palpitating.

The story of how ragtime 'died' is told in *Who Killed Ragtime? A Modern Nursery Rhyme* [g1520.pp(11)] which includes references to the supposed roles played by prominent public figures of the time, such as Emmeline Pankhurst and Lloyd George, showing that ragtime was very much within the spirit of the age. Another reason for rejecting ragtime is given in the song *Change that Rag into a March Refrain* [h3990.t(34)], written in 1915, which implores bands to 'Play a military march instead [as] that's the sort of tune we're needing now', suggesting that ragtime music was inappropriate in a time of war. The song ends:

> Goodbye to ragtime! We can do without it
> Play up that march tune there's a charm about it
> Change your evening dress to khaki brown and just bid your sweetheart goodbye!

Later, in a jazz song of 1919 [h3993.e(45)], ragtime is explicitly rejected in favour of jazz, and as this is the chorus of the song, it receives particular emphasis.

> Heigho, jazz it with me
> It's easy as easy can be
> It's better than ragtime or any zig-zag time
> Maggie come jazz it with me.

This song describes a man who 'was crazy on ragtime', but goes on to say that 'one fatal night he yelled with delight/"I've just learned to jazz and it's great!"'.

Initially, the use of the word 'jazz', particularly in song titles, added to the general confusion about what it actually meant. As musical styles tended to evolve and change much more slowly and infrequently than the associated nomenclature, fashionable words such as 'rag' or 'jazz' seem to have been applied to music and songs more or less indiscriminately, and had little meaning as names of musical styles. The *Dancing Times* reported as late as February 1920:

> It has become fashionable to call any band that has a trap drummer and some banjoists a Jazz band, but I am sure that in nine cases out of ten the nomenclature is wrong and the band quite harmless. (February 1920:350)

The fact that American syncopated styles had been the basis for most popular dance music in Britain from the late nineteenth century meant that jazz was perceived, initially at least, as merely another dance craze. The *Literary Digest*, an American magazine, reported:

> The latest international word seems to be "jazz". It is used almost exclusively in British papers to describe the kind of music and dancing – particularly the dancing – imported from America, thereby arousing discussions, in which bishops do not disdain to participate, to fill all the papers. (26 April 1919:28)

The speed at which various dances fell in and out of fashion meant that the names of the associated musical styles were often used synonymously for periods of time. Therefore, it was difficult for the distinctive characteristics of particular forms to be defined and understood. This was particularly true with pre-jazz instrumental pieces, where the terms 'ragtime', 'cakewalk' and 'two-step' were used interchangeably or in various combinations until at least 1905 (for example *The Manhattan Cake Walk: A Rag-time Solo for Mandoline* [h188.j(8)] and *General Jasper Jones: Cakewalk Two-step* [h1981.g(34)]), and a similar confusion in nomenclature is also demonstrated by contemporary song lyrics. The first three 'ragtime' songs published in Britain (in 1900-1901) all mention the cakewalk, the contemporary dance trend. The subject of *I Love My Little Honey* [h1654.rr(27)], described as the 'latest rag effusion', is in fact a visit to a cakewalk competition:

> The coons they had a cakewalk this summer
> Of course I had to take my baby Hannah
> Well when she commenced to dance
> The niggars knew they had no chance.[6]

The song *I'm Certainly Living a Ragtime Life* [h3986.ss(11)] seems to define ragtime as only a characteristic of cakewalk music, rather than a specific musical style. The song over-emphasizes the word ragtime, applying it as an adjective to everyday objects and practices, but as soon as music is mentioned the term is dropped 'cakewalk music fills the air/It can't be dodged because its ev'rywhere'. This suggests that in 1900, ragtime had yet to establish itself as a distinct musical style, although the word was widely used in society.

The lyrics of 'ragtime' and 'jazz' songs in the period 1900-1919 have many common themes, of which the link between music and dance is the most prevalent. Developments in social dancing in Britain in the twentieth century can be closely linked with the use of American syncopated music in the theatre. The show *In Dahomey* (1903) had solidified the popularity of the cakewalk in Britain, and subsequent revues brought numerous ragtime dances that were fashionable before and during the War. Towards the end of the War, revues began to include 'jazz' songs and dances, and the first songs to contain the word 'jazz' in the title were published in Britain in 1917. Shows throughout the period 1900-1919 generally utilized a standardized musical style and orchestration and this meant that there was an initial lack of musical distinction between jazz and other popular forms, such as ragtime, other than in terms of the characteristics of associated dancing. Initially, there were numerous references to jazz within the pages of the contemporary dance press, but there were no publications that dealt specifically with jazz as a musical style until *Melody Maker* and *Rhythm* in the mid-1920s. The verb 'to jazz' meaning 'to dance' (for example in the quotation from *Heigho! Jazz*

---

[6] Many of the song lyrics considered here use what would nowadays be considered offensive and racist language. It must be remembered that at the time at which these songs were written, terms such as 'nigger' and 'coon' were widely used and were not usually considered particularly offensive by whites.

it with Me above) was extremely common in song titles and lyrics and was certainly encountered more frequently than the noun 'jazz' denoting a musical style. The majority of early jazz songs contain the phrase 'jazz band', and describe the reactions of people to performances by these groups, including many references to dance.

The language used in connection with dance in song lyrics throughout the period 1900-1919 is remarkably consistent, and establishes jazz as part of a long tradition of American dance forms in Britain. Ideas associated with jazz were rooted in earlier ragtime songs, and in jazz songs the imagery is often taken further and made more explicit. The infectious nature of the music is often emphasized, and expressed through the inability of anyone listening to keep still, suggesting that the music had a strong power over the listener, for example the ragtime billiard player [h3988.uu(40)] 'often makes a thousand break/But he still can't keep still!'. The same idea is specifically linked with the music of a jazz band such as in *Stick Around for the New Jazz Band* [h3991.ii(5)] 'Lordy, honey, Oh! I can't keep still' and *When I Hear that Jazz Band Play* [h3996n(22)] 'Say what you will, you can't keep still while they're playing'. Several songs make the point that once you have started dancing it is impossible to stop: 'And if you take the chance, you will want to dance/Right through the night 'till the break of day' [h3993e(9)] and that this activity could result in exhaustion, as the ragtime band 'Makes me dance till I can hardly stand' [h3991t(44)].

The nature of the movements associated with dancing is also referred to in song lyrics. In ragtime songs, this tends to be a list of stylized dance steps:

> Inside the ballroom bands are gaily playing
> Ragging the music, see those dancers swaying
> Two-steps and tangos and ragtime fandangoes
> Argentine sliding and Gaby gliding.
> [h3990.t(34)]

Apparently jazz was initially regarded as an addition to this list. An advertizement for Rector's club in the February 1919 edition of the *Dancing Times* described 'foxtrotting and jazzing to the tune of a banjo band' and the editor of the *Dancing Times* had published *The Darewski Jazz Chart* (1919) which provided a diagram of the main step used for jazz dancing, with the comment: 'It is known as the jazz, and causes the couple to progress in a zigzag fashion, and should therefore be used sparingly in a crowded room'.

The extremely rapid evolution, apparently within just a few months, of the ideas associated with jazz dancing can be seen through the examination of contemporary dance magazines. An article in the April 1919 edition of the *Dancing Times* asserted that 'as for the Jazz dance – there is no such thing. There is a step that may be introduced into the foxtrot, one-step or valse which is called the Jazz step' (April 1919:248). Two months later, the magazine reported that 'the real trouble is that there is nobody to say with real authority what the so-called Jazz-step really is' (July 1919:439). In September, an article described 'The Passing of the Jazz-Roll', a step that dancer Josephine Bradley described as 'slow, quick, quick' but which turned into a 'long gliding movement' that 'revolutionised dancing' (Bradley, 1947:12) and then became absorbed into foxtrot dancing. By the time of the November 1919 issue, there was acknowledgement that 'the word 'jazz' refers to the music and not to the dancer's movements' (November 1919:86). This opinion may well have been influenced by Irene Castle, a leading authority on dance at the time, who asserted that:

> ... there is no such dance as the "Jazz" and anyone who tells you there is wrong ... the nigger bands at home [America] "Jazz" a tune, that is to say, they slur the notes, they syncopate, and each instrument puts in a lot of little fancy bits of its own ... . (quoted in Pearsall, 1976:56)

Articles in the *Dancing Times* indicate the increasing lack of specificity of 'jazz' as a dance and early recognition of its characteristics as a musical style that took place in Britain during 1919. Likewise, in later jazz songs, unlike ragtime songs, there are no references to specific dance steps, and lyrics emphasize the freedom now permitted to dancers. This indicates the increase in improvised dancing that developed alongside jazz music, confirmed by Josephine Bradley, who commented that 'Improvisation was rife' in the ballroom at this time (1947:13). W.W. Seabrook, writing in *Brightest Spots in Brighter London*, noted the individuality of dancing where formal steps were abandoned and described that in nightclubs there were 'so many people, each executing his or her own peculiar style of dance to the same tune' (1924:138). The song *Jazz!* [h3988.yy(1)] encouraged dancers: 'When you hear that rhythm – just go with 'em – jazz jazz!/For when the music's playing start in swaying – jazz jazz!'. One song even goes as far as to suggest that the intense physical activity associated with dancing to jazz could lead to serious injuries:

Let our arms entwine,
Come and bruise your knees on mine,
Till you dislocate your spine.
[h2452(33)]

The word 'swaying' is often used in jazz songs to describe the movements of the dancers: 'You can't resist you start to twist while you're swaying' [h3996.n(22)]. The word itself suggests that the music had an almost hypnotic power over the listener. The Javanese Jazz Band 'Makes you happy and it makes you dance' and when listening to the music 'You can't make your feet behave' [h3996f(43)]. Similarly in *Everybody Loves a Jazz Band* [h3993.e(9)] 'your feet 'er goin' to make your body sway'.

The increasingly improvisational nature of modern jazz dancing probably made this style intimidating for dancers used to the previously strict conventions of ballroom dancing. The *Dancing Times* encouraged dancers: 'Do not, if you are a temporary stranger to the ballroom, be kept away by fear of the Jazz. He is not so fearsome as the Press would make one think.' (February 1919:157). Similarly, song lyrics indicate that there was a perceived risk, expressed as having to 'take a chance', associated with the sort of dancing which required participants to lose their inhibitions to the music. Initially it was difficult to resist: 'You want to dance, so take a chance/Come on and hear that Jazz Band music!' [h3991.ii(5)]. Some songs take this idea further, describing the hypnotic power of the music, which has the ability to exercise control of the minds of the listeners. The performance of the Javanese Jazz Band 'Hypnotizes, puts you in a trance ... . Of those notes your mind is a slave' [h3996.f(43)], and similar power is attributed to the music in the song *Rag-Time Crazy* [h3995.jj(30)] 'That mysterious rag I cannot slip/I'm in the grip/I've got ragtime on the brain'.

The words 'craze' and 'crazy' are used very frequently in songs, particularly in connection with dancing. These are often juxtaposed and mixed even within the same song, as it is the overwhelming and infectious enthusiasm for music which is constantly heard and provokes a compulsion to dance ('craze') that drives people to a state of madness ('crazy'). Many songs emphasize the universal extent of the enthusiasm for ragtime: 'Ev'ry one has got the ragtime craze' [h3986.ss(11)] and jazz: 'Ev'rybody's got the jazz band craze' [h3996.u(24)]. The same idea is expressed in ragtime songs using the word 'rage', as in the song *The Rage of Ragtime* [h3984.yy(37)], but this word is never used in connection with jazz. The idea that music also has the power to make people crazy by controlling their minds is frequently explored in the lyrics of ragtime songs, in fact there are two songs called *Rag-time Crazy* [h3995.o(14) and h3995.jj(30)] which assert respectively that 'Ev'ry one seems crazy with ragtime on the brain' and 'Ev'ryones raving ragtime mad/The youngster the mother and the dad'. This is explored further in some songs such as *The Rag-time Craze* [h3995.j(46)] 'The music sends you simply mad' and ultimately in *Don't Sing in Ragtime* [h3994hh(10)] 'We're right on the brink of it, brink of it, brink of what? Of the lunatic asylum'. Similar ideas pervade jazz songs such as *The Jazz Band Cabaret* [h3994xx(47)]:

> Ev'ryone's crazy tonight.
> Oh! what a mad refrain,
> Gee! there it goes again,
> Join in this whirl of delight.

Surrendering to the power of the music through listening or dancing is shown in some lyrics to create a mood of reckless abandon, for example: 'Come and hear the Ragtime band play Dixie ... And you'll feel like jumping o'er the moon!' [h3991.t(44)]. A similar reaction is provoked by a jazz band 'Something they do, I never knew just makes me/Feel oh! so good that I could throw myself away' [h3996.n(22)]. In most ragtime songs the results of this are usually left to the imagination, but the risk associated with surrendering to the music is made clear in *Come and hear the Ragtime band play Dixie* [h3991.t(44)], which suggests that ragtime music is a threat to domestic stability: 'It's a tune I'd leave my happy home for ... . Put your arm in mine, for there's danger on the line when the band plays Dixieland'.

The nature of this 'danger' is shown more explicitly in jazz songs, which demonstrate that the music can provoke excesses of emotion: 'Oh! My it nearly makes me cry/Oh! Gee it seems to creep right over me does that jazzipated melody' [h3995.b(8)]. This can easily lead to possibly illicit romantic activity: 'I've got a heart so big, come on and hug me kid/Hug me and don't ask why.' [h3994.xx(47)]. The hypnotic power of jazz can have a similar effect, as in *The Jazz Band Cabaret* [h3994.xx(47)] 'While the band plays music to mesmerise/You'll find rapture deep in somebody's eyes'.

The link between dance and sexual attraction is made explicit in some later songs. The presumably 'ordinary' Rag-time Postman Bill seems to be universally popular with women due to his dancing abilities as 'When he goes by all the girls cry' and 'Parlour maids and nurse maids banish their pride/Throw their arms around his neck and do the wedding glide' [h3996.f(47)]. The syncopated characteristic of ragtime is used as a sexual image in the sentimental ballad *Ragtime Kisses* [h3990.o(1)]:

> I'll teach you how the syncopations go
> And I'll kiss you in ragtime while the band plays below ... .
>
> Just you and I dear together in Ragtime ecstacies quite new
> Those syncopating palpitating kisses and you.

Dancing, or 'jazzing' is used as a more direct sexual metaphor in jazz songs, with the new independence permitted by improvisational dance equating to the increasing sexual liberty and freedom of women in social situations. In *Heigho! Jazz it With Me* [h3993.e(45)], jazz dancing is linked with flirting: 'She wore the Jazz skirts and like all the Jazz flirts/Maggie didn't object to a squeeze'. In the same song, Maggie's uncontrollable flirtatiousness and promiscuity due to jazz leads to inappropriate activity:

> One day on a bus oh! There was such a fuss
> That poor Maggie she could not keep still
> She grabbed the conductor, a fat old conductor
> And Jazzed with him till he was ill.

In *The Coster Jazz Song* [h3991.r(24)] a woman describes how her partner Bill, a lower-class man, is able to mix with the upper classes and secure the affections of women due to his dancing ability: "E's took to dancin' nah and I'm as jealous as can be/'Cos all the gels 'e dances wiv gets mash'd on 'im yer see'. This song suggests that in 1919, jazz dancing was primarily an occupation of the upper classes, and a form of entertainment towards which those in the lower classes could only aspire. Certainly, in London at this time the venues for dancing to jazz, luxurious hotels, restaurants and clubs such as Ciro's and Rector's, would only be open to those with money and social connections. It was not until October 1919 that the opening of the Hammersmith Palais de Danse, which presented what P.J.S. Richardson, editor of the *Dancing Times*, called 'dances of a more popular nature', provided some opportunity for others to experience jazz dancing (Moseley, 1924:25). In *The Coster Jazz Song* his wife complains 'My Bill 'e's always jazzin' it', but is unable to stop him due to her lack of dancing ability: 'Oh lor! nah wots a gel to do? 'Cos I can't dance yer see'. In this song, 'jazzin' once again becomes a metaphor for sexual activity:

> My poor Bills' goin' orf 'is 'ead
> 'E comes 'ome at any time and flops in bed
> Dreams I'm somebody else instead
> And starts jazz-jazzin' it wiv me.

Moral objections were being made at this time to what some people saw as the overt sexual connotations of jazz dancing. For example, a writer in *The Times* in 1919 stated:

> I was amazed to see my girl handed by and handing young fellows with so much familiarity … . They very often made use of a most impudent and lascivious step called *setting* to partners, which I know not how to describe to you but by telling you it is the very reverse of *back to back.* (29 April 1919:15)

Explicit imagery in songs may have played a part in fuelling this publicly aired debate over jazz dancing, as it enabled people such as Canon Drummond, who 'had no personal experience of the art of Jazz dancing', to strongly condemn it as 'mean, low entertainment' (15 March 1919:7). Similarly, Sir Dyce Duckworth saw jazz dancing as a sign that 'the morals of Old England had become degraded' (18 March 1919:7).

As well as the sexual implications of inappropriate body contact between dancing partners, it can be seen that jazz was also developing metaphorical associations with other activities that were thought of by some as socially and morally inappropriate. In the song *That Ragtime Suffragette* [h3988.zz(14)], ragtime music became symbolic of a woman's suffragette activities in a portrayal which is clearly disapproving (my emphases):

> She's no household pet
> Oh mercy! while her husband's waiting home to dine
> She is *ragging* up and down the line a-shouting "Votes for women".
>
> *Bands are playing* as she swaggers by
> Banners are waving as the men all cry
> "Why don't you go home and bake a cake?
> One like dear old mother used to make?"

Paradoxically, alongside these prevalent images of social and moral impropriety, weddings are a surprisingly common theme in both ragtime and jazz songs, presumably because the musical styles were popular with younger people who were of the age to be getting married. In several songs, jazz or ragtime replaces the traditional wedding music, and in this way jazz acts as a metaphor for the increasing freedom of young people to usurp tradition:

Said the bridegroom looking stiff as starch,
We don't want any organist to play the wedding march ...
Old man Joe on your old banjo
Play a little bit of ragtime music.
[h3990.i(47)]

They jazzed it one day to the church down the way
And a real jazz choir sang as they wed:
Heigho, jazz it with me ... .
[h3993.e(45)]

Dull solemn music played down the aisle,
Give me a brighter style.
Often I wonder why no one has
Ever composed a real wedding jazz.
[h3670.a(25)]

Examination of song lyrics is extremely illuminating of the differences in the images of jazz and ragtime. The word 'ragtime' is often personified, as in *Who Killed Ragtime?* [g1520.pp(11)]. The number of songs that emphasize that ragtime permeated society confirms the theory that increasing cross-class popularity of music hall entertainment in the late nineteenth century was fully developed through the widespread popularity of American syncopated music, for example in *Rag-time Crazy*: 'No matter where you wander ragtime music fills the air/From the cottage to the mansion you can hear it everywhere' [h3995.jj(30)]. There are also many ragtime songs about 'ordinary' people including the milkman, postman, policeman, and motor man. *Rag-time Crazy* continues:

The poor old milkman down our street has lately lost his 'ead
Instead of singing milk he whistles ragtime tunes instead
The butcher and the baker's boy the dustman and the sweep
Are like a ragtime quartette as around the place they creep.

Ragtime is also shown in song lyrics to have permeated many aspects of everyday life, such as church and school:

Last Sunday in Church the parson exclaimed
He hoped he wouldn't do wrong
'Stead of preaching sermons he sang a ragtime song.
[h3995.o(14)]

Teacher said that little children now should keep up with the times
Said we must remember how to sing in 'rag-time' Nurs'ry Rhymes.
[h3986.qq(26)]

This idea receives extended and exaggerated treatment in *I'm Certainly Living a Rag-time Life* [h3986.ss(11)]:

> I've got a rag-time dog and a rag-time cat,
> A rag-time piano in my rag-time flat
> Wear rag-time clothes from head to shoes
> I read a paper called the 'Rag-time News'
> Got rag-time habits and I talk that way
> I sleep in rag-time and I rag all day
> Got rag-time troubles with my rag-time wife
> I'm certainly living a rag-time life.

Jazz songs rarely make the link between music and everyday life and more often portray exotic scenes and express escapist sentiments. This may have been as a result of the exclusive venues in which jazz was first performed, as well as the influence of World War One, which would have prompted a natural desire to escape from the unattractive reality of everyday life, an idea explored extensively in Chapter 3. Several jazz songs mention the ability of jazz bands to lift the spirits and take away the 'blues', for example:

> When you're kind of feeling blue
> I guess I'll tell you what to do
> You'd better come right down to my hometown
> Where they'll show you something new
> They've lately formed a big Jazz Band.
> [h3988.yy(1)]

The now legendary assumption that jazz is linked with excesses of alcohol and drugs is mentioned in two songs from 1919. The chorus of *Johnson's Jazz-time Band* [h3991.q(4)], which is set 'down in Sheriff Johnson's gin and fizz saloon', begins:

> When old man Johnson is serving out the grog,
> And the cabin's full of smoke like a London fog,
> Well all the coons are busy jazzing till your heart feels good ... .

The cover illustration of this song depicts three musicians clearly under the influence of alcohol, and two couples dancing to the music, but all the people in the illustration appear to be white. The exoticism of the setting of the song *That Mandarin Jazz* [g426.d(33)] is further enhanced by references to drugs ('Dream pipe dope is rife tonight') and the intoxicating power of these substances is compared to that of jazz music: 'When a chink gets busy on the tympanium/There's a sinister spell like opium.'[7]

---

[7] In the first decade of the twentieth century, a large Chinese settlement had became established in the Limehouse area of London and the Chinese opium dens evolved their own mythology (Kohn, 1992:18). Opium became illegal in 1916, but there was apparently a certain tolerance towards this drug, as 'Britain founded its Indian administration upon revenues from sales of opium to China in the eighteenth century' and it was considered mild in comparison with other drugs. (Kohn, 1992:61).

At this time, links were beginning to be made between drugs, people of 'exotic' races, and jazz. This was physically embodied in Edgar Manning, a notorious 'Dope King', who was a black Jamaican and played drums in a jazz band (Kohn, 1992:7). As the most fashionable dance music, jazz was naturally present in the upper class and bohemian social situations in which drugs were also prevalent. Jazz and drugs were ubiquitous in London's West End, which itself embraced all social classes:

> There was a continuum in West End society, from the street prostitutes and petty criminals at the bottom, through the chorus girls and actresses who might work as prostitutes between engagements, to those whose success in the entertainment world allowed them to mix with the social elite. (Kohn, 1992:6)

The formation of the underground drugs scene in the West End was encouraged, ironically, by war-time restrictions on alcohol and midnight curfews placed on London's clubs at weekends which meant that 'by the end of 1915, there were 150 illegal nightclubs in Soho alone' (Kohn, 1992:30). Jazz later provided the musical accompaniment for these underground activities. Although the drugs underworld seems far removed from the variety entertainment in which the songs considered here would have been performed, in reality the centrality of drugs in the West End meant that underneath the superficial respectability of stage acts, the two were inseparable. In this context, it is significant that the image of jazz as presented in contemporary songs is so consistent with the conventionally understood effects of drugs: addiction, swaying, hypnosis, craziness, abandon, excessive emotion, sexual desire, and escapism. In addition, there were clear links between jazz and intoxicating substances due to the freedom of women to both take drugs and dance to jazz; activities which became symbolic of their post-war independence. Edgar Manning himself recalled in 1926 that:

> The women ... seemed to go utterly mad with excitement. Dope had sapped away all their feelings of modesty and restraint. The wild syncopated rhythm of Africa's pulsing music – translated into American jazz tunes – did the rest. (Kohn 1992:158)

This description shows the compatibility of taking drugs and dancing as social activities, and also emphasizes the origins of jazz in 'exotic' Africa. Several songs of the period are set in exotic locations including China (*Miss Ching-A-Loo: The Ragtime Chinese Wedding* [h3992(35)] and *That Mandarin Jazz* [g426d(33)]), and Java (*That Javanese Jazz Band* [h3996.f(43)]). *That Jungle Jazz in Congo Land* [h3994dd(31)] uses a fictional exotic setting, while 'the Rag-time Coon' [h3989.f(42)] can be heard singing in Hindustan and the Indian Seas. American place names are used in a similarly random way to provide settings. The song *Jazz!* [h3988.yy(1)] provides a context of 'Down in Alabama where the cotton grows/ That's the place you've got to learn to shake your toes' and *Johnson's Jazz-time Band* [h3991.q(4)] performs 'Out in Arizona at the dead man's bluff'. New Orleans is used as a setting in two songs; [h3996.n(22)] 'You've heard of nearly ev'ry kind of band/But there is one that's come from Dixieland' and [h3993.e(9)] 'I heard 'em down in New Orleans'. Only one song, *You've Got to Sing in Ragtime* [h3990.zz(36)] of 1911, links ragtime with America in a 'patter' dialogue between the performer as representative of 'English' and a stereotyped American 'wearing a very light suit, baggy trousers, square shouldered coat, soft hat, bright red tie and yellow gloves. Has cigar in mouth at upward angle'. The Englishman announces to the audience: 'I don't know whether you like this rag-time or not. Anyhow, don't blame me, it's not my fault. It's an American idea. Over in America everything is rag-time.' The American then attempts to educate the Englishman as to the correct way to perform the song.

Certainly, very few songs give a clear idea of the specific geographical origins of jazz, except a general impression of exoticism created through references to the Orient or America. Arizona was probably as foreign to the majority of the British public as Java in the early twentieth century. An article in the *Dancing Times* even claimed that jazz had originated in China, and included a picture of a 'native Chinese Joss Orchestra' (February 1920:350). The fact that exotic settings appear to have been chosen indiscriminately indicates that for songwriters and the public, any setting outside the West could represent the 'other' and thus achieves the effect of establishing jazz as music of 'another world'.[8] This added to the appeal of jazz as an escapist music with the power to take the listener out of his or her own environment, with or without the help of drugs.

Significant numbers of songs specifically associate ragtime and jazz with the stereotypical 'nigger' or 'coon'. These caricatures would be familiar to the public through their use in minstrel shows and in a huge body of songs published in Britain from the late nineteenth century. Sufficient numbers of these were published to denote 'coon songs' as a separate category in publishers' listings of songs on the back covers of music. Familiar elements of the stereotypical portrayals of black people are presented in songs. The 'coon' is portrayed as a simple character, with nothing to do except make music: 'Who sang all day in such a pleasing way/That they called him the "Rag-time Coon"' [h3989.f(42)]. If engaged in employment, it is a menial task such as selling oysters and clams [h3651(45)], although even then the 'coon' is portrayed as being lazy as he 'takes things easy – goes along at a crawl'. The song continues: 'Jasper Jones wasn't born with a "silver spoon" stuck in his mouth/It was a shovel there isn't a doubt'. The established stereotypes often emphasized that Negroes supposedly had large mouths, and therefore loud voices, which are useful when selling produce: 'Ev'ry weekday morning comes a long thin greasy coon/A-shouting "Oysters" and A-shouting "Clams"!'. The association between 'coons' and shouting leads a rag-time milkman, his trade emphasising his 'whiteness', to distinguish himself and his trade from that of 'coons':

---

[8] Derek Scott has noted a similar non-specificity in the settings of Orientalist operas: 'I had first though it might be important to understand where [the operas] were set geographically. Then I began to realize that, for the most part, all I needed to know was the simple fact that they were set in exotic, foreign places'. (1998:309). He also notes that 'the Orient can begin in Spain, if the intention is simply to connote a cultural Other' (1998:326). Jazz, as an American music, is shown in these songs to be considered sufficiently 'Other' to be compatible with more conventionally exotic Oriental cultures.

Meelk! I'm not a coon
Meelk! it's my usual tune
It's always been the milkman's cry
Years before the ragtime coon came nigh.
[h.3983.gg(59)]

This is the most overtly racist song examined, as the chorus ends with a bitter claim: 'And when I hear the coons shout "well"/It makes my milk turn sour'. The grotesquely large features of the stereotypical Negro are emphasized in a cautionary tale to children:

Oh, that ragtime gollywog man
With his great big eyes and his great big hand;
When you see him coming that's the time to start a-running
And just run as fast as you can.
[g1520(50)]

Songs link the 'crazy' element of the music with the influence of 'coons', for example in *Rag-time Crazy* [h3995.o(14)] 'Ev'ry one seems crazy with the Coon song on the brain'. The chorus of this song most clearly links ragtime with the 'coon' stereotype:

Coal black coons and slivery moons,
All you can hear is ragtime tunes;
Honey and money and Lindy Lous
Singing 'come out in the moonlight do';
Mandy and Carolina dancing to the ragtime strain,
Ev'ryone's gone crazy with ragtime on the brain.

However, in the second verse, this appears to form the basis of a reason to reject ragtime: 'All the coons sing "ma baby my love is true"/Isn't it time we had something new.' This gives a new emphasis to lines from the first verse, which now reveal a mood of resignation rather than enthusiasm:

Some songs live for ever, some for a day,
Once all the rage then pass away,
But there's a song that's going to stay,
You know what I mean it's the coon song.

Few songs depict black performers of ragtime or jazz, and those that do are derogatory or patronising in nature, for example 'You ought to hear those crazy tunes/Played by all those crazy coons' [h3988yy(1)]. This is taken to extremes in *That Jungle Jazz in Congo Land* [h3994.dd(31)] which could be an innocent, slightly nonsensical song about jazz in the jungle, but could also have racial undertones. Written in 1919, it prefigures the pseudo-African 'jungle' music of Duke Ellington. The song begins:

Have you heard the latest news from Congo Land?
All the animals home from zoos in Yankeeland
Brought with them to kill the 'blues' that new Jazz Band
Now they make the forest ring each night.

These lines could refer to Negroes emancipated from captivity in American 'zoos'. The second verse compares jazz performers to animals:

Leader is a chimpanzee of great renown
Seems to play the tune all upside down
Makes the tiger, full of glee, act like a clown
Joy your heart is sure to syncopate.

The black origins of jazz were generally only mentioned in contemporary articles by those who wished to criticize jazz, just as at this time 'blacks' were generally blamed for the concurrent 'drug problem' (Kohn, 1992:66). The general lack of any associations between jazz and black performers in songs published in England is significant, especially when considered together with other statistics which suggest that overall numbers of songs about 'niggers' or 'coons' dropped rapidly in the second decade of the century when jazz was coming to prominence.[9] This indicates that jazz was *not* presented in songs as a black music, and that these origins of the music had become suppressed. This was probably due to the importance of the revues in introducing jazz to Britain, as these tended to present an image of white America as being responsible for the latest trends.

The number of songs that make detailed references to the characteristics of musical styles shows that it was not only live performances that could define jazz for British people. It is by examining the differences between the way that ragtime and jazz are described in song lyrics that conclusions can be reached about what distinguished jazz from other syncopated music styles heard in Britain. The first important point that emerges is that there is a strong link between ragtime and song, whereas the instrumental aspects tend to be emphasized when jazz is the subject. Singing in a ragtime style was a common subject for ragtime songs, for example *You've Got to Sing in Ragtime* [h3990.zz(36)], *Don't Sing in Ragtime* [h3994.hh(10)] and *Don't Drive Me Crazy with Your Ragtime Song* [h3996.e(26)]. Characters in ragtime songs are often portrayed either singing or whistling the music whilst going about their work, for example 'Ev'ry newspaper boy sings it in

---

[9] The following table shows the number of incidences of the words 'coon' and 'nigger' in titles of songs published in London in the British Library Collection:

	Nigger	Coon
1880-1890	6	2
1891-1900	9	69
1901-1910	12	140
1911-1920	3	23
1921-1930	2	0

the street' [h3995.j(46)]. The sheer number of songs that use this idea reinforces the tendency for ragtime to be portrayed as permeating everyday life, as discussed earlier.

The rhythmic aspect of ragtime and jazz is emphasized in several songs, and the word 'syncopation' occurs frequently, for example in *The Rag-time Craze* [h3995.j(46)]: 'Ev'ry new song you hear is a different rag/And it's filled to the brim with syncopated gag'. Rhythmic features of the music often appear to be emphasized when the song is set in an 'exotic' context, for example the ghost of the rag-time coon can be recognized 'When you hear that music of that syncopatin' air' [h3989.f(42)], in *Johnson's Jazz-time Band* [h3991.q(4)] 'You can hear them hitting up a syncopated tune' and in *That Mandarin Jazz* [g426.d(33)] 'That Mandarine is sure some guy/Ev'ry Jasbo rhythm he'll try'. It is possibly the rhythmic complexity of the music which leads to a lack of understanding in the derogatory portrayal of the composition process in *You've Got to Sing in Ragtime* [h3990.zz(36)]:

> When composing in ragtime, if you want to make hits,
> Take a sheet of music, cut it up into bits
> Paste it all together, never mind if it fits,
> Play it in gag time, that'll be ragtime.

The idea of 'ragtime' is retained in lyrics of songs written after the ragtime craze as a characteristic of jazz, such as in *Johnson's Jazz-time Band* [h3991q(4)]: 'Sammy with the bones is full of ragtime tricks' and *Stick Around for the New Jazz Band* [h3991.ii(5)]: 'Dan on the banjo as cute as can be/Picking out the rags in any old key'. References to ragtime within 'jazz' songs are associated with the most overtly rhythmic instruments, banjo and percussion, indicating that 'ragtime' was perceived as a primarily rhythmic characteristic. This may have been influenced by the prominence of the banjo in most performances of syncopated music before 1919, either as a solo instrument or as part of the bands that played for dancing. These performances reinforced the rhythmic characteristics of the music due to the origins (as an instrument to accompany dancing) and percussive, rhythmic nature of the instrument. The consistency of the image of the banjo in songs will be considered in detail in Chapter 5.

The drums are the most frequently mentioned instrument in jazz songs, and this emphasizes the centrality of 'noise' in descriptions of jazz, for example, when Johnson's Jazz-time Band are playing 'You can always hear the melody a mile away' [h3991.q(4)]. There is evidence of an actual and perceptual shift in focus from the omnipotent banjo to the drums as the provider of rhythmic drive and excitement in syncopated music from about 1919. As early as 1917, the *Encore* reported under the heading *Mr Jazz Arrives*:

> ... [jazz musicians] are certainly correctives against air raids, because no matter how loudly the anti-aircraft guns roar outside, the trap drummer inside with his colleagues of the trombone, etc. can be guaranteed to drown out all extraneous noise. (*Encore*, 11 October 1917)

In January 1919, a review of a 'jazz' performance at the London Coliseum, entitled 'The Art of Jazz: Drummer as Chief Conspirator', stated:

> The object of a jazz band, apparently, is to produce as much noise as possible; the method of doing so is immaterial, and if music happens to be the result occasionally so much the better for all concerned. The chief conspirator is the drummer ... . (*The Times*, 14 January 1919:11)

Reviews of the earliest 'syncopated' or 'jazz' bands often devoted space to descriptions of the 'trap drummer' and his extensive equipment, and visiting drummers such as Hughes Pollard (known as 'Black Lightening' [*sic.*]), Louis Mitchell and Alec Williams quickly achieved notoriety in the British press. The drums are normally referred to in songs as 'pans' and 'tin cans', of which the principle characteristic is the volume of sound produced, which is not always appreciated by the audience:

> There'll be sixteen iron pans
> And a set of old tin cans
> Twenty saucepans and a worn out bassinet
> Just fill your ears with chunks of cotton wool ... .
> [h2452(33)]

This idea was also reflected in the *Dancing Times*, in a description of a jazz band percussionist as a

> ... hefty and utterly unscrupulous young man who has previously made a tour of the marine stores and collected such curios as frying pans, tin-lids, fire-irons and such-like impedimenta – in fact he is well provided with everything BUT music! (January 1919:123).

One song is unusual in being a little more complimentary about the musicality of drummers: 'They get melodies from pots and pans/They get music out of old tin cans' [h3996.u(24)]. Similarly, Theodore Curson pointed out in the *Dancing Times*:

> We are authoritatively assured that "Jazz" is not music, but merely noise. However, as exactly the same thing was said of Wagner's music when it came to birth, it is possible that the process of time may change the critical pronouncement as to "Jazz". (February 1919:183).

The loud and unrefined nature of the sound, as produced by pots, pans and cans, was also the principle feature of performance of jazz on other instruments. An important characteristic of jazz performance as presented in song lyrics is the ability to produce odd noises from familiar instruments:

Hear that trombone with that peculiar moaning
That saxophone with that peculiar groaning.
[h3996n(22)]

They got a funny clarinet
And a man that plays cornet
In such a funny manner ... .
[h3993.e(9)]

This can even be taken to the point of 'producing sounds that pianos never ought to make' [h3991.q(4)] and creating the assumption that jazz bands 'play all out of tune' [h3996n(22)].

Whereas very few songs refer to instrumental performance of ragtime, more than half of the jazz songs examined contain the phrase 'jazz band' in the title. In addition, the description of performances of jazz on instruments including trombone, saxophone, piano, clarinet, cornet, trumpet, cello and fiddle suggests that the variety of instrumental effects was one way in which jazz was distinguished from previous American syncopated music. The accompaniments in many 'jazz band' songs are no longer merely functional, but contain features of musical interest, such as 'fills', breaks and counter-melodies, to a much greater extent than ragtime songs. In some cases, the piano parts are specifically illustrative of the elements of jazz performance described in the lyrics. There are also examples of contemporary piano pieces that try to 'describe' jazz in musical terms (for example *The Jass Band* by Henry Steele [h3284.yy(21)]), sometimes with appropriate annotations on the music to indicate to the player the effect or instrument that he/she should be attempting to reproduce or represent on the piano keyboard. This seems to indicate not only that instrumental effects were fundamental to the accepted *image* of jazz, but also that the genre had begun to develop a clear *musical* identity which was linked with the instruments on which the music was performed.[10]

Ragtime, on the other hand, was brought to prominence in Britain almost exclusively by revues, and unlike in America, the concept of 'ragtime piano' was virtually unknown in Britain (a situation that will be examined in greater detail in Chapter 5). Ragtime was understood mainly as the prevailing popular song style and dance music. There is little mention in song lyrics of any particular instrumentation of ragtime, suggesting that it was a general musical style that was applied to pre-existent ensembles, as the revues utilized the conventional pit bands in the West End. Finally, the fact that ragtime was portrayed as having been retained as a feature of jazz demonstrates that its main stylistic feature, the syncopated rhythm, was compatible within this new genre. Therefore, the emphasis on the instrumental characteristics of jazz in song lyrics can be understood, as it was the most appreciable difference between this music and the similarly syncopated ragtime.

---

[10] A similar phenomenon had occurred previously during the banjo craze of the late nineteenth century, where banjo effects were represented in piano accompaniments to songs that described banjo performances (see Chapter 5).

The perception of ragtime as the basic syncopated rhythm and jazz as instrumental colour, which is asserted in song lyrics, is also the basis of an early definition of jazz, written by R.W.S. Mendl, who provides the first retrospective account of the development of jazz from a British perspective in *The Appeal of Jazz*:

> Strictly speaking, jazz has nothing whatever to do with rhythm: it is solely concerned with instrumentation, and it would be possible to have jazz music that is not syncopated at all. You cannot play jazz music as a pianoforte solo: if you perform syncopated dance music on the pianoforte it is ragtime, not jazz. It only becomes jazz when it is played on a jazz orchestra. (Mendl, 1927: 45-6)

This definition is very different to the way in which jazz is generally described today. Improvisation, usually considered as inherent in the style, is not mentioned by Mendl, and is merely hinted at in only one song that I have considered:

> There's a charm you can't resist
> Ev'ry man's a soloist … .
>
> Ev'ry player gives it fits
> Puts in little twiddley bits … .
> [h3991.r(31)]

However strange Mendl's idea of jazz may sound, the fact that it largely concurs with the way in which jazz was presented in popular song suggests that it is an accurate representation of the image of jazz in Britain in the early twentieth century. This image can be understood with reference to the way in which jazz had evolved in preceding years. Jazz was perceived in Britain as part of a larger category of music defined by Mendl as 'modern syncopated dance music' (1927:25), as due to the geographical distance from the source of the music, the British public received only 'snap-shots' of the much more detailed evolutionary process that was occurring in America. Thus the word 'jazz' was initially a vague, all-embracing term for current syncopated dance music in Britain, as were 'cakewalk', 'foxtrot' and 'ragtime' before it. This meant that the first distinguishing characteristics that emerged became accepted and established as the definitive elements of the jazz style.

The image of jazz shown in song lyrics is significant as it must surely bear some relation to the perception and understanding of the 'ordinary' Briton as, in a competitive market, publishers would only be able to sell songs that would either influence or reflect contemporary attitudes. Therefore, the fact that image of jazz portrayed in songs is also consistent with the way in which it was presented by the Original Dixieland Jazz Band when they visited Britain in 1919, gives an indication of the strength of their influence in Britain. The ODJB was initially booked to perform within a revue at the Hippodrome, where the image of jazz detailed here had already been presented with such success, and this made their claims of authenticity undeniable. Although the word 'jazz' was being used a few years before the arrival of the ODJB in April 1919, and there were jazz songs and even a few 'jazz' bands in existence, it needed the commercial presentation of an American band to establish a clear musical meaning for the word. Arguably, the ODJB achieved emblematic status in Britain simply for being the first to present instrumental jazz that sounded different to other syncopated styles and to produce recordings.

The fact that performances of earlier syncopated music in Britain normally involved the banjo, whereas the ODJB did not include this instrument, established an image of jazz as being primarily concerned with the kind of noisy, comical instrumental effects that are presented in song lyrics and accompaniments. The rejection of the banjo, which was strongly symbolic of black music-making, by this group also implies a rejection of the black origins of jazz, which became explicit when later they claimed to have 'invented' jazz. This is reflected in the fact that black performers are rarely mentioned in songs, which suggests that the black origins of the music were not a significant part of the British image of jazz at this stage. The image of jazz that was presented in sheet music served to disseminate further and establish as seminal the performances of these white men who, in 1919, presented jazz in Britain in such a way that 'the blind prejudice felt by many towards what they think is jazz can be traced straight back to Original Dixieland Jazz Band's comic hats' (Harris, 1957:201, see Figure 6.1).

Chapter 3

The 'Jazz Age' in Britain

During the early 1920s, jazz became phenomenally popular in such a way that it provided the fundamental basis, in musical and evolutionary terms, for the formulation of later popular music genres. However, as John Lucas states, 'when in the twenties people spoke of jazz music they very rarely had in mind the real thing' (1997:126). This premise is clearly over-simplified and essentialist with respect to the notion of 'real' jazz, but this is nevertheless an important point. Certainly, the popularity and appeal of jazz in Britain during the 1920s and 1930s was balanced by the correspondingly strong outrage and antipathy that it provoked, often from people that had never actually experienced the music for themselves. It is not necessarily the precise musical characteristics of the presence of jazz in Britain, which may have been heard only by a limited number of people, but the representations and perceptions of the music and the function of the idea of jazz within contemporary society that are under scrutiny here. This is complemented by studies of the aural presentation of jazz in Part II.

The adoption of jazz may be viewed as another manifestation of modernism, which was an aesthetic that was clearly evident in other arts at this time. But, more specifically, jazz was so strongly representative of the mood and character of the 1920s that the decade has become known as the 'jazz age' after *Tales of the Jazz Age*, a collection of short stories by F. Scott Fitzgerald set in post-war America and published in 1922. These 'tales' define the 'jazz age' as one of:

> ... disenchantment and scepticism, of a failed and vulnerable romanticism that takes the place of lost belief in the old gods of order and progress, and of exuberant, inflationary excess in which the philosophy of *carpe diem* vies with the restrictions of Prohibition as the gap between the rich and poor expands to the point of collapse with the stock market crash of 1929. (O'Donnel in Fitzgerald, 1998:viii)

In Fitzgerald's work jazz becomes metaphorically and literally, through the inclusion of jazz dancing in the stories as an important social activity, representative of the modern age. Nor was this idea of the 'jazz age' a peculiarly American phenomenon. The fact that jazz came to prominence as a new musical genre in the unique post-war cultural, social and political climate, evolved alongside modern art, literature and 'serious' music, was disseminated through new technology and was popularized by the related rise of mass consumerism meant that this music also became strongly representative of the spirit of the era in Britain.

There is a danger that as we look back at history, we tend towards generalization, simplification and categorization of what are in fact complicated interwoven threads. In taking the 'jazz age' as a central concept here, it is important that we acknowledge that its characteristics could be said to be in evidence from as early as 1917 and extend into the 1930s (see Lucas, 1997:1, 3). Therefore, the label 'jazz age' can potentially cover a period that includes the varying political and social climates associated with events such as the end of the First World War, the post-War years, the General Strike, the Wall Street crash, and the build-up to the Second World War rather than just one static typified decade. Although jazz may be seen as a consistently important musical style across this wider chronological span, its function must necessarily change over time in line with shifts in social, political and economic circumstances. Similarly, the musical characteristics of jazz in Britain, methods of dissemination and modes of audience identification and engagement with the music are also at variance.

Contemporary writing can provide important indications of the changing reception, understanding and meaning of jazz in this period, and this chapter shall particularly draw upon theoretical writing on jazz by R.W.S. Mendl (1927), Stanley Nelson (1934), Constant Lambert (1934) and Theodore Adorno (1936) as the earliest extensive European criticisms of jazz. Mendl's book *The Appeal of Jazz* typifies the interest in jazz amongst the intelligentsia at this time. Nelson was the music critic for the theatrical trade paper the *Era*, and Lambert was a well-respected composer and critic. Whilst Adorno's views on jazz have been criticized as flawed through their limited scope, the fact that he was constrained principally by his restricted experience of the music, as like all Europeans he was geographically removed from the sources of jazz (he wrote 'On Jazz' whilst living in Oxford), means that his ideas are particularly valuable when considering jazz in Britain in this period. In fact, the extent to which these four authors concur in their thoughts on jazz is significant; and most fundamentally, they all recognized the idea of the 'jazz age' in their writing, which spans the period 1927-1936:

> ... [jazz is] the spirit of the age written in the music of the people. (Mendl, 1927:186)

> The intoxicating low spirits of jazz ... express, whether we like it or not, the constant tenor of our lives. (Lambert 1934/R1966:189)

> This is an age of speed; the pace at which we live is surely exemplified in the hectic rhythms of our music ... . The Victorian spirit has been too long dying out for any but the post-war generation to take kindly to the hiccoughing rhythms of Jazz. (Nelson, 1934:155)

> Jazz is pseudo-democratic in the sense that it characterizes the consciousness of the epoch ... . (Adorno [1936], trans. Daniel, 1989:50)

This chapter falls into two parts chronologically, the first dealing with the post-War period and the second with the 1930s. This broad generalization of what was obviously a less typified and more fluid historical evolution is used as a basic starting point for illuminating the changing function of jazz as popular music in British society. In both sections, the dissemination of and critical reactions to the music are examined. It will be noted that the critical writing cited above is used in both sections, as in most cases, the writers concerned make reference to earlier attitudes or these are embodied in their work as they begin the re-evaluation of jazz that is discussed in the second part of this chapter. The chapter concludes with a section entitled 'Defining and Understanding Jazz', which examines the influence of popular criticism, widely available in publications such as *Melody Maker* and *Rhythm*, on musicians and enthusiasts in Britain.

Modernism and the Post-War Period

The characteristics of the post-war period (which may be seen as the beginning of the 'jazz age') actually began to be formulated as early as 1917 in Britain, when the initial enthusiasm for war had waned, conscription was taking effect and the sheer scale of the death toll was becoming apparent. The futility and naivety of the original promise that the War would be 'over by Christmas' became apparent by the reality of conflict and everyday life in wartime. Soldiers had been told that they were fighting for 'civilization', yet they had seen its very destruction on the battlefield. Cynicism towards those who had sent them to war grew, and at the end of the War the establishment and the state, and particularly the 'old men' at the helm, became the new enemy.

There had been much speculation during the War as to what life would be like after it but, as peace came nearer, it became in some ways more daunting than war itself as speculation turned to anxiety and uncertainty. Lady Asquith commented in an entry in her diary on 7 October 1918: 'I am beginning to rub my eyes at the prospect of peace. I think it will require more courage than anything that has gone before.' (1968:480). This feeling culminated at the Armistice, which Hynes suggests was anti-climactic (1990:255). Virginia Woolf commented on the resulting feeling of disillusionment: 'in everyone's mind the same restlessness and inability to settle down, & yet discontent with whatever it was possible to do' (1977:216). Disillusionment was not just confined to the responses of society leaders. Ordinary soldiers felt that they did not receive the hero's treatment that they were led to expect during the War, as instead they faced poverty, unemployment and disability, and saw the new monuments as impractical, empty gestures, prompting riots on ceremonial occasions (Hynes, 1990:281). Women, who had taken on essential work during the War, were pushed aside by returning men and by 1921 a smaller proportion were employed than before the War. In some ways, the War served only to emphasize the inferior status of women, as they were excluded from the action, and the shortage of men after the War meant that some would never have a family, which added to their sense of worthlessness (Hynes, 1990:380). Asquith had set up a 'Reconstruction' committee that Lloyd George developed into a ministry as an attempt to make the War seem worthwhile, but this was abandoned in 1919 leaving the word with only ironic associations (Hynes, 1990:263). Thus, England fell into a post-war period founded mainly on disillusionment and disenchantment.

In the latter part of the War, art and literature had been infected with a new spirit of realism, which prompted the development of modern techniques, as pre-war 'academic' styles were inadequate to represent the horror of war. As the War began to draw to a close in 1918, there was a sense in the arts of 'looking to a new but unspecified future' (Hynes, 1990:241), which created a momentum towards experimentation in new artistic styles. Realism took a satirical turn, as soldiers expressed their hatred of war and increasing alienation from the country for which they were fighting (Hynes, 1990:242). The anti-hero in the shape of the 'damaged man' became a frequent and dominant character in literature from the middle of the War and much art, even by the official war artists, demonstrated an anti-monumental attitude through representation of total physical and emotional destruction, rather than propaganda-style glory of war.

Not surprisingly, two groups of artists developed during the War, combatants (i.e. War poets) and non-combatants (i.e. the 'Bloomsbury' group). During the War, civilians had taken over important editorial jobs, and became responsible for the new artistic directions. Soldiers returning from the War found that the arts had changed, and for many of them the War had taken up their formative years (Hynes, 1990:327). In this way, modernism can be seen as a personal solution for these combatant artists, as a way of constructing their own post-war styles, as well as a way of expressing the realities of war that they had experienced. This allowed the division between soldiers and civilians to persist after the end of the War. Middleton Murray commented that 'Modernism and hatred of war were...the same; and traditional art and traditional views of war were on the other side together' (Hynes, 1990:275). In this way, modernism could allow artists to express disregard for the 'establishment' by rejecting classical forms and devices.

The distinction between tradition and the avant-garde was sharpened due to the fact that the past persisted through the 'old men' who were seen to be responsible for the wartime destruction, and particularly the phenomenon of the 'lost generation', as they had sent the young to war. At the Armistice, people who came of age during the War were 'lost' either in the sense of death which meant that a generation of political or artistic leaders had been lost, leaving an unnatural cultural and social void; or, in the case of those that survived, 'lost' in the sense of being directionless and confused, with only irrelevant pre-war and horrific wartime memories from which to construct a future. In addition, there was the post-war generation, who came of age post-1918, and became the students and 'Bright Young Things' of the 1920s. Although they had not experienced war directly, they emerged into a world of disillusionment and disenchantment and took the destruction of the past for granted (Hynes, 1990:395). Hence, although the War created a gap in artistic development, it was also a driving force in encouraging the construction of post-war modernism, and was therefore the most important event of the twenties, although it did not occur within that decade. Both the post-war and 'lost' generations had to formulate modernist ideas to explain their lives and create a progression towards the future for which there was little foundation in the society and culture of post-war Britain. A modernist response was thus one of necessity, and as Pearsall comments, 'the Bright Young Things boasted of their emancipation, their freedom from the conventions that had constricted their parents, but in reality their reactions were predictable' (1976:18). Modernism can be seen to have been prompted dually by aversion to tradition and the need for artistic experimentation to express the nature of the modern experience, both ideas that are reliant on the prevailing disillusionment and dissatisfaction with the past in the post-war period.

On this basis, Bradbury and McFarlane have defined modernism as 'less a style than a search for a style in a highly individualistic sense' (1991:29). The pluralistic nature of post-war modernism that is implied in this definition can be seen in the adoption of jazz as the music of the age, as it was in itself a culturally composite musical style. In addition, it was interpreted by individuals on a practical level through improvisation in dance and instrumental performance and metaphorically through the numerous attempts to understand the essence and meaning of the music. Many of the characteristics of modernism which developed through the latter years of the War can be seen in jazz and its role in society, and in this way Fitzgerald's idea of the 'jazz age' can be understood.

Primitivism

The realist tendencies of early modernism were reflected in the increasing interest in the 'primitive' in the post-war period, showing a desire to return to a perceived basic, simple culture that contrasted with the decadence of Western civilization, which some moralists believed to have caused the War. Adam Lively has explored the links between the nineteenth century interest in the exotic, knowledge gained through colonialism, the *fin de siècle* encounters with 'primitive' cultures through Exhibitions and Darwinian theories of evolution, culminating in primitivism that is 'one of the strongest threads connecting the seminal works of high modernism' (Lively, 1998:99). Jazz can be seen as the musical expression of modernist primitivism, through its associations with black culture, which was perceived as 'primitive', and also through the idea that the music was founded on rhythm, an expression of the primitive. A similar two-fold manifestation of the 'primitive' idea can be seen in visual art of the period, where there is 'art which attempts to express the workings of the primitive mind' as well as examples of stylistic primitivism that was more directly imitative of non-Western art (Rhodes, 1994:7).

As we have seen, black performers had been interesting to white Britons from at least the nineteenth century. In the 1920s, the perceived simplicity and freedom of black culture could be something desirable for whites to emulate, rather than just observe or imitate, and jazz 'seemed to promise cultural as well as musical freedom' for young people (Frith, 1996:128). Although this was tinged with misunderstanding based on the long-held assumption that black art was the unsophisticated 'low other' of Western culture, this attitude seems to demonstrate genuine interest and appreciation of the perceived 'authentic' qualities of black culture. The values of black culture could act as a constructive replacement for the ruined past for 'lost' young Britons, and was also a way in which they could subvert tradition: 'Whites gravitated toward black music and black culture in general because they felt it expressed the abandon and hedonism toward which they liked to think they were moving' (Sidran, 1981:54).

Paradoxically, primitivism can also be read as the rejection of the whole idea of the modern age, with the Negro as a cultural primitive who 'maintained a kind of escapist innocence in the face of technology – a myth perpetuated by blacks who were gaining respectability in white society' (Sidran, 1981:54). Perry (1993:3) identifies a similar adoption of primitivism as an alternative to modernism by some artists. But yet, the tendency towards black culture in so many art forms in the 1920s, particularly through the art and literature of the 'Harlem Renaissance', established the 'primitive' Negro, ironically, as a primarily modern idea. Jazz was unique in presenting this 'primitive' culture in a way in which it could be assimilated, reproduced and experienced directly by whites, and thus 'became a cultural shorthand for that which was both supremely modern and, through its African roots, connected with the exotic origins of things. It was the music of the urban jungle' (Lively, 1998:99). The paradoxical expression 'urban jungle' is particularly apt when describing the simultaneous expression of 'supreme modernity' and 'the exotic origins of things' in London in the 1920s. Jazz encapsulates musically the metaphor of the 'urban jungle', as its modernity was expressed through its perceived 'primitive' rhythmic qualities.

Dance

Whites responded to jazz in a simplistic, 'primitive' manner through dancing that was becoming increasingly improvisational. Stanley Nelson describes the post-war embrace of 'primitive' culture through the adoption of jazz as dance music in his book *All About Jazz*:

> The War shattered many of our illusions and brought us nearer to earthy things. That is why the artificiality of the Victorians in their dance music was superseded by a dance music [jazz] which was unashamedly proud of showing its crude emotional stress. (1934:170)

Indeed, to an extent 'the reigning obsession of the 'jazz age' was not jazz but dancing' (Goddard, 1979:28). There was a huge increase in venues for dancing in the capital after the War, from the hotel restaurant dances and luxury clubs such as Ciro's and the Kit-Cat, to the London Club and the Hammersmith Palais, where the entrance fee was affordable by the middle class (Pearsall, 1976:78; Nott, 2000:154). Clubs were often decorated in a modern way, here the colour scheme is reminiscent of primitivist art: 'The floor was black ebony and the walls and furniture were in the prevalent jazz fashion of black and orange' (Bradley, 1947:8). (The underworld of London's nightclub scene in the 1920s will be examined in detail in Chapter 7). The dance hall was the only form of entertainment that could rival the cinema and public house, and crucially, dancing to jazz was specific to the young people of the 'lost or 'post-war' generations, and hence demonstrates many of the features of the modernist approach to the post-war period.

New dance styles provided another way in which young people could subvert tradition, as they could reject the long-established formal steps and music of dances. The tempi of dance music were much faster than previously, which in itself dictated the nature of the dancing, described by Josephine Bradley: 'the only thing one could do was walk, which we all did with energy and enthusiasm' (1947:16). Steps initially associated with jazz, such as the 'jazz roll', quickly went out of fashion, which meant that there was greater opportunity for self-expression through dance. This allowed various transient fashions to be set and for jazz dancing to remain modern, and together with the energetic nature of the dancing which necessarily confined it to fashionable young people, confirmed the division between young and old that had begun through the later years of the War.

Developments in jazz dancing in the 1920s hinged on the increased social and sexual freedom of women. During the War, women from the upper and middle classes had been permitted more contact than formerly with men through their work as volunteers, and women from the lower classes left domestic service which gave them increased sexual freedom. The philosophy of *carpe diem*, which promoted living for the present moment without concern for the future, was widely adopted in wartime and probably led to more extra-marital sexual encounters. Contemporaneously, writings by Stopes and Freud addressed sexual issues openly for the first time, and the traditional role of the woman as a mother was increasingly rejected by young girls who felt that they deserved their freedom through their role in the War.

War-work led to increasing practicality in the design of women's clothes, but the resulting freedom was also reflected by the changes in dress at this time. Hemlines rose steadily and an un-corseted simple silhouette became fashionable, showing the rejection of pre-war decadence and the return to basic ideas. Significantly, 'the thin young woman, who was so far from symbolizing the family that her dress minimized the maternal bosom, while exposing the legs, in the manner of a little girl' (Steele, 1985:230) was now the ideal image for women. Sexual freedom was demonstrated by these clothes that enhanced natural feminine beauty, and meant that 'a woman wearing twenties dress was much more touchable than a woman in Victorian and Edwardian dress' (Steele, 1985:240). The emphasis on 'youth' in the ideal image of the 1920s woman meant that it was the young rather than middle aged women who began to set fashion trends in the 1920s, once again underlying the division between generations that we have seen in relation to 'old men' and soldiers. Orientalism and primitivism also influenced women's dress, through the addition of turbans, scarves, beads and tassels and the use of cosmetics and perfumes (Steele, 1985:233). The use of elements of exotic cultures in this way created a mysterious sensuality reflecting the more explicit expression of sexuality and the need for escapism characteristic of the age.

Dance halls were the centre of the fashionable world, as the movements of dancing could show off dresses excellently.[1] Leading figures of the dance world, such as Irene Castle, the well-known American professional 'exhibition' dancer, set the trends not only for dance but also for fashion; she was said to have been influential in the trend for 'bobbed' hair for women in the 1920s (Steele, 1985:229). Dance halls gave women the opportunity to go out and enjoy themselves, and the associated activities of drinking cocktails and smoking became popular with young women of the 1920s as symbols of their emancipation

---

[1] Dance and dress fashions had been closely linked since before the War. Steele suggests that 'Perhaps more than any other single factor, the popularity of the tango and similar dances led many women to abandon orthodox corsetry in 1913 and 1914' (1985:229).

(Stevenson, 1984:384), with the availability of drugs in nightclubs adding to the heady atmosphere (Pearsall, 1976:78). Indeed, 'drug use was understood as a crisis of young womanhood; cocaine, especially, was a young woman's drug.' (Kohn, 1992:8). The movements of jazz dancing required close contact between partners, 'dancers had to adopt the style of the man pressing his head firmly on the lady's 'perm' to keep balance' (Bradley, 1947:12). Together with the nature of twenties dress which made the women more 'touchable' and the 'mysterious sensuality' of the exotic elements of fashionable dress, this meant that dancing was a more overtly sexual experience than previously. As jazz was the new dance music of the time it became inextricably linked with youth and freedom of sexual expression, which epitomized the rejection of traditional moral values. The adoption of jazz as representative of 'primitive' black culture and the sexual implications of the resulting modern dance also provided a basis for opposition to jazz at this time. Canon Drummond referred to jazz as 'a dance so low, so demoralizing and of such a low origin – the dance of the low niggers in America' (*Times*, 15 March 1919:7) and Sir Dyce Duckworth described 'wild dance – amid noises only fit for West African savages – held in London drawing rooms' (*Times*, 18 March 1919:7).

Jazz in the 1920s

Modernism, as we have seen, is founded on dissatisfaction with and rejection of the past, and thus raises the issue of people's relationship to time. Consideration of jazz as the music of the age can explain some of the complexities of this idea. As we have seen, the demonstrable roots of jazz in another culture gave particular relevance to the post-War youth who had seen their own past destroyed. However, whilst poets, artists, composers, writers and philosophers were wrestling with the problems posed by the destruction of elements of civilization by the War, many ordinary people were coming to terms with loss and the practicalities of its aftermath. Hence, while culture and society appeared fractured by war, there were elements of indestructible continuity, which hinged around the need for entertainment. Towards the end of the War, mass destruction had led to a spirit of *carpe diem* as described by Josephine Bradley: 'All the girls were having a very good time with men friends home on leave, who wanted to fit into each moment as much as they possibly could. Night life was at its height' (1947:7). Pearsall comments that a similar attitude existed in the immediate post-war:

> The optimism of the first year after the war – before demobilisation of the armed services threw hundreds of thousands of men onto the market to precipitate one of the evils of the age – unemployment on a massive scale – encouraged popular music to proceed as if the war had never happened. (1976:7).

Although the stasis demonstrated by 'high' art during the War can also be seen in relation to popular culture, the effect of war was less shattering on the course of its overall development due to the fact that popular music and dance had constantly functioned as a diversion from the realities of wartime life. In the post-war period, popular culture remained a reliable distraction in the face of the destruction of so many other elements of society and culture. According to Nelson, 'The intervention of the war left the civilized world in a mental chaos, and Jazz provided the very stimulant it required' (1934:13), and Mendl describes jazz as a 'musical alcohol' for soldiers returning from 'the horrors and hardships of the trenches' (1927:89).

An important feature of jazz in the 1920s was the novelty aspects and humorous presentation of the music: 'The god of the 1920s was novelty, whether it was in art, serious music, dance music and jazz, architecture or literature' (Pearsall, 1976:79). The idea of 'novelty' is consistent with the spirit of constant re-invention which must be inherent in modern art, as, broadly speaking, if a particular style becomes established as typically 'modern', by definition it can no longer be so. This led to a constant feeling of progression and development in the 1920s, especially when compared to the stasis in the preceding war years. In this way, jazz is an expression of modernism, and 'Its pulse reflects the restlessness and inexorable momentum of the pace of modern life' (Pleasants, 1961:157). However, as Ted Heath explained 'Jazz was a novelty and people wanted to dance and forget the horror of the First World War' (1957:28). Jazz was more than just dance music, as it also functioned as entertainment that presented a humorous diversion from everyday life. This explains the popularity of the Original Dixieland Jazz Band in 1919, and the replication of their novelty effects by British bands after their departure. It seems that when the saxophone was introduced it was regarded as the latest humorous novelty, as Nelson comments that:

> ... the saxophone is a stock jest to-day, and our foremost humorous daily weekly rarely fails to comment caustically upon it, while our music hall comedians have seized eagerly upon the instrument as a welcome addition to Wigan, mothers in law, and all other things that are fondly supposed to be intrinsically funny. (1934:17)

Jazz had the ability to encapsulate in one form the defining, often paradoxical features of the post-war age such as aversion to tradition and the progressive experimentation, constructive and escapist approaches to reality, and the Western and the 'primitive'. Jazz can be seen as an intrinsically modern music as it mediated the contemporary interest in primitivism, both as a way of deliberately subverting native traditions, and constructing a new past and future for those who felt that they had none. Jazz dancing as a social activity encouraged the division between young and old, and the liberation and sexual freedom of women. Jazz also permitted individual freedom of expression and interpretation in instrumental performance, dance and dress. Whereas modernism was a direct response to the reality of the War and post-war, and attempted to construct explanations of the meaning of modern life, jazz was adopted primarily as a reaction against reality, and fulfilled an important escapist function, acting as an antidote to the actual and metaphorical complexities of the period. Jazz was music with immediate impact, unlike some complex modern art forms, and was thus closely allied to the spontaneity of the *carpe diem* philosophy. As we have seen, the fact that jazz had 'primitive' associations meant that it was seen as 'a joyous revolt from convention, custom, authority, boredom, even sorrow' (Sidran, 1981:54). The new dance clubs were decorated in unusual, other-worldly colour schemes, and the prevalence of drink and drugs offered other sources of escape. Dancing was now a response to the basic rhythm of the music, rather than a formal series of steps, and required participants to become absorbed in the music. Dancing, together with the social freedom of women and the nature of their dress, also offered possibilities of sexual 'escape'. Jazz itself can also be seen as a musical form that constantly re-invents itself, and thus remains supremely modern, but through its escapist characteristics, can even be seen to transcend modernism itself, as it represents art which is 'independent of or else transcending the humanistic, the material, the real, [which] has been crucially important to a whole segment of the modern arts' (Bradbury and McFarlane, 1991:25). Jazz is thus representative of the escapist spirit of the age, and therefore Fitzgerald's idea of the 'jazz age' is a valid label and an important concept. This is reflected by Mendl, who wrote in *The Appeal of Jazz* in 1927: 'even if it [jazz] disappears altogether it will not have existed in vain. For its record will remain as an interesting human document – the spirit of the age written in the music of the people' (1927:186).

Jazz and the Culture Industry I: the BBC

Jazz was a music disseminated via technological means from its very beginnings due to the development of recording and radio broadcasting. The emotional need for jazz, as identified above, could be exploited by a burgeoning, powerful and regulated culture industry, in the form of the broadcasting and recording companies, which had a fundamental role in influencing the understanding of jazz in Britain. Vital to the continued presence and significance of jazz in Britain were important changes in its dissemination over the period due to technological developments. As we shall see, this prompted increased public interaction with the music and ultimately allowed jazz to be re-evaluated with increased knowledge and understanding.

Broadcasting and recording meant that many more people had access to performances by the top dance bands in Britain than they might have had without these industries. Radio and the gramophone represented a totally new dimension in home entertainment, which had previously been self-generated and centred around the piano, but was now available with little personal effort and with much greater variety. The fact that performances which were otherwise socially exclusive were now much more accessible was important in the evolution of jazz as the music of the age. However, broadcast and recorded material could gain an element of authenticity simply through being broadcast or recorded. This meant that the associated industries, often economically rather than artistically driven, became fundamental to the way in which jazz developed in Britain. Thus, the two main pillars of the culture industry in early twentieth century Britain, the BBC and the record industry, should be analyzed carefully in order to understand the way in which jazz was presented and perceived at this time.

Whilst 'the gramophone first entered the home as a novelty among the monied classes' (Chanan, 1995:40) several decades prior to the introduction of national radio broadcasting, the cost of players and records was generally prohibitive until later in the 1920s. The role of recording in the dissemination of jazz will be considered later. Radio, however, was relatively affordable as a crystal set cost about the equivalent of a week's wages for a manual worker (Pegg, 1983:47). The popularity of the radio was reflected in the rapid growth of licence holders, from 36,000 licences in 1922 to 2 million in 1926 (Stevenson, 1984:407) and 'by the end of 1926, about 20 per cent of the nation's households owned radios' (Doctor, 1999:19). Tuning into radio broadcasts had begun as an enthusiast's pastime, with the aim to pick up any sort of signal, the actual content of the broadcast being a secondary consideration since 'initially the fascination of the radio was its magical quality; its marvellous ability to generate sound from an apparently lifeless box' (Pegg, 1983:6). Instructions for building crystal sets to receive radio signals could be found in specialist magazines, of which there were around 30 titles on sale by 1924-26 (Pegg, 1983:45) and local or even national papers, and it seems that initially there was as much pleasure derived from building a successful set as from listening to the programmes that were broadcast. The absorption of radio into home life is shown by the more expensive radio receivers, which 'were free standing cabinets, considered by dealers and department stores in the same way as furniture' (Chanan, 1995:39).

The British Broadcasting Company, as it was initially, was formed in 1923 under the leadership of Sir John Reith, who was a man with strong views on the public role of broadcasting, and a commitment to the use of the radio for the education of the masses. In this way, 'Sir John Reith and his associates were determined to provide what they thought the public ought to have, not what it wanted' (Pearsall, 1976:10) and they largely rejected the idea of the provision of entertainment as a function of broadcasting. Reith famously commented in his book *Broadcast over Britain*, published in 1924:

> ... to have exploited so great a scientific invention for the purpose and pursuit of "entertainment" alone would have been a prostitution of its powers and an insult to the character and intelligence of the people. (1924:17)

If any entertainment was to be included at all in BBC schedules, it was to consist of items such as talks, plays and classical music that would 'widen listener's intellectual and cultural horizons and ... heighten their critical perceptions' (Doctor, 1999:27). Reith clearly viewed jazz as entertainment of a less desirable type:

> To entertain means to occupy agreeably. Would it be urged that this is only to be effected by the Broadcasting of jazz bands and popular music, or of sketches by humorists? I do not think that many would be found willing to support so narrow a claim as this. (1924:18)

The word 'jazz' does not feature often in the BBC programme schedules, as performances of popular music were usually referred to as 'dance music'. Jazz had certain undesirable associations, which were widely understood at the time and rendered music called 'jazz' unsuitable for inclusion on the BBC. Articles in early editions of the *Radio Times* show that jazz was considered to be a brief phase of development in dance music, outdated and unfashionable when compared with modern syncopated music. Although dance music was mere 'entertainment', it was still made to fit within the BBC's brief of providing material considered 'suitable' for the public. Dance music was considered acceptable entertainment as it was firmly associated with the respectable upper class venues from which it was broadcast and, after all, was not meant to be listened to seriously but was considered to be purely functional for dancing.

Moseley, writing in the 1930s, perceived that 'broadcasting has ... given a tremendous impetus to dancing and dance music' (1935:117). The importance of the broadcasting of dance music in the 1920s is shown through the *Radio Times*, which suggests that people did actually dance to the music. Features in the magazine idealistically emphasized both the social importance of these broadcasts, and that the BBC enabled music that was otherwise socially exclusive to become more accessible. In the 23 November 1923 issue, the *Radio Times* reprinted an extract from an article in the *Evening Standard* 'Dancing to Wireless: A Possibility of the Future' (p. 315), in which the author could foresee the broadcasting of dance music from larger venues to 'the smallest dance studio and even to the private dance rooms', providing better music than had been customary at such venues at an economical price. In the spring of the following year, an article on 'Radio in the Summertime' predicted that 'Open-air wireless will largely be popularized through loud speakers enabling impromptu dances and concerts to be shared by holiday and picnic parties' and promising that 'Dance music and songs and popular programmes by well-known bands will figure more largely in the fare to be provided in the coming months.' (*Radio Times*, 16 May 1924:308). Dancing to the radio was not a pastime solely of the lower classes, as shown by a description by the 'distinguished essayist' E. V. Lucas, who also points out the advantages of the radio over the gramophone:

> In a house in Buckinghamshire where I was staying recently everyone, at the moment for which they had been waiting, began to dance, not to any instrument in the room, but to the strains of the band at the Savoy Hotel in the Strand, thirty-five miles away. In ten thousand houses the same impulse probably was setting other couples capering. The tune lasted longer than an ordinary gramophone record, nor did anyone, at the close, have to leap across the room to remove the needle. (*Radio Times*, 5 September 1924:442)

The pleasure of dancing to broadcast music was further extolled in an article entitled 'Are you a Radio Dancer?' by Lydia Kyasht:

> To listen to a loud speaker delivering the perfect dance music broadcast, for example, by the Savoy Orpheans Band, is a delight to the heart of a real dancer. It brings the exhilarating atmosphere of the ballroom into your home...You are transported by the magic of radio, which overcomes distance. You believe that you are actually listening at close quarters to the band. (*Radio Times*, 2 October 1925:73)

Programmes of uninterrupted dance music were advertised in advance so that evening dances or afternoon *thé dansant* parties could be planned and, by 1926, the *Radio Times* reported 'an increasing tendency lately for listeners to organize loud speaker dances' (22 January 1926:195). Broadcast dance lessons were also transmitted and accompanying diagrams, photographs and written instruction published in the *Radio Times*, and in this way it can be seen that the BBC played a central role in perpetuating and disseminating the latest dance trends.

In both descriptions, the 'magic' ability of the radio to bring the atmosphere of a distant ballroom into ordinary, domestic settings remains an integral part of the overall experience. Such fascination with the technological aspects of radio permeates early editions of the *Radio Times*, which contained letters and articles on, for example, reception and oscillation. Increasing numbers of advertisements in the magazine also highlight both the interest in broadcast technology and the centrality of dance music to the radio output in the 1920s, for example advertisements for 'Western Loudspeakers' featured an illustration of couples dancing to music from the radio (see Figure 3.1), and used a similar idea in a written advertisement in the following year:

> The company is congenial, the surroundings pleasant, the occasion ideal, but the dance will not be a success if the music is poor. A Western Electric Loudspeaker will enable your guests to dance to the latest music, played in perfect time, by the well-known Savoy Orpheans and Havana Bands. (*Radio Times*, 15 August 1924:341)

Readers were encouraged to purchase 'Brown's Loudspeakers' to hear dance music to the best advantage:

> Radio listeners throughout the country look forward to their dance music broadcast through all eight stations from the Savoy Havana Band. It is safe to say that in very many homes the dining room table is pushed out of the way immediately the Band strikes up and a happy informal little dance takes place. And the leader of the dance is the Saxophone, a nickel-plated, highly polished Instrument which is quite a newcomer to orchestradom.

> To obtain the greatest pleasure from your Radio Dance you need a loudspeaker capable of rendering a loud and clear volume of sound without the slightest trace of distortion: a BROWN, in fact. (*Radio Times*, 25 January 1924:176)

In the 1920s, 75 per cent of letters to the BBC complained about reception problems rather than programming, the fascination with the technological aspects of broadcasting meant that the listeners were less discerning than they were to become later in the twentieth century (Pegg, 1983:37). The fact that the BBC held a monopoly over broadcasting and was perceived as an 'official' body, must have meant that the quality and content of the broadcast output was questioned less by the general public than it might have been. It is easy to understand how British audiences in the early 1920s accepted the popular music that was disseminated by the BBC, particularly as this was so consistent in terms of its style and presentation. The popular music that was broadcast on BBC radio was tightly controlled through the selection of reputable British bands and 'there was barely a

Figure 3.1   **Western Loudspeakers Advertisement (*Radio Times*,
                        14 December 1923:424, by permission of the British Library)**

hint of the quality which writers on jazz of the time called dirt.' (Pearsall, 1976:125) as the majority of the BBC senior staff were from 'dinner-jacketed Oxbridge and public school backgrounds' who were determined to lead rather than be influenced by public taste (Pegg, 1983:97). The BBC made a clear distinction between 'dance' music and 'hot' music, generally characterized as British and American respectively, remembered by Graves and Hodge:

> The BBC now provided dance music: plenty of the humorous and sentimental kind-Jack Payne and Henry Hall, for instance – very occasionally the really hot stuff, straight from America. (Graves and Hodge, 1940:237)

As Graves and Hodge suggest, the British version of jazz was dominant in radio output and was widely accepted as 'standard' popular music, with the American hot music as an occasional novelty. The infrequency of American performances was probably also linked with the idea that the BBC should be inherently British, with 'a commitment to the concept of a British National Culture' (Barnard, 1989:5). After all, the BBC had originally been formed with the intention of creating a monopoly in order to avoid the chaotic situation of American commercial radio. Hence, the American roots of popular music were hidden beneath a façade of Britishness, for instance the use of the term 'dance music' instead of the obviously American 'jazz'. Together with the BBC's commitment to providing suitable entertainment, this influenced not only the way in which the music was presented (formally announced, as bandleaders were not permitted to announce their own numbers to prevent 'song plugging'), but the generally restrained nature of the performance and the music itself, as there was little room for spontaneous displays of improvisation in the carefully scored arrangements.

The BBC ensured consistency in their dance music output through the close association with Savoy Hotel bands, considered extensively in Chapter 7, and a succession of 'house' bands, most notably the BBC Dance Orchestra under Jack Payne. Payne became one of broadcasting's first stars, and according to Moseley, 'received 50,000 letters, postcards and telegrams a year' (1935:118), and many other bandleaders also became household names through their extensive recording and broadcasting. The fact that national stars could be made through recording and broadcasting indicates the strength of the influence that the British 'culture industry' had over the population at this time, particularly when it came to setting trends in popular music. In fact, the strict control exercised over the 'dance music' that was broadcast meant that there was little distinction between the various bands, particularly 'through the medium of the primitive wireless set' (Pearsall, 1976:125). Hence the BBC was responsible for creating and disseminating a stylistically unified music, suppressing the whole spirit of individuality that was to be central to the future development and longevity of jazz. The standardization of popular music meant that by 1929 jazz was regarded merely as a briefly popular form in the post-war period. Listeners wrote in the *Radio Times*:

... the dance music of today bears no resemblance to the 'jazz' of the immediate post-war period. (1 February 1929)

Why will these antagonistic highbrow people still talk about 'jazz'? There is no such thing nowadays. It died years ago. (15 February 1929)

Maine, writing in 1939, commented that the BBC 'has helped to persuade listeners that dance music is a serious subject' (1939:126); certainly, the BBC appears to have had the capacity to influence public taste. However, not all listeners were mere passive recipients of the BBC's programming by any means, and it is interesting to note that apparently 'more vitriol and prejudice was espoused for the cause of broadcast music than for any other subject' (Pegg, 1983:200). This reflects both the centrality of music in the BBC's output – music accounted for two-thirds of the daily programme output in the 1920s (Doctor, 1999:39) – and the BBC's rigid categorization of music, where popular music was defined as 'entertainment' rather than culture (Barnard, 1989:8). This encouraged a polarization of 'serious' and 'popular' musical styles, which was taken up by the media. Whilst the popular press resented the monopoly enjoyed by the Company and urged the BBC to pay more attention to listener's tastes, 'critics in the serious press generally supported Reith's intention to raise public taste and oppose the popularizing or vulgarizing of music which they saw in "popular" music' (Pegg, 1983:200). In one week in 1925, 125 letters out of 8,000 received condemned 'dance music', suggesting that, unsurprisingly, lovers of 'serious' music were more vocal in their opposition to 'popular' music than visa versa. Although the presence of 'dance music' in broadcast schedules was both criticized and commended, its validity as a musical style was largely unquestioned. This shows that in the 1920s, the BBC had the power to dictate the stylistic features of mainstream popular music, as we shall see in Chapter 7, this was to affect the perception and evolution of jazz in Britain for several years to come.

Highbrow, lowbrow and Rhapsody in Blue

The *Radio Times*, first published in September 1923, was intended not only to provide information about future broadcasts, but also to make the BBC seem accountable to the public. For example, a memorandum to station directors about the intention to stop announcements by bandleaders to prevent song-plugging stated that 'It is possible that a certain amount of objection will be raised by listeners to the non-announcement of numbers, but this will be met by explanatory statements in the *Radio Times* as found necessary.' (BBC Written Archives Centre R19/244 19 February 1929). The BBC encouraged 'listeners-in' to write to the *Radio Times*, and published a selection of letters in each issue, stating from the outset that: 'We hope to give on this page each week a limited selection of typical letters from the BBC postbag. The points raised by the writers will be answered briefly immediately beneath each communication.' The 'Listeners' Letters' page often included contradictory opinions on particular subjects, suggesting that the BBC were trying to justify their programming simply by proving that it was impossible to please everyone. The selected letters presented stereotypical extremes of the 'highbrow' and 'lowbrow' listener, who, apparently, could be identified by their respective taste in music above anything else, which led to certain musical genres being stereotyped themselves as representative of these high and low categories. One reader attempted to define highbrow and lowbrow musics thus: 'High-brow music is appreciated more the more one hears it; low-brow music is likeable at first, but rapidly tires on repetition'. (4 December 1925:489). A correspondent concerned about 'wireless etiquette' recommended 'a few lessons on this subject to "high-brows" who grumble audibly when "low-brow" music is being broadcast, and to the jazz enthusiasts who spoil their companions' enjoyment by jeering when Beethoven is coming across the ether.' (3 October 1924:50). This letter demonstrates the extreme polarity that was perceived to exist between different types of music and their respective groups of listeners.

It seems that dance music and classical music were not regarded as different forms existing within the 'music' subset, but as representative of opposite extremes (highbrow vs lowbrow; autonomous art vs functionality and pure entertainment) of the BBC's output. The use of the term 'dance music' itself implies functionality, meaning that, unlike 'serious' music, it could not and should not be appreciated as autonomous art. Furthermore, dance music was not the responsibility of the music department of the BBC and was instead classified as 'variety'. This arrangement prohibited any comparison with highbrow classical music, as although both genres were established as important and suitable for broadcast, this was within their respective high or low classifications and there was no question of which was the 'better' music. This is shown by the fact that whilst classical music was presented as 'high' art, complete with broadcast or published explanation and information in the *Radio Times* to encourage serious and attentive listening, pieces of dance music latterly were not even identified by their titles due to song-plugging restrictions. Song plugging, where payments were made to artists to encourage them to perform certain numbers was, of course, totally against the philosophy of the BBC and the subject of long-running battles between the Corporation, venues and artists. In early 1928, Sidney Firman, conductor of the London Radio Dance Band, was found to be 'not guiltless in the matter of receiving monetary grants from publishers for song plugging' (BBCWAC R19/244 Dance Music), and from 1928 onwards, 'no song-plugging' clauses became a standard feature of contracts between artists and the BBC. Much correspondence on this subject can be found in the BBC Archives.

The overwhelming tendency to polarize 'high' classical and 'low' jazz began to be more profoundly disrupted by the radio broadcast of a performance of Gershwin's *Rhapsody in Blue* by the Savoy Orpheans from the Hotel on 15 June 1925 with the composer at the piano, the first time the work had been heard in Europe, and the fascinating interview with the composer in the *Radio Times* on 3 July 1925, entitled *When we have a Jazz Opera*. Seemingly as a direct response to 'high-brows' concerned with the corrupting influence of jazz upon classical music, Gershwin stated that: 'I do not think that serious music will ever be influenced by jazz, but it is quite probable that jazz will be influenced by serious music', predicting jazz symphonies and concertos, and citing his own ambition to write an 'opera for niggers'. He also refuted the notion that jazz was merely syncopation:

'Many people make the mistake of thinking that jazz is mere syncopation. But there is nothing new in syncopated music; it was written by Bach. Jazz is something more than that.' Crucially, he explained jazz as a fundamentally American music: 'I feel that through this medium I can express myself, my nationality, my soul'. *Rhapsody in Blue* made a significant impression upon listeners, for whom, influenced by the BBC's complete separation of dance and classical music save for the dubious practice of 'jazzing the classics', it represented 'the blending of two extremes of music' and a 'new era in music'. A correspondent to the *Radio Times* wrote: 'It would be interesting to know whether both high- and low-brows enjoyed it, or whether it appealed to neither.' (3 July 1925:55).

In the years after the broadcast of *Rhapsody in Blue* there were numerous broadcast debates on the relative merits of jazz and classical music. Gershwin's work had shown that jazz had aspirations towards becoming artistic and highbrow, and could no longer be cast aside as unequivocally lowbrow. The music now represented a direct challenge rather than a mere antithesis to classical music, and in this context, the word 'jazz', instead of the term 'dance music', was used to further heighten the distinction and opposition of the two genres. Debates and discussions included 'Jazz vs Classical' between Sir Landon Ronald and Jack Hylton with illustrations from the Wireless Orchestra and Hylton's band in July 1926, which sparked off a huge reaction from listeners in the letters pages of the *Radio Times*. Subsequently, Mr Sebastian Brown, Lecturer in Music at Chelsea Polytechnic, the music critic Percy Scholes, and even P.P. Eckersley, Chief Engineer of BBC all broadcast their views on the subject, but their debates and listeners' opinions were inevitably inconclusive.

The conflict between highbrow and lowbrow, if not jazz and classical music, was settled to some degree by the adoption of 'symphonic syncopation' as the main form of broadcast dance music: 'Classical syncopation, or symphonic syncopation, is a new development in the arts of musical composition and of syncopation, and is a combination of the two.' (*Radio Times*, 23 October 1925:201). In this way, the boundaries between highbrow and lowbrow music were broken down through combining elements of both in one musical form. Although in practice it was debatable how much effect this had upon standard dance music, the nomenclature nevertheless made syncopated music more acceptable as a musical form in its own right and to an extent legitimized it for staunch highbrows. Shortly after Gershwin's visit, Jack Hylton was defining jazz in 'classical' terms in the *Radio Times*: 'By jazz, I do not mean much of the trash which, whatever its popular appeal, does a great deal of harm to the serious efforts of composers who bring it to a high standard of technical accomplishment.' (27 November 1925:438). In a second article, Hylton took his arguments further, stating:

> I do not hesitate to declare my belief that, after the test of time, some of the syncopated music of to-day will merit the designation 'classical'.... . Symphonic syncopation is not 'jazz', that nerve-torturing riot of sound which made its appearance during the war, when everything, music included, was topsy-turvy. (18 June 1926:466)

Here the development of a more refined form of jazz is inextricably linked to a more stable situation in society, where things are no longer 'topsy-turvy' and the 'invasion' of jazz is brought under control.

Jazz Criticism in Britain

The attitude and policies of the British 'establishment' towards jazz, described above with reference to the BBC, are reflected in the emergent critical debates on jazz in Britain in the period 1927-1936. Ted Gioia has written that 'Almost from the start, European thinkers of note were inclined to treat this new music as a serious artistic endeavor; accordingly, much of the best jazz writing from the 1920s and 1930s came not from America but from across the Atlantic.' (1988:24). Although it has been argued by James Lincoln Collier that this commonly held view is not necessarily accurate (1983:249), it is true to say that many writers in Britain demonstrated the desire to understand this exotic new music in this period. The main problem with which these writers wrestled was the almost unique status of jazz at this time as both popular and art music, crossing over the well-established distinctions between 'high' and 'low' culture. The increasing recognition of the artistic status of jazz, which, as we shall see, was intimately bound up with greater knowledge of its ethnic origins, distinguished it from other popular forms of the day. This meant that jazz presented a direct threat to the integrity of the British artistic establishment, which many within it felt necessary to challenge, as well as suggesting important new directions to the avant-garde who, by arguing for the artistic status of jazz, were able to justify their endeavours in this area.

Jazz and Classical Music

Most of the early British writing on jazz shares the common feature of the use of classical music to provide the criteria against which jazz is evaluated. Supporters of jazz attempted to validate the music by pointing out similarities with classical music, positioning jazz within the canon and the evolution of music in a bid to make the music seem less radical and to emphasize its artistic qualities. Both Mendl and Lambert try to fit jazz into the evolution of dance music, a particularly interesting comparison as this focuses on the social function of jazz at a time when understanding aspects of its musical nature was proving problematic. Mendl addresses this in the first chapter of *The Appeal of Jazz*, entitled 'The Bond Between Music and Dancing', in which he identifies dancing as a fundamental response to the inherent rhythmic nature of music from its earliest days. In the following chapter, he explores the link between the work of the 'great composers' and dance music, noting that 'it is so common nowadays to set the symphonic art and dance music in antithesis to one another that we are apt to forget that the form of the sonata or symphony is largely derived from dancing numbers' (1927:13). Similarly, Nelson begins his book *All About Jazz* with a general historical survey of syncopation, in which jazz is allied with the rhythmic tendencies of recent classical music.

At the heart of many of the comparisons made between jazz and classical music is the assumption, made clear in the BBC's attitudes and actions, that classical music was simply better than jazz. Mendl notes that often in the 1920s: '"Jazz music" and "classical music" are set in antithesis to one another as though one were bad and the other good' (1927:25), which was hardly surprising since it was often classical criteria that were being used to make the judgements. The most obvious link between the apparently antithetical popular and serious styles was the common practice of 'jazzing the classics'. This meant that jazz was further deplored by 'high-brows' as it was seen as a force with the ability to corrupt sacrosanct classical music. A letter from one radio listener protested:

> Why, in the jazz age in which we are now living, when new dance numbers are being published literally by the score every week, must we fall back on some of our most famous classical compositions and thus cheapen them simply to satisfy the desires of a jazz crazed world? (*Radio Times*, 8 May 1925:294)

Adverse comparisons between jazz and classical music were a fundamental source for those that wished to denigrate jazz. Essentially, comparing jazz to classical music could show that jazz was simple and under-developed particularly with respect to its harmonic basis, and its supposed dependence on rhythmic aspects linked it with 'primitive' music, clearly identifying it as 'lowbrow'. This was a source of misguided criticism, particularly, as Mendl points out, from 'some of the most notable men in the musical world' (1927:60) whose views were often published in the national press and thus perpetuated the misunderstanding of jazz. The comparison of jazz with classical music forms the foundation of Adorno's views on jazz: 'the most striking traits in jazz were all independently produced, developed and surpassed by serious music since Brahms' ([1955], trans. Weber and Weber, 1967: 123). Adorno comments that jazz is not original because it only uses elements that have already been used in classical music, such as syncopation and effects of orchestration, which he sees as being constrained, rather than developed, within a standardized format of jazz.

Evaluating Jazz Composition and Performance

Reliance on classical criteria for criticism, even by those who were basically in favour of jazz, meant that it was more difficult for the traditional hierarchy between composer, performer and arranger to be reconsidered. This was necessary for the appreciation of jazz and particularly the recognition of the importance of improvisation in this style. Lambert is critical of jazz musicians who produce 'improvisations over an accepted basis and not a true composition at all' (1934/R1966:186). He comments that 'It is the greatest mistake to class Louis Armstrong and Duke Ellington together as similar exponents of Negro music – the one is a trumpet player, the other a genuine composer.' (1934/R1966:186).[2]

---

[2] The presence of Armstrong and Ellington in Britain in the early 1930s provoked comparison of their respective talents in improvising and composing that consequently fuelled discussion of the nature of jazz (see Chapter 9).

Lambert identifies improvisation as 'a number of frills that are put on by the players at the spur of the moment' (1934/R1966:186) and Adorno makes a similar observation about the superficiality of improvised elements as 'mere frills' ([1955], trans. Weber and Weber, 1967:123). Adorno was unable to acknowledge any freedom in improvisation in music that was subservient to the demands of the culture industry:

> The elements in jazz in which immediacy seems to be present, the seemingly improvisational moments – of which syncopation is designated as its elemental form – are added in their naked externiality to the standardized commodity character in order to mask it – without, however, gaining power over it for a second. ([1936], trans. Daniel, 1989:48)

Mendl, however, recognized that 'the performers are relatively of greater importance to this twentieth century popular music than they are in the case of the works of the great masters' (1927:77), as 'the jazz players will introduce actually unrehearsed effects into the performance' (1927:78). Mendl is able to deconstruct the notion of the unalterable 'work' and its composer, to whom the performer is subservient, as being at the top of the hierarchy, as he notes the importance of both performers and arrangers, who even have 'the privilege of changing the notes' (1927:79), in transforming an original composition into jazz.

Ultimately, several writers looked to composers to secure the future development of jazz by improving the basic musical material upon which it is built. For Lambert improvisation 'is all very well in its way' but is essentially limited by 'the monotony and paucity of musical interest in this perpetually recurring harmonic ground that eventually makes us lose interest in the cadenzas themselves' (1934/R1966:186-7), and Adorno is critical of the fact that 'the sole material [for jazz] remains popular songs' and resultantly the improvisations suffer from 'stifling limitations' of beat, metre, harmony and form ([1955], trans. Weber and Weber, 1967: 123). Although Mendl defends the practice of 'jazzing the classics', he points out that 'if jazz is to occupy a worthy place in musical evolution, it will have to stand on its own feet and invent its own melodies' (1927:161) and regrets that 'modern syncopated dance music has not yet been taken up by any composer of the front rank' (1927:12). Similarly Lambert concludes: 'The next move in the development of jazz will come, almost inevitably, from the sophisticated or highbrow composers' (1934/R1966:198).

Lambert sees jazz as intrinsically reliant upon developments made in 'sophisticated' music rather than the reverse as expounded by Mendl. Having found that jazz forms a limited basis for 'serious' compositions, Lambert suggests that it requires a more complex response than mere imitation from modern highbrow composers. Whilst in the past composers produced pieces based on popular forms that 'are either definite examples of unbending or definite examples of sophistication', modern highbrow composers could hardly hope to improve upon the 'popular' compositions of Duke Ellington, for example (1934/R1966:181). Lambert identifies a contemporary 'rapprochement between highbrow and lowbrow' in literature (1934/R1966:182), and seems to indicate that similarly composers might respond to the idea of jazz in a more abstract, postmodern sense, without necessarily making extensive use of its precise musical content: 'We need not expect the symphonic jazz of the future to bear any more superficial resemblance to the foxtrot of the night club than the scherzo of Beethoven's symphonies did to the minuets of the eighteenth-century salon.' (1934/R1966:193). The agenda of elevating jazz from its perceived low status is barely hidden in Lambert's pronouncements.

Mendl, Lambert and Adorno conclude by placing jazz in the middle ground between highbrow and lowbrow music, but for different reasons. Mendl explores the contemporary antithesis between highbrow classical music and lowbrow jazz and finds that it has been over-stated, as the 'works of the masters are chock full of light music' (1927:102) and also there is an 'intellectual element in the appeal of modern dance music' (1927:108). He argues that jazz 'has the best of two worlds' appealing to 'both those who are seeking for skill and wit and ingenuity, and those who care for sentiment or pathos' (1927:114). Adorno, however, observes the 'stabilizing' of jazz in the middle ground as a negative development symptomatic of its material functionality that requires it to have mainstream popular appeal:

> While beginning to split off into its two extremes, "sweet music" and the march, the core of jazz, "hot music" is being stabilized into a middle-of-the-road line of artisanal scrupulousness and taste which restrains the improvisational elements of disruption which were sporadically present in the original conception of jazz into symphonic simplicity and grandeur. ([1936], trans. Daniel, 1989:59)

Lambert sees jazz as 'the first dance music to bridge the gap between highbrow and lowbrow successfully', but this argument is based on the premise that jazz has only achieved this status as the result of the addition of sophisticated European harmony to its primitive rhythmic basis (1934/R1966:178), an argument, like many others regarding the relative merits of jazz and classical music, in which a racial agenda is nearly always implicit and often made explicit.

Jazz and Race

The adoption of symphonic syncopation as the main form of popular music by the establishment as described above, was closely linked to the contemporaneous rejection of the increasingly undesirable black origins of jazz, that were understood, although not overly apparent in Britain. The addition of symphonic harmony and orchestration meant, in effect, the white 'civilizing' of 'primitive' black music. This indicates the continuation of white Britons' preference for diluted or imitative black culture, already noted in connection with the nineteenth century minstrel troupes, and which became more strongly stated as racist attitudes developed in the post-war period and beyond. Race riots in 1919, considered in detail in Chapter 7, exemplified a negative attitude to black people in Britain, and racist attitudes also continued to be inherent in support of the British Empire. The 1924 British Empire Exhibition displayed 'natives' in such a way as to 'demonstrate their cultural, linguistic, intellectual and technological inferiority' (Sherwood, 2003). Although this provoked criticism from Africans in Britain and prompted the formation of the West African Students Union (Fryer, 1984:324), one of several organizations that expressed the solidarity of black communities in Britain in the 1920s, nevertheless, such public displays continued to confirm the well-established perception of the inferiority of black people and culture.

Even Mendl, who was generally a perceptive analyst of early jazz, says that it is unfair to criticize jazz just because it is a black music, as white musicians had since civilized and improved it (1927:72), and echoes the romantic view of slavery, which suggested that black slave culture was improved by their contact with whites. He describes of the evolution of jazz from 'little nigger bands – consisting, for instance, of a trumpet, cornet, clarinet and drum – [that] used to play weird syncopated strains in the back streets of the American towns' (1927:43). Mendl then credits 'Whiteman, Hylton and others' for improving the jazz band, bringing it 'to so much higher a level that the modern syncopated dance band can hardly be put on the same footing or appropriately designated even by the same name, as the primitive organisms from which it took its origin' (1927:49).

Although symphonic syncopation continued to influence the long-term development of British dance bands, there was a sense that the compromise was offered by this style was no longer sufficient for everyone as the music was not successful as either jazz or art music:

> Stabilized jazz is that which presents itself as "symphonic", as autonomous art, but which thus conclusively abandons all the intentions which previously had contributed to its appearance of collective immediacy. It submits itself to the standards of "artistic" music; compared with it, however, jazz exposes itself as lagging far behind. (Adorno, [1936], trans. Daniel, 1989: 59)

Rhapsody in Blue, which had initiated a compromise between highbrows and lowbrows and had become synonymous with symphonic syncopation, began to face increasingly criticism in the late 1920s. Mendl had described this piece as 'technically an extremely efficient composition … skilful in form … the work is a kind of instrumental fantasia written for jazz band' (1927:177-8). In an article published in *Dancing Times* in 1929, Roger Pryor Dodge was critical of the piece as being 'imitation jazz', and in 1934 Lambert described the piece as being 'neither good jazz nor good Liszt' (1934/R1966:195).

Jazz in the Great Depression

The rejection of 'symphonic' dance music around the start of the 1930s was both a result and an expression of a complex combination of social, economic and technological factors. Towards the end of the 1920s the public mood in Britain began to change, prompted by the General Strike (1926) and the Stock Market crash (1929). This was followed by severe economic depression and unemployment, which reached 'nearly 3 million of the insured population at its peak in late 1932' (Morgan, 2000:32), and 'as the Thirties dawned, the note of ominous disorder and historical nervousness grew stronger' (Bradbury, 2001:196). The Government appeared to be in disarray in the early part of the decade, and

Fascism was becoming a more organized movement through the British Union of Fascists under the leadership of Sir Oswald Mosley. Such developments promoted self-awareness, reflection and a sense of realism, and 'writers looked to society, reality and political comment' to provide inspiration and subjects for their work (Bradbury, 2001:137).

A significant author in this regard is Evelyn Waugh, whose novels present 'a cross-section of contemporary British society' (Stannard, 1986:197) that scholars have shown reflect his experiences and the people he encountered in the fashionable upper-class communities of Oxford and London, as recorded in his diaries (Patey, 1998:3). The subtle change in the predominant character of Britain in the late 1920s and early 1930s may be understood through a basic comparison between Waugh's novels *Decline and Fall* (1928) and *Vile Bodies* (1930). Both novels draw on the experiences of the post-war generation, who had been too young to fight in the war, and the protagonists are 'young men thrown into the world on their own, without guidance, while all around them the visible symbols of the passing order suffer change and decay, demolition and collapse' (Patey, 1998:57). Whilst in *Decline and Fall* Paul Pennyfeather is given a chance to re-invent himself and begin again, *Vile Bodies* ends with Adam Fenwick-Symes in the midst of a new war. Both novels are filled with 'the stage-properties of modernity, from cocktails and car-racing to aeroplanes, films, telephone chatter and the vogue of professionalized interior decoration' (Patey, 1998:34). However, *Vile Bodies* 'from the outset ... describes a darker world than *Decline and Fall*' (Patey, 1998:74) beginning with a crowded and stormy sea-voyage symbolic of the contemporary 'political and social unrest' (Stannard, 1986:197). The whole novel takes place under the threat of war, the world of endless parties has lost much of its appeal (as Adam exclaims in exasperation, 'Oh Nina, *what a lot of parties*' [Waugh, 1930:123]) and not even the gossip columnists are able to find anything interesting to write about ('My editress said yesterday she was tired of seeing the same names over and over again' [Waugh, 1930:50]). Waugh's novel indicates that the activities of the 'Bright Young Things' were 'consciously public' and came to exist purely to fuel the press (McKibben, 1998:28). In *Vile Bodies* Waugh describes the destructive consequences of the decadence of the 1920s, which ultimately is shown to lead to the death of several characters. The reporting of high society in gossip columns begins to influence society itself in an ever-decreasing and quickening vicious circle. The columnist Simon Balcairn is unable to keep up with the pace and commits suicide. Similarly, it is the circular motion of 'racing-cars speeding round a track' that leads to the death of Agatha Runcible. Flossie Ducane falls fatally from a chandelier in the bedroom as a result of her sexual promiscuity, and Adam and Nina conceive an illegitimate child. In *Vile Bodies* 'events move faster and faster until a whole world crashes' into war, and the novel concludes with the implied corruption of a character called 'Chastity' (Patey, 1998:74).

The uncertainty of the early 1930s did not bring about dramatic changes to everyday life for the majority of people, particularly in the cities, as depression and unemployment tended to affect the older industrial areas such as mining towns in the North and Wales. Insecurity in the present and future prompted a prominent mood of nostalgia, looking back to the period immediately after the War that was now remembered as euphoric rather than anti-climactic, and there was criticism of the heady days of the 1920s, of which the present predicaments were the result, as decadent and irresponsible. The growth of the suburbs of London with newly opened tube connections into the City and affordable housing began a new ideal of domesticity in this period. Those that were the jazz-loving 'Bright Young Things' in the immediate post-War period were growing up and settling down, but yet jazz remained an important part of popular culture in Britain, including in the newly emerging 'talkies':

> The curiously delocalized and declassed atmosphere of jazz was aptly symbolized in the film version of Noel Coward's *Cavalcade*. Whereas in the earlier part of the film the barrel-organ tunes were used to hit off the atmosphere of London lower-class life at a particular date, towards the end of the film the jazz song, "Twentieth Century Blues", was used to hit off the atmosphere of post-war life at any venue. (Lambert, 1934/R1966:189)

> In film, jazz is best suited to accompany the contingent actions which are prosaic in a double sense: people promenading and chatting along a beach, a woman busying herself with her shoe. In such moments, jazz is so appropriate to the situation that we are hardly conscious of it anymore. (Adorno, [1936], trans. 1989:62)

Constant Lambert wrote in the Preface to the second edition (1937) of *Music Ho!: a study of music in decline* that 'Compared to the vertiginous 'twenties' the 'thirties' are curiously static' and that in 1937 'things, particularly in the world of popular music, are very much as they were [in 1934].' (1934/R1966:27). As Arthur Hutchings points out in his introduction to the 1966 edition of the same book, in retrospect Lambert's work is similarly pessimistic as literature of the same period 'such as *The Shape Things to Come* and *Brave New World,* the latter appearing exactly a year before Lambert's book' (1934/R1966:19). Lambert repeatedly expresses the idea that jazz is representative of this new 'spirit of the age':

> ... jazz has long ago lost the simple gaiety and sadness of the charming savages to whom it owes its birth, and is now for the most part a reflection of the jagged nerves, sex repressions, inferiority complexes and general dreariness of the modern scene. (1934/R1966:184)

> The intoxicating low spirits of jazz ... express, whether we like it or not, the constant tenor of our lives. (1934/R1966:189)

> More than the music of any period jazz has become a drug for the devitalized ... . They make up for the threadbare quality of their own emotions by drawing on the warm capacious reservoir of group emotion so efficiently provided by the American jazz kings. (1934/R1966:199)

The escapist function of jazz in the 1920s as discussed earlier was retained in the early 1930s through nostalgic identification with earlier sources of the music. The forms of jazz that became popular in Britain in the early 1930s built on the style established by the small, 'Dixieland'-type bands, some American examples of which had visited ten years earlier, and thus prompted nostalgia for the immediate post-War period that was in line with a general feeling of the time. Bernard Tipping presented a series of articles in *Rhythm* magazine at this time entitled *Looking Back* in which he reminisced about the early appearances of jazz in Britain including Murray Pilcer and the Original Dixieland Jazz Band. At the same time, as we have seen, the widespread criticism of society in the immediate past (the 1920s) was also being applied to the 'symphonic syncopation' played by augmented dance bands that was representative of this period.

Jazz and the Culture Industry II: Recording

The development of recording technology was crucial in allowing Britons more direct access than ever before to jazz, particularly as performed by African-American musicians. At first, the recording industry like radio broadcasting was centred upon technological aspects rather than recorded material itself: 'the business was geared to the manufacture, first, of industrial equipment used to produce records; second, of consumer furniture to play the records on; and third, the records themselves' (Chanan, 1995:55). Gramophones, like radios, could be housed in splendid cabinets, and 'it was even possible to conceive of – and make – an object with the threefold purpose of being an artistic lamp, a provider of music and a decorative item' (Ward, 1978:20), and for early producers 'records appeared almost as a sideline to promote the sale of furniture' (Chanan 1995:55). Improvements in methods of sound recording, the manufacture of discs and players and the developments in international marketing and dissemination meant that recordings could now play a more important role in setting popular music trends. Previously British audiences could experience the music through the occasional jazz number performed by one of the British dance bands on the radio, or at exclusive London venues that would not have been accessible by all interested parties, and in the mid-1920s, records had been expensive:

> If there are any objections at all to the present-day gramophone record they are certainly not in regard to the musical results achieved. The price of a record, however, is still a drawback … it is only a comparatively wealthy man who can buy half-a-dozen records a week, and yet that is but a mere percentage of the gems issued monthly by the recording companies. (*Melody Maker*, July 1926:30)

As we have seen, although the consumer had some control of the technological aspect of radio reception, they had little input as to content. As records became more affordable and distribution networks between America and Britain became established, it was possible for Britons to hear a greater range of American music, including blues singers and small groups playing hot numbers as well as large dance orchestras. 'Ordinary' people were now no longer reliant on the BBC to provide them with popular music and through records (and later, in addition, the new commercial radio stations such as Radio Normandie and Radio Luxembourg) they could exercise greater choice in the music that they wished to listen to in their own homes. The fact that recordings rather than live performance (due particularly to increasing restrictions on American musicians performing in Britain) became the main way to experience the latest jazz was compatible with middle-class suburban domesticity at this time. Effects could be created which involved the listener further in the performances as electrical recording developed. By picking up the natural resonance of a room, the listener could be 'brought into' the atmosphere of the performing space. Conversely, by use of close-micing techniques, an effect of 'artificial intimacy' could be produced, 'as if the singer and the song are transported into the presence of the listener', which led to the development of the 'crooning' style (Chanan, 1995:59).

In addition to widening the stylistic basis of the popular music that could be heard in Britain, the growing availability of jazz on record was significant in that, unlike radio or a live performance, records permitted repeated listening. This feature allowed the music to be both evaluated by critics and imitated by musicians with greater depth and accuracy: 'broadcasting differs from recorded music in that the critic has one chance only to consider the radio version, while the gramophone critic can play over his material as often as he likes.' (*Melody Maker*, April 1927:329). The familiarity with a wider range of popular music through recordings was vital in provoking critical responses to both the dissemination and musical content of popular music, an extension of a public tendency that has been noted in connection with BBC radio. It is surely no coincidence that the earliest critical writing on jazz produced in Britain is contemporaneous with the availability of a range of good quality recordings.

Jazz as Art

Re-evaluating the Culture Industry

Jazz was the first musical style to be primarily disseminated through the 'culture industry'. Although, as observed in Chapter 2, sheet music was sold in vast quantities in the early part of the century, records sold not only musical works but also performances and therefore their domination could be viewed as more holistic. The contemporaneous development of jazz and recording technology meant that they were intrinsically linked; jazz was the first significant musical style with a complete recorded history. The role of the 'culture industry' in ensuring the popularity of jazz led to considerable debate about the resultant artistic status of the music. For those critics, most famously Adorno, who consistently adhered to 'classical' music to provide the criteria on which to evaluate jazz, the relationship between jazz and recording meant that it was impossible for jazz to be art as it had sacrificed its essential autonomy to the 'culture industry' in order to take on a social function as entertainment. Although a strong relationship between music and its context is undoubtedly important in ensuring its popularity, both Mendl and Lambert recognized a problematic future for jazz that was only able to reflect its surroundings. Hence both assert the need for a 'serious' composer to take up jazz to ensure its future as an autonomous art form. The omnipresence of jazz in society can lead either to resistance or addiction in critiques in which the listener that is recognized as a passive victim of the 'culture industry':

> [The lover of music's] objection to jazz music, such as it is. consists partly in fatigue resulting from its over frequent performance. Almost everywhere he goes, in the street, on the river, in the restaurant and the theatre, syncopated dance music is hurled at him by singers and players, good, bad and indifferent. It is a small wonder that he wearies of it. But this is only another way of saying that he is a victim of its immense popularity. (Mendl, 1927:75)

> ... it is no rare experience to meet people whose lives are so surrounded, bolstered up and inflated by jazz that they can hardly get through an hour without its collaboration ... . (Lambert, 1934/R1966:199)

> The more deeply jazz penetrates society, the more reactionary elements it takes on, the more completely it is beholden to banality, and the less it will be able to tolerate freedom and the eruption of phantasy, until it finally glorifies repression itself as the incidental music to accompany the current collective. The more democratic jazz is, the worse it becomes. (Adorno, [1936], trans. Daniel, 1989:50)

Recordings also prompted a deeper understanding of artistic and cultural validity of jazz that allowed it to be more easily appreciated in its own right without persistent comparisons with classical music. Mendl's work provides a counter-argument to Adorno's culture industry theory: 'It has been said that jazz making is an industry; so it may be, but that does not prevent it from being also an art.' (1927:163), although his argument that jazz is 'a form of music; and as music is an art, it follows that jazz is an art form' (1927:162) might be regarded as simplistic. The Editorial of the special 'Dance Music' issue of the *Radio Times* in March 1933 made the vague pronouncement that 'Modern dance music is more than an art, or a branch of an art; it is a vast business' (Editorial, *Radio Times*, 17 March 1933:651). In Lambert's assessment of Duke Ellington there is some remarkably progressive thinking in recognizing the potential for the recordings to become art works in their own right:

> ... the first American records of his music may be taken definitively, like a full score ... . Ellington's best works are written in what may be called ten-inch record form, and he is perhaps the only composer to raise this insignificant disc to the dignity of a definite genre. (Lambert, 1936/R1966:187-8)

Nelson addresses the apparent incongruity between popularity and art more directly, asking: 'Why is that, when anything is popular, it is immediately assumed that it has no artistic value?' (1934:18) He states in the opening chapter of *All About Jazz*:

> To compare modern syncopation with serious music as an art form is manifestly ridiculous ... . That there is a future for Jazz as an art form, I am convinced, but, as I shall show later, only in its best aspects and not as the super-orchestrated form of the most banal of tunes. (1934:14)

There is no attempt here to align modern 'dance music' with classical precedents, and in rejecting the common idea of comparing jazz to classical music, Nelson allows himself the possibility of evaluating jazz more freely. His work exemplifies the growing public awareness of the commercial motives of the culture industry and its products, which accompanied the expansion of the record industry. In this period certain types of popular music began to be designated 'commercial', in particular, the presence of vocals, especially when performed by 'crooners', was often an indication of a 'commercial' recording. Song lyrics enabled particular numbers to be distinguished more easily and thus more directly linked with sales of sheet music and recordings where significant income could be secured, hence the BBC's opposition to song plugging. Mendl points out that:

> We have to remember that jazz appeals to a large number of people who are not ordinarily keen lovers of music. Therefore it is reasonable to think that the words account in many cases for the popularity of certain syncopated dance songs. (1927:125)

Both Mendl and Lambert construct criticisms of the popularity of jazz around song lyrics, which they see as contributing to the standardization of popular music. Both note the tendency of lyrics to reflect the prominent mood of the day, with Lambert contrasting the 'general air of physical attractiveness, sexual bounce and financial independence' in songs of the pre-War period with 'modern' lyrics which assume that 'one is poor, unsuccessful and either sex-starved or unable to hold the affections of such a partner as one may have had the luck to pick up' (Lambert, 1934/R1966:182-3). Lambert notes that many song lyrics are simply reflective of the music with which they are associated: 'It is almost impossible to find a quick fox-trot, however, that does not inform us that it is in a particular variant of common time, and that it is very gay in consequence' (1934/R1966:184). Furthermore, for Lambert and Adorno writing in the mid-1930s, the addition of meaningless 'crazy' lyrics to jazz is 'a desperate attempt to hide the underlying boredom and malaise' (1934/R1966:183) and 'a chance word, as a scrap of everyday, becomes a jacket for the music from which it spins forth: "bananas" and "cheese at the train station" and "Aunt Paula who eats tomatoes" have often enough knocked their erotic and geographic competition out of the field' (Adorno, [1936], trans. Daniel, 1989:62).

Re-evaluating Jazz Composition and Performance

Nelson most clearly and consistently expresses criticisms of commercial element of jazz, of which songs are the basis:

> The "jazz" song is really the nucleus of the whole business. Very often screaming with banality, it is taken from its birthplace in Tin Pan Alley, and dressed cunningly in rich harmonic and rhythmic garb for performance ... . A song is not valued as a work of art, but by reason of its sales. (1934:29)

Therefore, it is unsurprising that he also identifies the 'paucity of raw material' as the main difficulty in the future of jazz (1934:156). Unlike Lambert and Adorno, rather than necessarily calling for better composers as the only course of action,

Nelson addresses the need for performers and arrangers to develop commercial material in their work and establishes a new hierarchy of performer, arranger and composer in jazz:

> It is the cleverness of the arranger, which takes its banal melodic line and builds it into the colourful tone poem, pulsing with rhythm, with which we are familiar ... . The bands of a few years ago simply played from the commercial parts, like their cinema and café confreres, allowing their individual players free rein in their interpretations. From these individual solos grew "hot" choruses, and the manner in which these solos were played came to be known as the player's individual style. (1934:63)

Whilst Nelson notes the need for ingenious arrangers in jazz (1934:16), and particularly credits the arranger Ferde Grofé as being responsible for Paul Whiteman's success (1934:28), he is disparaging of bands who 'play arrangements, note for note, instead of allowing the various soloists free rein, so that modern renditions are interesting only for their arrangements and the precision of the players' (1934:16). A large proportion of Nelson's book is devoted to identifying the players that he considers the best performers on particular instruments, drawn from a variety of British and American bands. This approach is clearly reliant on recorded sources, and demonstrates the growing interest in the improvisations of individual jazz musicians, whereas the members of large bands, with the exception of the leader, had often been anonymous. Nelson achieves a much greater level of specificity in this regard in comparison with both Mendl and Lambert, and his work is generally more successful in identifying the 'artistic' qualities of jazz, whilst also acknowledging its popular-basis. Adorno, too, attributes arrangers as the 'qualified musicians' rather than the composers and writes:

> It seems almost as if material which is completely indifferent is best suited to the jazz treatment. One of the best known virtuoso pieces for jazz, the *Tiger Rag* that orchestras love to use to show off their talents, is extremely simple in terms of its composition. (Adorno, [1936] trans. Daniel, 1989:55)

The two features that Adorno exposes as potentially progressive in jazz are firstly, the 'reintroduction into the composition of those who are reproducing it' ([1936], trans. Daniel, 1989:55), unlike the alienation between the composer and performer in artistic music and the lack of freedom of interpretation in new music and secondly, the 'working process' which is 'an obvious distribution of labor' ([1936], trans. Daniel, 1989:56). Although Adorno was aware of the practicalities of performance and importance of the roles of performer and arranger in jazz, he was unable to acknowledge any freedom in these roles and the resulting music as their function was intrinsically linked to the demands of the culture industry. Fundamentally, the pronouncements of both Nelson and Adorno are based on their recognition of the *inevitability* of the commercialism of popular music:

> Here we have a popular music industry, and the bands to exploit their product. The bands are dependent upon the public for their success, so they have to give the public what they are supposed to want. Sob-stuff of the crudest possible type is "plugged" until we shout the choruses in our sleep. As it is a case of Hobson's Choice, the long-

suffering public buys the records of the tunes produced by the leading bands. Such tunes are called successes, and the publishers get ready at once to introduce their next number ... . As the publishers are prepared to go to almost any length to induce leaders to play their tunes, there is little to be done about the further emancipation of Jazz. (Nelson, 1934:156)

... the demand on the composer that his work always be "just like" and yet "original"... cripples all productive power. (Adorno [1936], trans. Daniel, 1989:54)

Re-evaluating Jazz and Race

The increasing recognition of the importance of the black contribution to jazz was vital to the revisions of the value judgements that were being made about popular music, as in the case of 'symphonic syncopation'. Lambert states 'the only jazz music of technical importance is that small section of it that is genuine Negroid. The "hot" Negro records still have a genuine and not merely galvanic energy, while the blues have a certain austerity that places them far above the sweet nothings of George Gershwin.' (1934/R1966:186.) This presents an obvious contrast with Mendl's description of 'nigger jazz bands' making 'pointless noises' (1927:48-9) and is consistent with a wider appreciation of black art and culture that took place in Britain in the early 1930s.

Although racism remained inherent in British society, positive, if often controversial, images of black people could be seen in the public sphere. In 1928, Paul Robeson appeared in *Showboat*, where he altered the lyrics of *Ol' Man River* so that it became an anthem of resistance, rather than submission, to oppression and suffering (Cope, 2001:25), and following in the footsteps of Ira Aldridge, appeared in the title role in *Othello* (1930). Some of Robeson's early films also illustrated positive characteristics, although in later projects such as *Sanders of the River* Robeson's characters conformed to stereotypes (Cope, 2001:32). In 1934, Nancy Cunard published her anthology *Negro*, a large and lavishly produced book in which notable and mostly black writers recorded 'the struggles and achievements, the persecutions and the revolts against them, or the Negro peoples' (1934:iii). *Negro* was problematic in that Cunard asserted that 'the Communist world-order is a solution of the race problem for the Negro' as it 'wipes out class distinctions' (1934:iii). For this reason the publication was later criticized by Henry Crowder, Cunard's black lover who had helped her to make contacts in the African-American community, who also disagreed with her selection of material 'the thought and plan were brilliant, but they were very badly executed' (Crowder, 1987:118). Undoubtedly, though, the publication of *Negro* was 'a resounding refutation of racists, a proclamations of black achievement, and a celebration of black culture.' (Allen in Crowder, 1987:13). On a more practical level, Dr Harold Moody founded the League of Coloured Peoples in 1931, and later a journal, *The Keys*, to represent the interests of black people in Britain (Fryer, 1985:327).

Nelson's discussion of 'the future of jazz' demonstrates the most radical departure from the theories of his predecessors on jazz and race. Instead of expounding the theory that jazz is reliant on European composers to develop it, Nelson states:

It is my belief that most of the future development of Jazz will come from the coloured race themselves, and not from us. We have certainly played a great part in emancipating our present popular music from the crude form of the early cake walks, and we have standardized the instrumentation of the modern dance band. But our mania for order has run us into a *cul de sac.* We lack the spontaneity of the coloured people and their innate feel for the jazz idiom … . Their playing is characterized by its extreme fervour; instead of playing in the detached manner of white bands, these coloured artists subordinate every feeling to the job in hand. (1934:163)

Here Nelson expresses the self-critical tendencies of the period and the observation that 'our mania for order has run us into a *cul de sac*' might have been equally applied to the political situation of the day. In the face of such self-criticism, it was difficult to maintain a sense of European superiority. The discourse of primitivism remains inherent in Nelson's description of the 'spontaneity', 'feel' and 'fervour' of black musicians, whereas their white counterparts have been responsible for 'standardization' and a 'detached' style of playing. It can be seen that black music continued to hold similar escapist appeal as a cultural alternative to the complexities and failings of Western civilization as in the immediate post-war period.

Conversely, Adorno interpreted the widespread adoption of black jazz as a more superficial response based on the externialities of fashion rather than any deep understanding, maybe as a result of his experience of jazz enthusiasts in Oxford (see later), suggesting that that the whole idea of blackness in jazz had been fetishized and that 'the skin of the black man functions as much as a colouristic effect as does the silver of the saxophone' ([1936], trans. Daniel, 1989:53). Adorno rejects the 'wild' African origins of jazz, inherent in a common romantic 'primitivist' interpretation, suggesting instead the origins of the music were in 'the domesticated body of bondage' ([1936], trans. Daniel, 1989:53) with 'wild' gestures then analyzed as an attempt to break into the culture industry. Nelson's statement indicates that black music was now being appreciated in its own right for its complexity and quality, and is representative of the feeling that civilizing impulses were beginning to be recognized by many people as being unnecessary, superficial and even racist. As Simon Frith writes: 'whereas before it was critically obvious that white jazz was better than black jazz because of its refinement, now the same musical description led to the opposite judgement: black jazz was better than white jazz because of its lack of refinement' (1996:44).

The awareness of the workings of the 'culture industry' was an important part of the complex mixture of factors that assisted the increase in the popularity of black jazz in the early 1930s. African-American jazz was relatively obscure and profoundly different in sound to the frequently heard 'commercial' forms of popular music:

In the early days of jazz the Negro exponents were usually condemned by the experts as too crude … their jazz had a blatancy which was far from pleasing to white ears … in our opinion, their jazz was a poor thing beside the refined product of the best white bands. (Nelson, 1934:162)

In the early 1930s, the continuation of the 'primitivist' mode of reception of black culture meant that black musicians were now regarded as innocent of commercial motives ('They do not seem to be influenced by any dictates of commercialism' [Nelson, 1934:163]) and able to express themselves freely in the context of small groups. Although this was an essentialist notion that perpetuated stereotypical beliefs about black musicians, this contrasted with the overtly commercial, large, uniform and controlled presentations by dance orchestras that could be heard on the BBC and seen in established venues in the capital.

The increased awareness of the role of Jewish musicians in commercial popular music was also a factor in allowing the continued emphasis on black performers as commercial innocents. Lambert states in *Music Ho!* that 'most jazz is written and performed by cosmopolitan Jews' (1934/R1966:174), to whom he attributes the 'curiously sagging quality' and 'almost masochistic melancholy' of contemporary jazz (1934/R1966:185). A perception was that Jewish composers and arrangers, rather than black performers, profited from jazz, as Lambert writes: 'There is an obvious link between the exiled and persecuted Jews and the exiled and persecuted Negroes, which the Jews, with their admirable capacity for drinking the beer of those who have knocked down the skittles, have not been slow to turn to their advantage' (1934/R1966:185). This is commensurate with the sustained criticism of the musical material (popular songs) upon which jazz was based, which was often produced by Jewish composers.

The place of the Jew in British society in the early 1930s parallels the situation of black people in Britain earlier in the century, in that whilst they were generally admitted into the country legally, they were nevertheless subject to prejudice and discrimination and found sanctuary in the ethnically diverse West End communities of Soho and Fitzrovia that were to some extent isolated from mainstream society. Gerry Black outlines the gradual emigration of Jews from East to West London during the nineteenth century, which was followed by the trend of direct immigration into the West End where population peaked in 1925 (1994:20). Thus situated in the 'entertainment district' of London, Jews were well represented 'in the film industry in Wardour Street, the theatre in Shaftesbury Avenue, including theatrical costumiers, the music publishers in Denmark Street and the musicians who gathered in Archer Street.' (Black, 1994:54). In this environment Jews were publicly seen to be thriving, and the feeling might have been that this was at the expense of British workers. Criticism of Jewish success in Britain had been in evidence since their success in the industries of World War One (principally in supplying uniforms). Young Jews could often not fight for the British army and worked remuneratively whilst Britons of a similar age were fighting and dying (Lipman, 1990:141, 143). Ironically, Jews suffered in attacks in Britain against German people and property, and Fascists capitalized on anti-Jewish sentiment, which was probably exacerbated by the economic depression, leading to physical violence culminating in violent clashes such as the 'Battle of Cable Street' in 1936 (Lipman, 1990:185), which recalls the race riots that took place, particularly at Britain's ports, in the immediate post-War years.

Whilst the Jewish contribution to jazz was gauged through widely available sheet music, the growing familiarity with American jazz on record was vital in the development of different criterion of value for assessing jazz performance. Now, with access to recordings by black American musicians, many people in Britain began to discover the type of jazz that had been performed in America since the early 1920s but had not been widely heard in Britain until this point and this served to highlight the inadequacies of symphonic syncopation for many people. There was even evidence of a shift in the BBC's programming of jazz and dance music, as two articles (Duval's *The Genesis of Jazz* and Lambert's *The Future of Highbrow Jazz*, which was a rehearsal of the jazz content for *Music Ho!*) that recognize the importance of the black contribution to jazz were included the 'Dance Music' issue of the *Radio Times* (17 March 1933). Whilst the BBC clearly wished to continue to promote the performances of their own Dance Orchestra, which was pictured on the cover, the acknowledgement of the black contribution to jazz provides a basis for the criticism of modern, white, commercial forms of the music that the BBC was so keen to air. Duval's insightful account traces the black origins of jazz from Southern Negro music, through minstrel shows and ragtime and also, unusually for the period, discussed the origins and influence of the blues. He encouraged his readers that 'when you hear the modern Jazz Kings by records or radio, or see them on the talkies or on the stage, let your thoughts wander for a moment to the shadowy figures that preceded them' (*Radio Times*, 17 March 1933:658). Similarly, Lambert states in his article that 'the most vital qualities in jazz are due to the Negro mentality' (17 March 1933:659). The admission of such views into the *Radio Times* might indicate a more open view of jazz on the part of the BBC that was to allow Duke Ellington to broadcast a few months later. Indeed, the inclusion of these articles might have been intended to justify this decision.

Defining and Understanding Jazz

Undoubtedly, many people continued to enjoy the broadcasts given by the BBC Dance Orchestra under Jack Payne and later, Henry Hall and other similar bands in the early 1930s and beyond. Hence, the impact of recording on the dissemination of American jazz and its resultant influence upon popular music in Britain could easily be overstated. The majority of records available in Britain in fact disseminated a similar concept as BBC radio (civilized, white dance music as opposed to black hot jazz) and gave this style further validity. The bands that were regularly broadcast were, of course, in demand for recording but in addition the record companies appointed the leaders of these groups as Musical Directors whereby they had more control over the output of the label with which they were associated (Nott, 2002:49). It was a common practice for bands and individual musicians to record under different names and often for different labels, thereby standardizing the overall output still further. James Nott has pointed out 'imports [of records] were not large and the proportion of the home market for records held by British goods stayed at over 99 per cent for the whole period 1924-1935' (2002:18) and jazz, 'although available in Britain on HMV, Columbia, Parlophone and Brunswick labels, was poorly represented in terms of volume.' (2002:48)

Nevertheless, it is clear that from the late 1920s dance music and jazz began to become more clearly defined, rather than being either more or less synonymous or the former being regarded as an improvement of the latter, primarily as a result of the growth of the record industry and associated developments. In summary, records allowed more people to become acquainted with the sound of jazz, and to begin to understand spontaneous expression in performance as an artistic quality, particularly in relation to African-American musicians. This contrasted with the pre-meditated, standardized and carefully constructed dance music arrangements. At the same time, the growing realization and criticism of the commercial motivation of the dance music 'industry' contrasted with the relative scarcity of American jazz records. Whilst commercial dance music was reassuringly familiar, omnipresent and understandable through its use of standardized clichés, jazz remained exotic, mystifying and distanced from the mainstream. Jazz as distinct from dance music continued to flourish in societies that were outside the experiences of most people, such as nightclubs of Soho and the slightly more upper-class Fitzrovia in London's West End, and in addition, the universities of Oxford and Cambridge. However, records allowed ease of access to jazz for all, and a significant proportion of the records that *were* imported into Britain were for the new breed of 'jazz enthusiast' (Nott, 2002:18).

Popular Criticism

This interest in jazz on record was well supported by the periodicals *Melody Maker* (from 1926 onwards) and *Rhythm* (from 1927) that were vital sources of information for enthusiasts and professional musicians alike. An article on gramophone-record making by Percy Mackey to provide an 'introduction for those that find themselves in the studio for the first time' (January 1926:18) included in the first issue of *Melody Maker* demonstrates that these publications first appeared contemporaneously with the development of the record industry. The magazines helped listeners to choose which records to purchase as their record review pages featured extensive critical and comparative study of the latest releases and offered insights into the musical material and performance style. As such, they were extremely influential on the perceptions and understanding of jazz in Britain at the time.

In the first few years of *Melody Maker* the views of the editor, Edgar Jackson, infiltrated much of the material. Jackson's supposed neglect of black performers and his negativity in the reviews of the recordings by black musicians that he did choose to include has been interpreted as a deliberately racist policy (see Godbolt, 1986, Chapter 2). However, as increasing numbers of black performers were included this apparent bias probably also reflects the difficulties of obtaining their recordings, as the numbers of white American small group records also increased over the same period. The nature of the reviews of black performances, which although today would be regarded as racist, was to an extent compatible with general tendencies in the evaluation of such music resulting from the persistent attempts to apply inappropriate 'classical' criteria and the influence of the perception of black culture as 'primitive'. Reviews of groups led by Jelly Roll Morton, Fletcher Henderson and Duke Ellington were described respectively:

A band of which I have not heard hitherto, called Jelly Roll Morton's Red Hot Peppers is introduced to us in "The Chant" and "Black Bottom Stomp", both "hot" Charleston numbers. No one can say that the musicians are not wonderful performers. Nevertheless, we are treated to an exhibition of the bluest jazz, not as it should be to-day, but as it was about six years ago. The fact that this is about the best record I have come across for Charleston dancing owing to the "hot" rhythm behind it certainly does not excuse the fact that it is crude in orchestration and poor amusement to listen to it. (January 1927:43)

The ideas embodied in its orchestrations are really excellent – far better than those we are used to hearing from the average nigger band, and its technique better. It is a pity that its playing displays that slight crudeness which seems inseparable from all renderings of bands of the coloured variety, otherwise it could be one of the best 'hot' dance bands of the day. (June 1927:573)

… [despite the] usual failings of practically all negro bands, they still have some of the darkies' good features, such as style, lilt, and in many places, though crudely portrayed, soul. (June 1927:579)

The qualities that are generally praised in these recordings are those that were generally associated with black musicians, such as 'hot rhythm' and 'soul', and the classical features such as 'orchestration' and 'technique' are criticized (except in Henderson's case, where the quality of these aspects seems to surprise the reviewer). In addition, the music of the Red Hot Peppers seems old-fashioned in comparison to the 'sophistication' of modern dance music of 1927. This exemplifies the continued influence of primitivism upon the reception of black culture.

Although Jackson was unable to reconcile the 'crudeness' that he claimed to hear in all black bands, new criteria for the assessment of jazz is steadily formulated in *Melody Maker* as a response to the increasing availability of recordings of American bands. Early issues of the magazine uphold dance music as performed by Paul Whiteman and Jack Hylton as the 'best' popular music. Hylton wrote about jazz in sensational terms in the first issue of *Melody Maker*: 'Jazz came almost like a protest from the God of Rhythm against the public neglect of him.' (January 1926:14.) Jazz is referred to only in the vaguest sense in these early issues, and more often implied through the term 'hot', a concept that received increasing attention in the magazine and which will be examined in detail in Chapter 8. Few Americans are mentioned in the first issue in which British dance music is praised in articles by Jack Hylton and Paul Specht, although increasing numbers of white American dance bandleaders were included in subsequent months.

The difference between music variously referred to as 'straight' 'sweet' or 'legitimate' and that termed 'jazz' or 'hot' bubbles under the surface of the first twelve issues of the magazine, but was finally articulated clearly in a piece entitled 'Popular Music' in the January 1927 edition. The article describes the need for two bands in large ballrooms to provide two types of music, that which has a 'flowing melody' that can be played by a large orchestra and is easy to dance to due to its simple rhythm, and 'hot' music, that demands greater individuality from its performers and is not as suitable for dances in large halls. It is noted that many musicians may wish to play the latter style of music, but that the public still want to listen to the former type (January 1927:6).

In the issues of 1927 there are persistent attempts to try and identify the personnel of recordings, much of which is inaccurate and misspelled, but this does reflect an awareness of the importance of individual musicians in small hot bands. Spike Hughes points out that for jazz enthusiasts at that time 'It was not enough to hear and enjoy an unfamiliar record; we had to know exactly which player performed which solo, and it became a point of honour to be able to reel off the entire personnel in the most offhand manner.' (1951:105.) There is also increasing recognition of the importance of improvisation, for example the editorial of the February 1927 issue demands better education for 'the dance band musician who has very often to improvise', a review of a Bert Firman record confidently states: 'I am convinced that all the titles mentioned below are played from the ordinary orchestral parts issued by the publishers. Of course, they are not rendered note for note, the musicians extemporising as they go along' (February 1927:141). There are many more technical articles dealing with improvisation from this date. The growing awareness of American jazz meant that British dance bands, even Hylton's, faced increasing criticism for being behind developments in America (April 1927:306) and in an editorial entitled 'Scrap the Dance Teachers!' in July 1927, there was a demand for a more 'interactive' and less prescribed type of dancing that was compatible with hot music. Eventually, in May 1927, there was a breakthrough on the 'Gramophone Review' pages of *Melody Maker*, as it was recognized that the same criteria could not be applied in relation to all the records that were being reviewed. Instead, three separate categories were proposed: 'Hot Style Dance Record', 'Popular Dance Record' and 'Rhythmic Concert Record' (May 1927: 465).

Listening and Collecting

The ideas about jazz presented in *Melody Maker* influenced public perceptions and taste, simply due to the scarcity of information available from any other sources, but its impact was also due to the practical ways in which readers were invited to participate in the music. The availability of jazz on record prompted new modes of engagement with jazz in addition to dancing, which was now an activity that tended to be associated with commercial dance music. Increasingly, even at this early stage, there are signs that jazz was becoming music for listening to closely, as it came to be regarded an art form that demanded close attention. In the 1933 'Dance Issue' of the *Radio Times* the Editor commented: 'Whatever may be our personal opinion of jazz, it is, incontrovertibly, the most popular music of the day – despite the strange fact that the majority of those who listen to it with enjoyment do not dance to it.' (*Radio Times*, 17 March 1933:651). The rise of listening as opposed to dancing was encouraged through the analytical depth of reviews and articles in *Melody Maker*, where readers were called upon to note particular features of an arrangement or solo, whereas prior to the widespread availability of recordings the musical features of popular music had not been examined in such detail.

Nott indicates that the market both for the gramophone and jazz records was 'a predominantly middle-class group, whose demand was fairly inelastic despite changing economic circumstances' (2002:18) and Adorno observed that 'jazz permeates all levels of society, even the proletariat ... . Often, the lower classes identify themselves with the upper classes through their reception of jazz' ([1936], trans. Daniel 1989:50). Record collecting and listening to records were domestic activities that were compatible with middle-class suburban lifestyles and Rhythm Clubs allowed these hobbies to gain a social function within the particular communities in which they were founded. In newly constructed residential areas such as the outer London suburbs, various associations were being established that 'brought together people who had much in common but who would otherwise probably not have met' and became synonymous with 'friendship' (McKibben, 1998:97). The idea of forming groups similar to literary circles for listening to and discussing hot music first appeared in *Melody Maker* on 3 June 1933 in a letter from James P. Holloway. At this time, record collecting was becoming a distinct hobby, with letters to the magazine outlining the size and scope of individual readers' collections. Although American jazz recordings were not available in large quantities in Britain, collectors could visit specialist shops such as Levy's on Whitechapel Road where one could find 'all manner of rare recordings imported from America and issued with mud-coloured labels. It was at Levy's that we first encountered the music of Duke Ellington whose name was not yet known even to the expert collectors in this country.' (Hughes, 1951:322). The proposed 'Hot Circles' would allow extensive collections and rare records obtained by individuals to be shared. The idea caught on rapidly, with *Melody Maker* taking a co-coordinating role: 'Anybody desirous of commencing clubs of this nature should write to us and we will publish his name and address.' (1 July 1933:7) The first Rhythm Club was known as 'The Melody Maker Club No. 1' and met in premises in the West End of London, but the phenomenon spread rapidly across the country. By May 1935, when the British Federation of Rhythm Clubs was established, there were 90 clubs in existence (Nott, 2002:199).

The Rhythm Clubs launched their own publications, *Swing Music* and *Hot News and Rhythm Record Review*, in March and April 1935 respectively. These dealt specifically with hot music as distinct from commercial dance music, whereas *Melody Maker* maintained some balance between the various different forms of popular music. These publications articulate a clear 'pressure group' agenda that lay behind social and educative basis of the Rhythm Club movement, as it was felt that with enough members it would be possible for the British Federation of Rhythm Clubs to lobby the culture industries and 'indicate to the gramophone companies the records that they would like issued and re-issued, and to approach the BBC with reference to broadcasts of rhythmic music.' (*Hot News and Rhythm Record Review*, May 1935:23.) Publications and Rhythm Clubs played an important role in promoting, co-coordinating and supporting the dissemination of jazz in Britain through records by providing listeners with information and encouraging discussion and critical debate, and formalized the growing distinction between hot and dance styles.

Professional and Amateur Performance

The recruitment both of existing professional musicians and enthusiastic amateurs into dance bands was fast and widespread at this time (Ehrlich, 1985:202). Listening to records developed from a hobby into a necessity for young musicians emerging into the profession. Spike Hughes, an important musician and critic of the period, commented that 'We had learnt all we knew about jazz at second hand, from gramophone records and a very occasional short-wave broadcast' (1951:102). Many musicians that were influential in the development of jazz in Britain encountered jazz on records of this period in their formative years, whether this was in East London, at public school or in the university community of Cambridge:

> I had been listening to [Adrian Rollini's] bass saxophone playing on records and he was the greatest influence on my taking up that instrument and on shaping my style on it. (Harry Gold, 2000:35)

> I discovered that throughout the school [Stowe] were little cells of jazz lovers. Slowly I learnt something about the music and its history, most of it inaccurate, all of it romantic. I heard my first Bessie Smith record. (George Melly, 2000:386)

> I saw *Blackbirds* several times and I returned to the London Pavilion mostly to hear what went on in the orchestra pit. A more important factor in my growing interest in jazz ... was the issue in the spring and summer of 1927 of some unusual gramophone records ... . "Washboard Blues" was the first of a series of records of this type issued during the summer at Cambridge and their success in the University town encouraged the gramophone companies to put many more on the market. (Spike Hughes, 1946:307-8)

Records were vital in acquainting professional musicians in Britain with the latest innovations in American jazz, and listening to recordings was recommended by jazz publications as an educational method:

> A careful study of gramophone records of the best dance pianists will enable one to analyze their styles and reduce them to the essentials. It is then quite simple to take the best features from each, and form a style for yourself from the bunch. But in order to keep in the front rank, it is also necessary to keep up to date, and to do this a close watch has to be kept on the latest American records – for America is still the origin of new ideas for the dance band. (Nelson, 1934:44)

It was easy for a musician with a good ear, such as Spike Hughes, to learn to imitate recordings:

> ... I found it easy enough to pick out the bass notes of the childishly simple and monotonous sequence of chords which passes for "harmony" in modern jazz. Within a few weeks I was able to accompany any "hot" record played on the portable gramophone, if not strictly in tune, then at least in time; and within less than two years I

was voted Britain's Best Bassist by the readers of *The Melody Maker*. (Hughes, 1951:13)

However, as Cyril Ehrlich states, 'lesser talents followed similar paths' and 'popular instruments were easily picked up, by old hands doubling ... or newcomers plucking, blowing, banging and squeezing ... .' (1985:202-3).

The growth of amateur jazz performance in Britain was a direct result of the advances in recording technology which allowed closer study of the music, and it was a relatively small step from being a dedicated and attentive listener of hot jazz at a Rhythm Club meeting to performing it, and the clubs themselves quickly became arenas for live performance as well as 'record recitals' (Nott, 2002:199). The desire to perform was motivated by several factors. Popular music was seen as a burgeoning industry at a time of widespread unemployment, and the high salaries and glamorous lifestyles of the top dance band leaders such as Bert Ambrose and Jack Hylton were well-publicized. As previously noted, the public were generally aware of the commercial motives of the recording industry and would also recognize the opportunities that this presented for musicians. For amateur musicians hoping to find fame and fortune in a dance or jazz band, just as important as the records themselves were the record reviews and articles in *Melody Maker* and *Rhythm* that explained how the ideas that could be heard on records could be put into practice. *Melody Maker* invited readers to write in with their questions to be answered by instrumental experts (an early example featured responses from the American saxophonist Al Starita), and articles focusing on arranging for dance band and hot extemporization appeared frequently. For example, those on hot trumpet and trombone playing in *Melody Maker* in April 1926 drew on recordings by the New York groups the Goofus Five and the Cotton Pickers. Such articles relied heavily on conventional notation, rendering jazz instantly accessible to trained musicians and but also provided a short cut to apparent proficiency that avoided hours of careful listening and imitation, a less easy skill for enthusiasts to acquire. *Melody Maker* actively encouraged amateur performers, by organizing contests for amateur bands and providing arrangements of the latest popular songs with parts that could be extracted from the magazine. Amateur composers and arrangers could also submit their work to be scrutinized by professionals and their comments were printed in the magazine.

The universities of Oxford and Cambridge, which at that time 'were two main hubs of advanced recreational fashion: they were not merely suburbs of London, as they afterwards became' (Graves and Hodge, 1940:122), were important centres for amateur jazz performance. Hot music was new, exotic, fashionable and subversive for classically educated students. The Oxbridge communities were similarly socially exclusive and intrinsically linked with the London nightclub scene, where hot music could be heard live and to which students travelled for nights out (Stannard, 1982:103). The compulsory entrance examinations that were instituted after the War meant that Oxbridge undergraduates of the day tended to come from families that could afford to pay for a public school education (Leedman-Green, 1996:191). This in turn meant that students could afford to buy records, music and instruments. Evelyn Waugh was introduced to black American jazz at Oxford (Stannard, 1986:105), and Spike Hughes encountered jazz on record whilst living 'sub-undergraduate existence' in Cambridge ostensibly preparing for scholarship examinations (1946:242). Hughes also recalls making friends with Dan Chadwick who had 'discovered Red Nichols at Oxford at the same time as I had first heard Guy Naylor's [similar] records in Cambridge' (1946:322). The background of Oxbridge students also meant that it was likely they would have received musical training in their school education, and it was an easy step for them to begin to imitate what they heard on records. Fred Elizalde was able to form his first British band in Cambridge with his brother, who was studying at the university, and other students who were amateur musicians but enthusiasts for hot music. Importantly, amateur student performers were less constrained by the parameters of public taste than their professional counterparts, and were free to play whatever music they liked for their own enjoyment. This enabled progressive jazz to flourish in these environments.

Evelyn Wilcock's research confirms that 'in the [Oxford] university setting hot music was ubiquitous' (1996:65) and suggests that Adorno's remarks on amateur performers (and other subjects) in 'On Jazz' were influenced by his experiences of jazz when he was studying at Oxford. Wilcock points out that Adorno was interested in the fact that the amateur student bands were often more popular in Oxford than the professional bands that were brought up from London for the important dances of the year (1996:66). Adorno suggests that amateurs, through imitation and competition, perpetuate the commercial world, which he saw as the main restraining factor upon the development of jazz: 'his inventions are embodied within accumulated traditions ... the amateur ... imitates the clichés of current jazz music and guarantees the commercial opportunity to underbid it wherever possible'. The amateur has a perpetual fear of the music which means that 'he aspires to adapt himself to it, without, however, succeeding in it' resulting in his reliance on the products of the culture industry ([1936], trans. Daniel 1989:58). This means that he 'represents the extreme case of the public representative in the production of jazz ... the amateur is not the uncompromised and unsullied person whose originality asserts itself against the routine of the business; this idea is part of the mythic mystification of the black man.' ([1936], trans. Daniel 1989:57) Adorno's comparison between amateur and black performers, who in their very assertion of their freedom of expression in jazz are falling into a commercially imposed stereotype, provides an interesting premise for understanding the popularity of amateur bands and performance at this time. It may be that it was the anti-commercial stance and relatively unrefined sound of amateur instrumentalists that seemed closer to the hot American jazz that Oxbridge undergraduates heard on record than the polished sound of a professional British dance band. Hughes writes that musicians that he heard on record whilst at Cambridge

> ... brought a new charm to jazz, a technical dexterity which served an unusual inventiveness; and they had the added attraction of being 'uncommercial' and obviously playing to please themselves. It was this last quality which appealed most to us, for we were at a rebellious age, and while we were all prepared to hire a car and drive to London to hear Paul Whiteman at the Royal Albert Hall, we were naturally

proud to know that we appreciated the purely esoteric art of Real Jazz which was above the head of the rabble. (1946:309)

Hughes was shocked to find a more material reaction to the latest developments in jazz when he began working professionally in London. He summarized the view in the bandroom of a 'Very Smart Hotel': 'There was no room in the profession for any fancy musical ideas, as for all those American fellows they kept writing about in *The Melody Maker* – well, it was alright for chaps at Oxford and Cambridge colleges and that sort of thing, but the public hadn't got time for it; in business you had to give the public what it had got time for.' (1951:20.)

Naturally, there was some opposition to amateur or 'semi-pro[fessional]' performers from professional musicians at this time. *Melody Maker* summarized the prevailing view in April 1927:

> We all know what amateur would-be jazz performers generally are – full of such temperament, ideas and ambition as study of gramophone records and English bands has inspired, but hopelessly lacking in sufficient technical ability to put them into successful effect on an instrument. (April 1927:337)

The opinions expressed on the subject of amateur musicians in *Melody Maker* varied between 1926 and 1935, indicating the problems that the magazine had in supporting both professional and amateur musicians. Whilst the former were influential, the latter made up a significant proportion of the readership. An article in November 1926 warned against the 'Dangers of Amateurism' that was lowering rates of pay and opportunities for professionals, but yet competitions for amateur dance bands were an important activity of the magazine. In August 1927, under the heading 'Fleecing the Song-writer' the magazine warned amateur composers and authors about being exploited by publishing houses (August 1927:735), whilst offering a tutorial service for these composers. In November 1932 *Melody Maker* was advising 'semi-pros' that 'the profession is overcrowded, that competition has never been fiercer, that salaries are at a low level, that a musician's life, at best, is an unstable one' and proceeded to tell a cautionary tale of an amateur musician trying to make a living in London (November 1932:867). The policy of *Melody Maker* might be summarized as wishing to encourage amateurs to remain semi-professional. As a result of the nationwide popularity of dance music, 'the large numbers [of amateurs] that flooded the dance band scene in the 1920s and 1930s found the transition between amateur and professional status both easy and fast' (Nott, 2002:137). The demand for dance bands throughout the country ensured that there was generally enough work available, and there was a need for dance bands 'run by and composed of men who had other, more permanent jobs' (Nott, 2002:130), particularly to provide music in suburban and rural locations.

The Future of Jazz

An important development in the latter part of the extended 'jazz age' was that jazz, in the form of hot music, and dance music were becoming increasingly distinct through closer analysis and appreciation of the precise musical characteristics and function of these styles that was permitted by records. The rise and influence of hot music in Britain will be examined in detail in Chapter 8, but hot music was recognized as being a profoundly American innovation, even when the importance of the black contribution had yet to be fully appreciated. The contributions of individual musicians within ensembles were receiving more attention, particularly in respect to hot solos that were often improvised. Attentive listening was necessary for such detailed analysis, and this resulted in imitation of performances by musicians and calls for freer improvisational dance in response to the music. Greater public awareness of the 'culture industry' meant that hot jazz, with its relatively un-polished sounds and often produced by black Americans that were perceived as innocent of commercial motives, was understood as being much closer to the ideal of an autonomous art form. Adorno was forced to admit that 'this music, at least in Europe, has reached only a fraction of the general public' ([1936], trans. Daniel, 1989:64), and asserts that hot jazz allows 'the upper class to maintain a clear conscience about its taste' ([1936], trans. Daniel, 1989:51) whilst being unintelligible to the majority. As a niche market, it seems clear that both the enthusiast and the amateur were vital in keeping this strand of popular music alive in Britain at this time with the former importing hot records and the latter imitating them in their own performances with the support of information in *Melody Maker* and *Rhythm*. The best musicians who began as amateurs, such as Spike Hughes and Elizalde's Quinquaginta Ramblers, achieved some success and ensured that hot music was influential upon mainstream dance music.

Mendl, Lambert, Nelson and Adorno agreed that jazz had a future beyond the time at which they were writing, albeit often relying on their knowledge of the development of classical music by great composers to propose the nature of this evolution. Even Adorno, despite his reservations about jazz and contrary to the opinion expressed by some modern critics, did shift his position on jazz fundamentally, from bidding it 'farewell' in 1933 to considering the music as 'perennial fashion' in 1955. Certainly, even during the period that might be understood as an extended 'jazz age', jazz had shown considerable variation and development in its function, musical characteristics, methods of dissemination, cultural identity, ideology and modes of engagement, which ensured that it continued to remain relevant in Britain. Consideration of these aspects will provide the focus for analysis and comparison in the chapters that follow in the second part of this book.

PART II
THE EVOLVING PRESENCE OF JAZZ
IN BRITAIN

Chapter 4

In Dahomey: A Negro Musical Comedy

In Dahomey: A Negro Musical Comedy was composed and conducted by Will Marion Cook, an important figure in the history of African-American music in Britain as in 1903 he brought this show and also, in 1919, the Southern Syncopated Orchestra, to London. Both groups consisted entirely of black performers, and represented a conscious effort by Cook to promote black music and musicians. Cook had obtained a 'classical' music education, including studying the violin under Joachim in Berlin and at the National Conservatory in New York, which at the time was headed by Dvořák, who 'urged American composers to forge a new path using the indigenous musics of America' (Carter, 2000:207). Cook made his Carnegie Hall debut and received a promising review, but was clearly classified as a 'colored violinist' and realized that his career as a performer would be limited by the fact that he was black. He then devoted himself to composition, writing several musicals in his lifetime and influencing other black musicians and composers, most notably Duke Ellington (Dixon, 1992:14-15).[1] Cook first became well known through *Clorindy, the Origin of the Cakewalk*, which through his sheer determination was performed at the Casino Roof Garden in New York in 1898 (Dixon, 1992:15). Cook commented optimistically on the importance of this achievement for black artists: 'Negroes were at last on Broadway, and there to stay. Gone was the uff-dah of the minstrel! Gone the Massa Linkum stuff! We were artists and we were going a long, long way.' (Cook, 1947:233).

Cook came into contact with many black composers, librettists, lyricists and performers in New York that shared his aim to elevate the image of the Negro. He was a member of the 'All-Star Stock Company' at Worth's Museum that 'worked to train a professional group of show people that became the core company of many later shows' (Riis, 1989:26). Indeed, the show *A Trip to Coontown*, written by Bob Cole, who was the leader of this company, provided a precedent for *In Dahomey*, as it had:

> ... a continuous plot and a full cast of characters, and it provided a full evening's entertainment; it thus became the first full-length black musical comedy actually written, performed, and managed by blacks. It sparked many imitators and inaugurated

---

[1] Cook taught Ellington 'some of the standard devices for melody writing taught at conservatories' as he recognized that Ellington would never attend a conservatory himself (Collier, 1987:109). He encouraged Ellington to 'First find the logical way, and when you find it, avoid it, and let your inner self break through and guide you. Don't try to be anybody else but yourself'. Ellington wrote: 'That time with him [Cook] was one of the best semesters I ever had in music.' (Ellington, 1974:97).

a decade of New York shows patronized and applauded by both black and white audiences. (Riis, 1989:28)

Cook was one of a group of black artists that met at the flat of comedy duo Bert Williams and George Walker and then at Marshall's Hotel, both on West 53rd Street, for evenings of 'Southern Food, syncopated music, and stimulating dialogue on how, in effect, to remove the minstrel mask from the musical stage' (Carter, 2000:207). This group was to be the basis for the formation of the Memphis Students, who visited Britain in 1905, and the Clef Club, organized by James Reese Europe to assert the aims of the group more publicly. Specifically, Cook became acquainted with artists who were to be fundamental to the later success of In Dahomey such as Williams and Walker and poet and lyricist Paul Laurence Dunbar (Southern, 1983:231). Will Marion Cook's son, Mercer, recalled that In Dahomey was conceived specifically as an operetta for Williams and Walker (Cook, Mercer; symposium paper contained in IJS 'Cook' file, p.8). The formative years of Cook and the others in New York took place against a background of racially motivated violence and tension, which increased the need for solidarity in black communities. Ann Charters, in her biography of Bert Williams, describes riots in New York in August 1900, where 'mobs of whites assaulted Negroes, due to a murder of a white vice squad patrolman'. Walker was injured in the riots, and Williams was 'psychologically affected' (1970:54-55).

In Dahomey opened in New York in 1903, and was the first full-length black musical comedy on Broadway (Riis, 1989:91). Later in the year the cast sailed for Britain, opening at the Shaftesbury Theatre in London in May where the show ran for seven months (Sampson, 1980:25). The original cast remained touring in Britain until 1904, when they returned to America and were replaced by new performers (Riis, 1989:104). In Dahomey was not only the first black musical comedy to appear in Britain, but also the most significant, successful and widely influential (due to the length of its run) all-black entertainment to be staged in Britain since the nineteenth century minstrel shows. As such, an examination of the nature of this show and the responses to it is fundamental to understanding the role and reception of African-American culture in British society in the early twentieth century. The show is mentioned in the standard literature, but has only been considered in significant depth by Thomas Riis (1996), who mainly considers the show in an American context, and Jeffrey Green (1983a), who provides a sociological background to the London run through examination of contemporary newspaper reports. In this chapter I shall combine elements of these two approaches in an attempt to unravel the reception and significance of the show in Britain.

The very choice of Dahomey as the main location of the musical is significant. Dahomey had been conquered by the French in 1851, and so this setting provided an opportunity for the civilizing influence of white Europeans to be shown. However, before this conquest Dahomey had developed a reputation as an 'aggressive military power', whose people were alleged to practice human sacrifice and cannibalism (Riis, 1996:xix), thereby conforming to the widespread white myth of 'savage Africa'. Although in one way 'civilized', Dahomey still had the connotations of being exotic, remote and primitive that would provoke public curiosity in a show set there. This was a significant part of Cook's plan for the show, as it was originally entitled 'The Cannibal King' (Riis, 1996:xviii), and there is a reference to cannibalism in the first line of the *Caboceer's Entrance*, when the chorus sing 'We are the subjects of King EatEmAll'.

Riis suggests that Dahomey would have been familiar to educated African-Americans as 'the last major port-of-call for slave ships making the infamous "middle passage" in the early nineteenth century' (1996:xix). Inspiration for the show could also be traced back to the Dahomians that were features of American Exhibitions that Cook and Dunbar, as educated Americans, would have almost certainly visited in the late nineteenth century. In addition, Bert Williams and George Walker, who were to become the stars of *In Dahomey*, were even employed to take the places of some of the tribe who arrived late for the San Francisco Exhibition of 1894, and therefore gained some knowledge of customs and rituals:

> Bert and George were among the "natives" hired in the hoax, and for a few weeks they impersonated Dahomians, dressed in animal skins, posing among the potted palm trees. (Charters, 1970:25)

It seems that the writers of the show were trying to present an 'authentic' image of Dahomey, as Riis' comparison of *In Dahomey* with the 1864 writings of the British explorer and writer Sir Richard Burton on the Dahomian tribes demonstrates some significant similarities, for example the inclusion in both of 'pompous ceremonial activity, complete with caboceers, musicians, jesters, and griots' (1996:xx). This indicates that the writers of the show may have been influenced by the facts that were available to them at the time.

The British public had also encountered displays of African culture, although Dahomian tribes probably did not arrive in Britain until after the performances of *In Dahomey*.[2] Riis notes that 'Dahomey was not an obvious representative of all Africa; Egypt and Ethiopia had commonly been used for that purpose before' (1996:xix), and a programme for the Imperial International Exhibition in 1909 indicates the unfamiliarity of Dahomey compared to Egypt:

> ... one day the European tourist will go to far Dahomey as he now goes to Egypt in search of sunshine and merriment in the winter months. Until that time comes he must seek his amusement, instruction and entertainment in this Dahomey village ... . (Greenhalgh, 1988:94-5)

Therefore, the setting of Dahomey would have had particular exotic appeal for the British public, due to either its unfamiliarity or its legendary status for those who were well read and acquainted with Burton's account.

The Imperial International Exhibition programme refers to a 'tribal village' display, a feature typical of Exhibitions held in cities all over Europe around the

---

[2] Green's earliest evidence of the Dahomian Warriors in Britain is a group of postcards from 1905 (1998:11).

turn of the century that exploited the fascination of whites with the exotic. British Exhibition organizers had seen the potential in the 'tableaux vivants' at the 1889 Paris Exposition (Greenhalgh, 1988:90), and African tribes were brought to Britain and could be observed carrying out their daily routines in their specially created villages (Green, 1998:5). In England such exhibits emphasized the idea of imperial power conquering and ruling 'primitive' people, and had particular appeal for the Victorian public as they provided a glimpse of 'exotic' races that was undoubtedly a realistic but yet non-threatening experience, which allowed a balance to be maintained between perceived authenticity and good taste.

Crucially to the preservation of this equilibrium that ensured the success of the Exhibitions, Mitchell notes that 'two parallel pairs of distinctions were maintained, between the visitor and the exhibit and between the exhibit and what it expressed' (1992:297). The visitor was surrounded by but yet excluded from the reality of the exhibits as a 'safe' distance of separation between visitors and the exhibits was maintained, both physically through use of fences and enclosures; and also through the concept of the Exhibition in which the world was catalogued and presented in such a way as to give an false effect of order and certainty (Mitchell, 1992:290). Egyptian Orientalists visiting the exhibit of their own country at the Paris Exposition noted order even within the chaos, describing the exhibit as 'carefully chaotic' (Mitchell, 1992:291). Indeed, an exhibit, 'however realistic, always remained distinguishable from the reality it claimed to represent' (Mitchell, 1992:297). In particular, the realism of the exhibits was undermined by the underlying and reassuring presence of the commercial world from outside the Exhibition gates even in the Exhibition's most exotic areas, for example, buildings that appeared exotic externally could turn out to contain a conventional modern coffee house or shop. The commercial and financial potential of the Exhibitions must have been important to the organizers, and also to those being exhibited, but these motives were hidden from the public in favour of more lofty educational aims: 'When presenting African villages, the promoters did not tell the public that the living exhibits were seasoned travellers and semi-professionals. The image was the reality.' (Green, 1998:7).

Similarly to the Exhibitions, theatrical entertainment had long provided the British public with experiences of black culture that allowed distance between the performers and the audience through the conventions of the stage, and also between the show and the reality of the American South through the consistent use of expected clichés and stereotypes. Blackface performance extended the distance between minstrel shows and the reality of black life still further. Minstrel shows were considered respectable entertainment in the nineteenth century, possibly for these reasons, and provided the precedent for Negro musical comedies such as In Dahomey, which itself offered a suitably distanced but yet perceivably realistic experience of exotic culture. In Dahomey was generally regarded as acceptable entertainment, particularly after the company gave a performance of selections from the show at Buckingham Palace on 23 June 1903 to celebrate the birthday of the Prince of Wales. Later, in December, the show was advertised as 'Christmas entertainment' suitable for children.

It seems that the theatrical community was in a state of some stagnation at the time of the arrival of the company in London, and this contributed to the impact of *In Dahomey*. As the *Weekly Dispatch* stated with reference to the show, 'the first and foremost requirements of a jaded theatrical community is novelty' (31 May 1903:8). Sixth months later, *The Era* was still describing the show as a refreshing change from standard British entertainment:

The fresh and novel experiment of introducing to the jaded Londoner an American musical comedy played throughout by real coloured people, and written and composed by gifted representatives of the Negro race, with lyrics from the pen of the members of the same interesting nationality … . (3 October 1903:15)

Many newspaper reports of *In Dahomey* mention the novelty of a show that was entirely performed by a coloured cast, and this seems to have aroused considerable public curiosity. The review of the show in *The Globe* stated that '[the Negroes] attract and they amaze. Nothing quite like "In Dahomey" has been seen in London before, and the production should therefore be a success of curiosity, if of nothing else.' (18 May 1903:8). A preview in the *Daily News* on the morning that the show opened in London emphasized that 'Save that the scenery was painted by white men, this is a negro production throughout, the ninety persons in the company being all of that race'.[3] The company appeared alongside a Punch and Judy show and a troupe of performing collies at Buckingham Palace (*Era*, 27 June 1993:12). This gives an insight into the unique appeal of a show performed by an entirely black company as the latest novelty, which provoked curiosity from everyone, including the King.

The fact that the British upper classes could 'justify' the value of Will Marion Cook's work as he was a pupil of Dvořák and could successfully apply white musical values to this apparently black music probably contributed to the widespread acceptance and popularity of the show. However, others saw what they perceived as the intrinsically 'Negro' qualities of the music as the principal attraction of the show. The music of *In Dahomey* had several features that may have prompted comparisons with earlier British experiences of black and blackface entertainment. The choral style of some of the numbers recalls spirituals, which had been presented in Britain by the Fisk Jubilee Singers in the late nineteenth century and had become part of the later minstrel shows, as the standard and size of choruses had improved and enlarged (Hamm, 1979:138-9). The *Caboceer's Entrance* ends with a four-part chorale, which becomes harmonically adventurous through use of chromatic voice leading. This is reminiscent of religious songs, not only in musical terms, but also through the eulogizing lyrics: 'Brightest vision of the morning/Deign to glad our longing eyes', 'Great thy name and great thy station/ Caboceers long may ye reign'.

---

[3] This indicates that the orchestra for the show must also have been black.

Example 1   *Caboceers Entrance* **(bars 80-83)**[4]

The finale of *In Dahomey*, advertised on a poster as 'Special: At Finale of last Act will be presented a Grand Spectacular Cake Walk', is an extension of the traditional 'walkround' minstrel show finale in which couples improvised steps in competition with each other (Stearns, 1968:122). The show also contains important song types of the minstrel show, such as the sentimental love ballad and the 'Jonah man' song, which would already be familiar to British audiences.

The combination of the novelty value of the presentation of black culture by a genuinely all-black cast, but in a form that yet drew upon familiar themes and conventions associated with previous black and blackface entertainment, was clearly significant to the success of *In Dahomey* in London. But in addition, the fact that the show also fitted within contemporary popular culture in Britain in the early twentieth century was also extremely important. As was noted in Chapter 1, by the time of the performances of *In Dahomey* in 1903, musical comedy had taken over from music hall as the main form of popular theatrical entertainment. The quality of the music of *In Dahomey* alone, which was clearly exceptional within the musical comedy genre, ensured that the show was congruent within current theatrical fashions. *In Dahomey* also reflected the contemporary vogue for 'exotic' theatrical entertainment set in far-off lands. Race was initially the only way in which *In Dahomey* could be expected to be distinguished from other similar entertainment in Britain for one reviewer:

> … we had vaguely supposed *In Dahomey* to be like any other 'musical comedy', save in the complexion of its performers; and it was in an idle kill-time mood we visited the Shaftesbury Theatre … . Since Japanese performances of Sada Yacco[5] we had seen nothing so curiously disquieting as *In Dahomey*. The resultant impression left on our mind was one of strangeness, the strangeness of the colored race blended with the strangeness of certain American things. (quoted in Riis, 1989:103)

The popularity of *In Dahomey* was essentially due to the combination of the familiar and the unusual, and elements representative of black American and white

---

[4] The music examples and lyric extracts in this chapter are from *The Music and Scripts of In Dahomey*, edited by Thomas Riis, Music of the United States of America, vol. 5/Recent Researches in American Music, vol. 25, Middleton, WI: A-R Editions, Inc., 1996. Used with permission. All rights reserved.
[5] Sada Yacco was a koto (Japanese zither) soloist, who was in Europe in the early years of the twentieth century.

European cultures, which are used to great effect in Cook's music. In the *Caboceer's Entrance*, for example, Cook 'constructed a kind of musical evolution, from pseudo-African primitivism to African-American ragtime to European romantic transcendence' (Riis, 1996:xxxiii). The number begins with typical musical depiction of exotic savagery: a fifth drone bass, accompanied by a pentatonic melody that is vocalized wordlessly (see example 2).

Example 2   *Caboceers Entrance* **(bars 6-10)**

Syncopation is then dramatically introduced from the outset of the singing, and the number ends with a diatonic four-part chorale discussed above. Will Marion Cook clearly saw a combination of black spontaneity and Western training as essential to his work: 'Negroes are saturated with melody, and they only require training to exhibit magnificent results' (*Daily News*, 16 May 1903:6) – here he may well have been thinking of his own life.

Certainly, the music was considered by *The Star* (18 May 1903:1) as 'one of the best items of the production' and the *St James Gazette* declared that Will Marion Cook had 'considerable talent for a really tuneful score' (18 May 1903:15). Cook had a sound grasp of various styles, as there is a good mixture of musical material, including 'coon' songs, sentimental ballads, ragtime-style songs, and syncopated dances as well as numbers that are indebted to 'classical' music in *In Dahomey*. Cook also had the ability to exploit conventional Tin Pan Alley forms dramatically through structural extensions and adventurous harmonies; the skillfulness of his writing can be seen in extended numbers such as *Society* (see below).[6] Songs are frequently unified by motivic development, and the introductions often use material from, and thus balance, the central refrain. A similar balance operates in the large-scale structure of the work, as *On Emancipation Day*, the last song of the show on which the cakewalk finale was based, is used extensively in the overture, suggesting a cyclic form. The clear musical links and devices used to underline the drama would have contributed to

---

[6] Reviews such as *The Era* (3 October 1903) also praised the orchestration of the work as 'truly excellent', and various accompaniment textures can be seen in the score. None of the original orchestrations survive, but some parts are reconstructed in Riis's *The Music and Scripts of In Dahomey* (1996).

the understanding of an audience who had difficulties with following the plot[7] or understanding the dialogue, which reviews indicate were significant problems for the British audience.

The number of reviews that praise the show for its lack of crude humour seems to suggest that this was expected of a musical comedy at this time. The review in the *Daily Mail* (18 May 1903:3) said that there was 'never a suggestion of vulgarity. It will be well if some English concoctors of musical comedy take a lesson from the stranger within our gates' and *The Era* (3 October 1903:15) stated that 'the musical comedy is as harmless as it is amusing; and its humour, if simple, is never coarse or indelicate. Its popularity, therefore, can easily be accounted for.' Indeed, the comedy aspect of the show was widely praised, and most reviewers recognized the importance of Williams and Walker as the comedians who 'carried' the show (*St James Gazette*, 18 May 1903:15). The *Sunday Sun* reported 'on two [actors] – Bert Williams and George Walker – the success of the piece largely depends. They are both excellent comedians, and it would be difficult to find any better on the London stage.' (17 May 1903:6).

The humour of *In Dahomey* was essential to its appeal in Britain, being based on the slapstick and puns familiar to music hall audiences. *The Times* (18 May 1903:12) noted 'a number of dialogues [of Williams and Walker] that occasionally remind one of the pairs of "knockabout artists" at the music halls'. The *Daily Mail* (18 May 1903:3) compared Bert Williams's Jonah Man to the Christy and Templeton Minstrels (a blackface troupe) in its 'spirit of drollery', as the song *I'm a Jonah Man* humorously portrays a typical Negro who suffers from permanent bad luck:

My hard luck started when I was born leas' so the old folks say
Dat same hard luck been my be's fren' up to die very day
When I was young my mamma's frens to find a name they tried
They named me after Papa and the same day Papa died.

This song, which Williams wrote with Alex Rogers in 1900 (Charters, 1970:71), was representative of Williams's comic stage personality, and was interpolated into *In Dahomey* with great success.[8] The *Daily Mail* related how 'those who came to scoff remained to laugh. And they did laugh' describing the show as 'a captivating and attractive mixture, thoroughly irresponsible and vastly hilarious' (18 May 1903:3). The show, and particularly the performance of Williams, clearly loosened up a possibly inhibited or puzzled British audience as he 'upset the gravity of everybody, and the preservation of a rigid and decorous countenance became absolutely impossible' (*Daily Mail* 18 May 1903:3). The reviewer in the *Daily News* links Williams's abilities to the fact that he was black: 'In my opinion, no

---

[7] Even in retrospect the plot of *In Dahomey* seems extremely convoluted, with various sources contradicting each other. A brief suggested synopsis is contained in Appendix 2.

[8] This song is a clear precedent for *Nobody* (1905), another Rogers/Williams collaboration that became Williams's trademark song.

white American comedian can compare to Bert Williams when it comes to being funny' (16 May 1903:6).

However, the show's comic double act had serious ambitions for the show. Having encountered real Africans at the American Exhibition, Williams and Walker stated their intention to 'delineate and feature native African characters as far as we could, and still remain American, and make our acting interesting and entertaining to American audiences' (Riis, 1996:xx). This statement exemplifies the idea of the dual identity of the American Negro, described by W.E.B. Du Bois in his seminal work *The Souls of Black Folk*, published in the same year as *In Dahomey* was first presented on the stage (Carter, 2000:213):

> One ever feels his two-ness, – an American, a Negro; two souls, two thoughts, two unreconciled strivings; two warring ideals in one dark body, whose dogged strength alone keeps it from being torn asunder. The history of the American Negro is the history of this strife, – this longing to attain self-conscious manhood, to merge his double self into a better and truer self. In this merging he wishes neither of the older selves to be lost. He would not Africanize America, for America has too much to teach the world and Africa. He would not bleach his Negro soul in a flood of white Americanism, for he knows that Negro blood has a message for the world. He simply wishes to make it possible for a man to be both a Negro and an American, without being cursed and spit upon by his fellows, without having the doors of Opportunity closed roughly in his face. (Du Bois, 1903:3-4)

David Krasner has commented that 'Amidst deteriorating race relations between 1895 and 1910, African-American theatre found itself caught between two competing forces: the demands to conform to white notions of black inferiority, and the desire to resist these demands by undermining and destabilizing entrenched stereotypes of blacks onstage' (1997:1). Thus, the idea of Negro 'twoness' is clearly embodied in the dramatic content in black shows of the period such as *In Dahomey*. A prominent idea in the show is the striving of blacks to reach the exalted and respected social position enjoyed by whites, which was representative of the actual aims of many of the company. The enthusiasm that the performers exhibited was widely praised by British critics, as this could be interpreted as an attempt to attain these white standards and flattered the white audience. Paradoxically, *In Dahomey* also made 'an explicit appeal to black pride' (Riis, 1996:xxxiv), as many of the songs present positive images of black people. The show also references the conflicts between natives and African-American settlers that could result from the repatriation policies of the American Colonization Association. The lyrics of the song *On Broadway In Dahomey Bye and Bye* describe the expected transformation of Dahomey when the colonizers arrive, and show a stark contrast between the wildness of the place and the values and ideas which will be imposed upon it, although the tone of the song is humorous: 'You'll see on the sides of roads and hills/ "Use Carter's Little Liver Pills"' and 'then have Wagner sung by parrots every night'. However, *In Dahomey* concludes with the failure of the settlement and return of the colonizers to America, illuminating the need for African-Americans to be accepted in America rather than being segregated.

The theme of 'double consciousness' as expressed by Du Bois thus becomes a central pillar of *In Dahomey*, its subtleties being particularly evident in the music and lyrics of the show. It is significant that the songs that present positive images of black people use dialect and syncopation, representative respectively of black speech and black music, whilst those characters that aspire to white 'high society' usually have non-dialect lyrics and non-syncopated music. In this way, the combination of vernacular language and syncopation are used for dramatic effect throughout. The song *On Emancipation Day* is prominent in the show due to its extended use in the overture and finale. The lyrics describe the excessive joy of the freed slaves, and suggest that they have not only reached the social position towards which they have been aiming in earlier songs, but have in fact transcended whites in a spontaneous expression of joy of which whites are not capable:[9]

On Emancipation day
All you white folks clear de way...

When dey hear dem ragtime tunes
White folks try to pass as coons
On Emancipation day.

Example 3   Chorus from *On Emancipation Day* (bars 46-49)

The opening chorus of the show, *Swing Along*,[10] portrays the Negroes at leisure, and also indicates the exclusion of whites who can only watch in envy:

---

[9] Carter suggests that this song made 'a clear, perhaps even prophetic statement about the appropriation of African-American culture that would characterize the emergent popular music industry in subsequent decades' (2000:210).

[10] Mercer Cook recalled that Will Marion Cook composed *Swing Along* in London, and was determined to include it in the show. On the first night 'the curtain was delayed for twenty minutes while Jesse Shipp and others made a last attempt to dissuade him'. But it was eventually included and 'the audience, composed of supposedly blasé Britishers, cheered for ten minutes' (symposium paper in IJS 'Cook' file, p.10). *Swing Along* was clearly a popular song, as it exists in several arrangements published separately a few years later. This song was also included in the programme of the Southern Syncopated Orchestra under the direction of Cook on his return to Britain in 1919.

Swing along chillun, swing along de lane
Lif yo' head and ya' heels mighty high
Swing along chillun, t'ain't a goin' do rain
Sun's as red as de rose in de sky

Come along Mandy, come along Sure
White fo'ks a'watchin' an' seein' what you do
White fo'ks jealous when you'se walkin' two by two
So swing along chillun, swing along chillun, swing along.

Swing a - long chil - lun, swing a - long de lane, Lift yo' head and yo'heels might - y high,

Example 4   *Swing Along* **(bars 5-8)**

In contrast, the song *Leader of the Colored Aristocracy* describes 'the colonizer's
scheme to raise the social class consciousness of the Dahomians' (Riis, 1989:97):

Now to establish swell society for color'd folks I have a yearning
And from the high ton'd 'ristocratic white folks how to lead I have been learning.

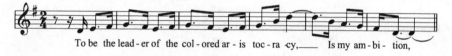

To be the lead - er of the col - ored ar - is toc - ra -cy,____ Is my am - bi - tion,

Example 5   *Leader of the Colored Aristocracy* **(bars 9-14)**

A strict dotted rhythm is used in the melodic line of the verses to suggest propriety,
and there is minimal syncopation and simple harmony in the chorus. The call and
response between the soloist and chorus used in this song is one example of the
way in which the show demonstrates the solidarity of black people in their aims.
Similarly, the use of chorale-like passages in the *Caboceer's Entrance* gives these
leaders of the black community pseudo-religious importance and the chorus
number *The Czar* demonstrates the solidarity of the community behind their leader:

He is the greatest thing
And known afar,
The black folks always sing
He is the Czar
His style is super fine
He's always right in line
He says 'the world is mine'
He is the Czar.

In the verses of the same song, the importance of the Czar as representing every type of leader for the community is emphasized:

> There's a man who's mighty grand
> Who rules supreme in Dixieland
> He's the president, the Mayor and the Governor,
> He's the citizen's private counsellor.

Despite the eventual failure of the Dahomian colony, there are indications that the aspirations of the characters in the show are fulfilled, but within a multi-racial society rather than a segregated colony. *In Dahomey* concludes with four instrumental numbers, the first of which, *March: On Emancipation Day*, not surprisingly is based on the chorus from the previous song. However, it begins with a section that uses a D minor melody, strongly reminiscent of the *Caboceer's Entrance* near the beginning of the show, except here there is greater use of syncopation:

Example 6   *March: On Emancipation Day* **(bars 11-14)**

In this way, the image of the 'primitive' that was presented at the start of the work is contrasted sharply and directly with the closing image of black people as free and joyful, and empowered to ask whites to move out of the way, and even leading white people to aspire to be black. Thus, in the music as well as in the drama of *In Dahomey*, we see a spirit of empowered optimism, which Riis defines as 'a synecdoche for the entire production' (1996:xxxiv).

In the context of the whole show, the vernacular style of songs such as *On Emancipation Day* and *Swing Along* contrast with numbers in a more operatic style demonstrating the presence of 'twoness' on a macrocosmic level. The Overture is of a substantial length, and uses a medley form, typical of nineteenth century operetta, with music taken from other numbers in the show. It has been carefully constructed, as some of the material is presented in different keys in the overture than in the individual songs, and short passages unique to the overture are used to link the various sections together. The *Daily Mail* (18 May 1903:3) reported that in the show 'there is one concerted chorus quite in the grand operatic manner, which secured immediate applause', and this probably referred to *Society*. This is one of the longest numbers of the show, but can be divided up into several contrasting sections, which are often motivically related, thus creating unity within the whole. The macrocosmic form of the piece is two sections, equivalent to two standard Tin Pan Alley songs, the first in 4/4 based around A minor and the second in 3/4 time in Bb flat major. A melodramatic, operatic section that includes recitative links the sections. (Riis, 1989:96).

In *Society*, the dramatic contrast between material aspiration and the sentimental love can be observed in the lyrics and music of each section. The verses of the first section show the ambitions of the colonizer Hamilton Lightfoot:

To get in high society I've always had an ambition
And since I've got the brass, now we're sure to have position
A royal prince my little girl shall wed
For since the days of lords and dukes have sped
It takes a prince to put you at the head of the best society

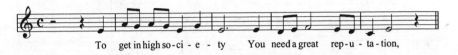

To   get in high so-ci - e - ty   You need a great rep-u - ta-tion,

Example 7   *Society* **(bars 5-9)**

In the first section of the number, the verses use C major with strong A modal/minor influence, with a simple melody and largely un-syncopated rhythm. After each verse there are contrasting passages sung by Pansy, Lightfoot's daughter and Leather, the bootblack whom she loves, and accompanied by the chorus singing sustained four-part harmonies. These repeat the last phrase of the lyrics of the verse that precedes it, and use contrasting tonalities and shifting harmonies. Both of these passages use the same rhythm, and are further linked through free inversion of the melody. The dramatic meaning of these sections is unclear, but the contrast in style and the way that the phrases are echoed between Pansy and Leather suggests that the lovers are absorbed in each other, and although repeating his words, possibly not paying full attention to Lightfoot's assertions:

Example 8   *Society* **(bars 22-26)**

The recitative at the start of the middle section provides instant and dramatic contrast, with a wide ranging vocal line over chromatically shifting tremolo chords, and finally resolves onto A major on the last word. The lyrics show that Pansy believes her father's ambitions to be ridiculous, and show that to her, Leather is indeed a 'royal prince':

> Surely you're only mocking
> Such levity is simply shocking
> Your prince for me would be too far above
> A royal prince is he I love.

Example 9   Recitative from *Society* bars (58-61)

Following the recitative, there is an immediate return to the A tonal centre of the opening, for a last-ditch attempt by Lightfoot to win his daughter round ('Just think of a house on some big avenue'). In the repeat of this passage he is joined by the chorus, who contribute to the dramatic tension by providing chromatic harmony to the static melody. The repeated monotonous rhythm emphasizes Lightfoot's determination and anger with his daughter, who has clearly spoilt his plans. Both the rhythm and tonality clearly link this to the earlier verses.

In the final section, the assertion of love over material ambition is marked 'by setting the text to a tender waltz' with two themes (Riis, 1996:xxxv) and a stable B flat major tonality which contrast with the shifting chromaticism of the earlier parts of the number:

Example 10   *Society* (bars 83-90)

The   hum - ble   cot_____   be - comes____   a   throne

Example 11   *Society* **(bars 114-118)**

Pansy's declaration that Leather, although a humble bootblack, is a prince in her eyes is also expanded:

> Love looks not at estate, oh no!
> 'Twere folly one should think it so
> The beggar maid becomes a queen
> Who through her lover's eyes is seen.
>
> The humble cot becomes a throne
> Whose dwelling place love makes his own
> So all man's heart and being sing
> Love is the King! Love is the King!

The music builds up to a splendid choral finale, marked *molto pesante*, with an operatic top B flat for the leading lady.

Carter suggests that the inclusion of 'realistic courtship', expressed here in the conventions of Western romanticism, rather than 'a burlesqued, unrealistic encounter' typical of minstrelsy, in shows such as *In Dahomey* was a way in which the authors attempted to remove the minstrel mask and to ensure its universal appeal (2002:209). The operatic style and proportions of some of Cook's writing in *In Dahomey* signifies not only the aspirations of the characters, but also the seriousness of his intention to elevate black musical culture away from minstrelsy. However, for Cook, the idealistic view of black empowerment as presented in the show itself was influenced by practical realism. In an interview printed in the *Daily News* on the morning on which the show opened in London, Cook stated that in *In Dahomey*, 'I have not strayed beyond themes that are light and amusing, and only here and there do I give glimpses of higher possibilities'. This indicates that he had an acute awareness of the nature of the audiences he was playing to on Broadway and the West End, possibly due to his contact with other black music theatre artists in New York, which inspired in him a more realistic approach to his compositional ventures and tempered his youthful idealism. Cook's approach to *In Dahomey* was clearly not intended to be a long term compromise of his artistic aims, as he stated that in the future he intended to 'produce a little musical melodrama of my own, conducting it myself; and after that ... I mean to rise to the heights of grand opera' (*Daily Mail* 18 May 1903:3). However, at this early stage it was important for his works to be performed and heard by as many people as possible to most strongly assert the position of black artists, and this meant making certain artistic compromises to ensure acceptance of *In Dahomey*. The original libretto, written by Dunbar, Cole and the Johnson brothers, had been revised by Jesse A. Shipp before it was performed, and Mercer Cook commented that 'the result was quite different from the ambitious operetta of which Dad and Dunbar had dreamed, but it was at least successful and brought in more money than the young composer had ever earned' (Cook, Mercer; symposium paper contained in IJS 'Cook' file, p.9). Even the 'operatic' numbers such as *Society* drew on familiar and expected Tin Pan Alley forms and clichés, and the obvious adherence to some conventions of blackface minstrelsy in the show enabled the work to be appreciated on a basic level by white audiences. However, in signifying on these conventions with references to the reality of the contemporary African-American experience, the group also presented more serious messages for those in the audience that could interpret these signs. The way in which 'twoness' is such an integral part of both the drama and the music of *In Dahomey* indicates certain self-awareness on the parts of black artists such as Cook, Williams and Walker. For this reason, in retrospect, the portrayals of supposedly stereotypical Negroes in *In Dahomey* take on a very different slant compared to earlier, particularly blackface, minstrel shows.

There is considerable evidence to suggest that contemporary British audiences did not understand the subtleties of *In Dahomey*. The reviews of the show do not generally relate it to contemporary debates on race, and, as Green points out, 'the show was not seen as a satire on the "back to Africa" movement' (1983a:23). As we have seen in Chapter 1, the popularity and familiarity of blackface minstrels ensured that by the end of the nineteenth century certain stereotypical ideas about black people had been firmly established in Britain, and this provides the context within which the contemporary reviews of *In Dahomey* can be understood. The combination of primitive savagery and the depiction of civilized, upper class Negroes, who are shown to be aspiring towards white standards, such as in the *Caboceer's Entrance*, is a paradox inherent in nineteenth century minstrel shows, which often emphasized the improving influence of whites on black slaves. The portrayal of Negroes as savages on one hand and civilized people on the other can also be seen with reference to contemporary Exhibitions, where 'African peoples were presented as conquered peoples, and paradoxically, as warriors and soldiers' (Green, 1998:7). Although the first Pan-African Conference had taken place in London only two years prior to *In Dahomey*, 'the press coverage contained little comment' and the Pan-African Association declined rapidly, due to the fluctuating black student population in Britain (Fryer, 1984:286-7). Thus, it seems that blackface and imperialist images of black people remained prominent in the perceptions of the British public at the time. In this way, *In Dahomey* appeared to British audiences to be little more than a twentieth century minstrel show or another Exhibition display.

There was genuine fascination that the show's black performers had so many different skin colours which reflects the familiarity with blackface shows, where all the performers would be made-up as a similar colour:

> *In Dahomey* is played entirely by a Coon company, and its plot, like its exponents, has various degrees of colour. (*Daily Mail*, 18 May 1903:3)

The company is a very large one, and all colours, from the slightest trace which the octaroon possesses to the deep purple of the full-blooded negro, are represented. (*Sunday Sun*, 17 May 1903:6)[11]

The show was often considered with reference to the expected features and stereotypes of black entertainment that had been delineated on British stages for several decades prior to the presentation of *In Dahomey*. The critic of *The Sphere* (23 May 1903:162) regretted that Cook had not included 'old plantation melodies', staple parts of minstrel show repertoire, in *In Dahomey*. The beliefs that a typical Negro was innately musical and often overly emotional influenced several reviewers of the show. For example, the 'natural dash and swing' (*Daily Mail*, 18 May 1903:3) of the performance was widely appreciated, and the *Pall Mall Gazette* stated that 'the music was utterly and completely negro. It had tune, prettiness, rhythm and catchiness' (18 May 1903:11). Will Marion Cook apparently conducted the Overture facing the audience and singing along, and the freedom of this unusual style was noted:

... the composer conducted with much vigour, singing most of the tunes with his band with a kind of untrammelled spontaneity that finds expression in the whole action of the piece, and more particularly in the dancing, which seems the natural expression of a racial instinct, not the laboriously acquired art of schools. (*The Times*, 18 May 1903:12)

Many reviewers praised the enthusiasm with which the chorus carried out their roles on stage: 'They play, and sing, and dance as if they thoroughly enjoyed the business' (*The Standard*, 18 May 1903:5). However, this was also offensive to British sensibilities, and furthermore, merely confirmed the nineteenth century claims of black simplicity and inferiority:

The chorus sang, as they danced, with an infectious enthusiasm and admirable training, but their general effect, like that of the orchestra, was distinctly too powerful. (*St James Gazette*, 18 May 1903:15)

Here was the coon in music, naked and unashamed, merry, pathetic, eager and alive with emotion; but always limited by a certain circle of not very wide ambitions ... . (*Pall Mall Gazette*, 18 May 1903:11)

... coon-songs and cake-walks are made to seem like the obvious expressions of genuine, if somewhat elementary emotions ... . (*The Times*, 18 May 1903:12)

Although the idea that Negroes were prone to an excess of emotion was even asserted by Will Marion Cook in an interview: 'We are more emotional than you ... . We are easily moved. But the Englishman – he is difficult to rouse, but

---

[11] Interestingly, Bert Williams wore burnt cork make-up. This may have been due to the lightness of his skin, but Hoefer suggests that this was part of a deliberate attempt to bring an artistic side to blackface, and to compromise with audiences expecting minstrel show conventions: 'Negroes were accepted only as minstrels and as they went into the Negro musical comedy era (1890-1910) there were many oppositions to overcome.' (Hoefer (n.d.) in 'Williams' file in IJS).

once you have roused him he is the greatest fighter on earth' (*Daily News*, 16 May 1903:6), these British reactions to *In Dahomey* show that it was not always successful in achieving Cook's aim to elevate black culture away from minstrelsy.

Ironically, the familiarity of British audiences with the blackface minstrelsy also meant that when confronted with *In Dahomey*, in which there was an attempt to delineate a more genuine African-American experience, there were criticisms that the show was not authentic and overly American. The *Daily News* suggested that 'it is just as far as it is characteristically racial that the performance is really interesting'. The reviewer regretted that there was no 'dreamy sentimentality, the gently appealing charm, the almost childish slyness of humour', characteristics that are the 'finest and most attractive in the negro's nature', and that in adopting 'Parisian fashions' on stage the Negroes had assimilated 'what is worst in European civilization' (18 May 1903:12). Similarly, the review in *The Globe* stated:

> Everything is thoroughly American and up-to-date. And that is our chief grievance against "In Dahomey" ... . What we really get is negro-America. We do not get the negro in the rough; we get him with a Yankee veneer. (18 May 1903:8)

In contrast, the more overtly 'African' elements of *In Dahomey* were generally well received in Britain. The popularity of the 'African' numbers seems to have led to their use the start of the show, rather than being scrapped completely, when the finale was restructured soon after the opening night. Riis explains that:

> What had been the first scene of the third act, a transformation scene set in Africa with several songs, was shortened and made into a prologue, thus allowing the retention of two strong "African" musical numbers, "My Dahomian Queen" and "Caboceer's Entrance." (1996:xxvi).[12]

Bearing in mind that Cook and Dunbar, as well as Williams and Walker, probably had some knowledge, through the Exhibitions, of what Dahomey was really like, these African elements were bound to have made a significant impression on a British audience, including the reviewer in the *Times*: 'When the scene changes to Africa ... a succession of apparently irrelevant pictures of native life are given'. These included a war dance, choruses 'sung with stentorian voices', and 'fine effects of costume and stage management' (18 May 1903:12). More likely though, the popularity of the 'African' numbers was due the use of typical 'Tin Pan Alley' formulas such as minor keys, modal melodies and drone accompaniments. The first song in the score, *My Dahomian Queen*, begins with an extensive introduction using diminished harmonies, which continue under the verse, undermining the tonality of the start of each verse. These features are all included on Derek Scott's

---

[12] The original position of the 'African' numbers in the finale is confirmed by a review in *The Sunday Sun* (17 May 1903), which states that 'the closing act, which takes place *In Dahomey*, was, it must be admitted, a fiasco, notwithstanding the fine duet of "My Dahomian Queen".' The song *My Dahomian Queen* later became the opening song of the show (see Riis, 1996:xv).

list of 'Orientalist devices' that form the 'Orientalist musical code' that was established by the late nineteenth century (1998:310). Scott shows that 'many of these features can be applied indiscriminately as markers of cultural difference' (1998:327), and could be used to broadly indicate the 'otherness' of any particular setting. The use of these musical features in *In Dahomey* meant that the fundamental exoticism of the African setting was understood and appreciated by British audiences. Therefore, it can be seen that the reception of *In Dahomey* in Britain was strongly influenced by the audiences' rather limited and standardized previous experiences of Negro and African cultures.

In examining the reception and understanding of *In Dahomey* in London, it is interesting to compare the British critical reaction with a review of the show in Britain by an American journalist, S.J. Pryor, in the *New York Times* (19 July 1903:3) under the heading 'Colored Folk in English Eyes ...The Inner Meaning of the Play at the Shaftesbury' (also printed in the *London Express*). Pryor describes the show as 'a perfect cinematograph of the "negro" life of New York, or of Boston, or of any other Northern American city today. It is a tragedy as well as a comedy'. He also recognized the two sides of the show, the presentation of the 'irresponsible, happy-go-lucky, old time darky character', which was clearly well understood by the British public, and the 'very pathetic and very serious and ominous other side of life of the coloured race in America' which was not.

Pryor himself believed that Britons did not understand that the show was representative of real life, and attributes the British lack of comprehension to the fact that the average Briton 'requires a guidebook' to understand the humour of the show, as they could not appreciate the slang as anything more than 'genuine American tongue'. This is confirmed by the London paper *The Sphere*, which said that the dialogue 'was too full of American slang to be comprehended on the first night' (23 May 1903:162) and the *Sunday Sun* (17 May 1903:6) which stated 'At present it is hard to follow the words'. This meant that the British public were probably laughing at the blatant, surface, slapstick humour, and were largely unable to understand the subtleties of the script. British reviews often emphasized the novelty aspects of *In Dahomey*, such as the cakewalk dancing, and the singing of the chorus, although criticized by some as overly powerful, also made a considerable impression on British audiences: 'the curious half-metallic, but not unpleasant, timbre of their voices afford a new musical sensation' (*Daily News*, 18 May 1903:12). However, Pryor praises the show in its own right, rather than as a mere novelty, for the 'supple-hipped, ball-bearing jointed dancing that only the blood of Africa puts into the limbs, it provides singing full of quaint catches and cadences that no white voice can imitate, and choruses that are a revelation to choristers'.

Pryor suggests that '*In Dahomey* is worth seeing in a serious mood' as 'the foundation of the show is solid fact'. Particularly, he cites the aspirations of characters in the show to have a land and nation of their own as 'a true dream' and the idea of a coloured aristocracy 'may seem comic, but is also sincere'. The serious aspects of the show seem not to have been widely understood or appreciated in Britain, as only one review, in *The Times*, indicates any understanding that that there was a serious element behind the comedy. The reviewer noted that 'a kind of ethnological purpose seems to run through the whole undertaking' and recognized that

> ... there may have been an intention to point the contrast between the dignity and picturesque surroundings of the African race in Africa and the absurd aping of men's ways which is perhaps the most pathetic thing in regard to the 'colour problem' of the present day. (18 May 1903:12)

As we have seen, to present an accurate and 'dignified' picture of Africans was one intention of the writers of *In Dahomey*, particularly in the light of the racism that they would have encountered in America. Riis suggests that the show was 'a visible symbol of co-operation and patience, as well as musical and theatrical creativity, in the face of persistent discrimination against blacks, against women on the stage and against actors in general' (1996:xiii). Whilst the British public may not have recognized that the show had a serious message, Cook indicated in his interview in the *Daily News* (16 May 1903:6) that the company was treated better by Britons than by their fellow Americans on their visit to London:

> There is no feeling against us here ... . We wanted to put up at the Cecil, and the management were willing enough to take us, but the [white] Americans stopping there objected to our presence, so we had to go to another hotel.

Later in the year a paper called *Mostly About People* declared 'They [Cook's company] are one and all charmed beyond expression with the manner in which they and their kind are socially treated on this side of the water' (15 August 1903, quoted in Green, 1983a:39-40). In addition, George Walker commented on the visit of the company to Buckingham Palace: 'We were received royally. That is the only word for it. We had champagne from the Royal cellar and strawberries and cream from the Royal garden.' (Sampson, 1980:80). Williams also remarked that the group had not been received at such a socially approved gathering in America (Green, 1983a:37). Apparently, also, 'men like the Duke of Connaught, Kennedy Cox and Cavendish Morton took Williams to their clubs and homes for dinner and conversation' (Charters, 1970:76). This indicates the extent to which the black performers were accepted in Britain, albeit as curiosities, and this patronage seemed to exert significant influence on the general public as well as providing the artists with all-important publicity. This apparent lack of racism that performers experienced in Britain compared with America may explain why the show remained in Britain for such a long period of time.

The company was also keen to be successful in Britain, taking criticism on board and making several significant changes to the show during its run at the Shaftesbury Theatre. Firstly, the problem of the language used in the dialogue was addressed. Riis states that 'nearly a dozen ... small emendations of the original script are scattered through the British libretto' with some lines cut and words altered (1996:xxvii). However, as we have seen, dialect remained an integral part of the drama and created a specific effect, especially when combined with syncopation in songs. The dialogue was also more substantially cut and re-arranged in the British script (Riis, 1996:xlvii) in order to more smoothly introduce the songs and also to attempt to clarify the plot. Almost all the reviews highlight the lack of a clear plot as a fundamental failing of the piece. *The Times* dismissed the show as 'an example of plotless drama' (18 May 1903:12), and although a synopsis of the story was printed in the programme it was still very hard to understand. The critic of the *Daily Mail* expressed his exasperation: 'What it is about we are unable, even with the aid of a printed "argument", to fully understand' (18 May 1903:3). Some reviewers picked up that the essence of the plot was 'some story of a lost casket and a bogus scheme for transporting negroes from Florida to Dahomey' (*The Star*, 18 May 1903:2). Misunderstanding persisted, even after the show had been running for six months. In October 1903, *The Era* stated with resignation 'of course, there is no pretence at connected plot in a piece of this sort. The intention merely is to provide a "go-as-you-please" entertainment, full of smart and attractive items; and this intention is completely carried out' (3 October 1903:15). It seems as though the comedy, the music, and later the dancing was enough to ensure the success of a show that was largely incomprehensible to the public.

The most criticized aspect of the production was the ending. The *Sunday Sun* critic saw this as the fundamental problem with the whole show and wrote optimistically: 'A more lively and convincing ending will doubtless soon be improvised, and then in all probability the play will go well from start to finish' (17 May 1903:6). The *St James Gazette* reported that when the show gets to Dahomey in the last act 'it goes all to pieces in a manner which is little short of bewildering' (18 May 1903:15). In all probability, the cast was equally confused due to a complete lack of dialogue for the last Act; the American script contains only a synopsis of the action. Most of the papers reported on the extraordinary occurrence that when the curtain fell on the opening night: 'the audience placidly remained in their seats, not a little puzzled, but patiently seeking Enlightenment' (*The Standard*, 18 May 1903:5). Apparently, nobody realized that the entertainment had ended until the National Anthem was played. It was not until late in May 1903 that dialogue was written for the last Act, but this did not make the plot any clearer, as Riis comments that 'the circumstances that motivate the characters are left unexplained, and the reasons for all of the action except the final decision to return home, are virtually non-existent. No wonder early audiences were confused' (1996:xxviii).

The addition of the cakewalk into the finale of the show more than compensated for the lack of clarity in the plot for British audiences. After the first performance of *In Dahomey*, the critic of the *Sunday Sun* had commented that 'the dancing to me was a disappointment. I had expected better things'. Dancing is mentioned specifically by very few of the early reviews, but after the rapid addition of the cakewalk into the show at the start of the second week of performances, it became a legendary part of the entertainment. *The Era* reported:

A real cake-walk has been introduced into "In Dahomey" ... . This item was omitted on the first night because it was believed that the dance had had its day in London. The number of letters received by the management requesting its introduction prove this idea to be incorrect. (23 May 1903:14)

The cakewalk had developed in America through plantation slaves, who learnt European dances and, combining them with traditional African circle dances, used them to satirize their white owners. Stearns comments that 'with its added emphasis on humorous improvisation, the dance was readily adapted to minstrelsy' (1966:11). Ironically, a member of the cast of In Dahomey, Aida Overton Walker 'was eagerly sought after by titled persons to teach them the cakewalk [dance]' (Sampson, 1980:438) when the show came to Britain, thus teaching the very class of people whom the cakewalk originally satirized. The cakewalk was recognized by Cook as a popular element in shows after the success of Clorindy, and it became fundamental to the success of In Dahomey, particularly due to its comic presentation by Williams and Walker: 'Walker did a neat cakewalk, much like the strut of today, and Bert Williams would follow behind him, doing a slow loose-jointed mooch dance' (Stearns, 1968:122).

The revised finale of In Dahomey presented a cakewalk competition, with couples trying to outdo each other by presenting novel steps, just as in the contests that had begun in New York in the late nineteenth century (Stearns, 1968:122). The Weekly Dispatch reported that at the Shaftesbury Theatre, the members of the audience 'signify their verdict by the volume of applause' (7 June 1903:8). The Era noted that the cakewalk had been 'made more effective by the introduction of a huge cake over six feet in height, and illuminated by one-hundred electric lights' and that the cakewalk competition now included a £10 prize for the person who 'wins the cakewalk prize most times during the week' (20 June 1903:12). The Royal Family also appreciated the cakewalk when members of the company performed at Buckingham Palace. The Era stated that 'the portion of the programme which created the greatest interest in the production was the cake-walk, the King being one of the first to recognize its merits' (27 June 1903:12), and by October 'the ubiquitous "cake-walk" is at the height of its popularity' (The Era, 3 October 1903:15). The addition of the cakewalk dancing proved so successful that subsequently 'several novelties were added to this already attractive and original entertainment', 'a troupe of dancers in Spanish costumes' and 'a minuet à L'Africaine by Miss Walker and a male chorus' (The Era, 3 October 1903:15). The increase in the dance content of the show indicates the expectations of a British audience that associated dance with black entertainment, an important feature of the later reception of ragtime and jazz in Britain.

The fact that the cakewalk was allegedly omitted initially because it was seen as dated is interesting. It could indicate that this assumption had been made with reference to the status of the cakewalk in America, and that therefore Britain was some years behind in its popular trends, which was to be a feature of the adoption of ragtime and jazz in Britain later in the twentieth century. The fact that letters were (supposedly) sent requesting the inclusion of the cakewalk supports Green's hypothesis that 'In the 1890s cakewalk dance was so associated with Black Americans that Britons expected it' (1988:85). This is also one factor that disproves the theory that the show introduced the cakewalk to London (also cakewalks had been published in London since at least 1890), although it did precipitate a huge craze for cakewalk dancing in Britain (consider, for example that the sheet music for at least 43 cakewalks were published in London in 1903,

compared with 10 in 1902 and 24 in 1904). There was even an instructional song
called *That's How the Cakewalk's Done* included in some versions of *In Dahomey*
(Riis, 1996:xxxix). *In Dahomey* demonstrated improvised dance in Britain, which
was to become a significant feature of dancing to later syncopated musical styles,
as well as providing a new sort of entertainment within the musical comedy format.

The interpolation of songs, common practice in the central part of minstrel
shows, was also important to the success of *In Dahomey* in Britain. Interpolation
accounts for the permanent and occasional inclusion of several songs in *In
Dahomey* that were not composed by Cook, and has resulted in the discovery of the
show in a variety of formats (see Riis, 1996:xv). A very large number of songs that
were included in the show at some stage have been located. From newspaper
reports of the opening night in London, for example, we know that *Annie Laurie*,
Sally in our Alley (*Star* 18 May 1903:1) and *A Rich Coon's Babe* (*The Times*, 18
May 1903:12) were interpolated on that occasion, and it seems likely that many
other songs could have been heard during the London run. Interpolation would
presumably have preserved public interest in the show over a period of time by
allowing its content to be constantly varied and also helped to ensure its popularity
by inclusion of familiar songs and thus contributed significantly to the length and
success of the London run of *In Dahomey*.

A core group of songs remained consistent in terms of their inclusion and
position within the show from the New York production in February 1903 to the
publication of the score in London during the second week of the show's run (see
Riis, 1996:xv). As the overture uses material drawn from five of these core songs,
these must have been permanent elements of the show. The London score includes
an Overture, twelve songs and concludes with the four instrumental numbers
necessary for the inclusion of the cakewalk and the extension of the finale.[13] The
fact that this score was published so soon after the start of the London run indicates
that the alterations to the finale must have taken place very swiftly after the
opening night, as the new order of songs and the dance numbers at the end are
included. This indicates the strength of the desire to make *In Dahomey* popular and
successful in Britain, in which respect the company achieved their aims.

Significantly, as a result of the combination of a lack of understanding of the
plot and dialogue and the strength of the blackface minstrel in the public mind,
British reviewers, unlike the American S.J. Pryor, were not able to appreciate the
idea of Negro 'twoness' that is shown on so many levels in the music and drama of
In Dahomey. In retrospect, the show's use of stereotypical Negro characteristics
indicates the self-awareness of the writers and the operatic tendencies show Cook's
aim to elevate black musical culture. However, in Britain in 1903, attempts to
portray African-American experience were largely lost on the British public,
whose experience and knowledge of black people was firmly based on stereotypes,
and ironically led to criticism that *In Dahomey* was not authentic. Disbelief was
expressed that *In Dahomey* was representative of Cook's serious aspirations
towards creating a new genre of 'negro opera', and reviewers even encouraged him

---

[13] In a later edition of the score, two further instrumental numbers were added at the end
(Riis, 1996:xv), which were also published separately.

to write 'work of a more solid and enduring character' (*The Era*, 23 May 1903:12). Therefore, Cook's intention to begin to 'remove the minstrel mask from the musical stage' (Carter, 2000:218) through *In Dahomey* was not particularly successful in Britain, although the show itself was undoubtedly popular.

However, it is fundamentally important to note that the lack of understanding shown by the British reviewers is not necessarily due to deliberate racism. Indeed, the *In Dahomey* company was apparently better treated in Britain than their native America and was certainly eager to please their audiences. As we have seen, they responded to criticism and made substantial alterations to the show in order to ensure their success in Britain. Nevertheless, the reactions to the performances of *In Dahomey* in 1903 show the extent to which the image of the blackface minstrel had permeated British society, due to its prominence on the British stage during the preceding century. Therefore, this indicates the context within which the reception of other forms of African-American culture, including jazz, in Britain in the early twentieth century must be evaluated.

Chapter 5

The Music and Symbolism of the Banjo

The banjo was present in all the forms of African-American music that were heard in Britain before jazz, and by the twentieth century the banjo had developed strong symbolism as the instrument of the stereotypical 'plantation Negro'. In Britain in the early twentieth century, the banjo had a unique status as the main instrument through which ragtime was disseminated, particularly by the bands of African-American musicians that were employed to play for dancing in exclusive London clubs. Therefore, the figure of the stereotypical 'black banjo player' was perceived in Britain to be central to the development of American popular music and, as a result, the evolutionary sequence of early syncopated forms towards jazz in Britain is demonstrably different when compared to that of America. In this chapter, the role of the banjo in both the actual musical and perceived symbolic evolution of black American music in Britain will be examined in order to understand the way in which jazz developed in Britain and in turn to explain some of the idiosyncrasies of the British perception of jazz.

The banjo became widely known to whites due to the transportation of slaves, mainly from West Africa, to colonies around the world from 'as early as the seventeenth century' (Sadie, 1984:151). It was known by various names in different countries, but is clearly described in several accounts written as early as 1621 (Epstein, 1975:350, Lloyd Webb, 1993:9). The banjo was used by slaves on American plantations to accompany their songs and dances, as it was suitably portable and was relatively easy to construct from natural materials such as gourds, wood, skins and gut (Lloyd Webb, 1993:9). Naturally, the singing and dancing of slaves was 'a source of interest and amusement for whites' (Oliver, 1984:24) on plantations. However, it was the unique social and political situation in New Orleans, Louisiana that allowed black culture to be more publicly disseminated to whites.

In the eighteenth century, the *Code Noir* 'exempted slaves from forced labour on Sundays and religious holidays … [and] shortly came to include Saturday afternoons as well' (Johnson, 1991:122). Although Sunday was a 'non-work day' throughout the American South, it was in Louisiana that slaves had 'the right to use their free time virtually as they saw fit, with little or no supervision' (Johnson, 1991:124). Slaves were often permitted to grow and sell their own produce at the market in New Orleans. The market place eventually became known as the infamous Congo Square where slaves and free people of colour danced on Sundays. Congo Square was established as a focal point for dancing, not only due to the market, which made it a natural meeting point, but also because of an early nineteenth century law which forbade dancing anywhere else. (Johnson, 1991:141).

The dancing in Congo Square was unique because it was still overwhelmingly African, whereas elsewhere in America pressure from evangelical religious sects which considered dancing sinful had led to the erosion of these traditions and acculturation to Anglo-American norms (Epstein, 1975:348, Johnson, 1991:141). The cultural diversity of New Orleans that allowed the traditions of individual ethnic groups to flourish and develop uniquely, including those of the large African population, as well as the French Creole's love of dancing contributed to the longevity of African music and dance in the city (Johnson, 1991:146). The fact that the dancing took place in a prominent location also allowed it to be observed and documented by visitors to the city, such as Benjamin Latrobe, an architect originally from Leeds. In 1819, Latrobe wrote an account of the dancing in Congo Square, in which he described the use of a banjo-like instrument (he also sketched the instruments that he saw):

> The music consisted of two drums and a stringed instrument ... which was no doubt imported from Africa. On the top of the finger board was the rude figure of a man in a sitting posture, & two pegs behind him to which the strings were fastened. The body was a calabash. It was played by a very little old man, apparently 80 or 90 years old. (Latrobe, ed. Wilson 1951: 46-49)

Latrobe's reaction to what he saw in Congo Square is typical of the white perception of black culture at this time: 'I have never seen anything more brutally savage, and at the same time dull and stupid, than this whole exhibition.' (Latrobe, ed. Wilson 1951:49).

Recent research has suggested that in fact the fiddle was a more central part of African-American culture, (see Linn, who cites Winans's work on runaway slave adverts that found mention of only 17 banjo players compared with 627 of the fiddle/violin (1991:42)), but yet it was the banjo that 'seems to have been the most widely reported and longest lived of all the African instruments in the New World.' (Epstein, 1975:351) and certainly developed the strongest imagery (Linn, 1991:49). This can be explained by the essential 'otherness' of the banjo, which was quite unlike any Western instrument (Linn, 1991:67), especially when compared with a fiddle, which even when played in a different style, retains its long-term associations with conventional Western music. It is easy to see how the banjo was congruent with the perceived 'otherness' of black-skinned people from a far-off land and thus became the instrument representative of black music, particularly for people without first-hand knowledge of African-American culture.

As a result of caricature in art and drama, 'the stereotype of a happy, carefree slave, dancing and strumming on the old plantation was known to English audiences well before 1800' (Epstein, 1975:347), and was even adopted by pro-slavery writers in England who regarded 'musical talent as quite compatible with innate inferiority' (1975:347). The deep-seated implications of the acceptance of such a simplistic view of black culture and the banjo specifically were matched only by the reaction of the abolitionists, who in their wholesale rejection of the 'Negro banjo player' also rejected the elements of truth within the myth. Latrobe witnessed a particular type of dancing with banjo accompaniment in Congo Square:

> They were formed in circular groupes [sic] in the midst of four of which, which I examined (but there were more of them) was a ring, the largest not 10 feet in diameter ... . Most of the circles contained the same sort of dancers. One was larger, in which a ring of a dozen women walked, by way of dancing, round the music in the center. (Latrobe, ed. Wilson 1951: 46-9)

The dancing that Latrobe describes strongly prefigures the circular form of the minstrel show 'walk-around' finales, which invariably took place in a plantation setting. Dancing to banjo music became an important element of the nineteenth century minstrel show. The Bohee brothers even apparently 'played the banjo while dancing, and may have been the first minstrel team to perform that speciality.' (Rouse, 1989:8). They were known to have performed highly rhythmic numbers as part of the climactic walk-around, thus perpetuating the traditional link between banjo and dance. Later in the nineteenth century, the walk-around developed into the cakewalk, a precursor of ragtime, and the result of complex cross-fertilization of African and European dance traditions. Few minstrel banjo players could replicate the reputed agility and dexterity of the Bohees, but for the banjoist the urge to dance was still present and expressed through 'tapping':

> It was not possible for him to dance, and yet he did not remain entirely motionless. In true Negro fashion he tapped out with one foot the regular beat of his music. (Nathan, 1962:59)

The practice of 'tapping' to banjo tunes is also mentioned in nineteenth century banjo methods. Nathan quotes from S.S. Stewart's Method:

> The time in the above jig may be tapped with the foot, 4 taps to each measure-which is the method generally adopted for playing jigs. It seems that the practice of tapping to banjo tunes came from the Negro, who still today considers a metronomic, percussive background indispensable to the vigorous rhythm he wishes to produce. (Nathan, 1962:190)

These instances clearly attribute 'tapping' to the stereotypical 'primitive' but yet innately musical Negro.

The banjo was not only familiar as an instrument of black culture, but specifically as the instrument of plantation slaves in Britain. This becomes even more significant when placed in context with Epstein's description of 'the most common and confusing legend about the banjo: that it was unknown to the plantation Negro.' (1975:348). In Britain, the black banjo player was more clearly associated with the plantation than any other setting, due to the repeated presentation of this environment in literature and drama. The lack of any evidence of Epstein's legend in Britain, rather, the unequivocal and repeated positioning of the banjo within a plantation setting indicates the strength of the 'happy, carefree slave' stereotype as a result of its presentation in songs and minstrel shows, genres that were well represented and understood in Britain.

The image of the 'Negro and his banjo' was a standard part of early minstrel shows, beginning with the pre-emancipation blackface troupes such as the Virginia Minstrels who visited Britain in 1843-45 (Lloyd Webb, 1993:11) including legendary banjoists Dan Emmett and Billy Whitlock. Indeed, it was 'the original and unique instrumentation of banjo, violin, bones and tambourine', quite unlike other music of the period, which enhanced the appeal of the minstrel show as new and different entertainment (Mahar, 1999:341). However, the white experience of supposedly 'authentic' banjo music was initially that which was transmitted as an exaggerated parody typical of blackface minstrelsy, where 'most of the banjo-playing, singing and dancing [of blackface minstrels] were casual and stereotyped imitations' (Blesh and Janis, 1917:11). Although the banjo was an element of 'authentic' African culture, and after Emancipation, enabled blacks to perform on the stage, performances had to remain within the boundaries of the stereotypes that had already been established by white performers in blackface. By performing in shows in America and all over Europe, black minstrels were disseminating and reinforcing white stereotypes, of which the banjo was an important part, as it was both a visual and musical symbol. Thus, the banjo became indicative of the paradox that was created and fuelled by whites:

> It casts both bright and dark shadows: banjo is frolic (but banjo is slavery); banjo is entertainment (but banjo is blackface); banjo accompanies the dance (but dancing in bondage, longing to be free). (Lloyd Webb, 1993:7)

The lyrics and music of popular songs present both literary and musical symbolism that indicates the nature of the understanding and reception of banjo music in Britain.[1] Black characters were 'sometimes found in English comic operas of the late eighteenth century, including some popular in America' (Hamm, 1979:110). One such opera, *The Wags* or *The Camp of Pleasure* by Dibdin, written in 1790, includes an early example of a song that connects the banjo with a portrayal of a stereotypical Negro. *The Negro and his Banjer* [g380e(15)], also introduces features that were to become typical of later 'banjo' songs. The accompaniment to this song includes a violin part that uses semi-quavers repeated on the same note, perhaps to represent the sound of the banjo. This depiction of the characteristics of the banjo on other instruments is common in accompaniments to later songs that mention the banjo. The song portrays the banjo as the instrument of the plantation slave, and the lyrics are written in a pseudo-Negro dialect that became a standard feature of such songs in the twentieth century:

> One Negro wi my banjer
> Me from Jenny come
> Wid cunning yei
> Me savez spy
> De buckra world one hum

---

[1] These songs will be referenced in the text using the British Library volume number. A full list of songs consulted with detailed information is contained in Appendix 3.

As troo a street a stranger
Me my banjer strum.

In later songs the banjo is clearly linked with both the positive and negative elements of paradoxical black stereotypes. In *The Old Banjo* [h3990q25], which in 1910 would have been considered a comic novelty song, various negative elements are presented. These include laziness: 'A nigger play'd on a banjo/The whole of the day, he'd sit and play'; cannibalism: 'I'm Lobengula/King of the Cannibal Nuts' who later fries his children for dinner; and excessive sexuality: 'The ladies all snigger because of my figger/I wear nothing else but an old banjo' and 'The next day they were wed/And quickly their family grew'. In this song, it is the banjo playing of his 72 children that drives Lobengula to shoot and eat them. Thus, the banjo is linked with the supposedly wild and uncontrollable nature of the black man.

On the other hand, *Ring de Banjo* [h1437(8)], a much earlier song of 1853, describes a dutiful slave who, having been freed by his master, returns voluntarily to continue to serve him. The endearing qualities of the slave described in this song are enhanced by use of pseudo-Negro dialect:

I could not go no farder
I turn to massa's door
I lub him all de harder
I'll go away no more

It is to the music of the slave's banjo that the master dies:

I on de banjo tapping
I come wid dulcem strain
Massa fell a napping
He'll nebber wake again

As in *Ring de Banjo* and *The Negro and his Banjer*, many songs link the banjo directly to the plantations. In *That Banjo Song* [h3992hh(6)] the music of the 'old banjo' is described as 'the sweet song of my old plantation home' and in *'Tis the banjo softly speaking* [h1788j(41)] banjo music is the accompaniment for the 'the whole plantation's singing'. The adjective 'old' is frequently used to describe the instrument in songs, for example the song *On Your Rag-Time Rag Shop Banjo* [h3990.i(47)] describes the performances of an old man on a banjo: 'Old Man Joe on your banjo/Play a little bit of ragtime music'. Linn points out that whilst nineteenth century banjo players in songs were generally young, 'by the 1920s the image of the Southern black banjo player was usually that of an elderly man' (1991:65), which showed that once he must have been a slave and therefore lent him a certain authenticity as plantation banjo player. Several later songs link the banjo with ghosts and life after death. In a song called *The Ghost of the Rag-time Coon* [h3989f(42)], the performances of the minstrel are described: 'Ev'rywhere he used to go/Playing cute airs on his old banjo'. After his death, it is the characteristic sound of his banjo that alerts people to the presence of his ghost:

'They'd hear the strains of the old banjo and this is what they'd say: It's the ghost of the rag-time coon…'. A similar image is used in *The Old Banjo* [h3990q(25)] in which the 'nigger' returns as a ghost: 'I'm dead and I'm gone/But I'm still going on/Playing gaily away on my old banjo'.

The consistency of this imagery illustrates that the banjo was widely used and well established as a symbol of traditional black music-making and, in later ragtime songs, the inclusion of the banjo acts as a metaphor for nostalgia. It also places the banjo within the popular myth of the 'Old South', which although more developed in America was also relevant and influential to the perception of the banjo in Britain at the turn of the century. Linn describes how the South had developed romantic and sentimental imagery that had captured the American imagination beginning with productions of *Uncle Tom's Cabin* and minstrel shows (1991:55). These particular manifestations were also present in nineteenth century Britain, and they included the banjo as representative of the music of the 'Old South'.[2]

The appeal of the sentimental mythology of the 'Old South' also was strong in the American North which was distanced from the reality of the South, and where people were often immersed in 'official' culture. The dichotomy that results from Linn's consideration of the differences between 'sentimental' and 'official' culture can also be used to explain the appeal of the banjo as a sentimental instrument for people immersed in official European culture (Linn, 1991:61):

(sentimental)	(official)
nature	civilisation
leisure	work
sensual	controlled
primitive	modern
emotional	rational
black	white
South	North
feminine	Masculine

The banjo appealed to British audiences in the late-nineteenth/early twentieth centuries as an 'other' instrument with no place within the history of 'official' Western music just as it appealed to those in American North. Most importantly, however, the banjo indicated the existence of an entire alternative culture, the otherness of which was heightened for British audiences that were even further removed from the sources of the 'Old South' myth. It is interesting to note that later in the nineteenth century, the banjo craze that swept both the American North and Britain did not affect the middle and upper classes in the South (Linn, 1991:18), indicating the importance of distance in developing the 'Old South' mythology of which the banjo was an integral part. Although the distance between British audiences and the American South helped to ensure the popularity of the

---

[2] Linn comments that Harriet Beecher Stowe's original novel *Uncle Tom's Cabin* does not mention a banjo, but yet the instrument appeared frequently in the films and shows of the book (1991:58).

banjo as representative of an 'other' culture, it also ensured that the 'plantation Negro' stereotype was more readily accepted as 'authentic' and this had a long term influence on the reception of black music in Britain.[3]

Contrary to the popular image of the 'plantation Negro banjo player' it is interesting to note that black banjo players in professional theatre, including Horace Weston and the Bohee brothers, the best and most famous black banjoists who visited Britain with minstrel troupes such as Haverley's and Callender's, were not necessarily from the South and often had no direct links with plantations. However, even if British audiences had known this, it is unlikely that it would have diminished their fascination for the black performers. The Bohee brothers were the most significant black minstrel banjoists to visit Britain, as they remained in the country for some time and continued to be popular in music halls after the minstrel troupes had left. The popularity of the Bohees was such that they formed their own minstrel group and 'were greatly in demand in London at society functions and private entertainments' (Reynolds, 1927:201). The act comprised 'banjo solos, duets, ballads, songs and dances, during which they accompanied themselves on the banjo' (Reynolds, 1927:202). The Bohees recorded on Edison in early 1890 (Schreyer, 1993:1), and were probably the first black artists to have recorded commercially (Heier and Lotz, 1993:74), yet again reinforcing the banjo as the main instrument of black music.

The continued appeal of the banjo as representative of a sentimental, exotic, primitive alternative to 'official' culture, led to banjo music becoming an important American musical craze in Britain in the 1880s. Two songs of 1889, *Banjo Mania* [h1260m(32)] and *Twang the Banjo* [h1260m(35)] specifically describe the concurrent 'banjo craze', which is shown to have permeated all layers of society: 'In hut and palace it is found/It pleases low it pleases high/They all adore it so' [h1260m(35)]. The song *Twang the Banjo* mentions that 'What's good enough for the Prince of Wales/Is good enough for me'. The Prince of Wales received banjo lessons from James Bohee[4] and this indicates both the acceptance of a black banjo

---

[3] In New Orleans in the early twentieth century, the guitar was initially more popular than the banjo, and it seems that many musicians only began to play the banjo as a result of the increase in popularity of the instrument in entertainment cities of the North in the 1910s. Johnny St Cyr reports that the banjo started to become popular around the time he was working with A.J. Piron in 1908-09 and this prompted him to construct his own banjo-guitar (Johnny St Cyr interview, 27 August 1958, HJA transcript p. 1). Danny Barker began playing a banjo-uke that his aunt bought as a result of a ukelele craze, and later obtained his first banjo from his uncle, Paul Barbarin, who was playing in Chicago with King Oliver (Danny Barker interview, 30 June 1959, HJA transcript p. 15). Emanuel Sayles's brother bought a banjo 'when they were popular' which Sayles borrowed (Emanuel Sayles interview, 17 January 1959, HJA transcript p. 5).

[4] In an interview in the *Radio Times* of 29 May 1925, the banjo maker Mr A. Weaver stated: 'I can remember [James Bohee's] excitement when he was commanded to appear at Marlborough House to give lessons on the banjo to King Edward [formerly the Prince of Wales], who later became an accomplished player. I made one hundred and fifty instruments for Jim Bohee alone. He and his brother came from America with the famous Haverley Minstrels about 1882 and went the round of the music halls for many years.' (p. 456.)

player into high society[5] and the extent of the vogue for the banjo. James Bohee and his brother George opened a banjo academy in London and Reynolds states that 'To learn the banjo became quite a craze amongst society folk' (1927:201).[6] Of course, this was not the first time that the banjo had been appropriated by whites, as the 'early nineteenth century banjo music and minstrel shows presented the first commercial use of African-American musical culture by white entertainers', i.e. blackface minstrelsy (Linn, 1991:5). However, it seems that by the latter part of the century, the banjo had developed such a strong symbolism that its 'otherness' could be evoked without recourse to such obvious visual or even aural prompts, as 'the actual banjo, the repertory, and the playing style offered by the white minstrel banjoists of the late nineteenth century increasingly had little foundation in black tradition' (Linn, 1991:48).

At this time, several prominent publishers and manufacturers such as S.S. Stewart and Clifford Essex attempted to elevate the banjo 'to a higher class of musical practice and a better class of people', bringing it within 'official' culture specifically by distancing it from its African-American origins (Gura and Bollam, 1999:248). In contrast with the image of the 'old plantation banjo', instruments became more highly decorated, as 'if the banjo were to become an instrument of a higher class of music, the object itself needed to be transformed into art, thus making it a worthy object for the parlor of a prince.' (Linn, 1991:13). Increased metalwork on the bodies of the instrument emphasized their modernism. Tutor books were published that advocated a 'guitar style' of banjo playing that was taught by Western notation, and large amounts of sheet music for banjo began to be published from the 1880s. The expansion of the banjo repertoire shown by sheet music is commensurate with developments in the minstrel show, which had begun to evolve away from the standard 'plantation' format towards variety theatre. Thus, shows increasingly incorporated music other than plantation material, and the performance of novelty pieces and arrangements (titles included the *William Tell* Overture and Dvořák's *Humoresque*) precipitated the development of a virtuosic banjo style. These pieces were extremely popular with the late-nineteenth century music hall audiences in Britain, and represented an alternative to the traditional 'sentimental' banjo repertoire. However, as Linn points out, attempts to elevate the banjo into 'official' culture generally failed, as the instrument never really lost its associations with the black musicians of the plantations (1991:36).

In America, as a result of this, the racially-based associations with 'other' culture that were at the foundations of the massive adoption of the banjo by whites were increasingly seen as inappropriate for black musicians. It was probably the strength of the racial symbolism of the banjo that resulted in a gradual decline in numbers of black solo banjoists from the second half of the nineteenth century as 'the banjo stood as a reminder of the old troubles of slavery, and the new troubles

---

[5] Horace Weston appeared in front of Queen Victoria, and 'so entertained her with the music of his banjo that she presented him with a gold medal, which he highly prized' according to his obituary (Linn, 1991:46).
[6] Rudyard Kipling wrote his poem *The Song of the Banjo* at the height of the banjo craze (1894).

of half-citizenship conferred by emancipation. In some quarters, at least, blacks expressed a desire to be rid of the banjo' (Lloyd Webb, 1993:17). Therefore, later developments in black music of early twentieth century America centred on other instruments such as the cornet and the piano, partially as a result of the negative associations of the banjo that featured less prominently in early jazz bands.

By this time, in addition to the strongly developed racially symbolic character of the banjo, contemporary songs show that the banjo had a clear *musical* identity that could be evoked without even using the instrument itself. Firstly, several songs feature vocalized banjo sounds, such as 'Tink a tank, tink a tank' [h3980cc(35)] and 'plunk, plunk, plunk' [h3992hh(6)]. Characteristics of banjo music are also frequently used in the piano accompaniment to songs, most often arpeggiated patterns, spread chords, and dotted rhythms and triplets that also sometimes find their way into song melodies. *That Banjo Song* [h3992hh(6)] also has a great number of phrases that begin on an offbeat (in this case the second quaver of a 2/4 bar) which are also characteristic of banjo music. The piano accompaniment in the song *Twang the Banjo* [h1260m(35)] is even marked *'sempre a la Banjo'*. It was the transferable nature of banjo music, particularly to the piano, as seen in these songs, that was to evolve into the ragtime piano style in America. The link between banjo music and ragtime has been well documented, for example Blesh and Janis state that 'Piano ragtime was developed by the Negro from folk melodies and from the syncopations of the plantation banjos' (1971:7). Scott Joplin met and heard the banjo player Plunk Henry at the 1893 Chicago Exposition and then 'developed the rudiments of piano ragtime from banjo syncopation' (Oliver, 1984:29).

Whilst in America around the turn of the century the piano took over from the banjo as the main instrument for the performance of syncopated music, the banjo remained prominent as the main instrument for the performance of syncopated music in Britain for a number of reasons. Piano ragtime did not make such an impact in Britain as in America, and there is very little evidence that any important ragtime piano players visited Britain until the 1920s (Rye, 1990a:45), which is especially significant in the context of most of the top American banjoists visiting this country in the preceding decades of the twentieth century. Eubie Blake, a ragtime pianist who performed in Britain in 1925, commented 'My playing of jazz seemed particularly astounding to the English musicians. They tried to classify it according to musical form, but failed.' (quoted in Rye, 1990a:53). This indicates that ragtime piano was not a familiar style to Britons.

This lack of identification with piano ragtime in Britain was probably due to the fact that ragtime was popularized in Britain primarily through revue shows, as discussed in Chapter 1. Within this context, piano ragtime would have been inappropriate both as a song or dance accompaniment, due to its lack of audibility, and also as a variety 'turn' in itself, as it lacked the visual interest of a band. Theatrical revues therefore tended to use orchestrated ragtime, which became the convention for dance accompaniment outside the theatre for similar reasons. Therefore, the British public associated ragtime with a variety of different forms including 'coon songs, ragtime songs and instrumental music' (Oliver, 1984:33), rather than predominantly with piano rags. This is particularly relevant to an understanding of the fundamental differences between the evolution of syncopated styles in Britain and America. In Britain, due to the absence of piano ragtime, there was a greater emphasis on the syncopated 'coon songs, ragtime songs and instrumental music', which have the banjo as a common musical and symbolic denominator.

Whereas in America 'the generally racist ideas that clung to the image of the black banjo player not only encouraged the abandonment of the instrument by blacks, in the end it discouraged the survival of the instrument as a viable vehicle for music making in American culture.' (Linn, 1991:75), the geographical and temporal distance from the reality of the South meant that the romance of the 'Old South' myth and the appeal of the banjo was intensified and persisted for longer in Britain where the association between black performers and the banjo was strongly maintained. This is shown by the fact that it is virtually the only instrument mentioned in nineteenth century songs that describe black music-making, and as the most frequently mentioned instrument in songs that describe performances of American syncopated music between 1900 and 1919. For example, in the 1917 song *Banjo Moon* [h3809b(25)], people in heaven are described as 'Playing the harp and singing see/Just like an everlasting Jubilee', but 'black folks' will 'want a banjo too'. The songs explains:

There's a great big banjo in the moon
So that niggers when they die
Can sit and play all the live long day
And raise their voices high.

The association between black performers and the banjo was maintained by the leading black banjo ensembles that visited Britain: Joe Jordan's Syncopated Orchestra (1905-06 and 1915), Dan Kildare's Clef Club Orchestra (1915-1920), and the Versatile Three/Four (1913-1926), who all used at least one banjo or derivative (banjoline, mandoline etc.) at a time when there was 'a growing vogue for Afro-American sounds in high-class dance clubs' (Rye, 1990a:46). These bands, initially at least, appeared in evening dress at exclusive venues in London such as the Savoy Hotel and Ciro's Club, which was 'extensively patronized by younger members of the royal family' (Rye, 1990a:46). The repertoire of these bands also reflected their civilized appearance. Dan Kildare's Orchestra played a mixture of popular, often sentimental, songs and dances, which were most often waltzes, and Hawaiian style numbers, incorporating typical glissandi between rapidly strummed chords in the banjo parts, that were apparently the craze at the time (e.g. *Hello Hawaii, How Are You?* and *Hawaiian Butterfly*). The Versatile Four performed a similar 'civilized' repertoire to Kildare's band, but also included a few pieces that made reference to the supposed plantation origin of the performers, for example, *Circus Day in Dixie* and *Down Home Rag*.

The respectability that the banjo had gained through the late nineteenth century banjo craze is reflected in these performances by black banjo bands but yet, as we have seen, the instrument still retained the strong associations with the perceived sentimentality and primitiveness of black music. This made the banjo the ideal vehicle for the dissemination of the type of non-threatening 'diluted' or 'civilized' black culture that British white audiences had preferred since the nineteenth century. Black banjo bands were the subject of the same upper class philanthropic interest that had permeated the British reception of black music since the minstrel show, as the fact that the groups consisted of coloured performers was their principal attraction. For example, Dan Kildare's 'Clef Club Orchestra' was re-named 'Coon Orchestra' shortly after its arrival in Britain. Several reviews of Joe Jordan's Syncopated Orchestra linked the music that the band performed with the spirit inherent in the nationality or colour of the performers:

> ... the latest American musical sensation – a band of gentlemen of colour who play rag-time music as if to the manner born. (*Era*, 5 May 1915:14)

> They come from America, and seem to have rag-time in their blood ... . (*Scotsman*, 1 June 1915:1)

It is interesting to note that many white banjoists of this period continued to perform 'characteristic'[7] material in mere imitation of black players, exploiting the stereotypical image of the banjo in the same way as whites had perpetuated and exaggerated black characteristics in blackface shows in the previous century. Although, as we have seen, some white players tried to reposition the banjo within 'official' culture through the performance of classical music, it was the white vaudeville banjoists that sustained the dying traces of minstrelsy, which was not an appealing form for black performers due to its associations with unflattering racial stereotyping. Hence, it was largely left to the black players to develop banjo music in new directions, prompting them to build upon rather than perpetuate the popularity of the minstrel show. The familiar figure of the 'black minstrel banjoist' was commonly perceived in Britain to have been absorbed into the new black banjo bands. A review of Joe Jordan's Syncopated Orchestra in the *Newcastle Evening Mail* (22/61915:4), states that the band 'are unquestionably one of the smartest combinations since minstrelsy was in its prime'. Thus, evolution from minstrel traditions was clearly seen to have taken place in performances by black, not white, banjoists, which placed them at the forefront of developments in syncopated music in Britain at this time.

The important banjo-based groups that visited Britain were closely linked with the Clef Club, that had been set up by James Reese Europe to allow black musicians to prosper and black music to develop. In practice, the club provided 'a central union, clearing house and booking agency for the employment of black musicians' as well as forming an orchestra to raise the profile of black musicians (Badger, 1989:50). Europe was not aiming to form a conventional Western orchestra; rather, he embraced the banjo as central to black music and the ensemble consisted mainly of banjos and derivatives. Although Europe himself did not visit Britain, the formation of the Clef Club and his later association with the famous Castles, who were at the forefront of modern dance fashions, ensured that black

---

[7] Defined as 'black-influenced or -derived music, which was seen as being "characteristic" of blacks' (Linn, 1991:6).

music gained respectability and popularity with the fashionable elite that allowed black banjo bands to make successful visits to Britain at this time.

An important factor in the domination of the banjo in the dissemination of early syncopated music in Britain was that the banjo was well represented in early recordings, as it produced good results due its restricted frequency range and percussive penetration, especially when compared to the piano. In fact, the number of banjo recordings made in Britain led to the situation where 'the British recording industry actually dominated in banjo solo and banjo ensemble sides produced' from the start of World War I to the end of World War II (Schreyer, 1993:4). It seems likely that the banjoists that recorded in Britain would have also given live performances. As the banjo was most often used in recorded performances of syncopated music, which disseminated the music increasingly widely, the instrument therefore became synonymous with the new musical styles in Britain. Conversely, technology did not allow pianists to record as successfully, therefore their performances were probably not as widely known as those of banjoists, and also they had no particular reason to visit and perform in Britain. It is interesting to note the role of the piano as an accompanying instrument in early recordings of 'solo' banjoists. Frequently, these involved the syncopations of the banjo against the steady on-beat, chordal accompaniment provided by the piano, and it was rare for the piano part to contain much melodic material. Even in vocal numbers, it was almost always the banjo and rarely the piano that played any countermelody or took a solo between verses. The piano fulfilled a similar underlying role in larger ensembles that included banjos, where it was relegated to the background due to a combination of the fact that the part it played was rhythmically and melodically uninteresting and the unsuitability of early recording techniques for capturing its sound.

The recordings of the black banjo groups that visited Britain illustrate both the technical problems with which bands were faced at this time and the suitability of the banjo for these early recording methods. The version of Dan Kildare's Orchestra that first recorded in 1916 consisted of banjo, banjoline, 'cello, piano, string bass and drums. The banjo and banjoline can be heard most clearly, the cello when used is reasonably clear, the piano faint and the bass inaudible. The percussion can only be heard when woodblocks are used. The Versatile Four, who performed on two banjolines, piano and drums as well as singing vocal numbers in close harmony, are more consistent in terms of the recording quality.

As banjos were responsible for providing both melodic and rhythmic interest in performances of these groups, this suggests that their prominence was pre-meditated and usual, not just the result of primitive recording methods. Indeed, banjo parts held melodic interest even in vocal numbers. In Dan Kildare's band, the banjos were used melodically to play decorative counter-melodies reminiscent of New Orleans polyphony and also play extensive variations in between the vocal verses on numbers such as *Where did Robinson Crusoe Go With Friday on Saturday Night?* Similarly, the performances of the Versatile Four incorporate rapid, decorative banjo counter-melodies under the vocal line, for example in *I Want a Doll*, vocal and instrumental 'breaks' and a sense of 'call and response' in some of the performances, where an ornamented banjo part is used to fill in the gaps at the end of the melodic lines.

It is the banjos in Dan Kildare's band that are responsible for the rhythmic drive, making up for the 'cello, whose legato counter-melodies frequently fall behind the beat. In fact, the group's second recording session in October 1916 omits the 'cello and has a lot more rhythmic clarity than the first. The banjos also have a clear role to play on the last sections of several numbers, such as *My Mother's Rosary*, performing with more vigour and often incorporating increased syncopation and cross rhythms into their strumming, thus anticipating the role of the drummer in, for example, big band jazz arrangements. In some pieces, the banjo and drums can be heard playing in rhythmic unison, which indicates that they fulfilled a similar rhythmic function within the group.

The recordings of the Versatile Four clearly prefigure jazz, as due to the use of the banjo their music often incorporates a strong sense of off-beat accentuation (on beats two and four in a 4/4 bar). The recording of *Down Home Rag* is certainly the most exciting and 'jazz-like' performance by this group that has survived. This number was rare among the early recorded output of this group as it is purely instrumental, and thus most clearly relates to later jazz ensembles. The tempo is very fast and the rapid melody must have represented a considerable challenge for the banjoists. The main melody uses a simple three note rising motive, whereby on the return to the starting note, which is metrically displaced, syncopation is created and the drum part emphasizes these accents. Most of the group's early recordings featured characteristically strong three-part singing, and it seems likely that the style of the songs and practicalities of having to play and sing restricted their banjo style to an extent.

Although the banjo bands were subject to the demands of their audience for sentimental songs and waltzes, they nevertheless were able to develop the banjo style rhythmically and by incorporating increasingly interesting and dense polyphony and embellishments into their arrangements. The bands mentioned above subsequently played at a wide variety of venues in London and the provinces, where they were generally well appreciated, and provided important models for the development of numerous similar groups and a foundation for the evolution of syncopated music in Britain. This can be seen with reference to the Savoy Hotel, which employed a banjo-based group, initially known as Murray's Savoy Quartette (because they also played at Murray's club), from 1915, which later included black drummer Alec Williams (Rye, 1990a:48; Savoy Archive). Their recorded repertoire shows considerable parallels with that recorded by the groups mentioned above, particularly Ciro's Club Coon Orchestra, and it can be seen that these two groups recorded the same numbers within months or even weeks of each other. This shows that a new musical genre had been firmly established in Britain, that there was constant cross-fertilization between various similar groups in London at this time, and that the 'modern' concept of the 'popular song' with a limited lifespan was developing.

Banjo-based bands and music remained popular in Britain long after the instrument was considered old-fashioned in America, as is demonstrated by the Versatile Four, who came to Europe in 1913, and were successful in Britain and the continent. However, when they returned to America in 1914, they found that work was not plentiful, as by this stage the banjo was probably considered old fashioned, certainly in New York where even James Reese Europe was recording without banjos or mandolins (Badger, 1989:53). Yet back in London shortly afterwards the Versatile Four played at significant venues such as the London Pavilion and Murray's Club (Lotz, sleeve note to DOCD5624). The centrality of the banjo to the performance of syncopated music in Britain is illustrated by a Savoy Orpheans concert programme of 1924. This provides a fascinating history of syncopated music as it was perceived in Britain, and states that banjo bands were the first to introduce syncopation to dance music: 'Syncopated rhythm of ragtime was introduced in new musical numbers about ten years ago, by orchestras composed of banjos with a piano'.

Although the perception by the British public of the evolution of syncopated music was based on the primarily *visual* and *symbolic* concept of the stereotypical Negro banjo player, initially as a solo minstrel and later as part of a black band, it was strengthened by a demonstrable *musical* evolution from plantation songs and dances to ragtime in which the banjo also had a central role, as crucially, there were elements of truth underlying the stereotype and the 'Old South' mythology. As we have seen, the banjo has a documental African and African-American history and was indeed used for accompanying dancing on the plantations of the South. This history of the banjo as an instrument for accompanying dancing permeates its continued use in this way in the twentieth century. For example, the practice of 'tapping' can be seen to have continued through the use of piano accompaniments in early recorded banjo music that emphasized a steady beat under the syncopated banjo melody. It is also interesting to note that two twentieth century banjo players refer to tapping. Johnny St Cyr mentioned in an interview that he doesn't usually 'pat' his foot, but that he is one of the few musicians that doesn't (Johnny St Cyr interview, 27 August 1958, HJA transcript p. 18) and similarly, Emmanuel Sayles mentioned that when recording 'almost everyone had to use pillows so their foot stamping wouldn't be picked up.' (Emanuel Sayles interview, 17 January 1959, HJA transcript p. 31). The reference to tapping in these interviews implies not only that tapping was considered central to the banjo style, but also that it extended to other instruments, indicating an evolution of multi-instrument jazz from banjo music.

The descriptions of 'tapping' may be favourably compared with the description of early performances of syncopated dance music in Britain in *The Appeal of Jazz* (Mendl, 1927), in which the universal appeal of jazz is attributed to the unusual sensation of dancing to syncopated rhythms:

> There was an instinctive delight in emphasising with your feet a beat which was not stressed by the players. We all felt, did we not, that we were playing our little part in the performance. (Mendl, 1927:84).

Therefore, the beginnings of modern improvisatory dance in response to the syncopation of the twentieth century banjo bands can be directly linked via the banjo to the dancing witnessed by Latrobe in Congo Square. Viewed superficially, the social setting of upper-class clubs in which groups such as Dan Kildare's Orchestra performed could not have been more different from Congo Square or the plantations. However, returning to the idea that slave banjo music was 'a source of interest and amusement for whites' (Oliver, 1984:24) it can be seen that a performance situation identical to that of the plantation was being artificially replicated, at the instigation of whites, in these London clubs. The fundamental difference is that these later banjo performances were given primarily for the enjoyment of the white audiences rather than the black musicians themselves.

The continued use of the banjo as the main instrument to accompany dancing was an element of African-American culture that had been preserved in the black banjo bands that visited and became popular in Britain in the early twentieth century, and this is vital to an understanding of the way in which jazz evolved in Britain. The banjo linked all the various forms of African-American music in Britain prior to jazz both symbolically and musically, thus establishing an evolutionary sequence that connected modern syncopated music to its black origins. Therefore, it is significant that banjos were included in almost all early ragtime and jazz ensembles in Britain into the 1920s, except for the Original Dixieland Jazz Band, who came to Britain in 1919. As this group had such a high profile on the stage and on record, they became responsible for defining jazz in Britain, as we shall see in the next chapter, and the main way in which the British public would have differentiated jazz from previous syncopated styles was probably, therefore, partially based on the banjo-less instrumentation of the group. This provides evidence that this white group were possibly attempting to deny the black origins of the music that they performed by deliberately omitting the instrument that had the strongest associations with this culture. Also, more significantly, the notable omission of the banjo indicates a reason why this group made such an impact upon their arrival in a banjo-dominated Britain.

Chapter 6

The Original Dixieland Jazz Band and the Southern Syncopated Orchestra

The year 1919 was marked by the arrival in Britain of two important American ensembles: the all-white Original Dixieland Jazz Band, and the Southern Syncopated Orchestra, an ensemble that consisted entirely of black performers. It is fascinating to compare the activities of these extremely different groups of American musicians who were performing new and individually unique musical entertainment in London contemporaneously. The role of these ensembles in disseminating jazz in Britain has been debated at length, but all too often such discussions focus on whether the music performed can be called 'jazz', and thus falter as a modern, 'evolved' definition of jazz is applied unsuccessfully to these early incarnations of the music. As we have seen, the word 'jazz' was on the lips of the British public by 1919, however, there was continuing discussion as to its meaning. This confusion was compounded by the appearance of 'jazz bands' that sounded no different to the familiar bands that had played for dancing for several years previously, due in part to the persistent inclusion of the banjo. Whether or not we now consider the music of the Original Dixieland Jazz Band and the Southern Syncopated Orchestra to be jazz, their performances were clearly seminal and definitive for those that heard them, and had considerable influence on the future development of jazz in Britain in the 1920s and beyond.

The Original Dixieland Jazz Band in London, 1919-1920

There have been many criticisms, particularly in modern literature, of the role in the dissemination of jazz and the commercial success enjoyed by the Original Dixieland Jazz Band supposedly at the expense of musicians of the black community in which jazz has proven roots. The implication is that because the group was white and commercially successful this somehow diminishes their authenticity as a jazz band and their importance within the history of jazz, and this view has clearly influenced many previous evaluations of the ODJB. However, the fact that members of the ODJB were white probably meant that their music made a much greater impression on the British public than if they had been black, and their race was certainly very significant in the way in which they were received in Britain. Essentially, racism in Chicago and New York, the northern American cities that acted as springboards to Europe for jazz bands, would have made 'a similar success for a comparable Negro group impossible' (Schuller, 1968:179), and thus only a white group could have been similarly precipitated into the international spotlight.

In Britain, as we have seen, black performers were inevitably compared or linked, consciously or subconsciously, to the minstrel stereotypes that had been embedded in the public perception; but these white men could perform without any 'cultural baggage' other than their American nationality. This meant that the focus was more on the content of their act rather than on the people performing it. Such strange music when played by black performers could be put down to their perceived eccentricities, but this music was less easy for British audiences to reconcile when the performers were white. This in turn meant that the music that the ODJB performed was more easily comparable by the British public to the performances of similar music by familiar, native white musicians. There were enough similarities between the ODJB and the few existent British 'jazz' bands to ensure that the ODJB was able to influence the performance of these native white bands. Bernard Tipping explained that the ODJB 'seemed to set a new standard for Jazz bands, and every musician who was anybody at all immediately copied or tried to model his own efforts on the style of this marvellous combination' (*Rhythm*, April 1930:20).

Only a few of the reviews of the ODJB in London specifically mention that the performers were white, for example the *Daily News* confirmed that:

> In view of the unkind and disrespectful things which have been said about Red Indians and negroids and West African savages it should be stated that the players are all white – as white as they possibly can be. (4 April 1919:5)

The fact that creed of the performers was rarely mentioned, and then only in passing, indicates that contemporary reviewers saw nothing significant in white rather than black men performing jazz. Even the most exaggerated parts of claims of authenticity made by the band were widely accepted in Britain, by a public who were not in the position to assess these objectively. This meant that the ODJB could define jazz as 'a specialized form of white dance music' (Gerard, 1988:17). In retrospect, it can be seen that this had the negative effect of weakening the understanding of the black roots of the music in Britain. However, twenty-first century attitudes and retrospective understanding should not be allowed to interfere with analysis of the past, and it seems clear both that the ODJB were fundamental in establishing jazz in Britain, and had significant long-term effects on the way in which jazz was perceived. This establishes careful consideration of the ODJB as central to an understanding of the way in which jazz evolved in Britain.

Early History of the Original Dixieland Jazz Band

The Original Dixieland Jazz Band was formed when entrepreneur Harry James arranged for a New Orleans band led by Johnny Stein and including Nick LaRocca, who was to become the leader of the ODJB, to go to Chicago to perform at the Schiller Cafe. LaRocca persuaded him to include Eddie Edwards on trombone and Henry Ragas on piano, who were to become founder members of the ODJB

(Brunn, 1963:23).[1] At this stage the band was known as 'Stein's Band from Dixieland', but one night, the story goes, a drunken punter shouted out 'Jass it up, boys!!' and so the word 'jazz' was incorporated into the name (Brunn, 1963:30). In May 1916, four members of Stein's band (LaRocca, Edwards, Ragas and Nunez, a clarinettist) left in search of better-paid employment (Brunn, 1963:38), and sent for drummer Tony Sbarbaro[2] from New Orleans to join them (Brunn, 1963:41). Soon Nunez was sacked, and Larry Shields taken on in his place, and thus the personnel of the Original Dixieland Jazz Band was complete (Brunn, 1963:44).

The band was successful in Chicago but also clearly ambitious, as Edwards began writing letters to New York with a view to securing employment in the city. Whilst the band was working at the Casino Gardens in Chicago, Edwards reported that 'all the celebrated actors and actresses would come to hear us' (*Second Line*, September–October 1955:10). Max Hart, a theatrical agent, visited the Casino Gardens along with performers from the show the *Ziegfeld Follies*. He signed the band to play at Reisenweber's Restaurant on Columbus Circle in New York (Edwards, 1947:5-6) where they were billed in advertisements as 'Untuneful Harmonists Playing "Peppery" Melodies'. Reisenweber's presented different entertainment on every floor, and the ODJB were the latest novelty. LaRocca recalled numerous actors that heard the band at Reisenweber's, including Charlie Chaplin, and said that 'till the dancers toppled over I'd stay there and play...they were all rich people, and they liked it' (LaRocca interview, 26 May 1958, HJA; transcript p. 65).

It is significant that the band appealed to a theatrical agent, suggesting that their performance must have encompassed more than solely musical entertainment. LaRocca credited his band with introducing jazz into the theatre in Chicago and New York (LaRocca interview 26 May 1958, HJA; transcript p. 62) and by the time the band arrived in England they were clearly experienced vaudeville performers. The band initially met with a poor reception in New York, and it had to be announced to patrons that the music was for dancing. However, the ODJB became popular during 1917, particularly with 'show people' who were sufficiently skilled and extrovert to improvise new dances to the music (Edwards, 1947:6) and made their first recordings. It was at the height of their success and fame in New York that the impresario Albert De Courville signed the band for a ten week run in *Joy Bells* at the Hippodrome, to commence at the beginning of March 1919 (Brunn, 1963:117). The presentation of jazz in Britain was therefore

---

[1] *The Story of the Original Dixieland Jazz Band* by H.O. Brunn (1963), who was a freelance writer and trombonist, but did not play in the ODJB (Squibb, 1963:17), is an important source for these early movements of the ODJB. However, some details are inaccurate, and the facts sometimes embroidered in fulfilling the book's function as a 'story'. Nick LaRocca was clearly a driving and influential force behind the writing of the book, as can be seen from letters in the files of the IJS. J. Russell Robinson, a pianist with the band, expressed his views on the book in a letter in 1960: 'In my opinion nothing good can ever happen from Brunn's mish-mash called "The Story of the ODJB". It only adds to the lies already written about jazz and it's beginning. And old debbil (*sic*.) Nick is the worst prevaricator of anyone before him.' (in 'Edwards' file, HJA).

[2] Also known as Tony Spargo.

linked to earlier American syncopated music and trends that had been introduced through the Hippodrome revues.

Arrival in Britain

The ODJB encountered problems even before the band left America, as Edwards, the trombonist, was conscripted and replaced by Emile Christian, and Ragas, the pianist, died from influenza two days before the band was due to sail for England. He was replaced by J. Russell Robinson (Brunn, 1963:120), who had learnt ODJB repertoire from their phonograph recordings (*Second Line*, September–October 1955:13). The band was granted an extension by De Courville, and eventually left for England on the HMS Adriatic on the 22 March, arriving in Liverpool on 1 April 1919 (*Liverpool Echo*, 1 April 1919). The band travelled straight to London and apparently spent their first night in London in the dressing rooms at the Hippodrome, as there were no hotel rooms available (Brunn, 1963:125). Similarly to the previous movements of the band within America, the visit to London seems to have been motivated by the promise of more money and fame. Musicians from New Orleans regarded cities of the American North, such as Chicago and New York, and even more so London and Paris in Europe, as full of promise, as there jazz was more of a novelty than in their home town and this could lead to inflated fees. A report in *Time* magazine in 1936 suggested that the ODJB's weekly income in New York was more than doubled in London (15 June 1936, contained in 'ODJB' file in IJS).[3]

The band had been previewed prior to their arrival in London, in the *Dancing Times* and *The Era* respectively:

> ... the "Dixie Land Jazz Band", for whom a special spectacular scene has been prepared [in Joy Bells]. This sextette will play Jazz, so I am told, as it is known in the Southern States and the West, and not as it is played in the Night Clubs of London ... . (March 1919:191)

> ... you will see, or hear, "the original Dixieland Jazz Band" – all the way from New Orleans, where the crocodiles come from! (19 February 1919:14)

The geographical origins of the band were emphasized, which influenced the perception that the band was representative of 'authentic' jazz, as well as creating interest through exotic references and indications that the performances of this band were different to the sort of music which British audiences had been used to hearing. The first performance that the band gave in England was on 3 April 1919, when they presented a special show between the matinee and evening performances of *Joy Bells*. The reviewers of this early performance continue to

---

[3] Financial factors also motivated the band's return to the States, which LaRocca attributed to the value of the pound falling (LaRocca interview, 26 May 1958, HJA; transcript p. 84). He also wrote in a letter to Gus Mueller in June 1920 that he had had an offer to go to Germany but declined as the exchange rate was not favourable (letter in the New Orleans Jazz Exhibit at the Old Mint, New Orleans).

stress the band's authenticity as 'the real original of all Jazz bands' (*The Performer*, 10 April 1919:25), an idea which seemed to have been impressed upon them by the promoter: 'I was told by Mr de Courville that this was the original Jazz band' (*The Performer*, 10 April 1919:23).[4]

The ODJB in Variety

The ODJB eventually appeared in *Joy Bells* on 7 April for one night only, which the paper *Town Topics* put down to the drummer contracting influenza (12 April 1919:2), a story confirmed by Sbarbaro himself (*Second Line*, September–October 1955:5). However, this was more likely due to the objections of the principal comedian, George Robey,[5] who 'approached de Courville in a seething rage and served his ultimatum: Roby [*sic*] or the jazz band would have to go – de Courville could have his pick' (Brunn, 1963:126). This is confirmed by Billy Jones, who took over from J. Russell Robinson on piano whilst the band was in Britain (in 'Jones' file in NJA). There was a subtle reference in the *Encore*'s column of rhetorical questions based on theatrical gossip, 'What does Geo. Robey think about it?' (1 May 1919:4), referring to Robey's probable displeasure when the band was asked to return to the Hippodrome for the 'Joy Bells Ball' in April.

On 14 April, the band began a two week run at the Palladium, performing three times a day as one act in a variety show, billed in a programme for the week beginning 21 April as 'The creation of Jazz. The sensation of America.'[6] The ODJB clearly received mixed reactions, as according to *The Era* they 'met with hearty approval' (23 April 1919:14), but the reviewer in the *Encore* stated that 'This is the most discordant and uninteresting entertainment I have yet seen at the Palladium' (17 April 1919:5). The band's previous experience in vaudeville and performing to audiences of actors and actresses in Chicago and New York meant that they were well placed for success on the British stage. The ODJB had appeared at the Hippodrome with a dancer, and their Palladium act used a male dancer, Johnnie Dale, and an unnamed lady who danced and sang. The addition of the singing and dancing to the band's performances shows their awareness of the requirements of variety theatre, in which acts had to be visually as well as aurally attractive, and ensured that this act was integrated well amongst the comedy, singing, dancing and bioscope projection which formed the rest of the bill.

It is significant that the *Encore* reviewer commented that 'After *seeing* jazz, musical studies are of no account' [my italics] (17 April 1919:5). This indicates the band's performances were perceived as an 'act' which was visually and choreographically, rather than solely musically, entertaining. The dance aspect of the act generally received more detailed comment than the music itself. *The Era*

---

[4] *The Performer* contains two separate reviews of the ODJB in the 10 April 1919 issue.
[5] George Robey (1869-1954) was apparently a very popular performer, and was particularly famous for his innuendo 'delivered dead-pan' (Pearsall, 1975:64).
[6] The band was usually billed in this way in Britain. On most billboards and posters, the ODJB usually appeared at the bottom but in similar size writing to the headline stars, suggesting that the band was an important novelty attraction (as shown in photographs and posters in the LaRocca scrapbooks, HJA).

described 'the lady singing a couple of numbers excellently. Johnnie Dale is the male jazz dancer, and his steps and gyrations are little short of wonderful' (23 April 1919:14). The review in the *Pall Mall Gazette* described 'Jimmy Dale' (*sic.*) as 'a dancer not easily to be equalled either in agility or grace. He turned catherine-wheels when he was a little boy, and ever since then he has turned them into fame in the front rank of the New York stage' (23 April 1919). The reviewer in the *Encore* was less complimentary, commenting that the female dancer 'almost danced without moving her feet; in fact when she danced with her partner later on, she was more danced against than dancing'. The male dancer 'came in and riggled [*sic*] himself about just like a filleted eel about to enter the stewing pot' (17 April 1919:5). These descriptions provide a basis for the frequent contemporary criticism of jazz and jazz dancing as being overly sexual and therefore immoral. The inclusion of dancing in the ODJB's act from the start prefigures the group's later development and rise to fame as a dance band in Britain.

The band did perform a few numbers on their own, without singing or dancing, at the Palladium, but it was still the visual aspects of their performance that received the most comment: 'The band itself gave "The Barnyard Blues Jazz" and the "Tiger Rag", in the latter a saucepan and bowler hat serving as accessories to the various instruments.' (*The Era*, 23 April 1919:14.) There are several aspects of the ODJB's performance that show that they were conscious of the visual aspects of their stage presentation. The saucepan mentioned in this review was probably one of the 'sugar cans' that the band had originally used as a receptacle for collecting tips at Reisenweber's (Brunn, 1963:57) and can be seen in photographs of the band in London. However, Lew Davis commented that 'the trumpeter tipped his instrument into one of the boxes and shook it; the trombonist did the same into the other. They were crude in those days' (1934a:7). Much comment has been made (see, for example, Harris, 1957:201) about the top hats that the band wore in performances at the Hammersmith Palais, which were painted with the letters D-I-X-I-E that could be read from left to right as the band stood on stage (see Figure 6.1).[7] LaRocca later defended these hats, saying that they were 'just to show who we were, that's all' (Rust, 1967:25). However, another photograph of the band in Britain in which they are smartly dressed in matching suits (see Figure 6.2), illustrates the ability of the ODJB to adapt to different performance situations and audiences.

The ODJB as a Dance Band

The ODJB began develop a new and significant role outside variety theatre when, about a month after their arrival in Britain, they were booked for their first dance gig. On 16 April *The Era* had reported that:

---

[7] The sugar can is present in this picture. There are two saxophones on the stage, and a smaller, cornet-like, trumpet and four black cones that resemble trombone mutes but may have been megaphones. The stuffed monkey that can be seen in this photograph apparently 'had electric lights for eyes and a baton that waved automatically (*Time*, June 15 1936).

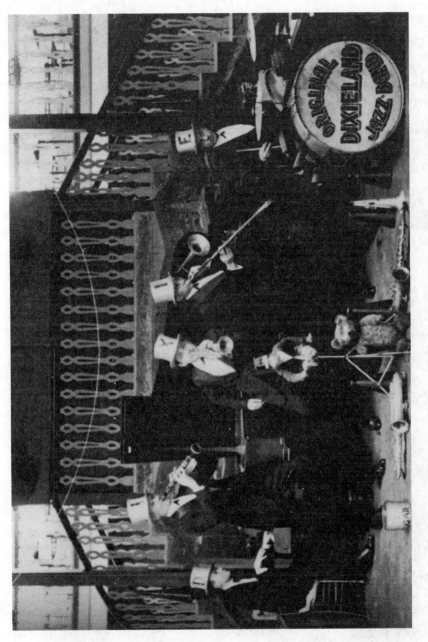

Figure 6.1   The Original Dixieland Jazz Band at the Hammersmith Palais, 1919 (Max Jones Archive)

Figure 6.2   The Original Dixieland Jazz Band, c. 1919 (Max Jones Archive)

Albert De Courville is fixing up a series of Jazz and other dances at a new club of his, to be called the Dixie. Moreover, he is planning to give, there or elsewhere, a dance to celebrate the success of his new Hippo revue. It is to be called "The Joy Bells Ball". (16 April 1919)

On 22 April *The Times* advertised that the ODJB would be appearing the following day in 'Albert de Courville's London Hippodrome "Joy Bells Ball"', with 'Dancing at 10pm'. As the band were advertised as appearing at the Palladium as well, this suggests that they played three variety shows then performed at the Hippodrome afterwards. The *Dancing Times* reported that the dance

... was well attended by members of the theatrical profession, who were somewhat divided in their appreciation of the extraordinary noise made by this orchestra. It is evident that dancing to true Jazz music is an acquired taste. (May 1919:321)

As we have seen, dance had been associated with the ODJB's performances from the start, when the 'gyrations' of the dancers performing with the band at the Hippodrome and the Palladium made a huge impression on variety audiences. A poster outside the Palladium advertised that the band 'made the feet ache to dance', although of course dancing would probably not have been practically possible in a theatre. Billy Jones stated that the ODJB 'was strictly a band for dancing to, really, not a show band in any sense of the word' (in 'Jones' file in NJA), indicating that he felt that the band was more at home in dance clubs than in variety theatre. Certainly, it was as a dance band that the group had most success in Britain, and this was as much due to the fact that their presence was timely with regard to the huge expansion of dance as a leisure activity and the evolution of modern dance in the post-War era as to the characteristics of the music that they performed.

The ODJB, having completed a fortnight at the Palladium, opened on 28 April at the Dixie Club on Bond Street, which had been bought by Albert De Courville (*Times*, 27 April 1919) and who had quickly changed its name from Martan's.[8] It seems that the club was certainly expensive and exclusive as 'The Prince of Wales used to come into the Bond Club [*sic*] almost every night to hear us play' (1947:6). This engagement marked the first extended period that the band was not employed as a variety act. De Courville had promoted the band as a dance group at the Joy Bells Ball, which together with the renaming of the club would have provided the group with some useful publicity and allowed them to establish a new profile away from the variety halls.

On 28 June the band caused a sensation when they played at the Savoy's Victory Ball in the presence of the King and Queen and various other dignitaries to celebrate the signing of the Versailles Treaty (LaRocca interview, 2 June 1958, HJA; transcript p. 88; Jackson, 1964:107).[9] The following day, the band began a

---

[8] The club was to be renamed again in December 1919, as the Embassy Club, with music provided by Benny Peyton's Jazz Kings, a group of musicians from the Southern Syncopated Orchestra (see later).

[9] Brunn reports that the band performed at Buckingham Palace for King George around this time (1963:129), a claim reiterated by modern writers although there is apparently no

new contract at Rector's Club. The ODJB remained at Rector's until their move to the Hammersmith Palais de Danse, the 'largest and most luxurious dancing palace in Europe', for the opening night on 28 October 1919. The *West London Observer* reported that:

> The music will be a feature of the Palais de Danse. By the employment of two exceptionally good Jazz bands, provision has been made for continuous music. One is the Dixie Band, now playing at a well-known West End club, and the other from the United States. As one band finishes, the other immediately strikes up, and so avoiding intervals. (24 October 1919)

The opening of the Hammersmith Palais, which could accommodate almost 3000 people, shows the extent of the dance craze in Britain at this time. The band remained resident at the Palais until they left England on 8 July 1920, and it is probably during this period that the ODJB made its most lasting impression. The Palais was revolutionary in that the admission prices were relatively small, and membership did not exist, whereas it was mandatory for the classy dancing establishments of central London, such as Rector's. In addition, instruction was available from '50 ladies and 30 gentlemen ...who will be constantly in attendance to dance with patrons' (*West London Observer*, 24 October 1919). Owing to the size of the Palais and the fact that it was open to anyone who could afford the entrance, the band would have performed to many thousands of more 'ordinary' people, especially when compared to the exclusive dance clubs of central London. The fact that the ODJB played in the newest and largest dance venue from its opening night for six months is significant, as their version of 'jazz' was widely disseminated and firmly established as the new dance music in Britain.

Reception and Musical Style

The fact that none of the reviewers of the ODJB's performances are able to critically evaluate the music itself is surely significant. Not only does this indicate that the attention of audiences was primarily drawn to the visual aspects of the act, but also that there was substantial confusion about the music that they were hearing. A lack of understanding can be seen to permeate the reaction of the British critics towards the ODJB, as there is little overt opposition to the band in reviews, but nor is the group particularly acclaimed. The reviewer in the paper *Town Topics* prevaricated, calling the performance 'a novelty not unartistic' (12 April 1919:2). Critics generally sat on the fence and avoided commenting specifically on the

---

primary source material to confirm it. Brunn credits Lord Donegall with arranging the 'command performance'. However, Donegall does not mention the event in a letter to the Editor of *Jazz Tempo* (1944, No. 17:21) in which he outlines his involvement with the ODJB. He recalled meeting up with LaRocca in New Orleans in 1936, the latter stating that 'he considered the greatest moment of the Band's life was when it played at the Peace Ball at the Savoy Hotel in London ... Earl Haig was one of the guests'. In addition, there are no records of the performance in the Royal Archives at Windsor. It seems likely that the source of this myth was that, as reported by Edwards, 'one time Shields and Spargo tried to crash Buckingham Palace and almost got shot. They just wanted to see the King' (1947:6).

music itself, and, as we have seen, tended to focus on familiar aspects of the performance, such as the singing and dancing.

The confusion demonstrated by critics also permeated audiences of the early variety performances. Lew Davis, who was a member of Lew Stone's band in the 1930s and recalled hearing the ODJB at the Palladium, stated that 'if truth must be told [the band] was a complete flop at the Palladium. Nobody understood it. I didn't either, but I was thoroughly interested' (1934a:8). A critic in *The Star* observed the audience reaction at the same performances:

> It is interesting to watch the faces of the audiences at the Palladium when the Original Dixieland Jazz Band, which is said to be the only one of its kind in the world, is doing its best to murder music. Most are obviously bewildered by the weird discords, but some, to judge by the cynical smiles, evidently think that it is a musical joke that is hardly worth attempting. Perhaps they are right. (19 April 1919:3)

It seems that this audience was not sure whether the band's performance was meant to be comical, or whether the music was meant to sound strange. Above all, it was the timbre and volume of sound produced by the ODJB that struck audiences most forcefully. Lew Davis describes the impact that this sound made upon him:

> They started playing when the curtain was still down, and, from the first note, I felt strangely stirred and exhilarated. To my uneducated ears, the music sounded like nothing on earth, but it certainly was exciting to listen to … . (1934a:8)

The timbre of the ODJB's music led some of the less open-minded critics to dismiss the band, assuming that little conventional musical skill was required to perform jazz:

> I've come to the conclusion that that the best qualification for a Jazzist is to have no knowledge of music and no musical ability beyond that of making some sort of noise on either a piano or trombone, or clarionet, or cornet, or trap drum, which I believe form the proper constituents of a Jazz orchestra. (*The Performer*, 10 April 1919:23)

> … musical studies are of no account … if I can only master a rattle on an old tin can my fortune is made … . (*The Encore*, 17 April 1919:5)

Town Topics conceded that there was 'a certain charm' in the music of the ODJB, but that this was 'dramatically broken by cheery jingles and a miscellany of noises such as one generally hears "off".' This is the only review that recognized the use of 'improvised' solos,[10] which were unprecedented in the experience of British audiences:

> At one moment the whole orchestra would down tools while one member tootled merrily or eerily on his own account, and then the whole would resume again, always ready to give a fair hearing to any player who suddenly developed a "stunt". (12 April 1919:2)

---

[10] The extent to which the ODJB included improvisation in their performances will be considered later.

The presentation of the band in Britain as 'the only one of its kind in the world', and advertising such as a poster outside the Palladium which asserted that the ODJB performed jazz 'quite unlike the various renderings already heard in this country' (Rust, 1972:10) exacerbated the difficulties in understanding and evaluating their performances. Critics writing on the early ODJB performances related them to previous experiences of jazz, and often commented on the common factors that defined the newcomers' performances as jazz for them. This is confirmed by the fact that part of the *Encore*'s opposition to the ODJB was their nationality, because as a variety act the band was not seen to be presenting anything better than or radically different from local acts:

> American jazz may be all right for those who want it, but I know some rattling good English acts walking about that can really entertain the English public as they love to be entertained. (17 April 1919)

The *Encore* continued its attack on the band after they closed at the Palladium, reporting that 'The [house] orchestra opened the matinee [at the Palladium] on Monday to a not over-crowded house with "Jazzmania", by Lawrence Wright, just to let us hear how real jazz music should be played' (1 May 1919). This indicates that this reviewer, at least, did not regard the music that the ODJB were playing as anything better, different, or more authentic than the music performed by British bands. Therefore, consideration of the 'native' presentation of jazz in Britain enables the reactions to the ODJB to be understood in context.

By 1919 jazz had already developed a clear image through sheet music, and the principal features of jazz, namely that it was novel and often comic entertainment, full of eccentricities, with the music consisting mostly of unrefined noise and mainly used as an accompaniment to unusual dancing; had already begun to be established before the arrival of the ODJB. The fact that the ODJB was initially presented in Britain as a variety act meant that these extra-musical, novelty aspects of their performance were emphasized. This provoked critics to make a superficial comparison with earlier 'jazz' bands such as those of Murray Pilcer and John Lester, fitting the ODJB within their existent understanding of jazz rather than providing anything more than a basic recognition of the musical differences involved.

Murray Pilcer was a white American drummer who came to Britain in 1916, performed in many West End venues with his band and remained resident in this country, probably until his death (Hayes, 1989:61-2). Pilcer was clearly an extrovert performer and 'a marvellous showman' (Tipping, June 1930:18). Tipping recalls 'the extraordinary tackle used by Murray Pilcer. He caused a great sensation at the time with the wild performance he put over with this collection of gadgets' (Tipping, June 1930:18). A photograph that accompanies this article shows Pilcer at the drums, in front of which is a frame hung with bells, gongs, and pans, which must have produced a real cacophony. Murray Pilcer made recordings of four numbers early in 1919, the first of a 'jazz' band in Britain. These were advertised with a suitably eccentric and extrovert description of Pilcer's performance in *The Sound Wave and Talking Machine Record*:

Having put his cannonading party in effective positions, he divested himself of all clothing decency would permit, and fitted his feet, legs, arms and head with mediums for extracting sounds from many and various instruments. (March 1919:101)

These performances were clearly seen as representative of true jazz, as a review of the Pilcer records explains:

The constituent elements of a Jazz band, consisting mainly of syren, rattle, buzzer, cymbals and drum, make revel in an orgy of cacophony which will rejoice the hearts of all true Jazzites. (*The Sound Wave and Talking Machine Record*, April 1919:165)

The surviving recordings made by Murray Pilcer, *Wild Wild Women* and *K-K-K-Katy*, indicate the influence of march repertoire and orchestration, but also show the prominence of banjos and novelty effects, such as the aforementioned 'syren' and exaggerated trombone glissandi, typical of British popular music of this period.

John Lester's Frisco Five was also reported to be giving 'auditors the first taste of Jazz' (*The Era*, 12 March 1919) touring the variety halls prior to the arrival of the ODJB. Jazz was clearly classified in *The Era* as a 'novelty', and whilst the 'banjo ensemble' itself was 'greatly liked', 'the applause hit of the show was invariably the Jazz dance by the Lester Boys' which featured 'difficult gyrations' and somersaults (12 March 1919). The Lester Boys were John Lester's sons, Harry and Burton, who had been touring the halls as 'The Jazz Boys' since late 1918 with an act that featured 'ragtime singing and dancing ... and eccentric and Jazz band antics' (*The Encore*, 31 October 1918).

There is evidence that the sound of the ODJB was particularly commented on simply because outrageous, loud instrumental combinations were a feature of the few early manifestations of 'jazz' in Britain. But in addition, the sound of the ODJB was profoundly different to most dance music in London clubs at this time, as Pilcer and Frisco were primarily variety acts. Bernard Tipping commented that he heard the band at the Hammersmith Palais and 'was amazed. I had never previously thought that real dance music could be produced by such a combination' (April 1930:20). Lew Davis explained:

Just to show how far in advance this band [the ODJB] was of the English conception of dance music at that time, I must mention that when the Dixieland Band had a night off, I used to go and dance at the Elysée Ballroom, Bayswater-quite a good class place. Music was supplied by a typically English combination of the day. It consisted of piano, violin, drums and two banjos! (1934a:7)

Josephine Bradley, who heard the ODJB at Rector's, also observed 'The band was of a different type ... . Whereas one might describe the Versatile Four [of the Grafton Galleries] as playing "sweet music", these virtuosi of Jazz "hotted it up" and "went to the town" in a big way' (1947:15). The ODJB's drummer Tony Sbarbaro commented that 'the average band that we had to buck up against [in London] ... was two banjos, piano and a drum' (Sbarbaro and Christian interview, 11 February 1959, HJA transcript p. 47). As the ODJB did not include a banjo, or indeed any string instrument (violins and string bass were often found in contemporary British bands) and featured a front line of cornet, clarinet and trombone, this surely meant that the band would indeed seem louder and brasher than familiar native ensembles. The ODJB reinforced the perception of jazz as 'noisy' music, primarily concerned with instrumental colour that had been established prior to their arrival.

In addition to their new and distinctive sound, the ODJB's rhythmic drive and tempi were different to anything which dancers had experienced before, and this seems to have thrown the conventionalists of the dancing world into panic. LaRocca commented that the band played one-steps, which were particularly appreciated by young people who were bored with the old dances (Rust, 1972:10). Interestingly, LaRocca credits Vernon and Irene Castle with provoking development of the ODJB's style:

> I played ragtime. The rhythm wasn't changed until I hit Chicago ... it was a dance team called ... the Castles. And the Castles was [*sic.*] bringing out a new dance like a straight dance – like a walk. Now ragtime music would fit it, but I noticed the general public, it was hard for them with the methods of music we were playing – that jumping music – so I decided to play in march time, slow down, making a fox trot of it, fast, making a fast march ... . (LaRocca interview, 26 May 1958, HJA; transcript p. 50)

In response to the new music, a new step, known in Britain as the 'jazz-roll', was invented, which Josephine Bradley describes as 'initially a slow, quick, quick' but which turned into a 'long gliding movement' presumably due to the speed of the music, which 'revolutionised dancing' (1947:12). LaRocca stated in the *Palais Dancing News* of April 1920, with customary exaggeration, that 'the jazz step ... typifies "pep", energy, push, advancement, the love of living, and the things that go with an up-to-date and modern world' (from sleeve note to Columbia 1087: *The ODJB in England*). Although articles in the *Dancing Times* suggest that the specific jazz step was fairly swiftly abandoned, the ODJB's fast one-steps were probably responsible for introducing a freer style of dancing in Britain. Although variety theatre at the Palladium and the Hippodrome was undoubtedly a popular form of entertainment, it was not until their appearance as a dance band that the ODJB were established as anything more than another novelty 'turn'. It was at the dance clubs that their actual *musical* performance was widely appreciated, through the response of those dancing, and in this context it is hardly surprising that the music of this band became synonymous with jazz in the minds of many people in Britain from the 1920s and beyond. A programme for the first anniversary concert of the Savoy Orpheans, published in 1924, stated a common perception in Britain that 'The history of jazz is practically the history of the Dixieland Jazz Band'.

Image

The members of the ODJB, and particularly LaRocca, were conscious of the image that they presented not only on stage, but also through what they said in public, and in this way were early examples of popular musicians who exploited media interest for their own publicity. It seems that LaRocca 'understood the golden rule of promotion, advertising and public relations: anything, repeated often and pervasively enough, will be believed, regardless of accuracy' (Sudhalter 1999:14). The band established an image of authenticity by billing themselves as the 'creators of jazz' and stressing that the band was the 'real original'. The consistency between jazz imagery and its manifestation in the form of the ODJB ensured that the band's claims of originality were widely believed by the majority of the British public, for whom the word 'jazz' had yet to develop a clear meaning as a musical style.[11]

The band projected an image that was consistent with their claim to be the originators of jazz. In the *Palais Dancing News*, April 1920 (from sleeve note to Columbia 1087:*The ODJB in England*), LaRocca was at pains to emphasize the originality, creativity and radical nature of their work:

> ... jazz is the assassination, the murdering, the slaying of syncopation. In fact, it is a revolution in this kind of music ... . I even go as far as to confess we are musical anarchists ... our prodigious outbursts are seldom consistent, every number played by us eclipsing in originality and effect our previous performance.

This led the interviewer to conclude: 'That they are musical geniuses is evident, for they are unable to read music; and play from memory, thus concentrating their attention on producing and inventing new, but appropriate and much appreciated, dance accompaniments.'

LaRocca was always at pains to stress the band's musical illiteracy, as if to prove their natural ability and spontaneous approach, a feature normally associated with the oral tradition of black musicians whose role in jazz LaRocca was generally so keen to reject. The omission of the banjo from the group implied a rejection of the black origins of jazz, but this was also stated more blatantly:[12]

---

[11] Nick LaRocca became increasingly passionate in his later years in his assertions that the ODJB invented jazz and was the first jazz band to travel to North America and to Europe. His scrapbooks contain offending articles that suggested otherwise, and he sent numerous vitriolic letters to magazines and individuals, stating his point of view (see 'LaRocca' file in IJS). A photograph in the New Orleans Jazz Exhibit in the Old Mint, New Orleans shows LaRocca and Tom Brown in 1955, moments before they came to blows in a televised debate over whose band was the first to go to Chicago. LaRocca deposited his scrapbooks and papers in the HJA at Tulane University in the belief that his version of events would be recognised as the truth by future historians.

[12] Many years later, in 1936, Nick LaRocca was to unequivocally reject the Negro roots of jazz in an article 'Jazz Stems from Whites Not Blacks' in *Metronome* magazine (October 1936:20) and in numerous letters attacking Marshall Stearns and Hughes Panassie who advocated the importance of black musicians in the development of jazz. Similarly, as Schuller has pointed out (1968:175n), Brunn's book also avoids mentioning the black musicians of New Orleans that must have had an influence on the musicians of the ODJB. LaRocca clearly intended this publication as another way of making his position and views clear, although he later claimed that material on the contribution of black musicians had been omitted for political reasons.

They will not have it that the word is of Red Indian origin, or that "jazz so" is a term of praise in the dialect of the negroes in the Southern States. (*The Daily News*, 4 April 1919)

Jack Weber stated that Eddie Edwards, the trombonist who did not travel to London with the band, was the only reading musician of the ODJB (Shapiro/Hentoff, 1955:60), and apparently 'the fact that Daddy [Eddie] Edwards could read music was a closely guarded secret for many years' as it was not compatible with the image of the band (Brunn, 1963:92).[13] Despite LaRocca trying to find a pianist to replace Robinson who could not read music (Ramsey/Smith 1957:51), Billy Jones, who had been a member of Murray Pilcer's band and could read music, took over and had an important role in the publication of ODJB numbers (Rust, 1972:16). Jones himself describes the group as a 'glorified band of buskers really; none of the boys could read a note of music – I was the only one who could. I'd run through the new numbers on piano once or twice, and then we'd throw the music away' (in 'Jones' file in NJA). LaRocca was proud of the fact that he could not read music, stating in 1936 'None of us can read a note of music and we do not intend to learn' (*Jazz Tempo*, 17, c. 1944:21). He also cited his musical illiteracy when defending claims that he had published New Orleans 'standards' as his own, explaining that since he was a faker rather than a reader, and learnt things by ear, 'bits of tunes came to mind and were incorporated within his compositions' (LaRocca interview, 21 May 1958, HJA; transcript pp. 8-10).

Authenticity

The ODJB's claims of originality have often been treated with scepticism by modern authors, fuelled by the open rejection of the black origins of jazz by their vociferous leader. Critics of the band include Christopher Small, who states that the ODJB 'simplified the idiom of the black musicians, substituting crude melodic formulas for their often subtle and flexible improvised melodic lines, and mechanical patterns for their vigorous rhythms' (1987:328) and Gunther Schuller: '[the ODJB] took a new idea, an innovation, and reduced it to the kind of compressed, rigid format that could appeal to a mass audience' (1968:180). However, what is most significant when evaluating the role of the ODJB in the evolution of jazz in Britain is that the musicians themselves (with the exception of Billy Jones, an Englishman) and the music that the band performed in London were clearly rooted in and representative of the New Orleans musical tradition. In that city, musicians were influenced as much by white march music as black blues, and jazz can be seen as a product of the tension 'between European, Euro-American, and Afro-American values' (Small, 1987:312). Bruce Boyd Raeburn has explained that in the city the 'demographic patterns which created a "crazy quilt" of mixed neighbourhoods also yielded an extremely eclectic musical amalgam' (1991:3). Jazz musicians, whether white or black, tended to all come

---

[13] J. Russell Robinson could also read music and published his own compositions, (see 'Robinson' file in IJS) but seems to have escaped consideration by both Weber and Brunn.

from certain areas of the city; for example, the white ODJB clarinettist Larry Shields was a neighbour of the legendary black trumpeter Buddy Bolden. Trumpeter and singer Wingy Manone recalled the racial integration of musicians in New Orleans:

> It was all mixed up there. Buddy Petit, Sidney Bechet, Freddie Keppard, Bunk Johnson, Nick LaRocca, the Bigards ... we were all in one area. The musicians listened to each other, and sometimes played together in parades ... . The young jazz musicians listened to everyone who came up who could play, white or coloured ... when the Dixielanders played, the coloured guys would go and hear them. There wasn't any prejudice if you could play. (Jones, 1987:149)

The ODJB itself included men of Italian, Irish and English origins, reflecting the wide racial mix of the city. LaRocca remembered hearing accordion-based bands on the riverboats and German brass bands on Sundays (LaRocca interview, 21 May 1958, HJA; transcript p. 2) and also experienced the strong operatic tradition of the city through his work as a lighting attendant at an opera house (LaRocca interview, 21 May 1958, HJA; transcript p. 12).

As well as the direct influence of the range of native music that could be heard in the city, the various ethnic groups had their own benevolent societies into which people paid money as 'insurance' against medical bills, and funeral and burial costs (which were significant, as in New Orleans bodies were buried above the ground on account of the high water table) and provided support for widows and orphans. These societies required bands for funerals, functions, and especially parades, which acted as advertisements, and hence provided opportunities for musicians to perform and be heard. Several of the members of the ODJB began their careers in Papa Jack Laine's various parade bands. Laine himself recalled 'I picked [LaRocca] up and brought him in the band, made a good cornet player out of him ... .' (Laine interview, 26 March 1957, HJA; transcript p. 16). There is evidence that the repertoire and style of the ODJB had been influenced by march music, particularly in the structure of numbers and in the decorative clarinet obbligato parts. Larry Shields was clearly a gifted and innovative player, as can be heard on his rapid descant on the band's recording of 'Lasses Candy. Papa Jack Laine also claimed that the origin of many ODJB numbers was in the repertoire of his Reliance Band, indicating that these pieces must have been well-known standards in New Orleans (Laine interview, 26 March 1957, HJA; transcript pp. 18-19). He resented LaRocca, claiming that he had learnt the numbers whilst playing with the marching bands, and then copyrighted and published them as his own compositions (Laine interview, 23 May 1960, HJA transcript p. 10).[14] Indeed,

---

[14] Laine claimed that LaRocca had 'double-crossed' him in monopolising on an opportunity to go to the North: 'Some fella from north came down here and wanted to speak to the leader, and get the band to go north. [LaRocca] jumps in and takes my place, see.' (Laine interview, 26 March 1957, HJA transcript p. 16). Laine also stated that initially LaRocca was allowed only to march and not play in the parades, that he never played at a funeral or Mardi Gras parade and that he was never considered to be one of the best cornet players (Laine interview, 23 May 1960, HJA transcript pp. 3, 19).

one of the most significant criticisms levelled against the ODJB was (and continues to be) that they claimed to have written tunes themselves that were in fact part of the standard New Orleans repertory. This led to some resentment of the success of the ODJB from black musicians such as Sidney Bechet:

> Some of the white musicianers had taken our style as best they could. They played things that were really our numbers ... it's awful hard for a man who isn't black to play a melody that's come deep out of black people. It's a question of feeling. (Bechet, 1960:114)

Further to this, Jack Weber recalled that in New Orleans 'Different bands had different names for the same tune, but they used variations and played the tunes in different keys' (Shapiro/Hentoff, 1955:60). According to Weber 'Tiger Rag was known as No. 2, [and] Sensation as Meatballs'. Jack Laine stated that *Tiger Rag* was known variously as Praline, Meatballs and Keep a Shufflin' (Laine interview, 23 May 1960, HJA transcript p. 4). Bunk Johnson suggested that *Tiger Rag* was based upon the 8 bar introduction that he played with Buddy Bolden's band before a quadrille (Shapiro/Hentoff, 1955:36). Band members Sbarbaro and Christian acknowledged that '"Tiger Rag" was always a New Orleans number in the first place' (Sbarbaro and Christian interview, 11 February 1959, HJA transcript p. 44).

A judge ruled in 1917 that the copyright of *Livery Stable Blues* could not be claimed by anyone, as the melody was not original but derived from 'More Power Blues' (Brunn, 1963:85). Preston Jackson, a trombonist, remembered Joe Oliver playing 'Eccentric', a number that appears to be very similar to the ODJB's *Livery Stable Blues*:

> He took all the breaks, imitating a rooster and a baby ... . The LaRocca boys of the Dixieland Jazz Band used to hang around and got a lot of ideas from his gang. (Shapiro/Hentoff, 1955:42)

Laine recollected that Yellow Nunez and Achille Baquet had composed *Livery Stable Blues* (Laine interview, 23 May 1960, HJA transcript p. 4). Furthermore, Schuller states that 'farmyard imitations were not new, having been "popular" musical fare for many years' (1968:179n).

Criticisms of the band in modern literature are based mainly on retrospective analysis that can place the claims of originality and authenticity into perspective within the context of a wider knowledge of the development of jazz, which was impossible for Londoners at the time. The reality, as we have seen, that the ODJB presented a version of jazz that was indebted to the music of New Orleans, lies somewhere between the understandable naivety of these early audiences, who accepted everything that they saw as intrinsically representative of the new music called jazz, and present day critics that feel able to disregard the band in retrospect. Fundamentally, however, British audiences were experiencing in the performances of the ODJB music that was not only new to them and perceived to be 'the real thing' but was also, basically, *actually* authentic.

Recordings

In addition to their much-publicized image, the fact that the ODJB were the first jazz band to record, and that so many of their recordings were made in London, certainly assisted in establishing the band as representative of jazz in Britain, and indeed world wide, as their records sold many thousands of copies. The ODJB were an ideal band for making recordings using the relatively primitive technology available at that time, as the group did not use instruments such as the double bass, the low frequencies of which were difficult to record and reproduce. Nick LaRocca described the band's early recording sessions:

> The cornet stood about twenty to twenty-five feet from the horn, the trombone was fifteen feet, the clarinet had a separate little horn ... . And he stood right near the piano. The piano faced me – right under the horn. The drums stood alongside me. (LaRocca interview, 21 May 1958, HJA; transcript p. 30)

The band initially recorded for Columbia, but the results were unsatisfactory. According to Eddie Edwards, this was due to disruptions caused by people putting up shelves in the studio whilst the band was playing (Edwards, 1947:6). A recording of *Livery Stable Blues* on Victor had been due to be released in England in November 1917, but the records did not in fact appear until June 1919 (Rust, 1967:24), after the band's arrival in Britain. The band cut their first sides for English Columbia, *At the Jazz Band Ball* and *Barnyard Blues* on 16 April 1919, and returned to the studio throughout the duration of their time in London, recording a total of seventeen numbers between May 1919 and May 1920.

Although it was with the up-tempo, brash and to an extent formulaic performances on numbers such as *Tiger Rag* and *Sensation Rag* that the band was and continues to be mainly associated,[15] careful analysis of the whole group of recordings shows that the ODJB was capable of greater variety within their repertoire and performance style than many modern writers are prepared to acknowledge. The ODJB recorded a mixture of popular and traditional New Orleans music, which was probably a representative sample of the repertoire that they performed 'live'. The recordings of popular numbers were mostly made in January 1920 when the ODJB was well established at the Palais, and were often drawn from American shows, but would have been known to some extent in Britain as they were all published as sheet music in 1919. There is generally less variety and musical interest in these recordings, which possibly reflects the fact that these would have been played for dancing and detail and variety within numbers was therefore less important. However, the two waltzes, *Alice Blue Gown*

---

[15] See, for example, Lyttelton in *The Best of Jazz: Basin Street to Harlem* (1980:15-25), who bases his evaluation of the ODJB solely on an analysis of *Tiger Rag*. It is interesting that these two numbers, which are most often cited as examples of the ODJB's formulaic approach, were the two numbers that were taken straight from the repertoire of New Orleans marching bands. Hence the ODJB probably simply used the original march form, with which they were mostly all familiar already, as an easy way of structuring the number, and saw no reason to alter this over the years.

and *I'm Forever Blowing Bubbles*, show that the band could perform with delicacy and respond to the demands of the British dancing public, who still expected waltzes. *Sphinx* uses typical Tin Pan Alley formulae to suggest the exotic, such as chromaticism, diminished chords and a drone bass, which shows that the band were aware of the techniques used by the popular song writers of the day. The syncopation of the upper lines against the driving rhythm of the piano and drums, for example in *Ostrich Walk,* is reminiscent of piano ragtime. The influence of the blues can be detected in *I Lost My Heart in Dixieland*, which features a trumpet lead over chalumeau register clarinet and trombone bass line. LaRocca uses vibrato and bends the notes, creating an improvisatory feel to his rendering of the melody. Numbers such as this show that the band did not produce a noisy cacophony all of the time, although it was this feature of their playing that naturally attracted public attention and, as we have seen, provoked some extreme reactions.

As well as performing a stylistically diverse repertoire, the band could also exploit their instrumental resources to create variety within individual pieces. As well as the classic rise in dynamic on the last choruses, some numbers make effective use of dynamic contrast, for example in *Satanic Blues,* which features a middle section in which the texture is lightened and the dynamic much softer. Several of the numbers feature breaks, most frequently for the clarinet, which provides a contrast with the prevailing polyphony. The full range of the clarinet is exploited, resulting in variation in the three-part front line polyphony of clarinet – trumpet – trombone in descending order of pitch, most often to trumpet – clarinet – trombone. The piano and trombone are also occasionally given the melodic lead, and there is use of dialogue between instruments. These ideas are most clearly shown in *Sphinx* and *Soudan*, the last pieces that were recorded by the band in Britain. In many ways, these pieces are the most musically developed of the set and reflect the prevailing vogue for the oriental and exotic. Woodblocks are used to particularly good effect on the former, and there is tonal variety with a major key section contrasting with the main minor tonality, whilst the latter uses a quotation from Grieg's *Hall of the Mountain King* as well as an unusual 'fade out' ending.

Although many of the recorded numbers sound loud and brash, this was probably the result of the primitive recording technology rather than carelessness. There is compelling evidence that the members of the ODJB were aware of appropriate dynamic levels for different numbers and venues, as Eddie Edwards stated that 'The Original Dixieland Jazz Band frequently played soft and ratty ... so that the shuffle of [the] dancers' feet could be heard (Edwards interview, 1 July 1959, HJA transcript p. 2). LaRocca mentioned that as the Hammersmith Palais was such a huge hall, the band had to play loudly (LaRocca interview, 26 May 1958, HJA transcript p. 84).

The use of the ODJB's recordings as evidence has led to generalizations as to the nature of their performances and their role in the evolution of jazz. According to John Chilton, the fact that the band recorded at all ensured that the musicians achieved 'a degree of eminence that was out of proportion to their musical skills' (Kernfeld, 1994:274) and Gunther Schuller has stated:

It is typical of the kind of nonsense perpetrated in the name of jazz in those early days that La Rocca and the other members of the ODJB could claim that they could not read music and that therefore their playing was *ipso facto* improvised and inspired during each performance, when in truth their recordings show without exception exact repetitions of choruses and a great deal of memorization ... . Contrary to being improvised, their choruses were set and rehearsed, and they were unchanged for years ... . The ODJB thus did not actually improvise. (Schuller, 1968:180)

Contextual analysis of the band's background, activities and recordings establishes these ideas as overly simplistic, and it is clear that the band, and particularly their use of improvisation, cannot be judged solely from listening to recordings. Most of the musicians in the ODJB were untutored in a formal sense, and would have learnt their instruments and the music upon which their repertoire was based through the musical and cultural mixing-pot that was New Orleans in the early years of the twentieth century. As they could not read music, they would have had to formulate an arrangement of a particular number through improvisational processes. Brunn suggests that improvisation was a significant part of the rehearsal process of the band, where arrangements and 'contrapuntal interest' developed as a number was played more often (1963:31). This is confirmed by Tony Sbarbaro and Emile Christian who stated that the 'tunes were written as a group while you were playing together' (Sbarbaro and Christian interview, 11 February 1959, HJA transcript p. 45). LaRocca was apparently the driving force behind the arrangements according to Brunn, (1963:90), as improvisation was 'in his blood' and compositions would evolve out of music that he heard in New Orleans. Shields's influence was also important for the effective clarinet breaks and obbligato lines that can be heard on recordings.

A 'set and rehearsed' approach would have been necessary when the band were part of variety shows or making recordings. In variety, the band was merely one act on a bill and presumably was given a set length of time in which to perform. As their act often, apparently, involved dance routines that may have been choreographed, these would have also required a precise musical structure and length. Similarly, when the band came to the recording studio, they would have had to work out a rigid structure for each number, firstly, and most basically, in order to ensure that the music would fit onto the limited time span permitted on the disc. Sudhalter suggests that this limitation also influenced the manic speed of the band's recordings (1999:17) and Squibb, in a 1963 review of the re-released recordings, points out that these ODJB records become 'more listenable' when the turntable speed is reduced, and that this slower speed may be a more accurate reflection of the band's live performances (1963:16-17). It would also be necessary to encompass in each number a sufficient variety of features such as solos and ensemble choruses to make the piece interesting. A pre-arranged structure was also important bearing in mind that unlike in the modern recording process, there were no editing facilities and there were presumably limited numbers of 'takes'. LaRocca commented on the pressure and restrictions on improvisation when recording as 'there was no way of me throwing in an extra lick here or there, because if I did and I missed out, that matrix was ruined and the whole thing was ruined' (LaRocca interview, 26 May 1958, HJA; transcript p. 64). Sudhalter also comments on the early studio conditions where 'a combination of factors – mechanical, temporal, atmospheric, acoustic and especially supervisory – could make the environment downright inhospitable for the kind of spontaneous interaction which lies at the heart of all good jazz' (1999:x).

Fundamentally, it is important to realize that many more people in Britain in 1919-1920 would have heard the ODJB's live performances than their recordings Conversely to the pre-arranged approach necessary for recording, it is likely that on their many nights as a dance band, the musicians would have extended the numbers which they performed, and may well have improvised extra choruses to keep themselves interested and to fill up time. The fact that the band did not perform from music certainly indicates that such flexibility was possible, and that the recorded performances that can be heard today were probably distilled versions of the numerous choruses that had been initially improvised, and then gradually refined during these rehearsals and dance engagements. The recorded numbers also represent only a sample of the band's repertoire, as it would have taken more music to fill their sets at dance clubs. In particular, in order to ensure successful sales of their recordings and to compete with British bands for popularity with dancers and audiences, the group clearly considered which numbers were popular, and themselves now distant from America, they would have been reliant upon British public opinion in formulating their choices of recording material. There is evidence of this from a report in the *Knights of Columbus News Bulletin* (contained in the LaRocca scrapbooks, HJA) on the Victory Ball of June 1919, where the band performed several popular numbers that they never recorded (including *Goodbye Khaki*, *Everything is Peaches Down in Georgia*, *If You Could Care*, and *That Rag*). LaRocca recalled that the ODJB learnt some numbers that were popular in Britain when the band was performing to the masses at the Hammersmith Palais, and that 'every now and then I'd slap 'em one of these snotballs that I had' (LaRocca interview, 26 May 1958, HJA; transcript p. 85). Once again, this demonstrates the band's flexibility to adapt successfully to different venues and performing situations, and this is also reflected in the fact that the band recorded more popular numbers and waltzes in their 1920 sessions. The extent of the influence of British preferences is shown in that when the band returned to America:

> ... their limited repertoire was not conducive to long-standing popularity, and the demand was for fresh novelties. While the long sojourn abroad had wrought few advances in their own style, the US had become more exacting and demanded something beyond the mere exhilaration of five musically illiterate youngsters. (Tonks, 1944:23).

Tony Sbarbaro recalled that 'after we returned to America, our old place at Reisenweber's was not the same. The rigor mortis of prohibition had set in and changed things up a great deal.' (*Second Line*, September–October 1955:5), and Billy Jones described how 'Show bands were all the rage in New York, and the Dixielanders couldn't compete' (in 'Jones' file in NJA). Subsequently, LaRocca even wrote to Mitchell and Booker, the owners of Rector's and the Hammersmith

Palais, seeking return engagements, but in a reply dated 6 June 1922, the owners stated that the fee that he had nominated was too high (LaRocca scrapbooks, HJA).

The Southern Syncopated Orchestra in London, 1919-1922

There are several reasons why the role of the Southern Syncopated Orchestra in the evolution of jazz in Britain has not often been considered in depth in modern literature. Firstly, the group was not initially very popular with Londoners (especially when compared with the ODJB); Lew Davis describes that the Southern Syncopated Orchestra 'played to crowds of twenty people and less' (1934b:6). This apparent lack of popularity appears to render the activities of the group irrelevant in an examination of jazz as a 'popular' music, although the performances were well received by the sparse audiences that they did manage to attract. *The People*, who had announced the forthcoming performances of the group in its 'Concert Notes' column, reported that 'The SSO has caught on well at the Philharmonic Hall. The entertainment is as delightful as it is original ... most of the vocal and instrumental numbers are vociferously encored at each performance' (27 July 1919:4).

Secondly, the group did not perform exclusively jazz, indeed, very few numbers performed by the whole SSO were actually specifically designated as such. However, it is the wide variety of musical styles in the repertoire of the SSO that makes the group extremely significant when considering the evolving presence of jazz in Britain. The performances of the SSO encompassed various African-American genres including 'spirituals, ragtime, plantation and coon songs, and formal compositions such as those of Samuel Coleridge Taylor' (Rye, 1990a:48). An early programme for the Philharmonic Hall concerts (included in Averty, 1969:22) includes several numbers by Cook, such as *Swing Along*, which had been made popular in Britain through the performances of *In Dahomey*. In addition, classical pieces such as *Hungarian Dance No. 5* by Brahms and Dvorak's *Humoresque* were on the programme. Bertin Depestre Salnave, a flautist recruited by Cook in Britain, recalled 'the orchestra had customarily borrowed several of the items in its repertoire from the classical domain. Thus we performed Grieg's Peer Gynt in a syncopated version, in other words, transformed into jazz.' (Rye, 1978:211). The conductor Ernest Ansermet who, according to Sidney Bechet, came to all the Philharmonic Hall performances (1960:127), described performances of ragtime based on 'the *Wedding March from Midsummer Night's Dream* ... [and] Rachmaninoff's celebrated *Prelude*' (1959:4), the latter being *Russian Rag*. The programme also included solos by drummer Buddie Gilmore[16] and Sidney Bechet. The juxtaposition of plantation songs and spirituals with instrumental ragtime and improvised blues thus provided in effect an illustrated lineage of the evolution of African-American music. Thus, the SSO linked the new

---

[16] There are several variations in the spelling of this drummer's name, Buddie/Buddy and Gilmore/Gilmour appear in primary sources in various combinations and are reproduced here as found.

styles of syncopated music with musical forms with which the British public would already be familiar.

The Southern Syncopated Orchestra was formed by Will Marion Cook towards the end of 1918, and was known before the European tour as the New York Syncopated Orchestra and then the American Syncopated Orchestra. Cook had the specific aim for his new group, just as with his previous British success *In Dahomey*, to elevate the status of black music as an art form. He remained dedicated to this task throughout his life, writing before his death:

> Let the Negro alone. Stop telling us how to be ourselves. Let us alone, and maybe the next generation will give us a healthy, honest, robust (not decadent) drama, beautiful, realistic, soul-stirring songs of the Southland, treated with the simplicity, the fervour, the grandeur of the Master – Beethoven, a Beethoven burnt to the bone by the African sun! (quoted in Cook, Mercer; symposium paper contained in IJS 'Cook' file, p. 20)

Europe's Clef Club Orchestra[17] was an obvious precedent for Cook's new group as, like the SSO, it included instruments such mandolins, banjos, bandolas, and guitars and consisted entirely of black musicians. Europe's Orchestra had performed a concert in Carnegie Hall on 27 May 1912, which as Badger points out, was an event of great significance, occurring 'twelve years before the Paul Whiteman – George Gershwin concert at the Aeolian Hall and twenty-six years before the Benny Goodman concert of 1938' (1989:50). This concert included similar repertoire to the SSO and demonstrated a significant commitment to black composers, including songs by Cook himself (Badger, 1989:50), who was involved in training the choir for the performance (from *New York Age*, 25 April 1912 quoted in Southern, 1978:73). Cook was critical of the later directions taken by the Clef Club and Europe in particular, with regard to his work with the Castles and his wartime 'Hellfighters' band, which he classified as belonging to a 'brand of brassy jazz and novelty bands on Broadway, which claimed to represent the Negro's music from New Orleans, as unworthy reflections upon the dignity of Negro music' (Schuller, 1968:251). Cook clearly considered Europe's work overly commercial and doing little to further the cause of black music as a serious art form, which may well have prompted the formation of his own 'syncopated orchestra'.

In March 1919, the British promoter André Charlot negotiated a contract for the Southern Syncopated Orchestra to come to London (Rye, 1990b:139), and approximately 24 instrumentalists 'who played violins, mandolins, banjos, guitars, saxophones, trumpets, trombones, bass horn, timpani, pianos and drums' (Rye, 1990a:48) and 12 singers arrived in three groups in June 1919 (Rye, 1990b:142). According to clarinettist Sidney Bechet, who was a recent addition to the group, the musicians travelled in a cattle boat, 'the trip took fifteen days and we were all as sick as dogs' (1960:125). The group was engaged to perform two two-hour

---

[17] Europe's 1912 Clef Club Orchestra should not be confused with Dan Kildare's Clef Club Orchestra that visited Britain, which, although an offshoot of the Clef Club, was primarily a dance band.

shows each day at the Philharmonic Hall, Great Portland Street, London from 4 July until 6 December 1919 (Chilton, 1987:36).

Figure 6.3   **The Southern Syncopated Orchestra (*Sound Wave and Talking Machine Record*, October 1920:698, by permission of the British Library)**

Reception

Reviewers at the time of the first performances by the Southern Syncopated Orchestra were wrestling with similar problems, posed by the orchestra's stylistic plurality, as modern writers, in that the entertainment could not be easily classified within existing musical categories. This, together with the general lack of popularity, meant that the group initially received few reviews compared, for example, the column inches given over to *In Dahomey*. British reviewers variously attempted to define and assess the performances as 'minstrelsy' 'negro folk music', 'religious music', 'art music', or 'ragtime', genres with which they considered themselves more or less familiar at this time. Many reviews clearly assessed performances of the SSO within the context of earlier styles of black music in Britain. For example, a review in the *South London Press* headed 'Minstrelsy at Kennington' (2 April 1920:11), reported that 'the entertainment is much in advance of any previous native coloured performance seen in this country'. Several reviews praised the Negro songs contained in the performance, indicating that spirituals could still fascinate and captivate British audiences, just as in the performances of the Fisk Jubilee Singers over forty years earlier. It seemed that these songs in particular had the power to evoke memories of these early British experiences of black music:

> The musical value of this body lies in its singers and their rendering of genuine coloured music, particularly of old negro plantation ditties ... . These quaint and semi-religious songs took one back to the atmosphere of "Uncle Tom's Cabin". (*The Referee*, 6 July 1919:4)

> ... some of the singing brings back the palmiest days of Mohawk and Moore and Burgess ... .[18] (*The Times*, 9 December 1919:12)

> Memories of the 'Jubilee Singers' and 'Haverley's Minstrels' were awakened by the performances of the American Southern Syncopated Orchestra ... . (*The Scotsman*, 21 January 1920:8)[19]

Although the performances were assessed as 'black' entertainment, the reviews themselves are in the main complementary and largely free from overt racism or racial stereotyping, and instead seem to indicate that there was a genuine interest in the music and its performers. In addition, reviews indicate awareness that what was being heard was in some way a genuine cultural experience as opposed to the mere 'imitations' that had been presented previously. The review in *The Referee*, although describing the band as 'more noisy than musical', concluded: 'We have had so much imitation coloured music that it is refreshing to hear the real thing rendered in the true manner, and the opportunity of doing so should not be missed' (6 July 1919:4). The reviewer in the *Musical Standard* recognized the importance of the racial and spiritual roots of the music, stating that 'This Negro Folk-music is quite an art-music of its own and is of course best when interpreted by those who truly love and understand the spirit of it as those 36 players do.' (2 August 1919, quoted in Rye, 1990a:49). *The Daily Herald*, in a review of the free concert which the orchestra gave at the People's Palace in the East End of London, took a more romantic view: 'At last we had the real thing. They had come straight from the cotton-fields of Georgia'. The reviewer also noted that the members of the audience were encouraged to become 'real internationalists':

> We were now being given an opportunity to study and enjoy the ideas and culture of another people. Some day, perhaps, we would be able to take to America something worth showing. One day there would be an end of hatred, and barriers of race and creed would be broken down, for at the bottom we were all merely men and women ... . (*Daily Herald*, 4 August 1919:3)

This idealism is given particular resonance considering that 1919 was the year in which the racial tension erupted into race riots between black and white people in many of the major cities in Britain, particularly at ports but also in the East End (see Chapter 7 and Jenkinson, 1986).

---

[18] These were British blackface minstrel companies that amalgamated around the turn of the century.

[19] Four of the vocalists associated with the Southern Syncopated Orchestra performed as the 'Exposition Jubilee Quartet' (Rye, 1990b:143), thus clearly continuing the tradition begun by the Fisk group and recalling the practice of inclusion of 'Jubilee' groups as acts in minstrel shows dating from the mid-1870s (Toll, 1974:238).

The performances of the SSO seem to have provoked an increased appreciation of the evolution and developments that had taken place in African-American music since the minstrel shows and performances of spirituals in the nineteenth century. There was some realization that performances of syncopated music by whites were somehow inauthentic and that audiences were now experiencing 'Real ragtimes by real darkies' (*Daily Herald*, 4 August 1919:3). Earlier black music genres were now beginning to be recognized as the fundamental roots of contemporary ragtime and jazz, and were perceived as more significant and permanent than the present day syncopated styles that they had spawned:

> [The performances of the SSO] can bring us back to the darkie folk-songs and melodies that will live long after jazz and rag-time have enjoyed their spell of popularity. (*The Times*, 9 December 1919:12)

> [The music of the SSO] serves to demonstrate how very far from its original sources nine-tenths of the ragtime we get howled at us has strayed. (*Musical Standard*, 2 August 1919, quoted in Rye, 1990a:49)

Felix Barker, in his history of the Coliseum (a venue in which the SSO performed later in 1919), put these various reactions into context:

> Never before had audiences in this country seen the spectacle of a large negro band on the stage. Never before had they had a chance to hear ragtime played by members of the coloured race responsible for its creation. (1957:191)

Even if this is not strictly accurate, this was certainly the first time that a large group of coloured performers had presented entertainment in a British theatre, which, unlike minstrelsy, was purely musical and had little or no dramatic content. The immediate precedents for the black musicians in Britain fall into two main categories; the ragtime bands such as Dan Kildare's Orchestra that performed in London clubs as an accompaniment to dancing, and African-American musicians, such as solo banjoists and drummer Louis Mitchell, who performed on the West End stage as acts on variety bills. In both cases, the musical value of the entertainment was secondary to the novelty visual aspect, whereas the SSO, initially at least, presented the music in the format of a traditional concert.

Despite good reviews, *The Times* noted that even after five months of performances by the SSO 'there must be thousands of people in London who have never heard of its existence' (9 December 1919:12), which meant that the recognition and appreciation of the importance of black music as described above was probably fairly limited. In addition, Will Marion Cook's aims for the orchestra were compromised due to the significant changes in the way that the SSO was presented and marketed to the public during its time in Britain.

Image and Marketing

Cook had returned to America in October 1919 and was replaced for a time as director by Egbert E. Thompson (Rye, 1990b:144). More significantly, the manager George W. Lattimore, a New York lawyer (The National Archives (TNA): Public Record Office (PRO) J4/9220 L. 175 Affidavit.100) appointed to look after the financial side of the orchestra as Cook 'was not a business man, but an Artiste' (TNA: PRO J4/9221 L. 542 A. 297), gained increasingly greater control of the group in Cook's absence. This was to result in lawsuits between the two men.

In marketing the group, Lattimore exploited the connection that critics and the public had already made between the SSO and minstrelsy, which was enhanced by considerable changes to the nature of the performances. In a full-page advertisement for a long-term engagement at the Kingsway Hall in 1920 in the *London Amusement Guide*, which includes his photograph, Lattimore asserted his position as the founder of the SSO:

> Mr George W. Lattimore presents the World-Famous American Southern Syncopated Orchestra of 50 Players and Singers ... .

> The American Southern Syncopated Orchestra was organized by Mr. G.W. Lattimore in 1918 under the name of the New York Syncopated Orchestra with a view of emphasising the wealth of art, distinctive and characteristic, to be found in the song and music of the American negro. (August 1920:63)

The accompanying illustration shows white faces with exaggerated features against a black background, caricatures that are strongly reminiscent of the blackface minstrel. The text of the advertisement emphasized stereotypical characteristics of black performers, promising 'Life, pulse, rhythm, tears and laughter' and 'Southern negro music ... [with] an honest native sense of rhythm and a spontaneous blending of the humour and pathos in music'. The light-hearted, novelty nature of the performance is stressed; the advert mentions visual delights such as the return of 'Buddie' 'repeatedly mopping his dark head' and an exaggerated description of 'the gymnastics of the tympanist ... [which] are quite an entertainment in themselves'. The Kingsway Hall programme included 'glees, darkie folk-songs, "spirituals", and various popular melodies', which tended to emphasize the Southern and exotic roots of the performers (for example, 'Wyoming' valse and 'Sand Dunes' African dances), but did also included a 'Suite de Concert by the distinguished negro composer, Coleridge-Taylor' (*The Stage*, 8 July 1920:8).

In October 1920, when the group was again performing at the Philharmonic Hall, they were advertised as:

> The American Southern Syncopated Orchestra and Singers In an Entirely New Musical Entertainment Depicting Scenes of Southern, Colonial and Plantation Life. (*London Amusement Guide*, October 1920:64)

A review of these performances mentioned 'A Plantation lullaby and an American-Indian love lament being very enjoyable' (*The Stage*, 4 November 1920:11). The entertainment was enhanced by new coloured lighting effects, which seem to have emphasized the exotic aspects of the show: 'The auditorium being darkened, a shaded green light was thrown on a white background, and in front of this were grouped some half a dozen singers in Beduin-like garments' (*The Referee*, 7 November 1920:3). It is clear that by this time the music performed was no longer the principal focus of the show, and that the visual and dramatic content was becoming more significant. A description of the company's performance at the Palladium in December 1920 clearly recalls the minstrel shows that depicted plantation life:

> This company of coloured performers open in a picturesquely arranged sit-round ... . The entire act ... gives a delightful impression of the everlasting youthfulness of the Southern coloured folk, and it is hugely enjoyed. (*The Stage*, 16 December 1920:12)

By the time the group was engaged to perform during August 1921 at The Dome in Brighton, 'humour' had become 'the predominating feature of the entertainment'. There is evidence that a stereotypical portrayal of black music-making was offered, as 'native music' was performed 'with inimitable fidelity to its ecstatic warmth of emotion, and those elements of grotesqueness and humour that are so different from anything to be found in the productions of the white races' (*Evening Argus*, 2 August 1921:4).

Later Engagements

Even before the introduction of this ruthless and ultimately degrading marketing of the SSO, by the end of the initial run at the Philharmonic Hall the orchestra had already 'achieved considerable popularity with a certain section of the public' (*The Referee*, 14 December 1919:7). The success of the group, particularly with upper class philanthropists, was such that the musicians had already been invited to perform at prestigious events, such as a garden party given by the King for his servants at Buckingham Palace on 10 August 1919. Sidney Bechet recalled that for this event Cook was 'going to take a quarter of the band and feature a quartet around me' (1960:128). This is confirmed by the report in *The Times* which refers to performances by 'the Southern Syncopated Orchestra from the Philharmonic Hall, and by a nigger "Jazz" band' (11 August 1919:13), the writer clearly assuming that these two groups were unrelated.

In November 1919 the band played at the Victory Ball held at the Albert Hall to celebrate the anniversary of the Armistice, one of the few occasions on which the whole group played for dancing. The organizers dispensed with an Empire procession 'which would cause too long a break in the dancing' and employed two bands at this event to provide continuous dancing which reportedly began at 10pm and continued until 5am (*The Times*, 1 November 1919:9). These ideas were no doubt popular with the dance-crazed London society. However, the *Dancing Times* criticized both the positioning of the bandstand in the centre of the Hall as 'there was a very unpleasant echo' and also the SSO whose 'dances were all tantalisingly short' (Christmas 1919:213). Nevertheless, the entertainment was undoubtedly enjoyed by all present. Soloman Plaatje, a South African Nationalist who was at the ball, reported that 'Vociferous applause from the spectators and revellers greeted the end of [the SSO's] pieces. They would repeat a piece two or three times, then strike up a better one while the throng still clamored for more of it' (quoted in Chilton, 1987:40).

In December, the orchestra moved from the serious surroundings of the Philharmonic Hall[20] to the more light-hearted atmosphere of the Coliseum. There is no doubt that the Coliseum, a variety hall, was a less suitable venue for the SSO, although it probably meant that their performances were heard by more people than if they had remained at the rather austere Philharmonic Hall. The two main problems identified by reviewers were the difficulty in condensing the SSO's two-hour show into a much shorter variety slot, and that the entertainment was simply not suitable for a variety bill:

> ... as a Coliseum turn their efforts were not particularly successful. The turn was far too long for variety purposes, and the plaintiveness of the majority of the songs and part-songs presented hardly in keeping with the general character of the Coliseum entertainment. (*The Referee*, 14 December 1919:7)

The *Times* also commented 'in three-quarters of an hour [a long time for a variety act] it is difficult to appreciate every point' and that the orchestra's contribution came as a strange contrast to the 'eccentricities' and 'frivolities' of the other acts (9 December 1919:12). Although the orchestra was still well received, this lack of compatibility with the variety format must have made it difficult for them to find employment. There is evidence of possible further artistic compromising, maybe in an effort to better integrate their performances and to conform to the expectations of the audience:

> One has grown to associate syncopation with musical fireworks and jazz drummers who hurl themselves at a dozen instruments in their efforts to extract noise from anything and everything. The Southern Orchestra can provide this kind of entertainment when required ... . (*The Times*, 9 December 1919:12)

These later activities of the SSO, together with the marketing style and changes to the nature of the entertainment do not seem particularly in keeping with the Cook's aim to promote respect for black music as a serious art form. Although many of these changes took place as a result of Lattimore's influence, later Cook himself was forced by financial circumstances to find work for the orchestra as a dance band and in variety.

The Disintegration of the SSO

After an important contract for the group to perform in Paris at the start of 1920 was broken, the gradual demise of the orchestra was almost inevitable. Lattimore occupied himself in a successful court case to obtain damages of £1733 from the Parisian theatre, but managed to find alternative work for the orchestra touring to

---

[20] The Philharmonic Hall appears to have been mainly used as a venue for films and presentations about explorers, for example Captain Scott and Ernest Shackleton (*London Amusement Guide*, May 1919 and March 1920).

Glasgow, Edinburgh and Liverpool (Rye, 1990b:165). Will Marion Cook had returned to Britain in January 1920, but he stated that Lattimore refused to allow him to return to the orchestra as conductor (TNA: PRO J4/9221 L.647 A.310), and this was corroborated by Fred Coxcito, a member of the SSO, who testified that Lattimore had said that 'he now had another Conductor and the Boys did not like [Cook] and would not work under him as Conductor' (TNA: PRO J4/9221 L.647 A.327). This, together with the fact that there were no funds available to pay the musicians (Rye, 1990b:167) led to a strike.

The main issue in the dispute between Lattimore and Cook was the ownership of the SSO. Cook claimed that he founded the orchestra then brought in Lattimore to help with the business side of the operation, and revealed that during the period when the Orchestra were at the Philharmonic Hall he 'was having constant trouble with the Plaintiff [Lattimore]. I demanded Accounts which he did not give me' (TNA: PRO J4/9221 L.542 A.297). Although the musicians who testified in these cases were loyal to Cook, as the disputes continued, the original orchestra personnel gradually disintegrated. Twenty-one of the musicians returned to London with Cook, leaving Lattimore with five singers and four instrumentalists (TNA: PRO J4/9221 L.542 A.297). This in turn led to the cancellation of the remaining engagements in Liverpool and temporary disbandment in February (Rye, 1990b:168). Cook found engagements for the orchestra at the Kennington Theatre, to which Lattimore reacted angrily by issuing a lawsuit against Ernest C. Rolls, the promoter (TNA: PRO J4/9221 L.542), and then against Cook, Rolls and André Charlot (TNA: PRO J4/9221 L.647) in an attempt to stop the musicians performing other than under his management.

Although the orchestra continued to exist in some form until 1922, it never regained its initial integrity and coherence after the disputes of 1920 as the personnel seems to have been constantly changing and 'the ranks of the Southern Syncopated Orchestra itself were soon swelled with non-American members of the African diaspora' (Rye, 1990a:50). Eventually, after the tragic sinking of the ship on which the orchestra was travelling to Ireland in 1921, white Britons such as trumpeter Tommy Smith, trombonist Ted Heath and pianist Natalie Spencer were also recruited. Billy Mason, a pianist who was recruited in Glasgow immediately after the accident, was apparently 'blacked up' to appear with the SSO, but none of the other musicians recall that they had to be 'disguised' in this way (Jones, 1960:12).

Ironically, the result of the gradual break-up of the SSO meant that both individuals and the group as a whole had more influence on the evolution of jazz in Britain than they otherwise might. The groups were forced to tour more widely in Britain due to the broken Paris dates, and the split between Cook and Lattimore meant that there were at times two groups in operation at practically the same time, which resulted in increased circulation of the music and musicians. Many of the disillusioned musicians who left the SSO sought alternative work in Britain[21] and thus disseminated the music even more widely around the country and into Europe

---

[21] Details of some these musicians can be found in Walker (1972:208) and Goddard (1979:61), and their later activities in Britain are considered in Chapter 7 and Chapter 9.

and remained active in Britain long after the final demise of the SSO. In addition, native musicians who were absorbed into the group to replace those who had left were able to learn about jazz techniques first-hand, especially through jam sessions which took place during orchestral strikes and periods of inactivity. Salnave recalled that 'It was during the orchestra's various strikes that I really began to play true jazz. Then I could vie for honours with the other coloured musicians. It was at this time also that I bought my first saxophone ... .' (Rye, 1978:215). It is in the accounts of the more 'unofficial' and informal activities of the musicians of the SSO, such as dance band work and jamming, that compelling evidence emerges which establishes the direct importance of this ensemble to the evolution of jazz in Britain.

Associated Dance Bands

The SSO was generally unsuited for playing for dancing and opportunities for extended extemporization were limited within the large ensemble. However, certain musicians who were clearly more proficient improvisers than others formed small groups and eventually ceased playing with the main orchestra (Rye, 1990b:144). The Portman Syncopated Orchestra, the first small group to be drawn from the orchestra, played for dancing at the Portman Rooms in Baker Street from mid-September to 20 December 1919 (TNA: PRO J4/9220 L.175, A.99). The *Dancing Times* simply reported that 'The Portman Dances will be held daily in the newly re-decorated Portman Rooms, Baker Street ... . Music by the Portman Syncopated Orchestra' (October 1919:33) and the *London Amusement Guide* describes the band as 'a combination of New York dance players, who are not only excellent musicians, but sweet singers as well' (October 1919:34).

In fact, two bands shared the work at the Portman Rooms, the Portman Syncopated Orchestra and the Red Devils. Bernard Tipping, although he mis-remembered the name of the band formed from musicians who 'originally came to this country as members of the SSO' recalled that they 'had a fine swinging tempo and ... always imparted to their playing that peculiar zest and vigour which can only be associated with coloured musicians' (November 1930:57). The group consisted of Fred Coxcito on saxophone (TNA: PRO J4/9220 L.175 A.99), and probably John George Russell (clarinet) and Pierre de Caillaux (piano) as their names did not appear on an October programme for the main orchestra (Rye, 1990b:143). George Smith (violin) joined on 15 October (TNA: PRO J4/9220 L.175 A.98), and Henry Saparo (singer/mandoline) on 14 November (TNA: PRO J4/9220 L.175 A.97). The latter was probably the only musician who also continued to perform with the main orchestra (TNA: PRO J4/9220 L.175 A.97). The engagement apparently ended when the club closed to allow a new floor to be laid and more new decorating to be carried out (*Dancing Times*, January 1920:307).

The SSO percussionist Benny Peyton was asked by Lattimore on the 18 December 1919 to lead a band at the Embassy Club on Bond Street (described by Bechet as 'a smart place where we had to wear white tie and tails' (1960:129)) and the 'Jazz Kings' finally opened on New Year's Eve 1919.[22] 'The Embassy Club' was in fact the 'Dixie Club', named after the ODJB who had played there earlier in 1919. The Jazz Kings were clearly much more commercially successful than the SSO, for a number of reasons. Firstly, they played dance music, which was praised by the magazine *Dancing World*: 'This combination of talented artists can certainly render dance music (much of it being of their own composition) in the most inspirited, lively and pleasing manner' (October 1920:4). Peyton had a good choice of musicians for his band as he was able to use the musicians who had been playing at the Portman Rooms, with the addition of himself and Sidney Bechet, who replaced Russell (TNA: PRO J4/9220 L. 175 A.79). The format of clarinet, alto saxophone, violin, banjo, piano and drums was similar to that of a standard dance band in Britain, but as it consisted entirely of black musicians and was a called 'jazz' band, the latest trend in dance music, it thus represented a desirable balance of the familiar and the exotic. The Jazz Kings were clearly popular, as they recorded some numbers for Columbia (although these were never issued) (Averty, 1969:23) and performed at the most important dance venues in the capital including the Hammersmith Palais de Danse from 3 October to December 1920, returning from April to September 1921[23] and at Rector's Club on Tottenham Court Road between December 1920 and February 1921 (*London Amusement Guide*).

The Jazz Kings were ambitious, and achieved musical and material autonomy from the SSO. When they found out that Lattimore had been taking a large share of their earnings, having stated that he was not making any money from the engagement, they negotiated their own contract with Albert De Courville, the proprietor of the Embassy Club.[24] This led to Lattimore attempting to sue De Courville as well as Peyton, Smith, Saparo and Coxcito, whom he claimed that under the terms of their work permits had to remain as part of the Southern Syncopated Orchestra or return immediately to America (TNA: PRO J4/9220 L.175 A.79), although they were all apparently unaware of this.

The Jazz Kings also seem to have paid careful attention to their image. A photograph (see Figure 6.4) shows them resplendent in matching striped costumes complete with turban-style hats, probably as part of the 'carnivals and frolics' that were included in the weekly programme at the Embassy Club (*Dancing Times*, January 1920:307). There is evidence that Peyton had picked up on the prevailing

---

[22] Although this group was known as 'The Syncopated Orchestra' until they appeared at the Hammersmith Palais later in 1920, they are referred to as the 'Jazz Kings' here for clarity.

[23] During April the Jazz Kings shared the billing at the Palais with 'Buddie' Gilmour's Syncopated Orchestra. The bands played 'alternately at each end of the hall' (*London Amusement Guide*, April 1921:8).

[24] Russell, not Bechet, was named in the contract that Peyton made with De Courville (L.175, A.79) and neither Russell, Bechet or De Caillaux were included in the legal action (1920 L.175). This may be because Bechet probably returned to the main SSO for a period during 1920, performing at the Kingsway Hall and the Philharmonic Hall (Bechet, 1960:129) and spent some time in Belgium or France playing with Louis Mitchell; although he did also play with the Jazz Kings on their French engagements in this year (Averty, 1969:23). This clearly shows Bechet's independent spirit.

idea of jazz as novelty entertainment in Britain, as in an interview he stated that 'We do our best to render Jazz music in a manner sufficiently good, we hope, to make the public like it, and to free it from monotony. But further than that, the "Jazz Kings" can entertain with tricks, stunts, solos and so on' (*Dancing World*, October 1920:4). The Jazz Kings were far more commercially astute than the SSO from the evidence of their costumes, financial deals and stated aims.

The other main dance group to spring from the SSO, known as Marion Cook's Syncopated Players, was formed in March 1920 from the musicians who left Lattimore in Liverpool and played for dancing at the Trocedero Restaurant (Rye, 1990b:169). It seems that Cook arranged this primarily to aid the musicians who were owed money from Lattimore and were probably becoming increasingly desperate. This engagement was advertised in *The Referee* as *Le Souper Dansant*:

> In the story of the furore of the dance, the introduction of dancing at the Trocadero marks an epoch. A Supper in the ultra-Trocedero style and an Orchestra worthy of the reputation of the restaurant. (7 March 1920:11)

The *Dancing Times* reported that 'the band, which is called Marion Cook's, is good, albeit some who do not like too much syncopation, might take exception to that feature of its playing' (April 1920:547), suggesting that the band were capable of playing suitable dance music, although this was possibly a little too modern for some. The engagement at the Trocadero continued until about August 1920 (*London Amusement Guide*).[25]

Jazz in the Performances and Rehearsals of the SSO

The SSO has been neglected in modern analyses of early jazz as initially, none of the material that the group performed was specifically designated as 'jazz', as discussed earlier. John Chilton has claimed that 'Will Marion Cook was determined not to use the word 'jazz' for any of the music performed by the SSO ... . Cook felt that the SSO's music would receive more careful listening, and more lasting acclaim, if it was not described as jazz.' (1987:35). However, since in Britain in the early twentieth century the precise meaning of the word 'jazz' was still very much open to interpretation, this was another description that could be variously adopted or rejected by critics in relation to the Southern Syncopated Orchestra's performances. British reviewers applied definitions of jazz that were based on their previous limited experience of the music, and it is significant that the performances of the SSO were generally seen as being appreciably different. The reviewer in the *Daily Graphic* stated explicitly that the music performed by the SSO was 'Ragtime but not Jazz' as it was a 'melodious species of ragtime [which] is quite distinct from Jazz, [and] has a special appeal to those interested in the folk-lore of plantation days' (9 December 1919:6). Reviews dating from 1920 begin to mention jazz in connection with SSO performances, but a review in

---

[25] Will Marion Cook's Syncopated Orchestra, a small group, also performed for dancing in the Australian Pavilion at Crystal Palace from July until about September 1920 (Rye, 1990b:172).

Figure 6.4   The Jazz Kings at the Embassy Club, 1920 (Max Jones Archive)

Sound Wave suggests that the SSO's performances of the music were rather different to the noisy and unrefined jazz with which Britons were familiar:

> The wildest orgy of jazz effects [in the SSO's performances] never reveals for an instant any real discord, for each artist plays with the harmonious objective of the complete performance uppermost in his mind. (October 1920:698)

However, there is strong evidence to suggest that the improvisatory essence of jazz was not only present in the small group and leisure time playing of certain individual musicians in the SSO, but as an integral part of the rehearsal process and performances of the full orchestra. Examination of these subtle references to the performance practice of the SSO is fundamental to an understanding of the way in which the whole group and individual players influenced the evolution of jazz in Britain. White pianist Natalie Spencer found that 'playing in an orchestra composed of people of an entirely different race was a unique, and, as it transpired, a pleasant experience' (1921:409). Her account provides a fascinating insight into the way in which the orchestral players 'with an artistic and elastic conductor' were able to introduce 'highly original bits ... not necessarily at rehearsals, but, should the spirit move one, at a show' (1921:410). Spencer's account suggests that although the band normally performed from printed music there was considerable flexibility for innovation and improvisation, governed by 'Mr. Cook's expression' that 'formed an unmistakable gauge of the success or otherwise of one's attempt' (1921:410). Improvisation was clearly part of the rehearsal and arrangement process, in which very good improvised embellishments were rewarded with a quiet smile 'and you knew that bit was 'in for keeps' and would be expected more or less in future' (1921:410). Her account leaves no doubt as to both the musical and humorous capabilities of her colleagues: 'An amusing occupation is "answering each other" – taking a phrase or bit of embellishment that you heard someone else put forth, and putting it in, (usually in another key) in another part of the tune.' (1921:410). Spencer's account suggests that although not all of the music that the orchestra played was jazz, the ability to improvise spontaneously was valued and expected from members of the SSO. Her description of SSO performances is confirmed by Ernest Ansermet, who stated that 'there are very few numbers I have heard them execute twice with exactly the same effects.' (1959:4).

Furthermore, some contemporary reviews suggest that the orchestra did not always use music, which may indicate that they learnt the music by ear and certainly that there was a freedom in their approach to playing in a large ensemble which would encourage improvisation, albeit within a limiting framework. For example, the reviewer of a performance in Bristol observed: 'All the singers and nearly all the instrumentalists know the music by heart, and are thus untramelled by the need of reference to the printed notes.' (*Bristol Times and Mirror*, 6 April 1920:5) and in Sheffield 'The whole programme was played from memory ... .' (*Sheffield Daily Telegraph*, 27 April 1920:4). Natalie Spencer also describes one instance when the brass and wind parts for a particular number were unavailable. After the instruction from Cook 'First strain in C major, modulating to A flat for

the second part, then back to C' the band proceeded to perform the piece
(1921:409).

Individual Jazz Musicians in the SSO

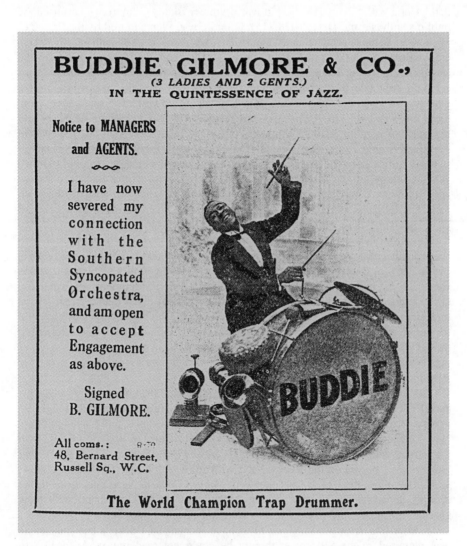

Figure 6.5   Buddie Gilmore Advertisement (*Performer*, 12 August
1920:27, by permission of the British Library)

The jazz elements of the SSO's show were most clearly demonstrated in the performances of the musicians that Will Marion Cook chose to feature, Buddy Gilmore and Sidney Bechet, who were to all intents and purposes jazz musicians working in an orchestral context. As such, both made strong individual impressions on the public, even before they branched out into small group work. Salnave stated that 'Along with Sidney [Bechet], it was drummer Buddy Gilmore who aroused the public's enthusiasm.' (Rye, 1978:215). Gilmore was even admired by the Prince of Wales and Salnave recalled that 'The Prince, who took lessons with Buddy, much enjoyed playing the drums. He appeared with the band every time he came to the [Savoy] club' (Rye, 1978:215). It was Gilmore's performance that led *The Times* critic to conclude that 'the Southern Orchestra can provide jazz entertainment when required' as they had 'a drummer who fascinated yesterday's audience – and more important still, the Coliseum's own expert – by his lightening dexterity and his knack of juggling with his drumsticks.' (9 December 1919:12). The reviewer in the *Dunfermline Press* also lauded him as an 'amazingly clever individual … [whose] antics keep the audience in continuous merriment' (24 January 1920:4). When Gilmore left the Southern Syncopated Orchestra for a time, he placed a large advertisement, complete with illustration, in *The Performer* to advertise his own act, 'The Quintessence of Jazz' (12 August 1920:27, see Figure 6.5) which had been the name adopted for his solo in the SSO show (see, for example, *The Scotsman*, 21 January 1920:8). Trombonist Ted Heath joined the band for a tour to Vienna, the last recorded appearance by a permutation of the SSO (Rye, 1990b:230), at a time when morale among many of the longer serving musicians was clearly at low ebb. Heath was 'terrified by the vicious arguments and when the knife fights started to break out, both Tommy [Smith] and I decided that it was high time we started for home' (1957:30). However, the experience was clearly a formative one, as Heath recalls learning from Buddy Gilmore (who had returned to the SSO) 'something about the different approach and technique necessary for jazz' (1957:30), thus leaving little doubt as to Gilmore's credentials as a jazz musician.

Sidney Bechet was undoubtedly the most significant member of the Jazz Kings, and if not the entire Southern Syncopated Orchestra. He was born and brought up in New Orleans, alongside jazz legends such as Buddy Bolden, and played in many New Orleans bands. Bechet made his way north to Chicago like the ODJB, with the Bruce and Bruce Stock Company, with which Bechet commented that 'sometimes I played on the stage myself with solos and things' (Bechet interview, 1958, HJA tape, Reel 1). Bechet met Will Marion Cook in New York prior to the group's departure for London, where Bechet was playing in a band with New Orleans musicians including Freddie Keppard (Bechet interview, 19 November 1945; HJA transcript p. 11). Cook must have recognized Bechet's potential as he was recruited to the SSO even though he could not read music. According to Averty, when Will Marion Cook was organizing the SSO for their departure for Europe, he 'kidnapped' Bechet outside the hotel where he was working (1969:23). It is clear from the interviews that Bechet gave for the Hogan Jazz Archive that he was in sympathy with Cook's aims to elevate black music, in particular showing respect for Cook's own perseverance against racial discrimination (Bechet interview, 1958, HJA transcript p. 27).

Although it was probably in the small group situation that Bechet could really shine, as in addition to improvising he had 'great talents as an arranger, at a time when this skill was as yet practically unavailable in Europe' and made instant arrangements on the stand (Rye, 1978:211). His improvisational abilities were immediately put to good use in the SSO, as he had his own feature in the show and seems to have been happy to be in the spotlight. As we have seen, improvisation was important when playing with the SSO, and Salnave recalled how once Bechet spontaneously improvised a clarinet obbligato to Abie Mitchell's *Madame Butterfly* solo, much to the surprise of Cook, who was conducting (Rye, 1978:210). Bechet may have been familiar with the aria due to the strong operatic tradition in his home city New Orleans.

Bechet's European travels were extremely significant to the development of the understanding of jazz in these countries, including Britain. Bruce Boyd Raeburn has commented that 'New Orleans was always right there with him, in his music and in his soul, and he gave the world a taste.' (1997:17). His upbringing in New Orleans meant that Bechet had been influenced by some of the great early jazz clarinettists, and his improvisational abilities and apparently already distinct sound made a great impression upon those that heard him in London. This led to him being one of the first individuals to be appreciated as a jazz musician in Britain, initially through his *Characteristic Blues* solo within the SSO show. Bechet's extemporizations were probably truly spontaneous and were certainly recognized as such. Bernard Tipping recalled that Berchet (*sic*) 'would conceive the most weird and clever ideas quite spontaneously while he was playing, and out they used to come all on the spur of the moment as it were' (1930:57). The reviewer in *The Cambridge Magazine* linked the performances of Bechet, 'who extemporizes a clarinette solo ... [and] compels admiration, so true is his ear and so rhythmical and vital his conception' with the abilities of slaves who 'having a great sense of rhythm they extemporised on any tunes, using subtle dissonances which are characteristic of them' (*The Cambridge Magazine*, 1919 quoted in Rye, 1990a:49). The origins of jazz and improvisation in black music were clearly understood by some writers at this time, and the use of the term 'subtle dissonances' suggests an awareness of the 'blue' notes must have featured in Bechet's solo.[26]

Bechet's playing of 'perfectly formed blues' prompted one of the earliest essays that recognized the significance of jazz by the Swiss conductor, Ernest Ansermet (contained in Williams (1959) *The Art of Jazz*). Bechet remembered Ansermet's numerous visits to the Philharmonic Hall: 'Many a time he'd come over to where I was and he'd ask me all about how I was playing and what it was I was doing, was I singing into my instrument to make it sound that way?' (Bechet, 1960:127). Obviously Ansermet had never heard a clarinet played in this way, and Tipping was also struck by the originality of 'a man who could glide and slide

---

[26] If Bechet's later recording of this piece is anything to go by, these early twentieth century audiences certainly experienced a blues performance, full of characteristic elements, which was unprecedented in Britain.

about on the clarinet as easily as if it were a slide-trombone' (November 1930:57). Ansermet recognized that what he was hearing was more than just a one-off novelty. Firstly, he understood the lineage of African-American music that was being laid out before him by the SSO, in which spirituals, rags, dances and blues were inextricably linked. Most significantly, however, he also recognized that this evolution was set to continue into the future, remarking that Bechet's improvised solos 'already show the germ of the new style' and suggesting that this may be 'the highway along which the whole world will swing tomorrow' (Ansermet, 1959:6).

Conclusion

Rigorous analysis of the activities of the Original Dixieland Jazz Band and the Southern Syncopated Orchestra establishes both of these groups as vital to the evolution of jazz in Britain. Although the two ensembles performed different repertoire, both were rooted in American music and were on the cutting edge of where jazz began to evolve from earlier American genres as a separate, new musical style. Although improvisation was not as central to the performances of the SSO and the ODJB as it was to become in later jazz, it was nevertheless very much present as a significant aspect of the way that both groups worked. The similarities between the way that these groups extemporized new ideas in rehearsal, that were then rejected or adopted in performances, are very striking, and it is clear that this provided a foundation for the development of improvisational practices in jazz.

This chapter has shown that the image of jazz and black performers that had been firmly established before the widely cited 'beginning of jazz' in 1919 were extremely influential on the reception of the ODJB and the SSO. The performances of the ODJB were established as seminal through their consistency with the way in which jazz was already understood in Britain. The group was understood to be performing authentic jazz, leading to British bands continuing to perpetuate this version and image of jazz after the ODJB had left Britain. This is confirmed by the number of photographs of five piece bands dating from the early 1920s, albeit including the ubiquitous banjo, but in dinner suits with the name of the band on the bass drum and often striking eccentric poses, that are contained in the Savoy Archive.

The SSO presented such a range of music that it was often simply classified as 'black entertainment'. Immediately this prompted comparisons with earlier instances of such entertainment in Britain, most notably the minstrel show. The familiarity and popularity of blackface minstrels became a useful marketing tool for Lattimore in an attempt to promote the group, but also became a straitjacket to which black performers were often forced to yield for their own survival in Britain. The feature of the performances that was often most appreciated by audiences was that the SSO represented an authentic cultural experience, unlike previous imitations. This reflects the change from the Victorian and Edwardian diluted and distanced experiences of black culture through the conventions of the Exhibition and the minstrel show to the post-war desire for realism, the deliberate embracing of 'alternative' cultures and the spirit of *carpe diem*. The SSO's performances led to some recognition of the fundamental roots of modern syncopated styles in black music. However, the word 'jazz' was not used by the main SSO until later in their time in Britain, by which time the idea of jazz that had been disseminated by the ODJB had been widely adopted. This meant that reviewers initially had trouble in defining anything that the SSO played as jazz, as it was said that it was too melodious and not noisy enough.

The difference between the reception and relative success of the two groups in Britain can be put down as much to the way in which they were presented as to the nature of the music that they performed. Cook's group was called an 'orchestra', appeared in black tie, included works by established classical composers, initially appeared at the Philharmonic Hall and were well received by audiences who were interested in music and culture. The attempts to adapt the SSO's show for variety theatre and dance accompaniment were generally unsuccessful. The ODJB performed from the start in London's most popular variety theatres and dance venues, to audiences who were merely expecting whatever was the latest novelty or dance band, and thus quickly permeated the British entertainment world. The fact that the ODJB were able to present jazz as dance music when new dance music was just what Londoners required in 1919 would ultimately ensured their success over an unwieldy orchestra, irrespective of race.

A more meaningful comparison can be made between Benny Peyton's Jazz Kings and the ODJB as similar sized dance groups, both of which claimed to be performing jazz. These groups performed in similar venues, which appears to indicate a lack of racial discrimination. Like the ODJB, the Jazz Kings were commercially aware and image conscious. However, the extent of the influence of blackface stereotypes meant that black musicians of the SSO were always destined to perform in the shadow of minstrelsy, and the Jazz Kings were probably only as successful as it was possible for them to be as black musicians. The ultimate success of the ODJB was due to long-standing white supremacy, and the fact that the population of Britain was predominately white. Most significantly, the ODJB were able to make recordings that gave them an emblematic status as the first jazz band for years to come. In contrast, the SSO, having been 'considered by HMV for recording ... the report to the committee was that they were not suitable' (Rye, 1990b:143), made no recordings and the Jazz Kings' recordings were never released.

The high-profile success of the ODJB in introducing jazz to Britain was clearly a transient phenomenon, and its importance has been to an extent exaggerated by writers over the years. The group was small, close-knit and impenetrable, and after they left Britain, their demise was rapid, and their reputation was disseminated in the proceeding years through their recordings as a new oral tradition. These recordings can easily give a misleading impression of the band and of jazz, and numerous imitators, keen to fill the shoes of the ODJB, but without a real understanding of the music, merely reproduced the superficial elements of their performances. Although the ODJB was significant in shaping an initial understanding of jazz and fundamental to the development of modern dance, their impact on the long-term musicological development of jazz in Britain is arguable.

The SSO and associated small groups disseminated jazz widely through Britain, performing in most main cities and in parts of Europe over a three-year period. Hence, many more people heard the SSO than ever heard the ODJB live, as the latter performed in a limited number of venues in London and were only in Britain for just over a year. The SSO established their authenticity and credibility through simply presenting the music of their own culture and this quality was recognized by those that heard them. Although the music of the SSO was viewed with interest and appreciated by audiences, it remained an experience outside white British culture and did not yet have the power to permeate and influence it, except through one vital route – the musicians themselves. The essential paradox in the history of the SSO was that collapse of the ensemble was vital in allowing the SSO to disseminate ideas on jazz in Britain, and especially to British musicians. In addition, several of the original American musicians found jobs elsewhere in Britain, no doubt encouraged to remain in the country by a relative lack of racial discrimination at this time, and helped to ensure the long-term development of jazz in this country. British musicians were absorbed in the band in their place, and could therefore experience the music first-hand at a time when strikes encouraged the members of the SSO to experiment and improvise at jam sessions, developing their own jazz playing still further. Significantly, it was the SSO, not the ODJB, which received serious musical criticism that began to establish black music and jazz as significant art forms in the twentieth century.

Chapter 7

Dance Music, the 'Plantation Revues' and the 'Underworld of London'

American syncopated music rapidly became central to popular entertainment in Britain following its introduction and dissemination in the early years of the twentieth century. American musicians continued to visit and perform in Britain in the 1920s but, in addition, increasing numbers of Britons began to compose and perform in new syncopated styles. Hence, jazz existed in 1920s London within three main situations: performed by dance bands, usually white, at socially exclusive venues such as large hotels and respectable clubs; performed by black music theatre companies, often accompanied by their own ensembles; and performed by small groups of musicians in West End clubs. The fact that in the former two situations the music performed was rarely referred to specifically as 'jazz' certainly does not render these irrelevant to the study of the evolution of jazz in Britain, and nor does this make the third situation of prime importance in such an enquiry. Rather, as the performances in all three situations were a response to experiences of jazz – both of its music and of its image – they should all be considered in order to gain a holistic perspective on the period.

Many white American dance bands visited Britain during the 1920s and performed in the capital's most exclusive venues, and numerous British dance bands were also formed in the same period. These have been considered at length in the standard histories of jazz. However, the BBC, rather than any one of these bands, can be seen to have had the most fundamental role in the first part of the decade in the regulation and dissemination of dance music to the general public in Britain. The relationship between the BBC and another key British institution, the Savoy Hotel, established performances of 'symphonic syncopation' given by the bands of this hotel as the standard for dance music in Britain to which other bands ought to aspire, and the effects of this will be considered in detail. African-American musicians also continued to visit Britain during the 1920s, but as they came to Britain mostly as members of bands accompanying revue shows, they were subject to artistic and practical restrictions on their performances as well as the increased risk of racial prejudice in the wake of the race riots of 1919. This situation will be examined through consideration of the two African-American companies that visited Britain to perform in the plantation revues of 1923, accompanied by their own bands.[1] Finally, jazz was also represented in Britain in

---

[1] 'Plantation revues' is a convenient term adopted by Howard Rye (1988b) to categorize the 1923 revues *The Rainbow* and *Dover Street to Dixie* that included African-American companies performing racially specific entertainment in a plantation setting.

the 1920s in the nightclubs of the 'underworld of London', and here it was largely unrestricted by the conventions of mainstream society.[2] It was probably only in nightclubs that black performers, whether American or resident in Britain, were able to express themselves artistically. The fact that jazz flourished in this environment, which had close associations with alcohol, drugs and prostitution, and also was increasingly understood as a black music at a time of growing racial intolerance, served to cement a negative image of jazz for the general public, distanced from the music not only geographically but through the pervasive and influential filter of the BBC.

Despite the fact that for Sir John Reith, the head of the BBC during the 1920s, the BBC existed primarily to educate the public, entertainment in the form of 'dance music' was an essential part of the broadcast output during this decade. Dance music on the BBC was subject to rigorous control to ensure its suitability for listeners, primarily through the formation of 'house' bands and the careful choice of outside ensembles that were broadcast, and this led to the creation of a consistent musical style and associated image for the genre. Radio in the early 1920s was a novelty in itself, and many people received radio transmissions through homemade equipment. Thus, the standardized 'dance music' presented by the BBC was given credibility simply because it was broadcast at a time when listeners were still captivated by the technological wizardry of radio rather than being critical of the broadcast material itself. Radio created an accepted and expected stereotype for dance music. This was particularly influential on the perceptions of the general public, especially provincial listeners such as one correspondent in the *Radio Times* who wrote: 'my knowledge of the London dance bands is due only to what I hear on the wireless' (1 January 1926:57).

Until 1926 most of the dance music on the BBC was broadcast from the Savoy Hotel, with the first broadcasts of the Savoy Havana Band and the Savoy Orpheans on Friday 13 April 1923 and Wednesday 10 October 1923 respectively. The Savoy Hotel had been at the forefront of fashionable life in London for the past thirty years, and the Savoy Quartette and other banjo-based groups had provided guests with musical entertainment in the early twentieth century. The Original Dixieland Jazz Band had introduced the idea of a band without banjo to Britain, and the next American group to come to London, Art Hickman's New York London Five, followed this principle and also replaced the clarinet with a saxophone. Although banjos remained part of many bands in Britain in the 1920s, they were now less prominent, and became a more significant part of the rhythm section rather than melodic instruments as formerly. The saxophone began to become more important in the 1920s, both musically, as it made 'the sound of 1920s popular music distinctly different from the piano and banjo ragtime of the previous decade' (Pearsall, 1976:65), and as a strong visual symbol of up-to-date dance music. W.W. Seabrook, in an article on 'London's Nightclubs' published in 1924, asserted that a nightclub proprietor 'knows that he may as well be out of the business without a saxophone player' (Moseley, 1924:139). The banjo group the Versatile Three/Four had begun performing as a saxophone quartet as early as July 1917,

---

[2] *The Underworld of London* is the title of a book on crime in London by Felstead (1923).

and although they never recorded as an all-saxophone ensemble, from late 1919 their recordings all featured Gus Haston on saxophone (Lotz, sleeve note to DOCD 5624). The Versatile groups kept pace consistently with the latest popular song numbers, and similarly the inclusion of the saxophone by this group must have reflected the fashion for this instrument at this time. Likewise, in 1919, when William F. de Mornys began to organize the Savoy Hotel's dance music, the Savoy Quartette was augmented by two saxophones and a violin to become the Savoy Dance Orchestra, possibly under his influence (Savoy Archives). In 1920, de Mornys was officially appointed Entertainment Director of the Savoy Group (Hayes, 1988:13). The Savoy Dance Orchestra was then reformed as a banjo-less quintet, and continued to be augmented until it was disbanded in 1923. By the end of 1920 the Savoy Quartette had made its last recording and left the hotel in January 1921.

De Mornys had already set up several clubs in London, including Rector's, and was aware of current fashions in dance music. He also had contacts with American musicians such as the ODJB and Murray Pilcer (Hayes, 1988:9) and recognized the importance of including Americans in his bands. According to Hayes, de Mornys 'often went off on visits to the States to seek crack musicians', and upon his appointment as Entertainment Director immediately began to employ American bands and musicians in the hotel: 'I decided that the hotel must have authentic music and I would bring over some Americans to carry the burden and put in some good-class jazz-minded British musicians.' (Hayes, 1988:15). Initially, de Mornys appears to have attempted to replicate the Original Dixieland Jazz Band, who had returned to America in July 1920, creating a band with the sound that he described as 'a piano twanging, the drummer hitting everything on his panoply of weird bits and pieces and the trombonist apparently blowing raspberries' (Hayes, 1988:15). In September 1920 he employed Bert Ralton, an American saxophonist, to lead the mixed American and British New York Havana Band, which became known as the Savoy Havana Band (Rust, 1972:31). His knowledge of the experiences of the ODJB in London also seems to have influenced de Mornys in the marketing of his new ensemble, as in 1922 he obtained a booking for the band in variety, an environment in which the ODJB had thrived and become popular. This enabled the band to perform to larger and less exclusive audiences than at the Savoy, and accordingly raised the profile of the band amongst the general public. De Mornys described the success of the band's variety performances at the Coliseum:[3] 'The public was clamouring for encores every night and poor Bert Ralton ... had to make speeches to say that they really could not play any more as there were other acts to follow.' (Hayes, 1988:16). De Mornys also recognized the commercial potential of the emerging recording and broadcasting industries. The Savoy Havana Band had made recordings from 1921, but Reith was initially reluctant to let the band broadcast as, according to de Mornys, he regarded jazz musicians as 'eccentrics and madmen'. De Mornys persuaded him to give the group a chance as a result of the band's success in variety (Hayes, 1988:16).

---

[3] In addition, a photograph in the Savoy Archive shows the 'Savoy New York Havana Band' billed at the Alhambra Theatre.

Figure 7.1   The Savoy Orpheans (*Radio Times*, 18 January 1923:141, by permission of the British Library)

In 1923 de Mornys formed a new band to replace the Savoy Dance Orchestra, an eleven-piece band that was named the 'Savoy Orpheans' because the musicians 'played like gods-like Orpheus!' (Hayes, 1989:69) (see Figure 7.1). De Mornys commented at the time:

> Jazz is becoming more dignified. Even in America, the nursery of jazz, there is no jazz to be heard any more. It has been replaced by symphonised syncopated music. So I have decided to form a new band featuring sweet music at the Savoy. I am certain that although the British public likes the rhythm, they want to hear the melody and dislike the music too swingy – they want melody and quality of tone. (Hayes, 1988:18)

Bert Ralton resigned as the new band was being formed, probably in objection to de Mornys' idea that performances should now be more restrained:

> We had a mixture of British and American musicians in the Orpheans and some of the Yanks had their own idea about jazz. When they got too 'hot' for the Savoy I sent them over to Claridges, where they soon had to quieten down. The restaurant manager went beserk if they played a note of jazz and rang me up complaining. (de Mornys quoted in Hayes, 1988:18)

The conductor of the Savoy Orpheans was also quick to disassociate the music of his band from jazz:

> Syncopation has come to stay, for a number of years at any rate. It is as different from the "jazz" music of a year or so ago as chalk is from cheese. Syncopation is a real music, not just a collection of noises. It requires, as I have said, real skill in its players, and hard study before it can be played correctly. (*Radio Times*, 5 October 1923:38)

> Dance music has completely changed its character in the past ten years – from the poorly constructed, poorly-orchestrated "Jazz" to the present-day syncopated music which takes advantage of every shade of orchestration and harmony. (*Radio Times*, 18 January 1924:141)

Hayes suggests that the band was formed as a result of a visit that de Mornys made to America, but the inspiration for this new venture may well have been nearer to home. It was in 1923 that Paul Whiteman made his first visit to London, directing his band in the revue *Brighter London* at the Hippodrome (Schiff, 1997:52). During their time in London, the band also played at numerous parties and at the Grafton Galleries for 'a party of pressmen and friends' (*Era*, 30 May 1923:14). Whiteman recalled the circumstances that brought him to London:

> We had come to London at the invitation of Lord and Lady Mountbatten, cousins of the Prince of Wales. We met this friendly and charming couple in New York, when we played at a private party given in their honor. They loved to dance, and after that they would visit us often at the Palais Royale, a famous Broadway dance palace of that day. Lord and Lady Mountbatten became loyal friends of every boy in the band.

> "You simply must come to London," Lord Mountbatten insisted. "The Prince must have a chance to hear the band – that's all there is to it." When he returned to England,

Lord Mountbatten arranged a six-week engagement for us in a musical called "Brighter London". Londoners must have liked us. We stayed on for six months. (Whiteman, (1948) from http://www.shellac.org/wams/wpaulw1.html)

The band was popular with the public and received many good reviews:

In the last scene, the Palais de Danse, Mr. Paul Whiteman and his band play jazz music on a varied selection of instruments with much skill and effect, and to the evident enjoyment of the audience, being loudly applauded ... . "Brighter London" had a rapturous reception at its London première. (*Era*, 4 April 1923:11)

Just as the Savoy Havana Band seems to have been de Mornys's response to the phenomenal success of the ODJB, his new band, the Savoy Orpheans, was influenced by Whiteman. De Mornys appointed Debroy Somers, 'a handsome, immaculate, soldierly man of immense charm, who had come from the Kneller [Royal Military] School of Music' (Hayes, 1988:18), and who was also not dissimilar in appearance to Paul Whiteman, as leader of the new band. However, the correlation between the Orpheans and Whiteman's band was more significant than the merely visual. On 12 February 1924, Whiteman presented his famous 'Experiment in Modern Music' concert at the Aeolian Hall in New York, for which he commissioned Gershwin to compose *Rhapsody in Blue*. In the concert, Whiteman apparently set out to present various forms of syncopated music, beginning with *Livery Stable Blues*, an Original Dixieland Jazz Band number, and demonstrated the skill of Grofé's arranging and the proficiency of his musicians. Similarly, the Savoy Orpheans presented a concert entitled 'Revolution of syncopated music from ragtime to symphonised syncopation' on their first birthday in October 1924, providing an opportunity for the audience 'to study syncopated music from its birth and origin, through its gradual phases and improvements, finishing with the modern symphonised music of to-day.' (Savoy Orpheans concert programme, 1924). As in Whiteman's concert, the programme cited the Original Dixieland Jazz Band, emphasized the importance of arrangements, and highlighted 'symphonized syncopation' as the most highly developed form of syncopated music.

In the following year, in which Gershwin performed his *Rhapsody* with the Orpheans, the band also gave concerts in the Queen's Hall, and in 1926 toured the country as the 'Savoy Orpheans Augmented Symphonic Orchestra' in order to 'endeavour to establish their claim that syncopated music such as Gershwin's "Rhapsody in Blue" deserves to be accepted as a serious contribution to art' (*Radio Times*, 16 October 1925:151). This shows obvious influence of the enlarged Whiteman band's concert performances, both in America and during a return visit to Britain in 1926, which included concerts at Alexandra Palace and the Royal Albert Hall (Rayno, 2003:129). The *Radio Times* even pointed out that 'the Savoy Orpheans have introduced scenery and modern lighting effects ... because they do not think that the atmosphere of the concert hall should be kept dull and severe, as has been the practice up to now.' (19 March 1926:580). Whiteman had used lighting and scenery in his concerts from the outset. The American tour of the 'Experiment' concert in 1924 was presented thus:

... a curtain of gold cloth with a silhouette of the Whiteman orchestra; this withdrew to reveal the orchestra dressed in its summer whites and seated in white bentwood chairs on tiers of dove grey trimmed with vermillion ... . To cap it all the stage was lighted (as it had been at Aeolian Hall) with shifting lights of green, yellow, pink and blue. (Schiff, 1997:61)

It was through the regular use of the Savoy Orpheans and Havana Band that the BBC ensured consistency and quality control in their early broadcasting of dance music. The relationship between the two institutions was mutually beneficial, on the one hand profiting the Savoy, whose management were largely eager to please in their dealings with the BBC, and on the other, the BBC's leaders relished the association with such a well-respected, upper-class, British institution (which was also conveniently close to the BBC's headquarters, and has been defined as an 'undercover branch of the BBC' [Pearsall, 1976:125]), which also allowed them to present an acceptable image for 'entertainment'. The Savoy Bands played in three late-night slots, on Tuesday, Thursday and Saturday during 1924 and 1925. Initially, dance music was restricted to the evenings but, from spring 1925, dance music was also broadcast in the afternoon, reflecting the popularity of tea dances at this time. The BBC's desire to cement the relationship with the Savoy led to an agreement being made on 11 September 1924 to broadcast Savoy Bands exclusively (meaning that other bands were not to be broadcast unless with the consent of the Savoy management).

The BBC made it clear through propaganda-style articles in the *Radio Times* that their association with the Savoy allowed them to present dance music of the highest quality. Early articles on the Savoy Orpheans allowed the care and expense taken to provide the dance music for broadcasting to be explained and emphasized: 'As you glide over the floor, it all seems so delightfully easy and simple. You know nothing of the months of hard work and expense that have been necessary to give you an evening's dancing to a good band'. The musicians were chosen carefully:

... we want a player who has been trained in syncopation; an ordinary musician is no good to us ... . (*Radio Times*, 5 October 1923:38)

Each member of the Savoy-Orpheans and Savoy Havana Bands is a soloist of the finest quality, procured at great expense and trouble ... each soloist is "discovered", brought to London, and, after much rehearsing, welded into the bands ... . (*Radio Times*, 18 January 1924:141)

The repertoire of the Savoy Orpheans was selected with similar attention:

... it is absolutely essential for the Savoy Hotel to have agents in every capital in the world searching for, and sending home new dance music. These new numbers are then considered by our special staff of arrangers in London and, where selected, are recast and orchestrated with every consideration for symphonic and syncopated beauty. (*Radio Times*, 18 January 1924:141).

As a radio audience would not, of course, be able to see the band in action, 'on broadcasting nights every effort is made to transfer to the listener by the music alone the true atmosphere of happiness.' (*Radio Times*, 18 January 1924:141). It is clear from these articles the phenomenon of outside broadcasting was still extremely new, both explaining that the band would 'play at the Savoy Hotel, whence the music will be transmitted by a land wire to 2LO [the broadcast transmitter at Marconi House on the Strand], and so, through the ether, to your receiving sets' (*Radio Times*, 5 October 1923:38).

Listeners gradually became less fixated with technological aspects of broadcasting and more critical of the BBC's programming. It is interesting that after the agreement had been made to broadcast the Savoy Bands exclusively, the BBC printed a letter entitled 'Too much Savoy Bands?' in the *Radio Times* in which a listener wrote:

> I should like to express the opinion ... that we are having rather more Savoy Bands transmissions at the present time than the average listener can appreciate ... . I would suggest that it is a style of music of which one quickly tires. (21 November 1924:385)

The editorial answer provided was that 'The Savoy Bands are broadcast only three times per week out of eight transmissions', but the timing of the publication of the letter suggests that the BBC were preparing to distance themselves somewhat from the exclusive deal with the Savoy, and possibly to convince the hotel management that this was a result of listeners' opinion. In the middle of the following year, the *Radio Times* printed the results of a survey by a listener in Cheshire, giving the opinions of a group of work colleagues on the BBC's programming: 'They gave it as their opinion that the Savoy Bands are not as popular as formerly. One or two originally thought these bands the only item worth listening to, and now apparently they consider them monotonous!' (*Radio Times*, 3 July 1925:72).

At this time the BBC wrote to the Savoy management 'We recognise that the Savoy, as pioneers of this form of broadcast service, should have preference, but realise that we can no longer give any particular band in London a monopoly for dance music', but promised that the Savoy should continue to broadcast the majority of dance music (BBCWAC R22/1 058/1 14 July 1925). The Savoy management responded 'we are inclined to think we should like to give the public a respite from the Savoy Bands. This would not of course prevent any novelty we might produce from time to time being broadcasted if you thought that desirable' (BBCWAC R22/1 058/1 17 July 1925). This suggests that they were concerned that listeners, such as the correspondents in the *Radio Times*, were tiring of the Savoy Bands' broadcasts and that the bands were beginning to lose public interest through over-familiarity.

The opening of the 'high powered' service from Daventry in 1925 allowed more flexibility in the arrangements for broadcasting of a wide range of music, with the London station and Daventry providing contrasting musical genres simultaneously. The *Radio Times* reported that 'starting on November 2nd, broadcast dance music will be available from Daventry every day, except Sunday, from the conclusion of the ordinary programme until midnight.' (2 October

1925:32), and the Friday broadcasts were extended until 2am (*Radio Times*, 16 October 1925:151). By necessity, more bands were required to meet the massively increased demand for dance music, and it was impossible for the BBC to honour an exclusive agreement with the Savoy Hotel. There was a huge growth in the broadcasting of dance music in 1925-27, both in terms of its proportion of the BBC's total broadcast hours (from 6.62 per cent in 1925 to 16.43 per cent in 1927) and as a percentage of music broadcasting, (from 9.94 per cent to 24.11 per cent) (Doctor, 1999:40-41).

BBC programme records enable comparisons to be made between output in the same week in successive years to be made, and it can be seen that during 1925 the BBC began to broadcast music from a wide variety of venues in the capital, although the Savoy Bands continued to feature frequently. For example, in the first week of March in 1925, the Savoy Bands provided all the late-night dance music that was broadcast, whereas in the corresponding week in 1926, Jack Payne's Hotel Cecil Dance Band, Jack Hylton's Kettner's Five, J Whidden and his Midnight Follies Dance Band from the Hotel Metropole, Firman's Carlton Hotel Dance Band and Ted Brown's Café de Paris Dance Band performed late-night dance music in addition to the Savoy Bands. In the first week of March in 1926 and 1927, every evening (except Sunday) ended with dance music. In 1927 these slots were filled with outside broadcasts from the most famous and exclusive hotels and clubs, including Ciro's, the Royal Opera House, the Riviera Club, and the New Princes Restaurant, continuing until midnight and beyond on the Daventry station.

The apparent variety of dance music on offer conceals the fact that broadcasting of the Savoy Bands almost exclusively for almost three years had the effect of standardizing London's dance music. The majority of the general public obtained their experiences of dance music from the radio, and therefore expected that dance music to sound like the Orpheans, whose controlled style also suited the image that the BBC wished to project. Even when the BBC began to obtain dance music from venues other than the Savoy, they still wished to provide what they viewed as 'suitable' entertainment and were obligated to an extent to satisfy listener's expectations. In the resulting vicious circle, British bands would have had to conform to the style laid down by the Savoy bands in order to be permitted to make the broadcasts necessary for commercial success. Thus, although in the later part of the decade a larger number of bands were broadcast, the basic style and presentation of the music remained generally consistent.

Radio broadcasts played an important part in the self-tuition of musicians in the new syncopated styles in the early 1920s and helped to ensure stylistic consistency across the country. Well-known British dance band musicians of the 1920s wrote tutor books, for example, the *Billy Mayerl School of Modern Syncopation* which was available as a correspondence course.[4] This further disseminated the British dance band style in print for aspiring professional musicians. Furthermore, as Paul Whiteman's band, an ensemble that, as we have seen, was demonstrably influential on the Savoy Orpheans, was also the most popular and influential band in America,

---

[4] Billy Mayerl's life and work is considered in depth in Peter Dickinson's *Marigold: the Music of Billy Mayerl* (1999).

this meant that many other American bands could be booked that largely fitted within the prevailing dance music style in Britain. Visits and broadcasts of bands led by, for example, Vincent Lopez, Paul Specht, Ted Lewis and Isham Jones, perpetuated this style further and this led to the exclusion from Britain of American bands that did not conform. Another important factor in the standardization process was that the activities of black musicians were generally under-represented in Britain at this time, which will be discussed further later. Leon Abbey's (black) band not only performed but also broadcasted in Britain in the twenties, but this was probably because they conformed musically to the expectations of a dance band (Gulliver, 1977:27). Fundamentally then, BBC policies severely restricted the popular music that could be heard in Britain, not only on the radio but also 'live' in venues all over the country.

The adoption of 'symphonic syncopation', a composed and notated style, meant that the mysteries of early jazz performances could be forgotten. The music was now accessible for performance by British musicians and could be imitated by British composers, who were widely considered to have surpassed their American counterparts in the mid-1920s. Whilst the Savoy Orpheans *First Birthday Book* (1924) promoted the group as an 'international orchestra' with players drawn from six countries, later sources emphasize that it was in the genre of 'symphonic syncopation' that British dance bands could be seen to be surpassing the American instigators of the music and making it their own. The bandleader Jack Hylton explained the 'improvements' made to jazz by British bands: 'When jazz first came to Britain, many people protested against this invasion of so-called barbarous "music". But I saw possibilities in it' and stated that he aimed to 'combine the colour of jazz music with that element of harmony which is so beloved of our race' (*Radio Times*, 27 November 1925:438). A report in the *Radio Times* was quick to point out that 'While syncopated music comes from America, the Savoy Orpheans are particularly anxious to add a British touch to it, by introducing some characteristic humour and comedy' (19 March 1926:580). Furthermore, when the Savoy Havana Band returned to the microphone in 1926 after a short absence, an article explained:

> When the Havana band started, it was practically an all-American band, but now it is practically an all-British band, competing with the Americans at their own game and importing its music through the medium of gramophone records into America, the home of syncopated music. (*Radio Times*, 6 August 1926:250)

The American roots of popular music were also undesirable for the BBC that wished to be seen to be providing the best *British* entertainment. The formation of the BBC Dance Orchestra represented the clearest attempt by the BBC to develop an ensemble that would seriously rival both American bands and other ensembles that performed in London hotels and clubs. The previous BBC house bands, the 2LO Dance Orchestra and the London Radio Dance Band, crucially lacked a well-known 'name' at the helm. However, in 1928 the BBC appointed Jack Payne, who was already a familiar figure in the dance band world, to lead the new band. The BBC executives trusted him implicitly, making a contract with him solely and thus allowing him to employ his own choice of musicians. The group was initially known as 'The BBC Dance Orchestra, personally conducted by Jack Payne'. Payne was commercially aware, if not also rather egocentric, and once his position at the BBC was secured he commented that the title did not suggest that he was in charge of the ensemble, and that his name was often missed out: 'That personal element which I think you will agree is so essential in appealing, from a show point of view, to the public, is entirely missing.' (BBCWAC 910 PAY August 1928). He proposed 'Jack Payne and the BBC Dance Orchestra' as an alternative that was in line with current industry practice. In November 1929 the name of the group was changed again to 'Jack Payne and his BBC Dance Orchestra', indicating Payne's fundamental input to the development of the band and his own increasing fame. The BBC Dance Orchestra was launched thus in the *Radio Times*, under the heading 'British Dance Music' (my emphases):

> A new era in studio dance music was marked by the engagement of Jack Payne, the brilliant young *British* dance band director, and his BBC dance orchestra. Jack Payne knows his job from A to Z. You remember his outside broadcasts of the past? They were first rate – but we had too little of them. He believes in plenty of variety in dance music, and the twelve men under his command are all versatile instrumentalists. Mr. Payne and his band are all *British* – and they mean to give *British* dances tunes a good showing. Though they have only been broadcasting for a few days, I have already received quite a batch of letters congratulating the BBC on its new acquisition. (23 March 1928:594)

Whilst the activities of all American musicians in Britain were increasingly opposed during the 1920s, *black* American musicians faced additional restrictions in Britain at this time. Most of the black musicians that visited Britain from America in the 1920s did so in connection with a stage show for several reasons. There was an expectation in Britain that black artists would provide minstrel-style entertainment due to the long-established synonymy between black performers and minstrels, which had already had a profound effect on the presentation and reception of black groups in the early twentieth century. In addition, at this stage black performers were not given the opportunity, either in America or in Britain, to participate as fully and as freely as whites in the commercial world of music through broadcasting and recording. It is clear that most black bands in the 1920s would generally be unable to compete with, for example, the publicity machine of the Paul Whiteman band. Therefore, in order to be successful in Britain, black performers had to conform to the public expectations of their performances to some extent. There was also the practical problem for American musicians of obtaining work permits, for which promoters had to prove that foreign performers could not be replaced by Britons. Clearly, native African-Americans could be more easily shown to be necessary for racially specific minstrel-type entertainment rather than purely musical performances.

It is significant that the only two notable groups of black performers in 1920s Britain that performed for dancing were not entirely imported from America. Victor Vorzanger's Famous Broadway Band was a mixed race band consisting of British and expatriate African-American musicians, such as trombonist Ellis

Jackson, who had been resident in Britain since he was a child and had been a member of the Southern Syncopated Orchestra (Rust 1972:45). It was probably a combination of the fact that the members of the band were resident in Britain and that not all the players were black that gave the group more freedom to 'compete' with white dance bands, as they were resident at the East Ham Palais de Danse in 1922-23. Leon Abbey's (black) band probably included British subjects (Gulliver, 1977:14). Abbey was also prepared to compromise his performances to fit in with British tastes, as is shown from his description of events after the band's first night at the Olympia Ballroom:

> The next morning a page boy came and said the owner would like to see me. I went over to his office. He was very friendly, offered me a seat, and said: "The way the boys carried themselves was fine ... the uniforms were beautiful ... BUT that screaming of the horns *isn't done heah!*" Now I had spent a lot of money on special arrangements but I went on the stand the following evening and I didn't pass any of them out ... just concentrated on melodies and popular tunes, and after that everyone was tickled to death. I stayed there quite a while ... went away and came back again ... I never did play those arrangements. (Gulliver, 1977:11)

The reviewer in the *Encore* noted that the band's success was due to the lack of adherence to what was considered as typically black performance style:

> ... we had also the excitement of a new coloured dance band who had just arrived in this country. Leon Abbey is the leader of the combination, who are away from the usual coloured entertainers in that they are more restrained, in spite of possessing wonderful rhythm and harmony. They made a complete success, and should undoubtedly soon also be performing on the music hall stage and broadcasting. They should certainly be heard by all. (*Encore*, 22 December 1927:10)

As a result, Abbey was successful in Britain, broadcasting several times on the BBC from December 1927 to February 1928 and recording for HMV (Rye, 1983b:207). It seems that as the sound of Abbey's band was compatible with the prevailing dance music style in Britain, the race of the band was considered less relevant, especially in the non-visual media of record and radio. However, black performers faced increasing union opposition from white British performers during the 1920s, and even Abbey's band faced problems in Europe at the end of the decade as they were 'perceived to be black musicians taking the jobs of natives' although in fact they were often British citizens (Gulliver, 1977:14).

Attitudes to black performers in the 1920s must be seen within the context of race relations in the post-war period. In 1919, the growing racial tension in post-war Britain erupted into race riots between black and white people in many of the major cities in the country (Jenkinson, 1986:182). During the war years, black people had played an important part as some enlisted and many helped to ease the labour shortage (Jenkinson, 1986:190), but at the end of the War there was fierce competition for jobs between these black workers and demobilized white soldiers. In addition, promises had been made by the government that after the War there would be greater economic security for workers, and improvements in health care and housing making Britain a better place to live. However, the reality for many was increasing poverty and unemployment, and this created a sense of disillusionment and anger (Gilbert, 1980:13). This situation initiated riots, particularly at ports, where competition for jobs was fierce and poorer blacks would accept lower wages (Jenkinson, 1986:185). There was also the perception amongst some whites that black people had taken housing that should have been available for demobilised servicemen and their families (Jenkinson, 1986:192).

Jenkinson also cites whites' sexual jealousy of blacks as a contributing factor to the riots, as there was the perception that black men had 'taken' white women made available by the absence of white men due to the War. Hence, 'sexual relations between black men and white women was mentioned as an anathema and soon the stress was laid on 'savage' instincts of the Black man' (1986:191). This jealousy was fuelled by the well-established and widely understood blackface stereotypes. The consistent reinforcement of negative ideas about black people through the continued presentation of these stereotypes in black shows contributed to the development of racism in Britain in the 1920s. Ironically, it was an African-American, Will Garland, who was a theatrical promoter and singer, that was primarily responsible for ensuring that the British public remained familiar with the Negro stereotype in the period between the original production of *In Dahomey* in 1903 and the plantation revues of 1923 through the presentation of shows that imitated American black cast productions. These included *A Trip to Coontown*, after a show of the same name originally presented in 1898 in New York, in 1906; a version of *In Dahomey* in 1905; *Coloured Society*, a title which recalls well-known songs from *In Dahomey*, in 1917; and various versions of *Brownbirds*, paralleling the series of *Blackbirds* shows produced by Lew Leslie from 1927 (see Lotz, 1997). Although the group included several white members it was known as the 'Negro Opera/Operetta Troupe' (Lotz, 1997:200). In October 1922, an article entitled 'A Black and Burning Shame: Coloured Artists who Disgrace the Stage' published in *John Bull* (28 October 1922:9) cited the supposed immoral behaviour of Garland's company, at that time touring Britain with the revue *All Black*, as reason for the opposition to C.B. Cochran's plan to import an American all-black company to Britain. This article shows how easily the negative elements of the stereotypes that black and blackface performers were delineating on stage could influence white judgements of all black people at this time.

The objections to black performers on the British stage in the *John Bull* article were exactly the same as the factors that Jenkinson identifies as the fundamental causes of the race riots in Britain in 1919. The first objection was based on economic factors and the perception that black actors would take employment opportunities that ought to belong to British performers. Referring to Cochran's plan to import an all-black revue, the article states that 'English actors and actresses, who have had a very bad time of it, contemplate this development with indignant anger'. Secondly, the article deals at length with the immorality of Garland's company. The excessive sexuality of the black performers, a widely believed stereotypical black characteristic, is emphasized: 'Garland protests that he has tried to stop coloured men and women living together. But he admitted that it had always gone on and several illegitimate children had been born'. Moreover, the article alleges that chorus girls were involved in prostitution, as they were only paid two pounds a week 'a wage upon which it is obvious that they cannot live honestly' and 'went into the street in their stage costumes, trying to find and talk to men, particularly those with motor cars!' Therefore, the immoral behaviour of the company posed a direct threat to white society in an interesting gender reversal of the sexual threat posed by black men in 1919: 'Garland admitted that his girls ran after white men and *visa versa*, and that he could not stop them'. The article concludes: 'We do not want low-class coloured people, who have an inferior sense of morality, to occupy our stage and elicit the applause of decent men women and children while they are living in a state of degredation [*sic.*] and moral filth.'

The *John Bull* article not only gave nationwide publicity to union opposition (principally from the Actors' Association and the Association of Touring Managers) to the importation of African-American performers but, significantly, it also seems to have brought this to the attention of the government. The government file (TNA: PRO LAB2/1187/EDAR954/1923) on the subject contains a typed copy of the *John Bull* article, and it was the Home Office that actually initiated correspondence with the Actors' Association in November in seeking to verify that their views had been correctly represented. Letters contained in this file from representatives of the Actors' Association once again detail the supposed negative economic and moral impact of coloured performers. In one letter to the Home Office, Alfred Lugg, Secretary of the Actors' Association, specifically recalled the visit of the *In Dahomey* company twenty years earlier and stated that he believed that many of the performers had remained in London living off white women. (TNA: PRO LAB2/1187/EDAR954/1923 5 December 1922)

The government concluded in March 1923 that in respect to the proposed importation of one black group:

> ... the performance which the members of the troupe are to give is of a special character and that it is not possible to obtain persons who can imitate it satisfactorily. In these circumstances, the Minister cannot regard the incoming of this troupe as displacing any British labour, indeed, the success of this particular item in the revue in question may tend to promote the employment of British people. (TNA: PRO LAB2/1187/EDAR954/1923)

This response demonstrates a lack of racism and fairness of judgement on the part of the British government, which Lotz also notes in connection with Will Garland's company when it had run into difficulties on a Continental tour several years earlier (1997:202). Despite this, following the *John Bull* article it was the views of entertainment unions including the Actors' Association, the Variety Artists Federation, the National Union of Theatrical Employees and the Musicians' Union, that condemned the proposed importation of black performers to Britain, that continued to be most often represented in the theatrical and national press. These opinions were particularly prominent in a series of articles written by Hannen Swaffer in the *Daily Graphic* in March 1923, prior to the appearance of the first 'plantation revue' at the start of April. Driberg notes that Swaffer, despite his Socialist stance, 'did not bother to hide a racial bias' in his caustic reviews and articles on black entertainment of this period (1974:137).

It was against this opposition that two black companies were brought to Britain to perform in the revues *The Rainbow* at the Empire Theatre and *Dover Street to Dixie* at the Pavilion Theatre by impresarios Sir Alfred Butt and C.B. Cochran respectively in 1923. Butt and Cochran had both been inspired to secure black companies for their revues having seen the cabaret at Sam Salvin's Plantation Restaurant on Broadway. Whilst Butt was unable to afford the actual performers from the restaurant, he hired another black company who had been performing a touring show, *Plantation Days*, in America and 'Robert Law, an American artist, to design a plantation setting' (*Daily Graphic*, 5 March 1923:7). In addition to the stage show, Butt also wished to replicate the cabaret setting of Salvin's within the restaurant of the Empire Theatre, which was to be decorated 'like a cotton plantation in one of the Southern States' (*Daily Graphic*, 3 March 23:4). Cochran, on the other hand, engaged the artists from Salvin's, including the star of the show, Florence Mills, purely for a staged performance. The similarity between the two shows was to lead to litigation between Butt and Cochran, adding to the publicity surrounding the revues.

Objections to the black companies did not cease even when their visits were inevitable, and the principle reasons given continued to fall with remarkable consistency into the 'economic' and 'moral' categories cited by Jenkinson and described in the *John Bull* article. Articles claimed that 'casual American turns' often failed to pay their Income Tax, thus defrauding British society (*Daily Graphic*, 6 March 1923:7), but the most frequent reason given for the opposition of the importation of African-Americans was that they would be putting British performers out of work:

> London's ordinary white actors and actresses are naturally gravely concerned about the question of unemployment which will be accentuated by the wholesale importation of negro artists into a country where they do not belong. (*Daily Graphic*, 5 March 1923:7)

Moral objections focused particularly on Butt's proposals to include black performers in a cabaret setting. Albert Voyce, Chairman of the Variety Artists Federation stated that:

> We have no objection to American artists coming to England ... . There are also in England negro turns, most respectable and most decent, who behave themselves and keep their place. But we view with the greatest apprehension a cabaret where black artists would actually mix with white folks at tables. (*Daily Graphic*, 6 March 1923:7)

Recalling the sexual jealousy of black men in the post-war period described by Jenkinson, Voyce goes on to detail what he considered to be undesirable relationships that developed between white women and black men of the *In Dahomey* company, suggesting that this might be the result of Butt's cabaret where members of both creeds could mix: 'some of the black chorus men [in *In Dahomey*] were spoiled by the kindness they received here. Some of them stayed in England, and for years afterwards lived on the earnings of white women.' (*Daily Graphic*, 6 March 1923:7). Swaffer also indicates the disgust felt by many at the time about mixed race relationships, even on film: 'No white woman film actress would act in a scene where a negro had to touch her, or make love to her, and, if she did, the film would be too revolting to show.' (*Daily Graphic*, 6 March 1923:7).

Black companies had already been blamed for unemployment and the decline of moral standards before the plantation shows had even opened in London and provided convenient scapegoats for problems that in reality they did little to exacerbate. Both revues included a substantial 'white' portion, and did not put great numbers of native performers out of work. In the case of *The Rainbow*, the black performers were only on stage for fifteen or twenty minutes, and Sir Alfred Butt pointed out that 'There is no "scandal" of coloured artistes. The "scandal" is that an attempt is being made to couple their engagement in this country with the appalling problem of the unemployed' (*Daily Graphic*, 10 March 1923). Butt refuted the charge that immoral activity would result from the Empire cabaret, stating that 'the cabaret is, and was, so designed and constructed from the first that all artists are divided by a railing from the audience, and it is an improper and absolutely unjustifiable statement to say that they would have any opportunity of mixing with the audience' (*Daily Graphic*, 10 March 1923).

In the context of the fervour of the surrounding debate, it is somewhat ironic that Butt's proposed cabaret, despite eventually obtaining the necessary permission from London County Council, never opened (Rye, 1988b:8) and also that *The Rainbow* made little impression and generally received poor reviews when it opened on 3 April 1923. The critic in the *Referee* wrote: 'To me ... "The Rainbow" as it stands (or stood) was simply vacant. There seemed to be no heart or meaning in it' (8 April 1923:8). Nor was the short plantation segment any better received. The *Daily Graphic* reported that 'The revue itself was mediocre, and the much-advertised nigger scene, "Plantation Days", unnecessary. Twenty-six niggers of various shades came on and made a lot of noise like rough children at a treat' (4 April 1923). Many reviews devoted considerable space to the incident that occurred at the end of the first performance of *The Rainbow*, where as the curtain fell a comedian, Jack Edge, shouted 'I was engaged as a low comedian in this piece, and I wasn't given a chance'. As Albert De Courville, the producer, came onto the stage there were shouts from the audience of 'We want Jack Edge' and 'Send the niggers back.' (*Encore*, 5 April 1923:12; *Stage*, 5 April 1923:14; *Daily Graphic*, 4 April 1923.) Cochran's revue *Dover Street to Dixie* opened on 31 May 1923 and was more successful. The second half performed entirely by the black company from Salvin's was generally considered to be better than the white part of the show, and Florence Mills was particularly praised:

> There was a little hissing; but they quickly carried their audience with them. They are so fresh and vigorous. To say they dance "like mad" is just to speak the truth ... above all, there is Florence Mills, a lithe, slender girl with eyes full of expression, a sweet voice, now strident, as when she reproaches a lover tending to slack off, now pathetic, and a way of dancing that makes a fool of perpetual motion! These plantation people made a huge success, and deserved it. (*Era*, 6 June 1923:11)

It is clear that both *The Rainbow* and *Dover Street to Dixie* presented conventional black stage entertainment, signified to the audience through the typical plantation setting. A review of *The Rainbow* suggests that the production presented nothing new in the way of black entertainment, despite its use of 'authentic' American black performers:

> "Plantation Days" ... is just usual darky song-and-dance entertainment ... . It would seem to have been a waste of time to bring these performers "all the way from the Southern States of America". There should surely have been enough resident coloured folk in London able to do the same thing with the same lack of distinction. (*Stage*, 5 April 1923:14)

These revues perpetuated blackface stereotypes, especially as in both cases the black performers were deliberately presented as a contrast to a white company. *Dover Street to Dixie* included the cakewalk, made popular in Britain by *In Dahomey* twenty years earlier (*Stage*, 7 June 1923:17), and a 'Jonah man' figure, typical of the minstrel show and delineated in *In Dahomey* by Bert Williams, was portrayed by Shelton Brooks: 'a very black faced droll dry comedian in a cleverly rendered down-trodden worm-husband number, "He Loves It"' (*Encore*, 7 June 1923:9-10). Similarly, the description of Florence Mills as 'a dusky damsel with flashing eyes and gleaming white teeth' (*Stage*, 7 June 1923:17) recalls the exaggerated facial characteristics of blackface minstrelsy. Reviewers also focused on the 'natural' exuberance and primitive tendencies of the black company, shown particularly through dancing in which women were 'displaying large tracts of brown flesh in the emphatically energetic performance of a number styled "Indian Habits"' (*Stage*, 7 June 1923:17).

The music of the plantation sections made a significant impression on the reviewers of both shows. Each black company brought its own band to Britain, led by James P. Johnson (*The Rainbow)* and Will Vodery (*Dover Street to Dixie*), which performed on stage as part of the act, rather than in the pit: 'The scene in the second half is laid in Dixie, with the Robert E. Lee moored against the landing stage with Will Vodery's coloured band arranged beside the side barrier.' (*Encore*, 6 July 1923:9-10). Reviewers did associate the music performed with 'jazz', noting that although the style of the music was familiar, the sound was unusual: 'There is a band, of course, but its "jazzing" sounds different.' (*Era*, 6 June 1923:11). Specifically, many reviewers noted the volume of sound that the bands produced:

> ... there was a band of nine that made a lot of noise. (*Daily Graphic*, 4 April 23)

> Much of the ear-splitting music, mainly of the Jazz order, is performed by Will Vodery's Plantation Orchestra (including Johnny Dunn), the band, controlled by Vodery without the use of a bâton, being seated beyond a palisade to the stage right of a picturesquely-presented Southern Plantation, and the trombone-players, in particular, striving to produce the maximum of noise, to be distinguished from melody. (*Stage*, 7 June 1923:17)

It seems incredible that the band in *The Rainbow* came all the way to Britain only to perform in a twenty-minute section in a revue show, but under the terms of their work permits they were apparently restricted from doing much else. Sir Montague Barlow, Minister of Labour, stated in answer to a question on the subject of the importation of coloured artists to Britain in the House of Commons: 'The permits were issued upon the condition that the troupe give a stage performance only. They will not play dance music without obtaining the prior consent of the Minister of Labour.' (*Performer*, 21 March 1923:5). In *Dover Street to Dixie*, in which the plantation entertainment took up the whole of the second half, the white orchestra even remained in the pit to play the national anthem at the end of the performance. (*Encore*, 6 July 1923:9-10). Nevertheless, a Musicians' Union Official had stated that 'There are something like two thousand of our union out of work. Many of them are unemployed because of the introduction of American negro bands, now in favour with certain dance clubs. British musicians could play quite as well' (*Daily Graphic*, 6 March 1923:7). This statement, made before the black companies had even arrived in Britain, shows the ease with which African-American musicians were blamed for British unemployment problems, yet it seems unlikely that black performers alone would have posed a significant threat to the livelihood of British musicians. As the activities of black musicians appeared to be sufficiently restricted and white pit orchestras were retained, there was little reason for the Musicians' Union to protest about the plantation revues, other than as a continuation of union opposition to foreign musicians dating back to the start of the First World War (Ehrlich, 1985:188) or in support of other entertainment unions.

Whilst these extensive debates over the importation of black performers were taking place, Paul Whiteman and his band arrived in Britain. Having learnt of the intention to engage Whiteman to perform in Britain, the *Encore* reported that:

> ... the Musicians' Union is up in arms that American bands should be imported into this country when there are so many of the home variety waiting for work. The Union declares that its opposition is not levelled against the musicians as musicians, but as potential ousters from employment of members of the Union. (*Encore*, 1 March 1923:3)

The opposition to the employment of this group of white Americans in Britain did not receive nearly such widespread publicity as the situation with regard to the plantation revue companies. This may have been for two reasons; firstly, that the unemployment situation for British musicians was not as desperate as that of actors, especially variety performers whose audience tended more towards the working class that were most severely affected by the economic depression and unemployment in Britain at this time. Secondly, this gives additional weight to the idea that it was *black* American performers that were most convenient scapegoats for the problems of unemployment amongst British performers. It is ironic that visiting white American bands such as Whiteman's, that represented more direct competition to native British bands due to their stylistic similarities, were given much more freedom than black groups and this was as a result of the contacts that such bands could develop in the highest ranks of society:

Lord Mountbatten gave a party for the Prince of Wales, at which only thirty-two guests were present. All were either direct descendants of the throne or related to the throne. The Prince, whom you may know better as the Duke of Windsor, went out of his way to put me instantly at ease with a flattering comment about our music. A warm friendship developed between us and I played at many parties at his request. (Whiteman, (1948) from http://www.shellac.org/wams/wpaulw1.html)

The work permits for Whiteman's visit were secured only through the direct intervention by the Prince of Wales (Rayno, 2003:64), and furthermore, although the Whiteman band were initially restricted to appearing only in *Brighter London*, pressure from the American government on the British Ministry of Labour in response to a telegram sent by Whiteman's manager allowed the band to perform for dancing at a variety of venues (Rayno, 2003:67). A report in the *Encore* under the heading 'Victory for British Musicians' describes a compromise agreement that had been reached between the Musicians' Union and the Ministry of Labour whereby 'foreign conductors bringing a foreign band must engage British musicians on a 50-50 basis'. In addition, if the Whiteman band was to undertake engagements 'other than for theatrical purposes, a band consisting of British musicians, of the same size as Mr. Whiteman's own band, under his personal training and supervision, should be employed' (*Encore*, 22 March 1923).

Although Whiteman did adhere to these conditions, it is clear that his band was much less restricted than the plantation revue bands performing in Britain contemporaneously. Cochran noticed the disparity between the government treatment of Whiteman's group and Vodery's Plantation Orchestra that performed in his show *Dover Street to Dixie*, and wrote in a letter to the *Star* newspaper 'the Ministry of Labour has one rule for the rich and another for the poor' (*Star*, 28 July 1923:11). Apparently, Cochran was hoping to offset the high costs of importing the company from Salvin's with additional income from Vodery's band playing for dances in the winter months. He argued that the decision of the Ministry of Labour to restrict the work of the band to the revue performances only would precipitate the closure of *Dover Street to Dixie*, thus putting the many British actors and employees involved in the show out of work. The Ministry of Labour stated to the *Star* reporter that 'It had been represented to us that the incoming of alien bands is acting in a way which results in employment for British bands being less than would otherwise be the case', saying that since the arrival of the Whiteman band in March they had tightened the conditions relating to the importation of 'alien' performers, and Cochran was the first to feel the effect of this (*Star*, 28 July 1923:11).

This Ministry statement is significant not only because it indicates the start of the increasing governmental restrictions upon visiting American performers, but also because it suggests that before mid-1923 there were possibilities for 'alien' bands and musicians to perform in venues other than that of their main engagements. As noted in Chapter 6, musicians in the Southern Syncopated Orchestra had to remain part of the group or return immediately to America under the terms of their work permits. However, this does not seem to have been rigorously enforced and there is evidence that the musicians themselves were unaware of these restrictions. Several musicians are known to have remained working in Britain having left the SSO. Similarly, the conditions and work permits that were issued to the black musicians performing in *The Rainbow*, presented just prior to *Dover Street to Dixie*, did not totally prohibit the band from playing for dancing, and it seems that at that point there was opportunity for further negotiation with the Ministry. This could explain Ellis Jackson's recollection of:

> Fred and Adele Astaire appearing at Ciro's Club accompanied by James P. Johnson and His Orchestra. He specifically recalled Addington Major being present. He also recalled Wellman Braud sitting in at Moody's Club in Tottenham Court Road. (Rye, 1988b:11)

It is difficult to ascertain exactly how strictly any work permit conditions for musicians were adhered to, and it seems possible that musicians from Johnson's and Vodery's bands might also have performed more frequently than they were known to have done during their time in Britain.

In summary, events surrounding the two plantation revues of 1923 had several important implications for black musicians in Britain. The revues themselves continued to present blackface stereotypes within a typical 'plantation' setting, 'but sought also to present an image of up-to-the-minute Harlem sophistication, sometimes with risqué overtones.' (Rye, 1990a:52). Thus, the sentimental idea of the 'Old South' still existed, but now the exotic appeal of the 'primitive' Negro had become more highly charged and sexual. This is commensurate with the increasing opposition to black entertainment on moral grounds, an important factor in the 1919 race riots and articulated in contemporary articles that were critical of the importation of black performers. This demonstrates the influence of the well-established, and now re-affirmed, blackface stereotypes in the treatment by some white Britons of black people in real life. Black performers were also blamed for the unemployment of British performers, again recalling the chief causes of the race riots. This idea was applied to musicians, although in reality the limited employment of visiting American black musicians had little effect on the situation. Although the government's treatment of visiting black companies was not overtly racist initially, it was clearly under increasing pressure from several trade unions which restricted the performances of most visiting African-American musicians to revue shows, where British performers could not so easily be substituted, thus perpetuating the vicious circle of racism rooted in stereotypes.

Black musicians responded to the open expression of racism in Britain during the controversy surrounding revues and the resulting increasingly restrictive government policies. Several black performers, even those who had been resident in Britain for some time, began either to move to the Continent, particularly to Paris, or to return to America. This was clearly a recognized trend, as Seabrook commented in 1924 that 'Coloured musicians, however, are no longer the vogue. London has grown tired of them, and most of these minstrels have gone to the Continent, and particularly to the Riviera.' (Moseley, 1924:138.) Nevertheless, there remained a notable black population in Britain in the 1920s, particularly in cosmopolitan central London, which was largely isolated from the flash points for race riots in poorer areas and at the docks. There were opportunities for musicians from these communities to perform, as government labour restrictions were vague once American musicians had gained entry to Britain, or not applicable to those of the black population who were British citizens. The disintegration of the SSO had meant that many non-American black musicians were employed in the group and had the opportunity to learn about jazz techniques first-hand, and it was from a pool of these musicians working at Moody's Club that Vorzanger's successful band was formed (Rye, 1990b:147).

The opportunities for black musicians in Britain at this time were limited and artistically restrictive. The public attitude towards black performers, influenced by the media, meant that they did not have the same opportunities as white musicians to perform at the most lucrative venues, and also risked becoming victims of racial abuse like the black company in *The Rainbow*. Black musicians were affected by the prevailing popular dance style of the period, which meant that even if they could secure a booking in a significant public arena, they would probably have to make musical compromises, like Leon Abbey at the Olympia ballroom. Rye comments that 'In general ... the black small bands seem to have confined their activities very largely to London clubs, and possibly this limited social and geographical base contributed to the decline in their fortunes after 1922' (1990a:51), but in context of the events of 1923 and their long-term impact this is hardly surprising. Black musicians could perform in certain clubs with more musical freedom and for racially tolerant audiences, and it is tempting to propose, for example, that the musicians in Vorzanger's band played popular dance music at the East Ham Palais for financial reasons, and then returned to Moody's to jam. The black jazz musicians that remained in Britain became associated with the notorious London nightclub scene, and this had a significant effect upon the image of jazz in Britain.

Many nightclubs had sprung up even within the relatively small area of Soho in London's West End in the post-war period, an area that Robert Fabian, a policeman in the 1920s, called 'The Square Mile of Vice ... where you can buy anything and see everything' (1954:10). There were in fact many different sorts of club in London at this time, embodying varying degrees of 'vice', and Seabrook, in his guide to London nightlife in *Brightest Spots in Brighter London*, wrote that 'London night clubs are not at all to be avoided as seats of Satan' (Moseley, 1924:137). At one end of the spectrum there were the underground clubs: 'There is the common night club kept by common folk and their dupes; there is the night club where gambling is the chief *motif*; and there is the night house to which the dope fiends and their victims resort.' (Moseley, 1924:137.) Fabian describes a 'shady' club that he visited in his official capacity as a police officer, which was considerably less glamorous:

> The club was up back stairs ... . It was just one room. The floor was bare and held half a dozen rickety tables with green wooden chairs ... . The "bar" was a trestle table across one corner, covered with green baize and a few strips of tinsel. (Fabian, 1954:21)

Then there were venues that Kohn describes as 'just above ground' and 'legitimate but tawdry' (1992:123). Murray's Club was probably typical of this sector of

London's nightclubs, as it managed 'to be regarded as both racy and reputable'. Although he attracted an exclusive and wealthy upper-class clientele, Jack May, the club's American proprietor, was also accused of inducing girls to smoke opium 'for vice or money or both' (Kohn, 1992:32). Finally, there were clubs such as Rector's, the Kit Cat and Ciro's, from which the BBC presented outside broadcasts of dance music in the second half of the decade, that were considered to be, at least outwardly, 'respectable'. This was probably because the more expensive and exclusive clubs had correspondingly more elaborate systems in place to protect the integrity and privacy of clients, for example, in the event of a police raid. The Metropolitan Police noted that conducting undercover work in clubs that 'cater for the richer classes, and where care is exercised as to the admission of members and strangers, it is very difficult, and sometimes practically impossible.' (TNA: PRO MEPO2/2053.)

Nevertheless, in the 1920s 'the very words "night-club" immediately suggest to some people the picture of something degraded and disreputable' (Meyrick, 1933:88), due to the fact that for most of the general public, knowledge of nightclubs was restricted to stories of scandalous activities that were published in newspaper reports. One case in particular gave significant negative publicity to nightclubs in the national press: the death of Freda Kempton. Kempton was employed as a dance hostess at Brett's club, run by Kate Meyrick, the most famous nightclub proprietor of the 1920s. Hostesses were employed to dance with rich men at the club in return for substantial tips and the possibility of a good marriage to one of their clients (Meyrick, 1933:210). Kempton inevitably became addicted to cocaine, a drug that 'answered the nightclub dancers' need to stay appealing and lively through long nights' (Kohn, 1992:124), and was kept supplied with the drug by the notorious Brilliant Chang. She died from a cocaine overdose in March 1922 (Kohn, 1992:128).

Following Freda Kempton's death, a 'war on drugs' was declared in the national press. Articles were published that sought to link her death with the availability of drugs through the presence of foreign dealers such as Chang in West End 'dance dens', resulting in unprecedented coverage of nightclub activities (Kohn, 1992:134). In a report in the *Daily Express* headed 'Nights in the Dancing Dens – When the Chinaman takes the floor' (14 March 1922:1), a reporter visited an underground club. Although he did not actually witness any drug use, his description of the scene involving dancing, alcoholic intoxication and the theatrical entrance of 'a Chinaman' presented a glimpse into another world and established a vivid image of the nightclub scene for the general public that had no personal experience of it. A cartoon was also published which shows a skeletal figure of Death as a doorkeeper to the 'Dope Dance Club', representing the fatal link between nightclub dancing and drugs that apparently 'caused' Kempton's death. Only two months later a film called *Cocaine* was released that disseminated similar imagery on the cinema screen and led to further newspaper articles on drugs and nightclubs. A civil servant reported that in the film 'The life of a Night Club is given in vivid detail. Many of the scenes are rather lurid and in some cases border on the indecent.' (TNA: PRO HO 45/11599.)

Although the image of nightclubs described in newspapers tended to be exaggerated, sensationalist and presented in such a way that it was seen as representative of all establishments, there were elements of truth contained within it. The clientele of clubs was very mixed, other than in the case of the classiest establishments, an indication that the underworld of London was separate from the hierarchy and regulation of 'normal' society. Meyrick describes a 'shady' nightclub 'patronised by the most undesirable types ... men of a really criminal cast, accompanied by pretty but flashy girls ... this dubious resort enjoyed a considerable vogue for a time among fashionable men of the West End' (1933:87). Criminal activity was rife in nightclubs of all types, and police records indicate that no establishments were above suspicion and therefore subject to police raids. This is not to say that there was not a certain understanding between the police and some proprietors, for example, Fabian knew that there was a secret exit from the 43 club to save the embarrassment of important patrons, such as politicians and royalty, in a raid, but he trusted Kate Meyrick not let anybody use it who was 'better in the hands of the law' (Fabian, 1954:12). Numerous instances of many different clubs being fined for selling liquor outside licensed hours or without a licence altogether and also holding dances without a licence can be found in police files of the period. West End clubs were potential targets for gangsters, and in her autobiography, Meyrick describes how these criminals, disguised in evening dress, terrorised doormen, often refused to pay for drinks and even used guns inside her club in the early twenties (1933:27-8) stating that 'in those days London was just as bad as Chicago, if not worse' (1933:44).

Despite the prominence of illegal activities of this sort, the primary purpose of nightclubs was to cater for the predominant vogue for dancing at this time. Meyrick described the centrality of dance to nightclub life: 'Everyone in London, young and old alike, had caught the dancing craze; almost any place with a respectable band and a decent floor was bound to make money.' (Meyrick, 1933:23.) Assuming that most of the nightclubs in Soho and the West End in the 1920s hired a band of some description, a great number of musicians must have been employed within the 'Square Mile of Vice' at this time. One way in which the status of a particular club was gauged, and can continue to be evaluated retrospectively, was the type of band that the management employed. The large, upper-class clubs could afford to engage and publicize large, well-known ensembles and American bands, usually consisting of white musicians. However, as the locations and names of underground clubs, never mind the bands that performed there, were never publicized in the contemporary media, the musicians that worked in this environment remain largely anonymous today.

Although it is difficult to establish exactly which musicians and bands played in underground clubs, in the light of the available evidence certain hypotheses can be proposed. The limited descriptions of music in underground clubs suggest that the music was certainly different to the conventional British 'dance music'. In any event, the restricted size of many of the clubs would have prohibited the use of a large 'dance orchestra' on practical grounds. The undercover reporter for the *Daily Express* described how in the 'dancing den' that he visited 'the band crashed out a really good foxtrot – a band 50 per cent. better than that in many a well-known and irreproachable dance club.' (14 March 1922:1). Even the music of Teddy Brown's band, an ensemble that was broadcast on the BBC, when employed by Meyrick in the 'just above ground' 43, 'possessed a subtle appeal that carried everyone away with it. Sometimes it was insinuatingly soft and crooning, sometimes it would swell up into a triumphant riot of crashing sound.' (Meyrick, 1933:156). These descriptions recall the difference between familiar dance music and that of Johnson's and Vodery's bands noted by reviewers of the plantation revues.

Whilst black people were suffering increasing racism in mainstream British society, there is strong evidence that they were probably much more welcome in the alternative communities of underworld of London. Indeed, the nightclub scene represented 'the negative image of daytime society; its hours the reverse of the conventional order, its values attuned to the pleasure principle, its economy only tenuously and dubiously connected with the authorised fabric of wealth creation.' (Kohn, 1992:125). Seabrook noted the racial mix in nightclubs: 'The types of frequenters are as diverse as are their races, colours and creeds.' (Moseley, 1924:138), and the areas of London in which there were many nightclubs, such as west of Tottenham Court Road, and the Seven Dials area of Covent Garden, were 'favoured by black men in particular.' (Kohn, 1992:141). Fabian describes that as a policeman on the beat in the West End 'I had a great deal to do with the African and West Indian boys in the West End, and got along with them very well' (1954:14). He describes the existence of 'coloured clubs', such as the 'Big Apple', and gives a fascinating insight into the music that could be heard in such places:

> I learnt all about jazz, boogie-woogie and calypso from my coloured friends years before they became known outside the murky little "coloured clubs". When we were all in the mood – which was often – I would persuade them to give me a "jam session" that would have opened new doors to any white musician, who had cared to spare the time to listen, in those days. (Fabian, 1954:15)

The nightclub scene was clearly a law unto itself, and it seems likely that proprietors that were regularly prepared to run the risk of supplying alcohol illegally would turn a blind eye to other indiscretions such as employing musicians without valid work permits. In addition, American musicians that continued to visit Britain with plantation-type revues or dance bands would have been able to 'sit-in' informally at clubs. Kate Meyrick, explaining how a night-club's standing can be indicated by behaviour at a police raid, describes that when 'one inferior establishment' was raided 'The members of the band vaulted their 'fence' and dived through a trap-door to a cellar below – why I have never been able to understand, since it seems unlikely that they would have been involved in any trouble.' (1933:89.) Meyrick does not state the race or nationality of the musicians, but it is possible they may have been working in the club illegally.

Whatever the nature of the music performed and the precise statistics on the numbers of black musicians working in London clubs, illegally or otherwise, it is clear that the negative aspects of blackface stereotypes, which had continued to be enforced through the plantation revues and racist attacks, fitted particularly well within an environment which was publicly perceived to embody immoral and decadent behaviour. Dark-skinned foreigners such as Eddie Manning and Brilliant Chang were principally blamed for supplying drugs to vulnerable young white girls, and in this context, it is interesting that Moody's Club, known to feature black musicians, was subject to an extensive series of detailed police observations soon after Kempton's highly publicized death (TNA: PRO MEPO2/2053). The increasing presence of black people in the underground nightclub environment in the 1920s meant that they could be held responsible for its associated social problems, just as black companies on the revue stage were being blamed for the unemployment amongst British performers.

Jazz began to develop a specific image and status in Britain in the 1920s, and was increasingly recognized as black music as simultaneously racist attitudes developed in Britain towards Americans, and black Americans in particular. The black origins of jazz had been highlighted by some people as a negative aspect of the music even prior to the 1920s. As has been observed in Chapter 2, although few songs of 1919 depicted black performers of jazz, those that do are derogatory or patronizing in nature, and the black origins of jazz were generally only mentioned in contemporary articles by those who wished to condemn jazz. Adverse criticism of jazz based on race became more common now that jazz was more specifically identified with black musicians. Mendl, in a chapter entitled 'The Dislike of Jazz Music' in *The Appeal of Jazz*, suggests that people in Britain were averse to jazz in the twenties because of their 'antipathy towards everything connected with the nigger' (1927:71). He also notes that the principal objections to jazz were that it was sensual, noisy, stupid and grotesque: a description that correlates with the typical negative perception of black people.

In conclusion, in the early 1920s, jazz was established by the Savoy Hotel and BBC, albeit indirectly, as African-American music at a time when black Americans were unpopular in Britain. The Savoy Hotel presented civilized white 'dance music' rather than black 'hot' jazz, and the process of 'symphonizing' was representative of the white civilizing of black American jazz which rendered it acceptable to be broadcast. This formulation of what was identified as an improved, British style of popular dance music diminished the significance of the American performers and the understanding of the origins of the music in Britain. Several factors meant that black musicians were unable to redress the balance between the prominence of white dance music and under-representation of black jazz in Britain in the 1920s. Black performers were still expected to conform in some way to the long-standing minstrel stereotypes, and furthermore governmental restrictions meant that it was generally difficult for them to obtain work permits perform non-racially specific entertainment. Although the government tightened regulations for all visiting performers, in practice it can be seen that black musicians were more restricted than their white colleagues. As circumstances encouraged black musicians to seek refuge in the nightclubs of London's underworld, an autonomous community that represented a mirror image of the conventions of mainstream society, they became linked with vice.

It is hardly surprising that according to Mendl, jazz was regularly denounced in the 1920s as 'vulgar, coarse and crude and ugly; it is described as a debased product and its popularity is said to be the sign of a decadent age' (1927:25). A common British understanding of jazz in the 1920s is epitomized in J.B. Souter's painting, *The Breakdown* (see Figure 7.2). The painting depicts a black man in evening dress playing the saxophone. In the 1920s, as we have seen, jazz was increasingly identified as a black music, and the saxophone was adopted as a distinctive new musical timbre and a clear visual symbol of modern dance music, hence this figure represents 'jazz'. A naked white woman, a shingled, androgynous figure, dances to the music of the saxophonist, representing 1920s youth. The saxophone player is seated on a shattered Greek statue, possibly Minerva, a goddess associated with virginity, wisdom and the arts, traditional values with which the figures in the painting are apparently in disregard. The corrupting influence of jazz as a black music is clearly implied in this painting.[5] Similarly, it is clear that due to the increasing representation of jazz as black music, and the concurrent move of black musicians into the nightclubs, by the end of the decade jazz was firmly positioned, metaphorically and literally, as the musical accompaniment to the other perceived evils of the underworld of London.

---

[5] Souter, a Scottish artist, submitted *The Breakdown* to the Royal Academy. The picture was included in the 1926 Summer Exhibition and viewed by George V and commended as 'a work of great promise executed with a considerable degree of excellence' by the President of the Royal Academy, Frank Dicksee (Matthew, 1990). However, after only five days the picture was removed from the exhibition under instruction from the Colonial Office, as the subject 'was considered to be obnoxious to British subjects living abroad in daily contact with a coloured population' (Royal Academy Annual Report, 1926:13), showing continued governmental concern for imperial integrity.

Figure 7.2   J.B. Souter: *The Breakdown* (1926) (from RA Illustrated
               Catalogue, 1926, by permission of the Royal Academy of Arts
               and the Souter Estate)

Chapter 8

Hot Jazz: Jack Hylton, Bert Firman and Fred Elizalde

Jazz, having been absorbed and often suppressed within mainstream popular dance music in Britain in the early 1920s, once more began to develop a clearer individual identity around the time of the introduction of electrical recording, meaning that 'jazz' and 'dance music' were no longer synonymous. Initially this identity was constructed through social as well as musical factors, and the association of jazz with African-Americans and the notorious underworld environment of London had negative consequences for the serious appreciation and understanding of the music. However, the increasing availability of good quality recordings allowed much wider access to jazz than was formerly permitted by London's nightclubs. Jazz could now be analyzed and understood in much greater depth by critics, enthusiasts, amateur and professional musicians that formed a relatively small, but active, audience for the music in Britain. The critical responses to jazz in magazines and books that resulted from the awareness of its musical characteristics that have been discussed extensively in Chapter 3 are complemented this chapter, which will focus on an exploration of the musical presence and responses to hot jazz in Britain.

> I who had danced so often to Herman Darewski, had listened-in so enthusiastically to the Savoy Havanas, and was so fond of *Kitten on the Keys*, as played by my Jewish friends, had never heard anything like the terrific strident, hard, highly-organised machine jazz of Red Nichols and His Five Pennies, Miff Mole's Molers, Venuti's Blue Four, Rollini's Goofus Washboards to say nothing of the negro bands. Even the titles of this new music were different ... *Clarinet Marmalade*, *Get with*, *Buddy's Habits*, *Mental strain at dawn*, *Boneyard Shuffle*, *Prayin' the Blues*, *Black and blue bottom* and *That's no bargain*. I felt that I had never heard a clarinet before, never felt the real impact of a drum-beat, never grasped the tone of a trumpet. The imagination of these instrumentalists, making their dazzling hot-chorus arabesques on the slender basis of a melody which was often completely lost to the ear, this lifted them into a category quite different from the palais bands and Savoy players. Hot jazz was a thing apart, and after I had once got my ear attuned to it I could never again care two hoots for "sweet society" playing or the commercial product of ordinary English bands. (Nicolson, 1941:64)

As the distinction between jazz and dance music developed, the word jazz was rarely seen in print without the prefix 'hot', or the music was referred to by 'hot' alone, to distinguish it from 'sweet', 'legitimate' or 'symphonic' styles of popular music that were often more commercially oriented: 'we never talked of "jazz".

Dance music was either "hot" or "straight"! In Britain we then had little knowledge of jazz history.' (Francis, March 1974:4.) Throughout this period, the growing distinction between hot jazz and dance music caused dilemmas for bandleaders whatever their musical preferences. Even for those inclined towards hot jazz, there was a need to compromise by playing 'sweeter' arrangements, including ubiquitous waltzes and vocal numbers, to ensure that they would retain bookings in the most prestigious upper class venues. However, there was also a need for the large dance bands that were comfortably resident in such places to incorporate some hot jazz, as this was the latest trend in popular music. McKibben comments that 'jazz was now going the way of classical music, with a decreasing audience for "pure" jazz and an increasing audience for an eclectic jazz which was liked simply as an element in the much larger category of commercial popular music.' (1998:401) Thus, the tendency of dilution in the British responses to American musical culture that has been traced in previous chapters can continue to be observed holistically in Britain in this period.

This chapter will consider the influence of hot styles on British musicians, by way of direct contact with American musicians and through records. The activities and reception of the hot groups of Bert Firman and Fred Elizalde in the late 1920s will be considered in depth, but in addition, the reactions to hot styles by the dance bands and the cultural establishment will be examined to provide context for their work. The importance of personal contact between American musicians and their British counterparts that occurred throughout the period cannot be underestimated as this was vital for the development of jazz musicianship and criticism which would sustain jazz in Britain through the restrictions on the performances of American musicians that were imposed by the government in 1935. The continuation of the opposition to 'alien' performers in this period served to limit such contact and some dangerous precedents in the reciprocity of musicians between Britain and America were established by 1930.

The Meaning of 'Hot'

Cross-referencing recordings with contemporary comment shows that the word 'hot' was generally used from around the mid-1920s to identify musical qualities that are considered inherent in a modern understanding of jazz. Initially, 'hot' was primarily applied to the rhythmic aspects of the music, which were often enhanced by homophonic scoring and the omission of sustained string or saxophone harmonies and legato melodic lines that could be heard in dance music. The first issue of *Melody Maker* identified the latest releases by Hylton's Kit-Cat Club band under the leadership of American saxophonist Al Starita as 'red-hot syncopated rhythm with a good deal of "dirt" thrown in' to 'appease the appetites of "jazz" lovers' (January 1926:31). One of these numbers was *Riverboat Shuffle*, the Hoagy Carmichael number first recorded by the Wolverines a year earlier than the Kit-Cat version. On the latter, the band mainly plays in rhythmic unison in a rather sluggish tempo, as opposed to the vigorous New Orleans-style polyphony and driving 'stomp' of the former. Most notably, the 'swung' quavers are much more exact on the Kit-Cat version whereas the Wolverines utilize a more laid-back style. The Kit-Cat arrangement is imbued with novelty effects that were expected of jazz in Britain in this period, including numerous breaks played by different unusual instruments, such as pizzicato violin and Wurlitzer organ, and the violin solo and banjo breaks are also typical. The trumpet solo paraphrases Beiderbecke on the Wolverines recording, but Ted Heath's trombone solo seems more innovative and he attempts to push the tempo along.

The term 'dirt' often appeared alongside 'hot' to describe the particular timbre of the blues inflections that were incorporated into the melodic line or harmony alongside hot syncopated rhythms: 'If you like the "dirtiest" stuff played really "hot", the Memphis Five have catered for you' (*Melody Maker*, June 1926:53). Groups that were regarded as being hot were even criticized for a lack of 'blue' features, which were clearly expected:

> Of the American combinations recording for this Company, *The Goofus Five* again stands out as being something exceptional. This combination is red-hot in its rendering, but is becoming much more orthodox in its harmony. Personally, I am rather sorry about this. Although one could not stand extremely "blue" harmony continually from every dance band, enthusiasts seem to look for it in a combination like the Goofus Five, and its absence takes away some of the individuality. If there is an advantage in the absence of "blueness" from such a combination, it is that its records are more easily understandable to the man who is only used to "legitimate" scoring. (*Melody Maker*, January 1927:141)

The importance of soloists in hot music was increasingly recognized, and hot breaks, solos and ensemble choruses were transcribed from records and analyzed in *Melody Maker* (see for example, articles on hot trumpet and trombone based on the Cotton Pickers and Ross Gorman's Orchestra in April 1926). Joe Crossman, an American saxophonist working in Britain, expressed the perception that improvisation was reliant on notation:

> There are two distinct manners in which extemporisation is obtained. The first is by embellishing or altering the score at sight; the second is by scoring out the embellishment or alterations beforehand ... the more instruments extemporising and the "hotter" the style of the rendering the more essential it is that the parts are written out in advance ... . (*Melody Maker*, September 1926:57)

'Hot' was therefore regarded as an effect that could be added in performances of popular music through small spontaneous alterations to the printed parts by soloists and, more significantly, through the style of the arrangement. The results of this perception were solos that basically paraphrased the melody, and an increasing emphasis on virtuosity and novelty effects in ensemble hot choruses, as discussed in relation to *Riverboat Shuffle* above. Advertisements appeared in *Melody Maker* with offers to provide notated hot choruses that could be inserted into arrangements: 'write stating instrument and tune' (October 1926:30).

American Hot Jazz in Britain

Although *Melody Maker* might be criticized for excluding or reviewing negatively certain, especially black, American bands, the publication included increasingly more American records in its reviews section. The content of early issues of *Melody Maker* and *Rhythm* seems to be representative of the general British experience of American jazz in the mid-1920s, which was based almost exclusively on familiarity with the recordings of white dance bands and small groups. Harry Francis for example was exposed to records featuring 'Beiderbecke, Nicholls [*sic.*], Mole, the Dorseys, Lang, Venuti, Rollini' (March 1974:7). Similarly, Spike Hughes initially encountered jazz through the Red Nichols and the Five Pennies and subsequently listened to Bix Beiderbecke, Eddie Lang, Joe Venuti and Adrian Rollini in 1927 (1946:308). Records made by Fletcher Henderson, some of which included the early work of Louis Armstrong, were an important early exception to the domination of white groups.

American hot jazz was most often represented in Britain by recordings made by the numerous five-piece groups of white musicians in New York (listed in Charters and Kunstadt, 1981:124), such as the Original Memphis Five. This represents a continuation of the trend for such ensembles that had been established by the success of the Original Dixieland Jazz Band. These two groups had been active in New York contemporaneously prior to the ODJB's visit to Britain, dividing the city and the repertoire between them (Sudhalter, 1999:106). Whilst the ODJB were absent in London, the Memphis Five developed their musical style and had always incorporated popular songs into their repertoire, an approach in line with the prevailing fashion of the 1920s. Sudhalter comments that retrospectively the Memphis Five fill a perceived hiatus in American jazz history between 1919 and 1922 (1999:105). Similarly, such bands were vital in presenting British audiences with a transition between the music of the ODJB and more modern hot jazz in the 1920s. The Memphis Five releases referred to in the 1926 review cited above, *Chinese Blues* and *Taint Cold*, are a hybrid of the collective improvisational Dixieland style, incorporating individual solos as well as some more rigidly homophonic arranged parts.

This amalgamation of styles demonstrates the development of the 'Original Fives' in New York during the 1920s into a style sometimes referred to as 'hot jazz chamber music', implying a small group version of 'symphonic syncopation'. Groups that began as 'fives' expanded and by the end of the decade frequently included more than five members although often retaining the numerical designation regardless. Recordings made by groups such as Red Nichols and his Five Pennies were good examples of a style which was 'derived from the hotter music that the Original Dixieland Jazz Band had brought to New York, but their restraint and rehearsed polish took much of the sting out of the virulent attacks that were being made on jazz.' (Charters and Kunstadt, 1981:127). Joe Crossman wrote in *Melody Maker* 'At the moment there is a craze amongst the small "hot" combinations (as distinct from the large symphonic) for a form of rendering which, while being decidedly 'hot' is – so far as the melody instruments (as apart from the purely rhythmic) are concerned – played legato', a style that he saw as perfected by

Nichols (July 1926:46). Numbers such as *Alabama Stomp* and *Brown Sugar* by Nichols's Red Heads were reviewed in *Melody Maker* as 'far and away the finest records I have ever heard … the renderings consist of a mass of solos by each instrument in turn in that very modern style' (March 1927:247). These records still include New Orleans-style ensemble sections, but these are generally more refined than the Memphis Five. The arrangement of *Alabama Stomp* incorporates significant rhythmic complexity, especially in the introduction, which gives the impression that the number is in three-time until Mole's trombone break. The solos by musicians of the calibre of Miff Mole, Jimmy Dorsey, and Nichols himself are of very high quality. In 1935, an important achievement of the Rhythm Clubs' lobbying cited in the first issue of *Swing Music* was persuading a record company to reissue some Red Nichols recordings (March 1935:2), indicating that this music was still regarded as the epitome of hot. It is not surprising that although Nichols was the subject of widespread adverse criticism in America throughout the twentieth century, an approach that compromised between hot jazz and more refined popular music appealed to the British public. As Sudhalter states, these white groups 'satisfied more exactly the musical criteria inherent in their listener's own musical educations' (1999:136).

Despite the popularity of small groups in New York and Britain, it was clear that the best opportunities for musicians were in the larger dance bands, and at the same time it was desirable for bandleaders to include musicians that could play hot solos when required. For this reason, the members of the Original Memphis Five had joined Sam Lanin's dance band as early as 1919 and even Paul Whiteman was able to recruit some of the best hot players for his band (Sudhalter, 1999:107). Hence, small hot groups could exist as offshoots of the main orchestras, such as the Georgians from Paul Specht's band and the Goofus Five from the California Ramblers, but other more *ad hoc* groups of musicians also performed hot jazz outside their main employment, often for the purpose of recording.

It is clear from extensive discographical research that has been undertaken into the personnel of New York white bands, that although the large dance orchestras were reasonably consistent in their personnel at least in the short term, the constituents of the small groups was extremely variable from session to session. It has been conjectured that some of these small groups did not perform live, more likely, however, was that they did perform 'out of hours' in small, underground venues for which documentation is non-existent. It is also possible that different combinations of musicians than are represented on recordings performed in this way. The best musicians in New York certainly recorded for many different bands on different labels, and the bands themselves were contracted to several companies and even appear on the same label under many pseudonyms. This did ensure a certain consistency in the recorded music that reached Britain and as a result, a clear understanding of what hot music sounded like, even if the processes by which it could be produced were still unclear. Thus, hot music emerged as a clear American trend that could be easily imitated by British musicians where appropriate.

Hot Jazz in the British Dance Band Repertoire

Reasons for Incorporation

Most British bands reacted in some way to hot music, but the nature of this response varied depending on the size of the group, the venues and function for which they performed, financial resources, and the capabilities of the musicians. At one end of the scale, musicians such as Bert Firman and Fred Elizalde formed ensembles to perform hot music specifically, some of which existed mainly as recording groups. At the other extreme, there were several reasons why larger well-established British dance bands felt a need to somehow incorporate hot tendencies into their performances to some extent. Firstly, an impetus might have been the preferences of the musicians, as a *Melody Maker* editorial acknowledged that there was a clear difference between the sheet music that was being bought by the public and the arrangements that most bands wanted to play (January 1927:6). The best popular musicians in Britain would normally aspire to be members of one of the top dance bands, which represented secure and extremely lucrative employment but could be musically limiting. Although Spike Hughes's experiences with the musicians in the band at a 'Very Smart Hotel' seemed to indicate apathy towards the latest developments in hot jazz (1951:20), this was probably a reflection that many musicians in the top dance bands were classically trained and were already professional when they became under pressure to become involved in the dance music boom in the immediate post-War period (Ehrlich, 1985:203). The opportunities to acquire jazz skills had not been so readily available to these musicians as to the younger players who began to join established bands from the late 1920s. Musicians such as Harry Gold and Ted Heath had been able to experience hot jazz through records and direct contact with American musicians, in Heath's case with the Southern Syncopated Orchestra, developing skills that could be utilized in their main employment in dance bands when required.

A second factor in the adoption of hot elements by dance bands was fashion. Ensembles performed at venues that catered for people at the centre of the fashionable world, which necessarily provided entertainment that would reflect the latest musical trends. For example, the craze for the tango was catered for by the employment of tango bands at the Savoy throughout the 1920s (Savoy Archives). Dance bands would be expected to perform the latest popular song hits in an up-to-date style. There was a growing awareness of American fashions of all types that influenced popular culture in Britain in this period. McKibben suggests that '"Society" as it was understood at the time, was ... a significantly Anglo-American affair ... . Americans wanted to conquer the English social system and the English wanted to obtain support for a decaying Empire' (1998:27). The growing awareness of the American roots of jazz and popular music, as well as the fashionable exoticism of American music, led to the visits of several important American white dance bands in the late 1920s and early 1930s. These included many bands that performed at the Kit-Cat Club such as those led by Ted Lewis, Ben Bernie, Irving Aaronson, Paul Whiteman, Abe Lyman and Johnny Hamp. Although the style of music performed by these bands tended to relate more closely to dance music than to hot jazz, such groups provided some useful examples of how hot features could be integrated within the performances of British dance bands. Top bandleaders in Britain such as Jack Hylton and Bert Ambrose increasingly looked to their counterparts in America to provide the direction for developments in popular music.

Methods of Incorporation

The main function of dance bands was to present familiar melodies for people to dance to, which limited the possibilities of hot playing. In an article entitled 'How to Write or Extemporise a Hot Chorus', Joe Crossman stated that:

> Modern extemporisation is nothing more than
> 1. The introduction of a note, or short phrases made up of the correct notes and passing notes of the proper chords, and/or repetition of the melody notes, to precede certain notes of the melody (counter-melody or obbligato) and to act as 'leading in' phrases to these said certain notes
> 2. Introducing arpeggios consisting of the correct notes and passing notes on the proper chords and/or repetition of the melody notes, in place of sustaining sustained notes of the melody (counter-melody or obbligato) their full length as written in the part.
> (*Melody Maker*, January 1927:85)

Similarly, the leader of the Savoy Havana Band, Reginald Batten, asserted that hot choruses for violin 'should follow the direction of the melody' and 'include as much of the original form of the air as possible' (February 1927:177). As a result, 'paraphrase' solos necessarily dominated British dance music of the late 1920s. In addition, British musicians who were capable of improvising hot jazz solos were not plentiful at this time. American musicians were often employed as leaders or prominent soloists with British dance bands to enable leaders to incorporate hot music into their performances when required. This at least gave the superficial appearance of being fashionable and up-to-date even if in practice these musicians were often musically restricted.

Harry Gold's early career, related in his autobiography, demonstrates that as he worked his way up through the dance band profession, the possibilities for jazz performance diminished. Gold began working in five-piece groups in the mid-1920s in which he 'played from commercial printed parts and also tried some extemporisation.' (2000:24). Gold auditioned successfully for Vic Filmer's band in the late 1920s in response to an advert for a player who could read and extemporize. He recalled working for Filmer at the Melton Club on Kingsley Street 'from 11pm until the last customer left ... . We always got a good breakfast, and, for those days, eight pounds a week was very good money'. This work involved reading, improvising and playing requests (2000:34). In a band led by Jack Padbury at the Princes Restaurant, Piccadilly, Gold recalled that 'Much of what we played was purely commercial music suitable for dancing but occasionally Jack would put on a short jazz set.' (2000:42). Next Gold joined Roy Fox, ostensibly a 'better' engagement but he comments 'It was obvious where my heart lay – with jazz – albeit that the music I was involved with then with Roy was a far cry from the original Dixieland Jazz Band, which I had first heard, or from Bix, Trumbauer, Nichols, Venuti, Lang, Rollini and the others that had come later' (2000:54).

The Savoy Hotel continued to be at the forefront of developments in popular music in the late 1920s. Under the management of de Mornys, the Savoy Orpheans and Savoy Havana Band had always included some American musicians since the early 1920s. It has been noted that a clear majority of American musicians employed at the hotel, and subsequently in London as a whole, came from Boston, Massachusetts (Hill, 1993:26, and Sudhalter, 1999:775). This lineage can be traced back to Bert Ralton who took over leadership of the Havana band in 1920, and Carroll Gibbons, Howard Jacobs and Joe Brannelly who also worked at the hotel. When de Mornys's contract with the hotel expired at the end of 1927 (Savoy Archive), this coincided with and even helped to precipitate the resurgence of interest in American music in London, as the American musicians that were at the Savoy became spread more widely through different dance bands in the capital. At this time Jack Hylton was in such demand that he formed other bands that could perform under his name at multiple venues in the capital (including the Kit-Cat Club, the Piccadilly Hotel and the Ambassador's Club) and employed American musicians Al and Ray Starita, formerly members of the Orpheans, to lead these groups. Bert Ambrose employed many American musicians in his band that also tended to be from Boston, as they were often recruited by Joe Brannelly. The need for American musicians at the Savoy after the reorganization was met by the employment of Fred Elizalde's band, which included several notable Americans, to play opposite a newly constituted Orpheans, known as 'Savoy Orpheans (1928)' and later as the 'Savoy Hotel Orpheans'. The new leader of the Orpheans, violinist Reg Batten, also recruited America musicians, including Sylvester Ahola and Irving Brodsky.

Several of these musicians that came to Britain as individuals in the late 1920s had already visited earlier in the decade with American dance bands. Trumpeter Frank Guarente had come to Britain in 1923 with the Paul Specht Orchestra, and led the Georgians, a small group drawn from the larger band, that achieved great success in Britain and secured a residency in Paris. After touring with the Georgians in Europe, Guarente returned to London to play lead trumpet with the Orpheans and other groups (Sudhalter, 1999:114-5). Sylvester Ahola, who took over Guarente's place when the latter left the Savoy, had also visited previously with Specht, in 1926. This indicates that the previous experiences of these musicians in this country had been positive and that the pay and conditions proposed for their return visits were favourable. Ahola certainly enjoyed his time in London, where he explored the sights and frequented the Duke of Cumberland Wine Lodge in addition to his musical duties (Hill, 1993:13-14). Sudhalter recalls that his father was also approached by Brannelly for the Ambrose band, but 'Swayed by family objections, [Al] Sudhalter turned down the Ambrose offer, which he recalled as generous and quite tempting.' (1999:775). Art Rollini reported that his elder brother Adrian, who joined Elizalde's band, 'did well in London financially' (1987:10). Art himself came to London to earn money to help his recently widowed mother (1987:12), where he met a stockbroker who was 'earning just a little more than half my salary' (1987:16). Sylvester Ahola recalled that the musicians in the Savoy bands enjoyed excellent facilities and privileges, including recreation rooms, waiter-service dinner, free beer and porters to look after the instruments (Hill, 1993:27-9). Of course, Britain also had the advantage for Americans of not having Prohibition in force. The main drawback for American musicians was that if they stayed in Britain for too long they would limit their opportunities upon their return to America, having missed out on the latest developments in jazz. Frank Guarente, who had warned Ahola not to be tempted to stay too long in Britain for this reason (Hill, 1993:27) was himself 'able to find top-of-the-line work in New York – but not as a jazzman' upon his return to America (Sudhalter, 1999:116).

A further way in which British bandleaders were able to incorporate hot qualities into their output did not rely as much on the jazz capabilities of individual musicians. The understanding of hot as merely the latest trend in popular music meant that, like other novelty effects, it could be viewed as a particular style that could be applied in the arrangement of the popular song material that formed the basis of the dance band repertoire. This idea is reinforced in contemporary sources that repeatedly express the idea of 'renderings' of popular songs that incorporate 'hot' or 'dirty' qualities. In this way, it was easy for arrangers to incorporate such features into some of the pieces that they were preparing, and this allowed hot numbers to be balanced within the overall repertoire of the group and also for the hot elements to be controlled within individual compositions. This approach is also commensurate with a general lack of understanding and skills in improvisational practice amongst British musicians at this time, as all the hot material could be prepared in advance.

Jack Hylton, who was one of the most successful and influential bandleaders in Britain in this period, clearly recognized the importance of American musicians. He was involved in the visits of American bands to the Kit-Cat Club and was instrumental in bringing Duke Ellington to Britain. Hylton also apparently imported American records of the latest style 'so that he could learn from and keep abreast of whatever was on offer from the birthplace of jazz' (Rust, sleeve note to RTR 79024). However, Hylton used British musicians in his own band at a time when, as we have seen, Anglo-American bands were commonplace in Britain. It is clear that some members of the Hylton band could play hot improvised solos when required, including Lew Davis (trombone), Jack Jackson (trumpet), Edward 'Poggy' Pogson (saxophone) and Hugo Rignold (violin). Rust points out that on two versions of *I want to be bad* recorded a month apart by the same personnel, the trumpet and trombone solos are completely different, suggesting that they were improvised (sleeve note to RTR 79024). This indicates that the best British dance band musicians were capable of improvisation in this period, but in many other bands were not always given the opportunity to do so (on record), as this was normally the role of the imported Americans.

However, several of Hylton's arrangements demonstrate an approach where an impression of hot jazz could be created by drawing as much on the skills of arrangers as the individual musicians in his band. As a clear rendition of the melody was important in dance music, 'paraphrase' solos, which were within the capabilities of most dance band musicians, developed into paraphrases scored for an instrumental grouping, often the saxophones, playing in rhythmic unison and close harmony in virtuosic fashion. This did not require any particular skills in hot jazz, but often a high level of technical capability. *Buffalo Rhythm*, recorded in October 1927, has hot passages scored for groups of trumpets, saxophones and strings that are typical of this approach. Although combined here with individual hot solos, dance bands without the resources to employ personnel skilled in hot jazz could easily imitate such effects.

It must be remembered that hot numbers would represent only a fraction of any dance band's overall output. Mindful of changing fashions and the ever-fickle public, Hylton was aiming to create a show band that presented diverse but generally inoffensive entertainment. Faint states that Hylton's repertoire in 1931 ranged from 'Lehar's *The Merry Widow* and Rachmaninov's *Prelude in C# minor* through the current hits of the day, to tunes that were already deemed to be jazz classics, such as *St Louis Blues*, *Tiger Rag* and *Limehouse Blues*' (Faint, 1999:28). Musicians had to be extremely versatile, and certainly would not be able to play hot music continually. Similarly, despite the high salaries that they commanded, visiting American musicians seemed to have little overt influence on the musical output of the bands with which they were working beyond taking an occasional solo, adding to the perception of hot jazz as a superficial effect. Whether hot jazz was incorporated through the introduction of a few talented players, complex arrangements or both methods there was a sense that all British dance bands had to balance any hot numbers within the holistic entertainment that they were expected to provide. Hence the prevailing style of dance music actually changed very little in this period.

Hot Jazz Education

Despite the restrictions on both British and American players within their regular employment in dance bands, the presence of such a large number of talented jazz musicians in London playing alongside young musicians who wanted to learn how to perform the hot music that they had encountered on record was undoubtedly important with regard to the development of jazz in Britain. In addition, contact between British and American musicians was encouraged, albeit indirectly, by the government in this period. Although a significant number of American bands visited Britain in the 1920s, the government placed increasingly tight restrictions on this activity. American bands were limited to spending eight weeks in the country, and promoters were required to employ a British band to play opposite the American group. However, the practicalities of having a venue large enough for two bands, and the possibility that large clubs such as the Kit-Cat could simply import a new American band every eight weeks, thus ensuring a continuous American presence, led to the government to refuse to issue permits 'in respect of complete dance bands save in special circumstances' (TNA: PRO AR278/41/1925). Although the regulations remained vague and lax, allowing American bands to continue to visit Britain, the formation of Anglo-American bands was actively encouraged and the Savoy's application in 1925 for seven

American musicians to become members of their otherwise British groups was used as an example of good practice.

Often, it was outside the confines of the formally constituted ensembles that employed Americans in Britain that the most beneficial contact between these musicians and their British counterparts could take place, just as had been the case with the musicians of the Southern Syncopated Orchestra. Although the official policy for visiting American dance bands was that the musicians were not allowed to play collectively or individually outside the venue for which they were engaged, this was hard to enforce, particularly when performances took place in London's underworld. The London nightclub scene provided many suitable venues for after-hours jam sessions:

> De Mornys had all his musicians under exclusive contract and they were not allowed to play anywhere else, but of course some of them did behind his back. He really caught them one night when we went to the famous 43 night spot in Gerrard Street ... and found them playing in the band there after doing their stint at the Savoy! (Hayes, 1988:33)

Harry Gold recalled a visit of the Ted Lewis band, which included Muggsy Spanier, George Brunies and Jimmy Dorsey who sat in with the Filmer band at the Melton Club. Gold countered the frequent criticism of Dorsey's improvisational abilities, probably derived from his frequent representation on dance band recordings, when he commented that 'I can vouch for the fact that on that night at least he ad libbed like crazy!' (2000:36). Several British musicians recalled playing at the Bag O'Nails club after they had finished work. Nat Gonella recalled jamming at the club (Brown, 1985:57), which he described as a situation where dance band musicians could 'let their hair down' socially and musically. Pianist Gerry Moore similarly recalled that musicians went to clubs to relax and play after they had finished work in hotels, where they had to read music rather than extemporize. Moore was resident pianist for a time at the Bag O'Nails, which he recalled would be full of musicians, especially on a Saturday night, playing into the early hours of the morning. Amongst the musicians that Moore played with were Harry Carney and Danny Polo. Harry Gold was also present at these jam sessions in the 1930s (National Sound Archive Interviews with Gonella, Moore and Gold).

Ironically, in encouraging individual rather than groups of American musicians to visit Britain, it was more difficult for the government to monitor their activities. A Ministerial reply to a letter from the Trades Union Congress admits that the government had not kept records of permits and extensions for individual musicians, but that these were only granted when they commanded substantial salaries (generally £25 per week and upwards), or where they presented some other evidence of outstanding ability. The Minister also acknowledged that in relation to the extension of work permits 'Different considerations do, however, arise in the case of an alien who has been in this country for some years' (TNA: PRO AR528/2/1929). The extra work that was available to musicians took place during the day in recording studios where the anonymity of musicians could be easily secured if necessary, and was therefore difficult to detect in practice. British bandleaders who wished to include Americans on their hot records exploited this loophole. Bert Firman recalled that:

> ... musicians moved from one label to another, fictious titles for bands were devised, but with often the same personnel ... hotels and rival record companies contrived to stop their stars recording under pseudonyms and the whole recording scene became a jungle ... . (1984:80)

In fact, the exclusivity contracts enforced by employers rather the conditions of governmental work permits seem to have more greatly impeded the activities of American musicians in the late 1920s. Sylvester Ahola, trumpeter with the new Savoy Orpheans and then with Ambrose at the Mayfair Hotel, recalled that 'when I started doing extra recording work I had to sneak my trumpet out of the [Savoy] hotel in a velvet bag.' (Hill, 1993:29). Ahola recorded frequently with bands led by Ray and Al Starita (Hill, 1993:30) and Bert Firman, and also in bands that accompanied popular singers of the day. (Hill, 1993:32). He recalled signing the pre-release agreements for the studio with various fictitious names when recording with Firman: 'Every week I would have a different odd-ball name, such as Ankanneers Dell, Grover Drivel and Cleat Boyle', although Edgar Jackson, writing in *Melody Maker* in May 1928, suggested that his identity had been deduced (Hill, 1993:40).

Bert Firman

Figure 8.1   Bert Firman (Courtesy of Pete March and Ned Newitt)

It was by no means only Ahola that 'sneaked' out of the Savoy and other similar venues to play in groups where proficiency in the hot jazz style was welcomed and encouraged, such as Bert Firman's groups on the Zonophone label. Firman, a violinist, was the youngest of four brothers who were all active in the music profession. Firman became leader of the Midnight Follies Orchestra at the Hotel Metropole in 1922, and progressed to become Musical Director for the Gordon Hotels group and of Zonophone records by 1925, which allowed him considerable success in both live and recorded performance. The security of Firman's residencies at the Carlton Hotel and then at the Devonshire Restaurant, combined with some artistic freedom at Zonophone represented the ideal for musicians at this time.

Firman's autobiography[1] illuminates many important experiences in his formative years as a musician that ensured his success and ultimately led to his employment by NBC and Hollywood. Firman had good contacts in the music business through his father and brothers but quickly developed these in his own right. His confidence as a young man enabled him to negotiate effectively with managers of venues and record companies. After only a few years in the dance band profession he had made his first records, taken part in an experimental broadcast and had been approached as a possible leader for the 2LO band prior to his brother Sidney being recruited for this role (1984:61). As well as musical contacts, Firman became conversant with the ways of high society. Edward, the then Prince of Wales was a personal fan and groups led by Firman performed for royal parties. As a result, Firman was in demand to provide the music for lavish private functions on the 'Belgravia/Mayfair circuit' (1984:55).

Firman's personality as portrayed in his autobiography is determined, ambitious and self-centred. He left his first employment as a bandleader at the Metropole Hotel as he was 'dissatisfied with the lack of focus on the band' in a venue where the cabaret performance was the main entertainment, whereas at the Carlton Hotel the band was the centre of attention (1984:68). Firman saw the importance of securing the services of the best musicians for his bands. As early as 1924 he recognized that:

> If I were going to stay at the top ... I needed to gather around me the finest musicians available in London. Money was no problem, but the right musicians were not easy to find. You had to search for them. There are always some musicians unemployed, sometimes deservedly so, sometimes not. But in this new world of jazz and dance music, gifted exponents were still rare. (1984:59)

Initially Firman sought out the best players through listening to other bands in London, including those that played a different style of music to his own. Around 1924 he 'bought and listened to every available gramophone record of dance bands or "novelty orchestras". The latter title was particularly interesting. It often meant that the orchestra was "jazzing" it.' (1984:59.) It was on one of these 'novelty'

---

[1] With thanks to Pete March for lending me the original copy of Firman's autobiography. Some of this material is also available online at http://www.jabw.demon.co.uk/firman1.htm. I am also indebted to Pete for lending me Bert Firman's band parts.

records that he first heard Ted Heath, who he eventually discovered in a café, apparently sitting in for a saxophonist (on trombone!). Nor did Firman discount unemployed musicians who were busking on the streets, suggesting that he found a trumpet player in this way (1984:60). It is notable also that many musicians employed by the Savoy played on Firman's recordings, an activity that took place without de Mornys's knowledge. Even after de Mornys's departure from the Savoy, Carroll Gibbons had to remain anonymous and uncredited for his recording of *Rhapsody in Blue* with Firman, as the Savoy had apparently 'tied him up' contractually (1984:101).

Firman's awareness of the musical world was increasingly extended beyond London towards America. Firman was using American arrangements even prior to the widespread availability of electrical recordings of American bands, and realized that the possibility of broadcasting demanded 'more musicians, new arrangements, perhaps even a new sound' and to find these things he 'might even have to go to New York for a few weeks' (1984:66-7). Such a visit was Firman's first action having been appointed as musical director for Zonophone records, as a result of the manager's realization that 'the sales of dance music records were beginning to take off. Zonophone was in danger of being left behind. Someone was needed to organize several recordings each week and every week. Someone who was a name and someone who knew musicians and arrangers.' (1984:73) Firman went to New York 'determined to lay the groundwork for making Zonophone the top-selling dance music label' (1984:75). Jocelyn, who he met on the SS Mauretania, became his 'guide to the night hot spots. We went to hotel rooms, restaurants, fashionable speak-easies and disreputable dives. We traversed Manhattan from Harlem to Greenwich Village ... I listened to record after record and talked to every musician, composer and arranger who cared to spend time with me.' Before returning to London, Firman also spent time in Chicago (1984:76-7).

A consideration of Firman's career more widely than the often-cited Rhythmic Eight recordings illuminates a musician who was able to negotiate a path successfully through the commercial and musical demands of the late 1920s. Like many bands of the period, Firman's groups recorded under numerous pseudonyms, and this enabled Zonophone to use Firman almost exclusively but creating the illusion of a wide variety of different groups recording on the label. This confusion and anonymity also allowed Firman to utilize freely the American musicians that were in London at the time. It seems that American musicians were incorporated into Firman's groups almost as soon as they arrived in London, and the proportion of Americans increases over the period 1924-28 in parallel with their numbers in the capital. Firman enjoyed a close friendship with Bert Ambrose, and there was an open arrangement between the two bandleaders that allowed Firman to use Ambrose's musicians on his recordings, and with the advantage to Ambrose being that as the musicians could freely supplement their income this would encourage them to remain in his band. Sylvester Ahola confirmed that 'there was no written contract like I had at the Savoy, and because it was only a verbal agreement, Bert Ambrose didn't mind if I recorded with anybody else. There was no contract to break.' (Hill, 1993:43). Firman had even encouraged Ambrose to move to the Mayfair Hotel and augment his band to give him a larger pool of musicians from which to choose (1984:109). Ambrose included many musicians that had formerly worked at the Savoy in his Mayfair Hotel band, including Breed and Ahola, which would have made it easier for Firman to use them on his recordings.

In practice, similar musicians featured in all the Firman bands, and there was a considerable overlap in the styles recorded by the various groups. The repertoire was mainly drawn from the latest popular songs as the concept of jazz 'standards' permeated the thinking of British bandleaders only to a very limited extent. The repertoire of the bands varied continuously, as they were under pressure to record new material with alarming regularity to keep up with the latest trends. Therefore, hot jazz bands in both America and Britain were still largely dependent on the music publishing industry to supply them with the basic material from which to perform. Publishers continued to issue sheet music of the latest popular songs, usually now accompanied with a 'stock' orchestration from which a basic performance could be given (Nelson, 1934:65). Bands that wanted to play hot jazz could adopt the same two basic approaches as the dance bands, to rely on the stock orchestrations but try to introduce as much variation as possible in the performance, or to write their own arrangements. Firman combined elements of these two methods, using stock orchestrations, but often altering them significantly. These were then performed by musicians who knew how to transform the printed music on their stands.

Firman's approach to hot jazz can be traced through his recordings between 1924 and 1928, and despite some radical stylistic developments it is clear that the quality of the recordings both on a technical and musical level is consistently extremely good for the time at which they were made. *Oo La*, a one-step recorded in Firman's first session with the Midnight Follies Band in 1924, is typically clipped, with the ensemble, including a ubiquitous banjo, playing in rhythmic unison. Variation is introduced exclusively through orchestration and the melody is repeated without variation or embellishment. Opportunities for hot breaks are largely neglected and often a note of the melody is merely sustained through these bars.

In 1926 the Devonshire Restaurant Dance Band recorded *Jig Walk*, a number that Duke Ellington wrote for *Chocolate Kiddies*, an all-black revue that had been performed Britain earlier in the year accompanied by Sam Wooding's band. This exemplifies the continued reliance of British bands on musical theatre and related sheet music in forming their repertoire and stylistic interpretation. The style of the performance is less clipped than the 1924 recording and there is more of a sense of swing. There is evidence of subtle embellishment of the melody in its repetitions in the trumpet part and the arrangement itself is more interesting, featuring some effective polyphony. Whilst Firman plays the violin with characteristic *portamento*, a tantalizingly short saxophone improvisation towards the end of the number provides a modern touch. *Melody Maker* noted that the musicians in Firman's band:

... display what can be done without any form of arrangement. I am convinced that all the titles mentioned below are played from the ordinary orchestral parts issued by the publishers. Of course, they are not rendered note for note, the musicians extemporising as they go along, which would probably be fatal in the case of the mediocre band artist; but when one has at command such as group of musicians as Firman employs, the result leaves nothing to be desired. (February 1927:141)

The approach that this writer suggests is clearly evident in the recording of *Jig Walk*. The performance is clearly reliant on the printed parts, a stock arrangement by Arthur Lange imported from America, but it is clear that in addition to the embellishment and rhythmic variation of individual lines there has also been considerable re-arrangement. Most basically, the number is performed using less musicians than the orchestration suggests, with second trumpet, trombone, banjo and bass saxophone (probably an alternative to the bass) all omitted. The orchestration is also altered, and this allows the incorporation of Firman's violin. Furthermore, several of the more sustained backing figures shown in the parts are omitted or performed with more interesting syncopated rhythms. The use of a smaller ensemble, which allows the players greater freedom, and an increased emphasis on rhythmic interest is commensurate with ideas about hot jazz that were emerging at this time.

In 1927, a time when Fletcher Henderson's records were becoming available to British enthusiasts such as Spike Hughes (1946:308), Firman recorded two numbers from Henderson's repertoire. It seems likely that the recording of *The Stampede* by Henderson's band in 1926 was an important source for Frank Skinner, who scored the orchestration, which is in turn varied in Firman's performance of it, creating a version twice removed from the 'original' within the space of a year. Particularly interesting in this respect is the saxophone solo originally played by Coleman Hawkins in Henderson's band and by Arthur Lally in Firman's band. The solo provided by Skinner in the printed part follows the Hawkins original solo very closely, with some of the more complex moments having been simplified. Lally varies parts of this still further, demonstrating that the common 'paraphrase' approach could be applied to notated improvisations as well as the basic melody.

In another Henderson number recorded by Firman, *Sugar Foot Stomp*, the indicated trombone solo (a transcription of that which can be heard on the 1926 Henderson version) is replaced by a completely different solo by Firman himself on violin, in which there is a clear attempt to incorporate blues inflections. This is followed by an extended trumpet solo played by Frank Guarente. In the notated parts, the arranger Elmer Schoebel has provided a transcription of the solo that originated from the King Oliver recording of the same number under the title *Dippermouth Blues*. After the first chorus, Guarente plays a version of the third chorus which differs from the written part in one notable instance: at the start of the chorus he disregards the written oscillation between the sixth and fifth degrees, and instead plays a long note, the sixth superimposed upon the tonic harmony, which is a feature of Armstrong's solo on the Henderson recording. This suggests that Guarente at least had heard the Henderson recording and was influenced by it, despite being a personal friend of Oliver (Sudhalter 1999:113).

Firman's experiences in America seemed to have crystallized his approach to the music business that was behind the peak of his activity in the late 1920s. A few years earlier, Firman had heard the violinist Albert Sandler in London, and realized that although the music was 'old-fashioned' it was still relevant for certain audiences in particular venues. Firman writes that 'Subconsciously, he exerted an influence on my own attitude towards dance music. This subsequently made me something of a musical Jekyll and Hyde, depending on when and where my orchestra was playing.' (1984:73.) In America, Firman heard music that was modern and progressive, and thus representative of the diametrically opposite side of popular music to Sandler's performances. This resulted in the emergence of what Firman describes as a 'spilt [musical] personality':

> I realised that playing for dancing in hotels or night clubs frequented by high society required a different set of values from that for recording. The reason why couples went to smart restaurants was to have fun, drink and dine well, to chatter light-heartedly and, perhaps to flirt for a few hours in splendour. Dancing on the postage-stamp floor, allowing the closer proximity of bodies, established a romantic mood hopefully to be consummated at a more discreet time. The music was therefore a background. People wanted to hear it, not listen to it. It should never intrude, then, on the other hand, records were bought to be listened to. So my orchestra at the Carlton, and later, the Devonshire Restaurant, mostly played arrangements that were "sweet" and emphasised the melody. I considered it a serious criticism if guests ever refused a table because it was too near the band. A different set of values applied to recordings. The orchestra placed more emphasis on the beat and the musicians were encouraged to play in a less inhibited fashion. (1984:79-80)

It seems that Firman was influenced in the approach to performing and recording taken by white bands in New York in this period, that developed smaller ensembles drawn from the larger pool of musicians for the purposes of recording hot jazz for minor record labels. Even *Melody Maker*, whose contributors unsurprisingly appear unaware that all the Zonophone groups were led by Firman and consisted of similar musicians, noted in September 1927 that although 'previously there was little to choose between the styles and types of renderings' of Bert Firman's Dance Orchestra and the Devonshire Restaurant group, the former was now playing popular numbers 'exactly from the commercial arrangements in a bright and vigorous manner likely to appeal to the vast dancing public' and the latter 'blossomed out as quite a "hot" American style band this month' (September 1927:889). This manifestation of Firman's 'split personality' was a precursor to the first recording session of a new Firman group called the Rhythmic Eight in November 1927, contemporaneously with the more widely publicized work of Fred Elizalde.

Fred Elizalde

Figure 8.2   Fred Elizalde and his Savoy Music, 1928 (Max Jones Archive)

Fred Elizalde came to Britain in 1926, joining his brother Manuel, known as 'Lizz', in Cambridge where the latter had been a student since October 1924.[2] Although Lizz took exams in Spanish and Engineering he did not complete the Ordinary BA degree for which he was studying, and Fred never studied at the University (he had already attended Stanford University in California [Chilton, 1997:106]). Lizz is listed as a member of the band for the 1926 Cambridge Footlight's production of *May Fever* (http://www.footlights.org/past/). Several of the musicians that performed in *May Fever* and as the original Quinquaginta Band for other gigs in Cambridge in 1926-27 (Chilton, 1997:106; Walker, 1984:15) were the basis for Fred's first band in Britain and made their first recordings in May 1927. Dan Wyllie, a saxophonist with the group, recalled that 'the results were shambolic! We were incredulous; it was hard to believe that we were so bad. It was agreed that four titles only should be released and issued for restricted sale in Cambridge only' (Walker, 1984:13).

Hot music had significant presence at the universities of Oxford and Cambridge, as discussed in Chapter 3, and the band adopted by the Elizalde brothers was one example of numerous similar bands that existed at these universities in this period (for example, an Oxford band called the Oxcentrics was mentioned in *Melody Maker* in June 1927). Recordings were undoubtedly vital to the success of the Elizalde brothers in Britain in that they allowed them to become known outside Cambridge. Although the band were known locally as the

[2] Information from Cambridge University Archives.

'Quinquaginta Ramblers' they recorded under names that exploited their university connection more obviously, the 'Varsity Band' and the 'Cambridge Undergraduates'. The scheme of limited release of the first recordings may have acted in the band's favour, in that it added to the mystique and exclusivity surrounding the Cambridge setting for those that were not involved in it. The *Daily Chronicle* reported that 'Elizalde has lately been studying at Cambridge, and so far "Elizalde and his Music" has not been heard outside the limits of a few smart private parties' (6 January 1928) and apparently 'much of the publicity they received was undoubtedly due to the fact that they were Cambridge men.' (Nelson, 1934:137). As Walker points out, that Quinquaginta Ramblers' records could allegedly be bought in London in the summer of 1927 might have meant that the limited release agreement was not honoured. This could also indicate that the records were in sufficient demand amongst the hot music fraternity as to be imported into London. Elizalde had sent a telegram to *Melody Maker* inviting a representative to hear the band play for a Footlights ball, asserting that 'Cambridge knows that the Quinquaginta Ramblers is the best dance band now playing in this country' and as a result eliciting some positive coverage from a reporter who wrote that the group 'as a modern dance band is, in style, in advance, I honestly believe, of any other now playing in this country' (April 1927:337). The brothers subsequently contributed articles to *Melody Maker* that acted as further publicity.

Walker identifies a trend for modern writers to be generally disparaging about the band's capabilities on their early records (1984:14), and numerous stories have been perpetuated regarding the Cambridge students' lack of musical knowledge. In fact, the recordings show that the Elizalde brothers had been able to find capable musicians with a desire, if not the practical knowledge, to play hot jazz from within the University environment. The musicians involved were by no means beginners, and perform the written parts competently, but certainly the hot content on these early recordings results mainly from Elizalde's arrangements and individual contributions from the brothers, with solos mainly restricted to Lizz's alto and Fred's piano. This approach to hot jazz was similar to that of contemporary British dance bands, which incorporated hot into their output through complex arrangements and the occasional short solo by a suitably skilled musician.

However, the music produced by Elizalde's band was subtly different from other British hot music of this period. Whilst leaders based their recordings on alteration of stock arrangements of popular songs with solos often produced through the technique of paraphrase, Elizalde's arrangements were innovative; tended to feature his own compositions and early jazz standards, taken, for example, from the repertoire of the ODJB; and allowed increasingly more space for individual improvisation. Such a liberated approach could be readily pursued within the Cambridge University environment, and Nelson recalled that 'With kindred rhythmic fiends for the players, and unhampered by any dictates of commercialism, [Elizalde] went all out for "hot" music, and was one of the pioneers of this form of playing in this country' (1934:49). Fred Elizalde's compositional voice shows through in his arrangements, with their extended introductions and succinct codas, and in his piano solos, which feature harmonic quirks. Dan Wyllie recalled that 'Fred's arrangements were by no means easy to learn or play for professionals, let alone amateurs like us.' (Walker, 1984:13). Edgar Jackson commented that Elizalde's work offered a challenge to other arrangers to 'put out some scores in which there is more than the stereotyped and boringly orthodox ideas, which they excuse on the grounds that they are commercial, but with which we are all becoming thoroughly fed-up.' (April 1927: 339).

The response to this latest hot music from the institutions of dance music was rapid, with both Ambrose and the Savoy Orpheans commissioning and recording arrangements by Elizalde in 1927. As a result, Elizalde began to make close links with better musicians in London and incorporated the likes of Joe Crossman, Joe Brannelly and Max Bacon into his recording groups in July–September 1927. The Savoy Hotel management, once again at the forefront of developments in popular music, seized the opportunity to secure the latest phenomenon in hot music for its ballroom at a time that conveniently coincided with the end of de Mornys's contract to provide the bands for the hotel. Fred Elizalde and his Savoy Hotel Music gave their first performances on New Year's Eve 1927-28 alongside the reformed Orpheans. Whilst, as we have seen, most bands in significant venues in London were trying to balance hot styles within their output as individual groups, the Savoy instead employed two separate groups that represented contrasting trends in popular music. Thus, despite the presence of some hot musicians such as Ahola in the ranks of the Orpheans, 'the hotel policy left little for [the Orpheans] to do that could not have been successfully accomplished by any competent dance band' (Rust, 1972:53) as they had to play 'sweet' to Elizalde's 'hot'. Ahola recalled that the Orpheans played 'popular dance numbers – we were the "sweet" band', and he considered Elizalde 'far too advanced for the British, especially for those at the hotel' (Hill, 1993:27).

In the latter part of 1927 Lizz Elizalde had been sent to America to recruit musicians for the Savoy band, returning with Chelsea Quealey (trumpet), Bobby Davis (alto saxophone and clarinet) and Adrian Rollini (bass saxophone, goofus and hot fountain pen[3]). The inclusion of more musicians who had specific ability in hot music and who could play solos was vital to the development of the group, particularly as the solos by the American musicians move away from the paraphrase style prominent in British dance music. The significance of the importation of these particular musicians to Britain was that they were active in a circle based around the California Ramblers, which was largely different from the group of Boston musicians that provided a significant majority of previous American musicians in Britain. The California Ramblers and the numerous associated groups had been well represented on recordings that were available in Britain and their performances were familiar to fans of hot music. One of the most frequently mentioned hot groups in *Melody Maker* from its earliest editions was The Goofus Five (sometimes known as the Goofus Washboards), which was one of many pseudonyms for the Little Ramblers, a small group derived from the California Ramblers. Whilst the style of the California Ramblers was 'quite formal

---

[3] For further information on the use of these distinctive-sounding and rare instruments, see the informative article by Norman Field: http://www.normanfield.fsnet.co.uk/rollini.htm.

... with occasional hot solos', the recordings of smaller groups such as the Goofus Five tended to use the same musicians playing more freely (Sudhalter, 1999:169).

Elizalde's approach to running his own bands in Britain appears to have drawn on the business model of the California Ramblers and associated groups as well as more directly on their personnel and repertoire. The Ramblers' manager Ed Kirkeby particularly exploited the college associations of the group. The musicians were 'clean-cut, good-looking, well-spoken and musically no worse than anyone else' (Sudhalter, 1999:161) and were popular in the affluent suburb of Westchester (Sudhalter, 1999:163). The Ramblers achieved success amongst audiences of students at their own Pelham roadhouse which was 'the most fashionable spot on Long Island for dinner and dancing after the college football games. The crowd knew most of the band by their first names and there was a general air of fraternity-dance hilarity.' Outside New York, 'the Ramblers' recordings ... were so much a part of the college life of the twenties' (Charters and Kunstadt, 1981:127) that Elizalde himself, as a student at Stanford, would surely have become aware of their success. Small groups recorded as the 'Varsity Eight' and the 'University Six', drawing on the college associations. Kirkeby's marketing was crucial to the success of the Ramblers, a scrapbook details his 'exploitation of radio, newspapers, popular magazines, and trade journals; deals with instrument companies ... ideas for publicity stunts, product tie-ins, hometown pitches focussed on individual band members' (Sudhalter, 1999:165).

Elizalde must have thought that success similar to that of the Ramblers was possible for a band with associations with an exclusive university in Britain. The change of name of Elizalde's group to the Quinquaginta *Ramblers* and use of other names that linked the group to the university setting, as well as his particular choice of American musicians for his band, belies this influence. Whilst at the Savoy Hotel, Elizalde recorded with two groups, 'His Music', initially a ten-piece ensemble, and 'His Hot Music', which was half the size, similar to the Ramblers/Goofus Five concept. Generally, the large group played complex arrangements of popular songs that included some hot solos, whereas the smaller group drew on standards, Elizalde's own compositions and featured more extensive improvisation. This group also performed more of the Goofus Five's recorded repertoire than is represented in their own recorded output (Tanner, 1971a:28 and BBC Programme Records).

Comparison of common numbers in the output of Elizalde's 'His Music' and the California Ramblers and Elizalde's 'Hot Music' and the Goofus Five perhaps indicates some more general tendencies in Elizalde's approach to this music. *Singapore Sorrows* was recorded by the California Ramblers in January 1928 and by Elizalde's group in April 1929, just after a new influx of American musicians into the band. Elizalde's skill in orchestration is a notable factor in this comparison and adds considerable interest to the performances. The instrumentation is frequently varied within choruses and phrases and the arrangements also include effective use of dynamics. There are significant differences in the approach to a hot statement of the melody, which in both arrangements can be heard towards the middle of the arrangement. Whilst the California Ramblers perform a rather weak hot paraphrase of the melody, Elizalde alternates hot phrases on trumpet, clarinet and saxophones with simple statements of the melody on the strings to great effect. Particularly notable is the use of a string bass (played by Tiny Stock), which can be heard to great effect playing on all four beats of the bar, rather than the first and third as in the California Ramblers' version, significantly aiding the rhythmic drive of the performance. The backing figures towards the end of the number prefigure the riff-based big band arrangements of the late 1930s. In Elizalde's version, the linking passages are more concise, and this means that overall, the structure of the number feels more coherent in his hands.

Elizalde's arranging skills also played an important part in the recordings of the 'Hot Music' group. *Arkansas Blues* was recorded by the Goofus Five in April 1927 and Elizalde's version of less than a year later in March 1928 features the same core musicians, Quealey, Davis and Rollini. Unsurprisingly, as Tanner points out, the opening chorus of the piece is similar in both instances (1971a:28). However, there are many differences between the two versions. Firstly, the tempo of Elizalde's version is significantly faster, possibly indicating the need for the arrangement to function as dance music, whilst the Goofus Five adopt a more laid-back feel. Elizalde's version features a characteristically unusual sounding introduction based on a pentatonic scale, whereas the Goofus Five begin with a simpler diatonic vamp. Whilst the solos in the Goofus Five version simply follow one after the other, Elizalde has clearly made a more complex arrangement featuring shorter 'breaks' and *tutti* interjections before and during the main solos. Arguably, the solos are of higher quality on this later version, where Elizalde allows the soloists the same amount of space as in the Goofus Five version, but within a more distinctive and varied arrangement. It was the combination of the quality of the arrangement and the hot solos that was so influential on British musicians at this time.

Although he did not go to Kirkeby's lengths in the marketing of his band, Elizalde was clearly aware of the importance of publicity, as is shown in his contributions to *Melody Maker*. In particular, his articles on American musicians and hot playing in 1927 helped to reinforce his increasing prominence in London. These subjects are intrinsically linked in contributing to the British understanding of the possibility of spontaneous individual expression in jazz, which was dependent on aural identification of individual musicians and recognition that improvisational processes were not necessarily reliant on notation. The Elizalde brothers' series of articles from May 1927 entitled 'Who's Who in American Bands' provided the detail about the musicians that could be heard on American recordings. This had often been the subject of guesswork and inaccuracy in Britain prior to this, and established the brothers as prominent authorities on hot music. Fred Elizalde's article 'Phrases or the meaning of "hot" choruses' is an important early explanation of improvisational practice. His ideas are reinforced in the editorial of the same issue ('"Hot" Music to the Rescue: Why it is essential'), which notes the near synonymous function of the composer and improviser in providing hot material, but clarifies that only 'When this is not scored in advance this is extemporisation.' (June 1927:531). Elizalde encouraged musicians to move away from paraphrase improvisation, introducing ideas that clearly present a significant departure from what had previously been written on the subject in *Melody Maker*:

> ... there is nothing in the melody through which you can show that you have a soul instead of being just a music (?) producing machine. To get soul into our playing we must have decent phrases to play and *there is the whole secret of modern dance music. These phrases are not given to us, so we must make them for ourselves ... .* [American musicians] do not just spilt long melody notes into shorter ones, or double notes. They make up beautiful phrases based both on the original melody notes and their harmonies. Sometimes they even alter the harmonies to fit a special phrase of which they have thought. These phrases, as well as having melody, are so designed to produce clever rhythms ... . (June 1927:585, emphases as in the original).

Despite the presentation of radical ideas in words and music, Elizalde achieved considerable success in Britain, which was undoubtedly due to his ability and willingness to adapt his group to the demands made upon him by the performing environments of the Savoy Hotel and BBC broadcasts, although it is unclear whether this was enforced or suggested by these institutions. Either way, the 'Fred Elizalde and His Music' recordings included waltzes in the first session of January 1928 and a violinist and vocal numbers were incorporated from April 1928. Further enlargement in July included three violins and a harp, and also pianist Jack Russin, another musician from the California Ramblers' circle, which allowed Elizalde to take the role of leader and one assumes conductor, a typical feature of British dance bands.

In October 1928 the Savoy Orpheans were suddenly sacked from the hotel, and were replaced by Elizalde's enlarged band.[4] The resulting prominence of the band at the Savoy allowed Elizalde to incorporate extra Americans including Rollini's younger brother, Art, Max Farley and Fud Livingston, who joined in March 1929. At this point the band had doubled in size from its debut at the Savoy. Art Rollini recalled that: 'The orchestra was truly superb, resembling Paul Whiteman's great orchestra in the USA.' (Rollini, 1987:14). Recordings from this period consist of sophisticated 'orchestral' arrangements that exploit the extended instrumentation that was now available. The enlargement of the band enabled Elizalde to split the band into two groups led by Adrian Rollini and Bobby Davis to play for the tea sessions on alternate weeks (Rollini, 1987:14). Some rest time was clearly required by the musicians as the Elizalde's band opened at the Palladium in April in addition to their Savoy commitments. Art Rollini recalled that 'we had to play three shows a day, plus both tea session and late evening session at the hotel.' (Rollini, 1987:18).

Despite the incorporation of appropriate numbers into the group's repertoire, (advertised as 'The Hall-mark of good dance music Fred Elizalde specially features

---

[4] This was the result of the band misbehaving on the bandstand in the absence of their leader, Reg Batten. Ahola recalled that 'on several occasions [Batten] failed to turn up to "front" the band, and one night we went onto the Grill Bandstand without him, and played as usual' but that they began to stand up to play their solos, which was deemed unacceptable by the management (Hill, 1993:42).

at the London Palladium The Waltz Success "Alone in a crowd", also the Great New Comedy Hit "My Only Consolation"' (*Era*, 1 May 1929:8), the band was not a great success at the Palladium:

> Fred Elizalde and his music from the Savoy compared unfavourably with Hylton and Somers. His arrangements are weirdly unwonderful, and I was at no time able to pick out a complete melody. Jean Barry and Dave Fitzgibbon leavened the deadly dullness by some excellent dancing, but the fact that two people I know fell asleep during the band's playing is proof enough that all is not well. It wants the strong hand of a real producer and the artistic touch of a clever arranger before it can be termed a classic. (*Encore*, 2 May 1929:8)

The accompanying dancers 'of the whirlwind or acrobatic order' (*Stage*, 2 May 1929:11) and even the 'the setting and ever-changing lighting, which placed the value of the band immeasurably higher' (*Performer*, 1 May 1929:11) tended to be reviewed with greater enthusiasm than the music itself in the theatrical press. Audiences were clearly accustomed to the high standards of visual presentation of dance bands when appearing on the variety stage. Edgar Jackson had warned that 'From a purely commercial point of view it may be found that the public will term the Band too "hot", since Elizalde's arrangements are very advanced, being based on modern harmony after the school of Debussy, Stravinsky and such like.' (*Melody Maker*, April 1927:337).

It has been suggested with reference to contemporary criticism that both the Savoy Hotel and the BBC were sufficiently opposed to Elizalde to stop him from performing. In fact, Elizalde broadcast from the Savoy alongside the Orpheans and a tango band every Thursday and Saturday from 10:30 pm until midnight from New Year's Eve 1927 until March 1929, with only a two month break in August and September 1928 (BBC Programme Records), during which the band toured to Paris and Ostend (Cundall, 1946). The reason for the eventual cessation of broadcasts from March 1929 was that the existing contract between the Savoy and the BBC came to an end and was not renewed. Elizalde continued at the Hotel until July 1929 when his contract with the Savoy also expired (Savoy Archives). This suggests that Elizalde's concessions to dance music were sufficient to ensure that he was not immediately dismissed, but that his hot tendencies did not encourage his long-term future with these establishments and his music may have been regarded as just a passing novelty. The opposition to Elizalde was probably more moderate than is often suggested. Tom Cundall, who heard the band's broadcasts as a teenager, recalled that:

> The band was widely acclaimed by all the rhythm enthusiasts who heard it in person and over the air, but the more conservative patrons of the Savoy and listeners to the BBC were, as usual, quick to voice their disapproval ... but ... in general the band received the praise that Elizalde's courage and rare talent so richly deserved. (Cundall, 1946)

The oppositional reception of the group exemplifies the emergence of a specific audience for hot music aside from that for mainstream dance music. Elizalde's music could have been the first exposure to hot music for young aspiring musicians and other members of the public. The juxtaposition of Elizalde and the Orpheans in the BBC broadcasts elucidated the differences between hot jazz and familiar dance music. Musicians and enthusiasts of hot music would have admired Elizalde for bringing this style of music to the fore in accessible formats such as radio broadcasts and variety shows. The popularity of the group with musicians was undoubtedly aided by *Melody Maker's* championing of Elizalde. The presence of American musicians that audiences had already read about or heard on record authenticated Elizalde's band: '[the American musicians] were already well-known to us as members of various recording groups in the States, notably, perhaps, of the California Ramblers' (Francis, April 1974:18).

The presence of Quealey, Davis, and Rollini was undoubtedly influential for the British musicians that played alongside them or heard them at this time. Adrian Rollini's playing was a direct inspiration for Harry Gold 'he was the greatest influence on my taking up that instrument and on shaping my style on it' (2000:35), and his influence on Arthur Lally's baritone saxophone with Firman's Rhythmic Eight is aurally apparent. George Hurley, a violinist that who had began opposite Elizalde in the Orpheans but later played in Elizalde's group recalled 'hearing Rollini every night – why, it was like going to school again. The Americans were virtually being teachers without knowing it. They were enjoying themselves and we were learning, because this was entirely new.' (quoted in Sudhalter, 1999:175.) Billy Amstell recalled being recruited for an audition for Elizalde's band (a position eventually filled by Philip Buchel) whilst sitting in with Leon Abbey at the Deauville Club, and that to him 'Fred Elizalde was the jazz King' (1986:18). In addition to their work at the Savoy, the American musicians from the Elizalde band were active in the clubs and recording studios of London alongside British musicians, including work with Bert Firman and Spike Hughes, who was 'able to persuade famous American stars, currently playing with Fred Elizalde's orchestra at the Savoy, to come and spend and afternoon with us making records' (1951:65)

Whilst the performances of the group on BBC radio and in variety brought Elizalde's unique arrangements and some fine instrumental performances to the general public, it was, arguably, the minority rather than mainstream activities of Elizalde's band, such as the *Melody Maker* articles and 'Hot Music' recordings, that influenced musicians directly and therefore had a more significant impact on the evolution of jazz in Britain. Similarly, at tea dances only half of the full complement of musicians was used and new, often hot arrangements could be tried out (Tanner, 1971b:218). These dances took place in the afternoon when some fellow musicians were free and therefore potentially able to go and hear the band's experiments (see Ahola's description of attending the tea dances of other bands in Hill, 1993:14). Some of these tea dances were also broadcast.

Melody Maker arranged a free concert of Elizalde's band at the Shepherd's Bush Pavilion for British musicians on a Sunday afternoon, 23 June 1929. Such was the publicity that the band had received though their recordings and presence in *Melody Maker*, that 'Rapturous applause by an audience of Three Thousand: Two Thousand turned away' was reported in a special supplement to the July 1929 issue of the magazine. Pete Tanner was drummer in his school band at the time and hence eligible to attend: 'Before an audience of over three thousand fellow musicians, the twenty-three piece Elizalde orchestra presented a cross section of music in their considerable repertoire.' (1971a:29) Although Elizalde's arrangements for his large group and his symphonic jazz work *Bataclan* were the main features of the concert, there were also hot numbers performed by a small group billed as 'The Jazz Band', in which solos normally taken by Livingston and Quealey were instead performed by Arthur Rollini and the young British trumpeter Norman Payne (Tanner, 1971a:29). These numbers were particularly appreciated:

> Their style is modern – one might say ultra-modern – but they have the great advantage of wonderful versatility ... the marvellous improvisations of the famous "hot" section; when they did their stuff in tumultuous enthusiasm, especially Adrian Rollini who made us alternately laugh and gasp at his tricks with bass saxophone, "hot" fountain pen, and goofus ... . The concert was an undoubted success ... . (*Performer*, 26 June 1929:9)

> ... to say they brought the house down would be to put it mildly ... . Anyone who thinks hot playing is not appreciated ought to have heard the thunderous applause which followed this ... . (*Melody Maker*, June 1929 supplement: ii)

One of these hot numbers was *Nobody's Sweetheart*, which had been recorded by an Elizalde dectet in the previous month.[5] The recorded performance, like *Singapore Sorrows* discussed earlier and which was also included in the concert, omits Rollini's bass saxophone and consequently has a lighter, swinging feel. The arrangement begins with a *tutti* hot paraphrase of the melody, which is followed by individual solos for many of the musicians, ending with a brief 'Dixieland' style coda, thus omitting obvious statement of the melody. The encores to the concert, *Sweet Sue* and *Tiger Rag*, would have been familiar to the audience of musicians and hence Elizalde's versions made a great impression:

> ... everyone was given a chance to shine, and hot choruses of the most marvellous kind, to the accompaniment of a rhythm section, which many who attended the concert claim is the finest in the world, bar none, tumbled over each other. Adrian Rollini, with his goofus, particularly seemed to capture the imagination of this very appreciative throng. (June 1929 supplement: iii)

As much as any music that the band presented, the success of the event set an important precedent for *Melody Maker* to actively promote concerts to enable musicians to take advantage of American jazz musicians: 'I would go as far as to say that, had this concert not been the success that it was, the Melody Maker would have never sponsored those given for Duke Ellington and his orchestra' (Tanner, 1971b:217). Such concerts enabled American musicians, who often performed in situations in which their repertoire and performance style were restricted, to

---

[5] Arthur Rollini recalled performing this number on board ship on his way to England in March 1929 (1987:13).

perform more freely for the benefit of significant numbers of their British counterparts.

Firman's Rhythmic Eight

Elizalde may well have been an influence on Bert Firman's output from 1928, particularly in the development of the Rhythmic Eight, which has often been noted for its consistent hot jazz content (see, for example, Scott, 2002:88 and Godbolt, 1986:66). Like Firman's numerous other recording groups, the Rhythmic Eight (which usually consisted of more than eight musicians) featured American soloists such as Sylvester Ahola and Perley Breed backed up with proficient British players. The evidence suggests that the Rhythmic Eight was more than yet another pseudonym for a Firman-led group on Zonophone, indeed, the name itself stands out as it does not identify the group as a 'dance orchestra'. Like many similar American small groups, there is no record of the Rhythmic Eight performing live. If this did occur, it would certainly have had to have been late at night in a club, as most of the musicians involved held regular positions in dance bands including those at the Savoy Hotel and Ambrose's band that would have been playing every night. Thus, the Rhythmic Eight had a specific function as a recording group that was much less constrained by the demands, that were clearly understood by Firman, of live performance of music that was intended for dancing. Hence the arrangements of the material are sometimes quite adventurous. For example, the introduction of *Back Beats*, composed by Frank Guarente, features an unusual introduction that feels in three, rather like the aforementioned *Alabama Stomp* by the Red Heads. After the slow blues opening on *I Left My Sugar Standing in the Rain*, the arrangement suddenly moves into double time. Most significantly, the (re)arrangements allow space for more extensive solos, which can deviate away from the melodic paraphrase style of improvisation.

Although the group was not as constrained as a 'dance orchestra', they clearly still wished their records to be successful in the marketplace and thus struck a compromise, balancing hot instrumentals with more commercial numbers. Thus, in addition to some impressive improvised solos, the Rhythmic Eight recordings included vocal refrains, a hallmark of commercial music in this period, 'many novelty numbers and waltzes with little jazz interest' (Newitt, sleeve note, *The Rhythmic Eight Volume 1* MELLO 0004) and use novelty instruments such as the xylophone, which are selectively ignored by those compiling CD re-releases in favour of tracks with clear 'jazz interest'. A balance between hot and commercial is also evident within the content of individual numbers, which could contain both vocal refrains and hot solos, sometimes even at the same time (for example, Ahola's obbligato to the vocal on *Can't Help Lovin' Dat Man*).

It has been identified that hot qualities were introduced into popular music in Britain through the arrangements used and the contribution of individual, often American, soloists. Elizalde's groups stood out in that both the arrangements and solos were of consistently outstanding quality. The Rhythmic Eight output built on the approach to hot jazz developed by Firman with his other groups, adapting stock orchestrations of popular songs. According to Sylvester Ahola, it was British saxophonist Arthur Lally that 'routined all of the Firman records, and did all the brainwork for that outfit, making up all the sketchy routines', although he was 'always receptive to new ideas', allowing Ahola to contribute to some of the arrangements. (Hill, 1993:41). However, the Rhythmic Eight did not rehearse regularly, the personnel was variable and the arrangements were often made on the day of the recording, unlike Elizalde's musicians, who played together every day, used specially written arrangements and could try out new ideas at tea dances. Although Firman used the best musicians that were available, he was reliant on a few key players to provide hot solos, usually Ahola and Breed, whereas Elizalde had a large number of proficient musicians from which to choose and some of his small group recordings feature as many as six different solos. Consequently, the Rhythmic Eight, when their output is considered holistically, falls stylistically between Elizalde's two main groups, as they were to an extent both musically unable and commercially unwilling to break free completely from dance music conventions.

The End of an Era

Just as Elizalde's contributions to hot jazz in Britain were beginning to be recognized and adopted by groups such as the Rhythmic Eight, events occurred that were to diminish the possibilities for British musicians to experience hot jazz directly and to play alongside American jazz musicians. The stock market crash in October 1929 froze Elizalde's funds, the Rollini brothers returned to America when they realized that they wouldn't be paid (Rollini, 1987:21). Quealey and Davis had already left without warning prior to the Shepherd's Bush concert apparently 'on the receipt of disquieting domestic news' (*Performer*, 26 June 1929:9) but Nelson reveals that 'it is now averred that their income tax arrangers were responsible for their flight' (1934:139). Allegations of income tax fraud were also made to the Ministry of Labour, demonstrating that economic grounds continued to represent a significant reason for the opposition to alien musicians. Certainly, American musicians working in Britain began to come under increasing scrutiny from the authorities from this time.

Although the almost continuous succession of bands for the Kit-Cat Club had provoked concern from the Unions in 1925, the Ministry of Labour was clearly prepared to be persuaded that American bands were highly specialized and had something different to offer that could not be provided by British groups. In practice the procedures continued much as before and as we have seen, significant numbers of American bands and individuals entered the country between 1925 and 1929. Certainly, the regulations governing the admission and employment of American musicians seem to be far from clear or rigorously enforced in this period. However, the worsening global economic situation from around 1929 was key to the increasing restrictions that both British and American musicians faced when they wished to work across the Atlantic. Entertainment unions and governments were under pressure to give jobs to native musicians rather than aliens, although foreigners often had special attributes that appealed to audiences. It is important to recognize the similarity of the situation on both sides of the Atlantic at a time of a general increase in unemployment, particularly amongst musicians, as the 'talkies' made their services redundant in cinemas. British dance bands became popular in America in the same way that American jazz bands were fashionable in Britain, particularly after the first transatlantic broadcast of Jack Hylton's band in 1931 (Faint, 1999:30).

In fact, in May 1929 Hylton's band received an offer of an engagement at the Roxy and Paramount Theatres in New York, but the American Federation of Musicians threatened to strike if the performances went ahead (Faint, 1999:24), which made the fulfilment of the engagement an impossibility. The AFM regulations apparently required musicians to be resident in the country for six months before they could join the Union and undertake engagements (see correspondence in TNA: PRO LAB2/1188/EDAR528/2/1929). The widely publicized opposition and cancellation of Hylton's visit to America contrasted with the significant presence of American musicians in the London dance band scene, with newspapers asking why Ted Lewis was at the Kit Cat Club if Hylton was not allowed to go to the States (Press Cuttings, Jack Hylton Archive). This raised the issue of reciprocity that became the focus of the re-opened debate surrounding American musicians in Britain in the early 1930s.

Letters and deputations to the new Minister of Labour, Miss Bondfield, from the Musicians' Union, the British Empire Union, the London Trades Council and the Trades Union Congress in 1929 reported problems in ensuring that American musicians did not take on extra work outside their main engagement, which was clearly a widespread practice at this time; the ease with which extensions to work permits could be obtained, and the lack of Ministerial consultation with the Musicians' Union on the employment of aliens. In reply, it is clear that although the Ministry had a policy that a British band should be employed alongside the American band, and that no more than 25 per cent of any band should be American, there was little regulation of individual musicians once they had been admitted, and that a stalemate situation with the Union whereby they 'opposed permits in every case' rendered these negotiations meaningless. The Minister considered that the existing procedures regarding the importation of alien bands were sufficient, and the Unions' expectations that a Labour government would take action were disappointed (TNA: PRO LAB2/1188/EDAR528/2/1929).

Consequently, a dance band section of the Musicians' Union was formed at a meeting in August 1930, with a policy of 'the tightening of restrictions upon the entry of aliens and the ultimate exclusive employment of British musicians' (*Melody Maker*, September 1930:739) as well as improving pay and conditions, in response to the hard line being taken by the powerful AFM. It was considered that the government had not co-operated with the Musicians' Union and that they were 'scared at the possibility of international reprisals if Britain were to apply the [1920 Aliens] act rigorously' (*Melody Maker*, September 1930:739). Although bandleaders such as Hylton and Ambrose recognized the importance of visits from American musicians of the highest quality, *Melody Maker* reported that the 'feeling of the meeting was strongly in favour of closing the doors to further importations'.

Hylton and Ambrose would have had the most to lose from a ban on American musicians rather than a resolution of the situation with the establishment of a reciprocal scheme, since it was in America that these bands could potentially 'earn the best money', just like American bands and musicians in Britain (*Melody Maker*, September 1930:740).

An 'informal conference' involving the Musicians' Union, the Hotel and Restaurant Association and Ciro's Club was convened by the Deputy Secretary of the Ministry of Labour in November 1930. The general opinion was that the improvement in British bands was such that whole American bands had less to offer in terms of entertainment or educative potential for British musicians, but that importing some American individuals and bands could still be justified 'to produce certain specialities and new developments' and that 'a way must be left open for the admission of new ideas' (TNA: PRO LAB2/1188/EDAR528/2/1929 Minutes of Informal Conference, 3 November 1930). For several years a flexible policy was maintained whereby American bands could perform in variety halls and in dance halls only when the resident British band was retained, but not in restaurants, where free admission was perceived to act to the detriment of British bands by depriving them of their audiences. It was under these regulations that the visits of Louis Armstrong and Duke Ellington took place (TNA: PRO LAB8/1926 Foreign Dance Bands, 26 September 1934).

Chapter 9

Louis Armstrong and Duke Ellington

Although the black roots of jazz were increasingly recognized in Britain by 1930, and the music was acclaimed and condemned as a result; in practical terms, black musicians were generally under-represented in Britain in both live and recorded performance. After the controversial plantation revues discussed in Chapter 7, black music theatre productions such as *Blackbirds*, which made a significant impression on Spike Hughes, Constant Lambert and Evelyn Waugh amongst many others, remained a constant presence. A succession of black bands including those led by Sam Wooding, Leon Abbey and Noble Sissle visited Britain. Although this ensured the continued representation of black music, these performers functioned primarily as novelties in the theatre or dance hall and often provided entertainment that often served to perpetuate racial stereotypes that were unhelpful to the serious appreciation of jazz. It is not surprising that such stereotypes and particularly the discourse of primitivism continued to remain relevant in the reception of black performance in the 1930s.

The participation of black musicians in British dance bands was limited at this time. Although British dance bands presented attractive opportunities for American musicians in the late 1920s, but those that were employed in this context were exclusively white. In conversation with the West Indian bandleader Ken Johnson, Bert Firman acknowledged the problem of employing black musicians in 'swank hotels and restaurants', saying that one such musician in a band 'would be a novelty. But a second one? I'm afraid he would have to be better than anybody else. I'd do it, but I'd have to work hard selling him to management' (1985:278). Integrating black musicians into dance bands in their upper class venues could be problematic, and contemporaneously the British government was ensuring that it was more difficult for entire American bands to visit and perform in the country. Therefore, it was difficult for Britons to experience live performances by African-American musicians.

Spike Hughes emphasizes the sense of dislocation that British musicians felt from the American sources of jazz:

> ... the contact with a distant transatlantic world was more important to jazz musicians of my generation than is generally realized ... to meet the few visiting stars of American bands which came to this country, even to talk with new arrivals from the States who brought hitherto unknown records or a titbit of personal information about some of our idols, was a stimulating experience. (1951:102)

Recordings represented the main way in which African-American jazz could be experienced in Britain. However, whilst 'almost anyone could, and many did, possess very good collections of negro jazz' before the 1930s (Tanner, 1971:218), this was by no means a common situation. For Eric Hobsbawm, and many other enthusiasts in Britain in the early 1930s, experiences of jazz on record were limited by financial considerations: 'The sort of teenagers who were most likely to be captured by jazz in 1933 were rarely in a position to buy more than a few records, let alone build a collection' (Hobsbawm, 2002:80). Recordings by black musicians were not as readily available in Britain as either hot white American groups or, of course, British dance bands. In addition, as we have seen, although Morton, Ellington, Henderson and Armstrong were reviewed in *Melody Maker* in the late 1920s, their work was not generally supported with the same endorsement and depth of analysis in the publication as that of many white bands at this time. Spike Hughes suggests that 'it was only towards the end of 1931 that the public (*via* the gramophone companies) was first able to hear [the Negro's] music to any great extent' (1951:146). Hughes had become a record critic for *Melody Maker* under the pseudonym 'Mike' in April 1931, with the Editor's intention that he would 'bring new ideas and new angles of criticism to our monthly discourses on the latest issues of dance records'. (April 1931:307).

Spike Hughes as 'Mike'

Hughes's radical stance on contemporary popular music was made clear in his first batch of reviews. He criticized established dance bands, for example Billy Cotton: 'what his band really needs is good, modern arrangements built round the players'; Jack Payne and BBC Dance Orchestra: 'I was reduced nearly to desperation by the monotonous lack of colour and variety in the arrangements, the heavily accented 1st and 3rd beats, and, above all, the unimaginative tempi'; Ambrose, whose 'arrangements, played, of course, with the familiar polish and intelligence, are a trifle stale if not actually dull' and Jack Hylton's band which he regarded as 'too big to make effectively rhythmic records' (*Melody Maker*, April 1931:307, 317). Hughes was, however, prepared to praise bands that he considered had made an effort to introduce hot or modern elements into their commercial offerings, but these were often groups with which he was associated. In April 1931, amongst the criticism of many other dance bands, Percival Mackey's *Folly to be Wise* selection was reviewed by Hughes as 'full of ingenious harmonic turns and thematic construction, and little hot passages for "the boys"'. Hughes had certainly worked with Mackey and might have performed or arranged the music on this recording. Hughes was able to exploit his anonymity as 'Mike' to promote recordings made by his own bands, referring to himself in the third person. For example, in his first review column he advised readers to listen out for *Some of these Days* 'which Spike considers one of his best efforts to date' (April 1931:309). Hughes articulated in his reviews that he considered jazz and dance music to be fundamentally American, and promoted the work of American musicians which set the standards to which he believed British musicians should aspire:

If we are to criticise English dance records then we can only see how they compare with those from America, for dance music will remain essentially American for many years. (May 1931:396).

Hughes typically reserved his highest praise for Duke Ellington: 'Ellington's is the band that appeals to me more than any other, and particularly when it lapses into the dreamy style of *Mood Indigo*' (April 1931:317).

In pursuing a comparative agenda between British and American bands in subsequent issues of the magazine, Hughes 'began to be ruder and ruder about the novelty fox-trots and so-called "comedy numbers"' produced by British bands (1951:112). Consequently from October 1931 *Melody Maker* allowed him to become a specialist reviewer of 'Hot and New Style Records', and 'Pick-up' (aka Dan Ingman, see Hughes, 1951:112) was recruited to deal with the commercial releases. Although Hughes's column was important in bringing new records to the attention of the readership and providing criticism, analysis and guidance for musicians and enthusiasts, his decided and inflexible opinions dominated discussions of hot music and jazz in *Melody Maker* particularly as he was doubly represented (as Spike and 'Mike') as a respected expert whose opinions would have carried significant weight within the profession.[1]

Early Musical Responses to Armstrong and Ellington in Britain

Although American jazz recordings that Hughes recommended were relatively rare in Britain, determined musicians and enthusiasts sought them out from shops such as Levy's in Whitechapel. Therefore, several years prior to the appearances of Armstrong and Ellington in Britain, their recordings were already exerting direct influence on British musicians, as can be observed with reference to Hughes and Nat Gonella respectively.

Nat Gonella

Nat Gonella had been given a gramophone and records by Gracie Fields, who was choreographer for the show in which Gonella was performing with Archie Pitt's Busby Boys in the mid-1920s (Brown, 1985:37). By the time he joined his first dance band in 1928 'Armstrong's records were playing an increasingly important influence on Nat's trumpet technique' (Brown, 1985:42) and he was also beginning to imitate Armstrong's vocal performance (Brown, 1985:45). Gonella quickly realized the inadequacy of the available sheet music for jazz performance, having sent for the sheet music of *Wild Man Blues* and discovering 'how much extemporizing Louis had introduced on to the recording' (Brown, 1985:43) and began to transcribe arrangements from records (Brown, 1985:46). In an article Gonella wrote for *Melody Maker*, he indicates how important records were as sources of jazz for British musicians, describing how he began by simple imitation

---

[1] Hughes held uncompromising views on female composers and jazz musicians that are expressed in his autobiography *Second Movement* (1951).

of Armstrong's tone, range and singing voice as well as learning his solos by heart. He recalled that he then began to work short Armstrong phrases 'into other numbers where the harmony permitted' and finally through variation and experimentation, 'it was but a short step to originating whole phrases. I had, in a word, learnt to play hot.' (July 1932:577.)

After playing with a succession of provincial dance bands, Gonella was recruited in 1930 by Billy Cotton where he was encouraged to continue his impressions of Armstrong, and was featured performing *Ain't Misbehavin'* with 'a brown mask over his head with holes cut for eyes, plus a crinkly wig perched on top of his head' (Brown, 1985:48), a description which recalls blackface performance. It was with Cotton that Gonella made his first recordings, and by the time of Armstrong's visit he had already recorded his own versions of several Armstrong numbers including *That Rhythm Man*, *Bessie Couldn't Help It* and *Tiger Rag*, and would have included these and others in live performances. It is likely that Gonella's performances would have been more widely heard in Britain than Armstrong's in the early 1930s, and Gonella recalled that he was quickly identified as 'the British Louis', probably before the arrival of Armstrong himself (NSA interview).

Spike Hughes

Although Spike Hughes had bought Ellington records in 1927, when Ellington's name 'was not yet known even to the expert collectors in this country' (1946:322), it was not until after 1931 that Ellington began to exert a great influence on his work. This suggests the importance of his 'first contact with genuine American Negro artists' (1951:104) that occurred when he was playing in Cochran's *1931 Revue*, as a formative experience. Buddy Bradley and Billy Pearce, African-American dancers involved in the show, had just arrived in Europe, and Bradley played Hughes 'a handful of records by Duke Ellington which had not been issued in Britain'. (1951:107). Hughes comments that the Americans brought 'not only the new jazz records not yet issued over here, but gossip from the streets and alleys of Harlem itself' (1951:102). This combination of experiences precipitated changes in his compositional style:

> As far as my own development as a jazz composer is concerned, I feel it is not without significance that I did not start to compose jazz until I had discovered the Negro's jazz for myself. While under the influence of Red Nichols and his white contemporaries I had been content to play the part of arranger, twisting the tunes of the day and the previous decade to provide the band with the material which was the everyday cud chewed by exponents of "hot music". The Negro, on the other hand, brought something which, while it was new in my experience of jazz, struck a familiar and welcome note in my own musical mind, something which I had unconsciously found to be lacking in dance music as I had known it: the application of music to lyrical and dramatic expression. (1951:146)

However, just as in Gonella's relationship to Armstrong, Hughes's initial response to Ellington was to imitate his style as a way of formulating his own.

Having already recorded Ellington's *Misty Morning* in December 1930, Hughes then recorded his own arrangements of spirituals and an adaptation of Ellington's *High Life* in his first session after Cochran's *1931 Revue*. He also augmented the brass section of his band to include three trumpets and two trombones, and the resultant sound of the band apparently caused 'a mild sensation in the profession' (Hughes, 1951:118), as it was noticeably different from most contemporary British dance bands. Later in the year Hughes composed *A Harlem Symphony*, influenced by Ellington's *Creole Rhapsody* (Tanner, 1981:11). Encounters with black performers also influenced Hughes in his choice of musicians for his bands from this date. As Hughes's groups existed primarily for recording rather than live performance, this allowed him a freer choice of musicians irrespective of any complications that might result for similar bands that were on view and subject to the prejudices of hotel or restaurant managers. Hughes used the African-American singer Joey Shields in his recordings of spirituals, and recalled that Shields was even credited on the record label at a time when 'no ordinary dance band had ever thought to mention its singer's name' (1951:118).

Leslie Thompson

The West Indian trumpeter Leslie Thompson also impressed Spike Hughes sufficiently to be included in his bands in the early 1930s. Although many young people in Jamaica aspired to leave the country and families usually saved up for a passage to New York, Thompson was amongst a minority that decided to emigrate to Britain. Thompson had visited Britain twice prior to settling in this country, firstly to attend Kneller Hall, the Royal Military School of Music, in 1919 (Green, 1985:27). He then returned to Britain to perform at the 1924 Empire Exhibition with the West Indian Regiment band (Green, 1985:44). The band also included Louis Stephenson and Leslie Hutchinson, who were also to become permanently resident in Britain from the mid-1930s. Thompson recalled that in 1929:

> I had an inflated optimism and decided to go to England. I recalled Egbert Thompson's success in France,[2] ... and my happy days in England in the army, so I packed all my instruments, bought a ticket, and left Jamaica for England. (Green, 1985:53)

Thompson was absorbed into the close-knit community of coloured people in London, which included several musicians (Green, 1985:54, 60-61). Although he was a classically trained trumpeter, and had not been involved in the limited dance music scene in Jamaica (Green, 1985:20-21), he soon formed a band with other coloured musicians, some British born and others fellow immigrants. Andrew Simons suggests that Thompson's aim to form an all-black dance band was influenced by the work of Marcus Garvey, who established the United Negro Improvement Association in Jamaica whilst Thompson was still resident there (sleeve note to TSCD781:12). Thompson recalled reading *Negro World*, the newspaper of UNIA, in the early 1920s (Green, 1985:36). His first group was not a

---

[2] Egbert Thompson (no relation) had told Leslie Thompson 'of the work and pay available in the commercial music world of Paris' (1985:44).

success as 'we sounded like little children against those American bands' (Green, 1985:61), but Thompson believed 'that a good coloured band would have got work in England at that time ...[as] the sounds of Armstrong, Ellington and Lunceford, and all those big bands, were all the fashion' (Green, 1985:61). Thompson attributed his eventually successful career to being 'the only coloured trumpeter in London when Louis's records became the talk of the music business, and so my face was my fortune.' (Green, 1985:65). He recalled:

> I had never heard anything of him [Armstrong] in Jamaica ... the style was new to me, and that swing, that beat, was tremendous. Everyone was listening to the records, and certainly I had never heard bands with that beat before. Our hotel bands were just milk and water by comparison. That beat and punch, and swing. It taught me a lot, and I knew my concept of trumpet playing was lacking. (Green, 1985:65)

Although the British experiences of African-American jazz prior to the arrival of Armstrong and Ellington may seem to be limited to the availability of recordings that provided direct experiences of their music for a minority, musicians such as Gonella, Hughes and Thompson then brought this music to a wider public through the filter of their own performance, composition and criticism. Therefore, recordings contributed significantly, if often indirectly, to the raising of certain expectations that influenced the reception of Armstrong and Ellington in Britain. Humphrey Lyttelton recalled the importance of Gonella in raising Armstrong's profile in Britain in Gonella's obituary:

> What he was actually doing was his own East End cockney version of Louis Armstrong, both singing and playing, and so his records led me to Armstrong. Nat was king and Armstrong was the emperor. What was important about Nat was that he was the first musician in Britain really to recognise the worth of Armstrong. Many musicians in the early 1930s regarded Louis as being, musically, on the rough side. Then because of Nat's showmanship – old clips show him singing versions of Armstrong's songs and playing the trumpet in the style of Armstrong – attention started to be paid to Armstrong himself. (Obituary in the *Guardian*, 8 August 1998)

Thompson's experiences in Britain demonstrate that there was a demand in the early 1930s, prior to his often-cited development of an all-black band with Ken Johnson, for black musicians to provide what were often perceived as 'authentic' performances of jazz. The popularity of jazz as black music was not an isolated development at this time as noted in Chapter 3, and Thompson himself recalled: 'there was a peak of Negro success in London in the 1930s – Robeson, of course, with those films, and on stage, and that magnificent voice; and Nancy Cunard had published *Negro*' (Green, 1985:89). Jones and Chilton have observed in relation to Armstrong's 1932 appearances that:

> The timing of his visit was favourable ... . The hard core of enthusiasts among dance musicians and fans was numerically strong enough to support him. Earlier, Armstrong would have found Britain unprepared for him. (Jones and Chilton, 1975:158)

Armstrong and Ellington in Britain

The circumstances surrounding the visits of Louis Armstrong and Duke Ellington to Britain in the early 1930s have been described in depth in the extensive literature. Here I propose to focus on contextualizing their initial performances and reception, focusing primarily on the period surrounding their first engagements, which was in both cases a fortnight at the London Palladium beginning on 18 July 1932 and 12 June 1933 respectively (both musicians subsequently toured nationally).[3] At the Palladium, a variety theatre which had played host to the ODJB over a decade previously, the Americans encountered a diversely constituted audience ranging from the most knowledgeable fans of their music, such as Nat Gonella, Spike Hughes, and Leonard Feather; to the regular variety show audience, who might not have been familiar with their music but had their own equally clear ideas about what to expect from the evening. Their success or failure depended to a large extent on their ability to address the diverse expectations of these audiences within the restrictions of a spot on a bill.

Motivation for the Visits

Both Armstrong and Ellington had decided to come to Britain for similar reasons as many American musicians had visited during the 1920s. Armstrong said 'I decided I needed a good rest and vacation, and that I would like to see Europe' (quoted in Jones and Chilton, 1975:157). Giddins illuminates further that he was also threatened by a lawsuit against him when he received the offer to appear in England (2001:102). *Melody Maker* reported that Ellington's 'proposed trip is more in the nature of a holiday ... . As Mr Mills told us ... the boys will be glad for a break and a change of scenery' (January 1933:66). Nicholson suggests that Ellington had 'become disenchanted with the music business, even entertaining dark thoughts of abandoning his career' despite his undoubted success in America at this time (1999:131).

Although, as Collier states 'for some years before 1933 it had been widely understood by black show people that Europe was a species of heaven, and meant to go and see it for themselves' (1987:153), black jazz was often presented as a mere novelty in British variety shows and the social situation was far from utopian. The musicians might have expected a lack of racial prejudice in Europe, but arrangements regarding their accommodation in London proved problematic. Dan Ingman of *Melody Maker* had to telephone endless hotels to find rooms for Armstrong and his party (*Melody Maker*, August 1932:616), and although Ellington stayed at the Dorchester, 'the other musicians were scattered around a number of small hotels and rooming houses' (Collier, 1987:155). These situations

---

[3] *Melody Maker* predicted accurately that 'in the provinces, or even in the suburbs, we fear that Louis would be too much for the general public' (*Melody Maker*, July 1932:530-31). The visitors did encounter prejudice and poor reviews of their performances and broadcasts outside London. However, both Armstrong and Ellington were well received during their visits to Scotland.

may have resulted from the insufficient planning for Armstrong's visit, and a normal arrangement where Ellington would reside in a better hotel than his musicians, but nevertheless were reported in outraged tones in the press (Ulanov, 1946:134). This demonstrates the paradox of the presence of racism in British society but yet strength of resistance against it, in print if not always in practice.

Preparation and Publicity

Despite the apparent similarities between the formats of the two visits, consideration of the publicity and logistical arrangements exemplifies important differences between them that influenced the reception of Armstrong and Ellington's performances in Britain. Louis Armstrong's visit to Britain was only announced in *Melody Maker* a few weeks prior to his opening night, and in the August 1932 issue of *Rhythm*, which reported that 'News of Louis Armstrong's arrival in England came too late for publication in our last issue' (August 1932:27).[4] However, Duke Ellington had been anticipated for at least seven months prior to his arrival. Irving Mills, whilst in Britain in November 1932 (just as Armstrong returned to New York), confirmed a rumour that Ellington was considering a visit (*Melody Maker*, November 1932:861), having 'found British musicians well-informed and appreciative of Ellington.' (February 1932:121). It was probably during this visit that Mills entered into discussions with Jack Hylton, who personally guaranteed Ellington's visit (Nicholson, 1999:132). A 'tentative agreement' with the Palladium was announced in January (*Melody Maker*, January 1933:66), and confirmation of new details about the visit appeared in the magazine in every subsequent month. This contributed to great sense of anticipation, especially amongst musicians.

Ellington's success in Britain was undoubtedly due, at least in part, to the efficiency of his publicity machine under Irving Mills and Ned Williams (Collier, 1987:154), as well as Jack Hylton's role in the visit. This ensured that Ellington 'was preceded in the spring of 1933 by a terrific advertising and publicity campaign' (Ulanov, 1946:130). In his *Portrait of Duke Ellington*, Nicholson reproduces an Advertising Manual that provides fascinating detail on the way in which Mills wished Ellington to be represented in the media (1999:152-59).[5] Armstrong was not marketed in such a strategic way until Joe Glaser became his manager after his return from Europe in 1935 (Giddins, 2001:108). Of particular interest is Mills's insistence that Ellington should be sold 'as a great artist, a musical genius whose unique style and individual theories of harmony have created a new music' (Nicholson, 1999:153). Although the manual dates from after Ellington's first European tour, the similarity between several of the reviews of

---

[4] Confusingly, material in the issue of *Rhythm* dated August 1932 was written before the contributors had heard Armstrong play. The first review of his performance appears in the September 1932 issue.

[5] It is interesting to note that one of Mill's sample press stories in the Manual draws heavily on Ellington's success in Britain, particularly with royalty, to promote and legitimise the group (1999:157-8).

Ellington in Britain with Mills's suggestions indicates that it is likely that the British press were briefed in a comparable way. Notable in British reviews is frequent use of two phrases suggested in the manual as 'Punch Lines'; 'Harlem's aristocrat of jazz' and 'Creator of a new vogue in dance music!' the latter being Ellington's billing at the Palladium. In addition, Mills even arranged for a limited edition six-record commemorative album of Ellington recordings to be issued in England to coincide with his visit (Lawrence, 2001:196).

Ellington was subject of extensive consideration in the trade press before his arrival. *Rhythm* included an article apparently by Ellington himself in the June 1933 issue, which laid particular emphasis on the importance of the rhythm section and provided an introduction to the personnel of the band.[6] In the concluding part of the article, Ellington explores the idea of his work as art rather than mainstream popular success: 'popularity amongst musicians has meant a lot more to me than monetary gain', and of jazz as the expression of his race: 'What we could not say openly we expressed in music, and what we know as 'jazz' is something more than just dance music.' (June 1933:34-37). Similar ideas were expressed by Spike Hughes, whose championing of Ellington in *Melody Maker* through articles and record reviews was important in building Ellington's profile and contributing to the prior knowledge of his music in Britain. Hughes was keen to emphasize in exaggerated language that Ellington was a serious artist:

> ... one of the few great artists that America has produced; certainly Ellington is the first serious contribution the New World has made to the history of music...his great personal charm and humour, his very infectious smile and that quiet dignity and self-confidence that mark the man of genius ... . (*Melody Maker*, May 1933:353)

Contemporaneously with the confirmation of Ellington's appearance later in the year, Hughes had left Britain for an extended visit to America, where he reported his experiences in a series of articles in *Melody Maker* entitled 'Day by Day in New York'. These accounts would have had the effect of further validating Hughes's opinions and emphasizing his status as a knowledgeable jazz expert. In May 1933, a report of Hughes's first encounter with Duke Ellington appeared in which Hughes attempts to distance his idol from the commercial side of jazz through pure conjecture:

> One of the most encouraging things about him is his very healthy dislike of the pretentious noises which pass for jazz on Broadway ... . Duke even mistrusts some of his own music; I am quite sure he does not think so highly of his "Sophisticated Lady" number as others do hereabouts. (*Melody Maker*, May 1933:353)

The introductions to the members of Ellington's band that were published in *Melody Maker* and *Rhythm* provided information on a concept that was still relatively unfamiliar in Britain, whereby each musician had a distinctive solo role

---

[6] Mark Tucker has suggested that 'the editors at *Rhythm* may have worked over these articles fairly thoroughly, due to uncharacteristic turns of phrase' (1993:46). Also see footnote 7.

to play within the ensemble. Although acknowledging the importance of the band musicians to Ellington's work, Hughes is keen to attribute the overall effect to Ellington, describing the group as 'completely and utterly a mouthpiece for Duke's own ideas. There is not a note which comes from the remarkable brass section, or from that rich tone of the saxes, that is not directly an expression of Duke's genius' (*Melody Maker*, May 1933:355). Expanding this idea in a later article, Hughes wrote 'Unlike many less fortunate composers of the past, Duke Ellington carries around with him the ideal instrument upon which to play his music – his own orchestra' (*Daily Herald*, 13 June 1933:8), thus apparently aligning Ellington with the 'great' court composers of the Western art music canon. Hughes also went into some detail on the 'treatment of the tunes', mentioning Ellington's use of different mutes for the brass, his scoring for saxophones and the use of percussion (*Melody Maker*, May 1933:355). He was, however, critical of the Cotton Club, in which he had heard Ellington's band, particularly with reference to the unusual racial situation: 'A place where no Negroes are admitted, though as a concession the more distinguished members of the race, like Paul Robeson and Ethel Waters, are allowed, rather apologetically, to sit away in the corner.' Hughes 'walked out of the opening night proceedings in disgust. I was more than infuriated at having to pay an immense sum for the privilege of hearing Duke play chords of G, to introduce the spotlit celebrities that were present.' (May 1933:353). The combination of praise for Ellington and his musicians and criticism of the presentation and content of the performance was to characterize Hughes's subsequent influential writing on Ellington in London.

In comparison with the detailed and extensive previews of Ellington's visit, the few articles that appeared immediately prior to Armstrong's first stage appearance in London are generally vague in their indications of what audiences could expect from his performances. *Melody Maker* reported that Armstrong was arriving without a band, and there was concern that 'Even if he arrives within the next few days he will not have time to rehearse a stage act' (July 1932:530). This indicates that there was some confusion about what Armstrong was actually expected to do in his performances. The later announcement in *Rhythm* could only report that 'an English orchestra, made up of West End musicians', would accompany Armstrong (August 1932:7), which did not turn out to be the case. *Melody Maker* attempted to link the forthcoming performances with music with which readers were familiar in an article entitled 'Imitation without apology: Why do I Copy Armstrong?' by Nat Gonella (July 1932:577) discussed above, in which Armstrong was unsurprisingly presented as the 'greatest dance trumpeter on earth'. Conversely, *Rhythm* included an article apparently written by Armstrong entitled 'Greetings to Britain!' (August 1932:27-8)[7] which emphasized his originality: 'I have tried to be a creator, to give the public something they have never heard before' and similarly in a tribute by Paul Whiteman: 'His style is individualistic, almost impossible of duplication.' (August 1932:28).

---

[7] The story that the article that appeared in *Rhythm* in August 1932 was written by Armstrong whilst at sea (*Rhythm*, September 1932:9) seems somewhat apocryphal.

According to Max Goldberg, trumpet players would be most interested in the technicalities of 'how Armstrong obtains those wonderful top notes' (*Rhythm*, August 1932:7). Whilst *Melody Maker* expected that he would receive a 'tumultuous reception' from musicians, 'what sort of reception Louis Armstrong will receive from the general public' was less clear to contemporary commentators. It was predicted optimistically that after initial 'stupefaction' the Palladium audience would 'take Louis to their hearts' as they were 'educated up to the unusual in entertainment' (*Melody Maker*, July 1932:530-31). Similarly, an article in *Rhythm* expressed the opinion that 'to the laity his remarkable style is a little bewildering, and we watch the result of the Palladium experience with interest' (August 1932:7) There was some concern that Armstrong's performances would not be popular, and a 'Sensational Matinee Scheme for Melody Maker Readers' was devised to provide reduced price tickets, and readers were encouraged to attend: 'The chance to see and hear in the flesh the world's greatest dance trumpet player is one that may occur only once in a lifetime.' (*Melody Maker*, July 1932:531).

Arrival in Britain

As a result of the relative amount advance publicity and preparation that they received, whilst Ellington was met by crowds and newspaper photographers upon his arrival at Southampton, and 'the same scenes repeated *ad libitum* and *fortissimo*' at Waterloo station (*Melody Maker*, 17 June 1933:1), Armstrong had to make his own way to London where he was met by a solitary journalist, Dan Ingman of *Melody Maker* (August 1932:616). Ellington also broadcast a short interview on BBC radio with Jack Hylton on the day on which he landed in England, outlining the instrumentation of his band and some thoughts on the future of jazz. At the conclusion of the interview Ellington had emphasized the importance of his band to his success, a remark that was noted in *Melody Maker* as being 'typical of his unassuming modesty' (17 June 1933:1). By the time Ellington and his band arrived in London, several concert and dance engagements had been secured in addition to the Palladium appearances, including a studio broadcast on the BBC, a *Melody Maker* concert and dances within and outside London. (*Melody Maker*, 3 June 1933:2). Many of these additional engagements took place during the Palladium fortnight, and the advance planning meant that Ellington could commence his provincial tour immediately after closing at the Palladium. Armstrong, on the other hand, was restricted mainly to variety appearances throughout his time in Britain and was forced to 'rest' for two weeks having finished at the Palladium whilst more engagements were arranged (Rye, 1980b:185).

Figure 9.1   Duke Ellington and his Orchestra upon their arrival in Britain, with Spike Hughes (*centre, back row*) and Jack Hylton (*seated, holding hat*), 1933 (Max Jones Archive)

Reception at the Palladium

The reception of Louis Armstrong at the Palladium was extremely mixed, partially because the audience had little idea of what to expect. A review by outspoken critic Hannen Swaffer summated the contradictory reactions to Armstrong's performances under the heading 'Storm over Negro trumpeter' (22 July 1932:13), reporting that Louis Armstrong was 'now arousing furious arguments as to whether he is, or is not. Hundreds cheered him as though it were Kriesler, and others went to the bar' and concluded that 'None of these modern Trans-atlantic turns please everybody.' These reactions to Armstrong are confirmed by contemporary comment and reminiscence. For example, there are many 'eye witness' reports of audience members walking out of Armstrong's Palladium performances:

> Nat Gonella remembers 20 or 30 disgruntled customers leaving on the opening night, and more on subsequent evenings ... . Nat and his brother Bruts ... sat wherever they could and when protesters walked out, tried to trip them in the darkness. (Jones and Chilton, 1975:157)

> Even at the Palladium, where he was topping the bill, I saw a handful of elderly members of the audience get up and leave the theatre in high dudgeon. (*Melody Maker*, August 1932:663)

However, Max Jones recalled a more favourable reception:

> I don't remember any walk-out to speak of when I saw Louis; but I believe I attended one of the four matinees, at a reduced price for *Melody Maker* readers, which took place on the Wednesdays and Thursdays of the run. Audiences at these special shows naturally included a high proportion of musicians and fans. (1975:157)

Dan Ingman's review in *Melody Maker* also referred to a matinee performance packed with musicians so that unsurprisingly 'When his number came up on the indicator board there was a terrific burst of applause' and Ingman noted that Armstrong's 'reception beggars description' (August 1932:617).

Aside from these extreme reactions to Armstrong's performance, Swaffer also suggested that some people were indifferent or confused as they were simply unable to understand the performance on either a musical or linguistic level. He reported a member of the audience as saying 'That man, why, he did everything with the trumpet but play it', someone else demanded to be told 'whether he was right to think it was dreadful' and another critic could not understand what Armstrong was saying, apparently confirming *Melody Maker*'s prediction of public 'stupefaction'.[8]

Duke Ellington was generally very well received by all sections of the audience at the Palladium:

---

[8] Max Jones recalled Armstrong using 'faintly alien expressions' at the Palladium, such as 'Way down, way down', 'Keep muggin' ... lightly, lightly and politely', and 'Swing, swing, swing, you cats' (Jones and Chilton, 1971:164).

My chief impression of the English debut of Duke Ellington and his orchestra last Monday at the Palladium is the enthusiastic, almost frenzied reception which he got from a crowded audience. (*Sunday Referee*, 18 June 1933)

Scores of smartly dressed English people came to rave over them, and did. Many hundreds of people in the hinterland of the Palladium also raved and shouted and applauded. (*Daily Express*, 13 June 1933:11)

[The opening night at Palladium] scared the devil out of the whole band, the applause was so terrifying - it was applause *beyond* applause. On our first show there was 10 minutes of continuous applause. It was a tremendous thrill. In fact, that entire first European tour in 1933 was a tremendous uplift for all our spirits. (Ellington in *Downbeat*, November 1952:7)

It seems that the advance publicity for Ellington's arrival which meant that 'British dance band musicians and fans were wound up with expectation' (Collier, 1987:154), resulted in corresponding excesses in many of the reviews of his Palladium performances:

I realise that these words are too perfectly inadequate to describe what I have just heard and seen. (*Rhythm*, July 1933:9)

How to describe in so many words the most vital, emotional experience that vaudeville in England has ever known? An orgy of masochism, a ruthless exercise in sensuality ... it mined deep the fundamentals of every human in that multitudinous audience ... . I am not ashamed to say that I cried during the playing of Mood Indigo. Here was music far removed from the abracadabra of the symphony; here was a tenuous melodic line which distilled from the emotions all heritage of human sorrow which lies deep in every one of us. (Nelson in the *Era*, 14 June 1933:1)

Ellington's music did also have some potential for 'stupefaction', particularly amongst the uninitiated:

More than half [of the audience] ... was bathed in an ecstatic adoration ... the rest had bewilderment plainly stamped on their faces. "Is this music?" said my neighbour. (*Era*, 14 June 1933:1)

Max Jones recalled that a few members of the audience expressed some displeasure during *Black and Tan Fantasy* by throwing pennies onto the stage and walking out (Lawrence, 2001:202). In general, any negative reactions to Ellington were far removed from the public exodus that had attended Armstrong, although some critics, whilst noting euphoria in the public reception of Ellington, acknowledged that the music had limited appeal for them personally:

This too hot jazz music just does not appeal to my particular taste. (*Sunday Referee*, 18 June 1933:11)

In short, a very good dance band, playing ingeniously orchestrated music. I do not pretend to appreciate its merits to the point of fashionable ecstasy; but I like it – as a dance band. (*Daily Express*, 13 June 1933:11)

Armstrong and Ellington as Variety Acts

Both Armstrong and Ellington were often evaluated within the expectations of the audiences and critics of variety shows such as the Palladium. Although British dance bands had been appearing on the variety stage for many years, they had evolved features to appeal to the specific demands of an audience which expected 'acts'. Jack Hylton had advised:

> Scenic backgrounds and artistic effects are useful to a stage band, but easy good humour and a fair leavening of comedy is a necessity, because no music-hall audience can be kept serious for a long time without signs of restiveness. They pay to be entertained. (*Radio Times*, 8 February 1929:319)

Melody Maker's concern prior to Armstrong's arrival about the lack of time to rehearse a stage act belies expectations that primarily musical acts in variety shows would include visual interest as well as carefully rehearsed musical routines in their performances. Harry Gold recalled that the Roy Fox band presented a balanced programme in their variety appearances in the 1930s:

> We would be playing in variety theatres, to seated audiences as top of the bill. The idea was to give them a complete entertainment, with good music. There would always be one comedy number, but most of the show would be made up of swing pieces ... and ballads ... . (Gold, 2000:72)

Although it might seem surprising that Armstrong had come to Britain without his own band, this was in fact consistent with his working practices. In America in the years prior to his appearance in Britain he was featured as a soloist with big bands on the variety stage, including appearances in the show *Hot Chocolates*, in which he featured playing *Ain't Misbehavin'* (Giddins, 2001:86). In Britain there were some problems in obtaining a suitable ensemble to appear with him at such short notice. It seems surprising that given Armstrong's reputation amongst musicians that securing a backing band was so difficult, with Hylton and Hughes both apparently unable to arrange for their musicians to play. However, the Palladium management really wanted a black band to accompany Armstrong. Rudolph Dunbar, a black clarinettist resident in Britain, was approached to provide 'a coloured band, formed of English Negroes' but apparently found 'there were so few coloured musicians in this country that it would be impossible to form a worthwhile band' and 'a complete band of coloured musicians from Paris' was eventually arranged (*Melody Maker*, August 1932:616).

The insistence on a coloured band suggests an attempt to not only provide the necessary musical accompaniment for Armstrong, but to enhance the exotic and novelty appeal of the 'act' through a visual means that would be easily understood. The critic in the *Performer* wrote that the band provided 'a necessary background for the leader, but otherwise negligible' (20 July 1932:10), and most reviewers agreed that the band that performed with Armstrong were below standard:

The band, on the other hand, are not so hot, and that's all I need say about that! (*Era*, 20 July 1932:19)

I wish the act had been longer... [and] that the supporting band had been stronger ... . If Armstrong's own band could not be brought from America, an English band might as well have been employed. This one was imported from Paris. (*Daily Express*, 20 July 1932:15)

Beyond noticing that [the band] was painfully under-rehearsed (naturally) and had very little of anything, I didn't notice it. [Armstrong] should have had – and could have had – much better support. (*Melody Maker*, August 1932:617)

The consistency of this criticism in both the national and trade press and the fact that a group led by Billy Mason took over from the Parisian musicians after the Palladium performances suggests that it may be well-founded.[9] This experience led a writer in *Rhythm* magazine to express the hope that Ellington 'will bring his own men, and not engage a bunch who have, perhaps, no recording connections to worry about.' (June 1933:11). The criticism of Armstrong also indicates that the expectations of both the musical style and presentation of bands on the variety stage were foiled. The *Stage* noted critically that 'the playing of the band is mainly used as a mere background' (21 July 1932:3), expecting that ensemble would play a more significant part in the entertainment, but the review in *Rhythm* pointed out:

It would be distinctly unfair to criticise his act because it was not, strictly speaking, "an act". This is probably why the critics were so bitter in their description of his performance. They expected a band act and did not get one. The band apparently forms a rhythmic background for his amazing trumpetics. (September 1932:9)

Armstrong's musical performance was generally not considered in much depth in contemporary reviews, suggesting that reviewers generally found this difficult to evaluate. It is clear that for variety audiences, the music was more extreme than they would normally expect: 'Armstrong is, no doubt, a marvellous trumpet player, but one would like to hear him play something less hot.' Apparently the other turns on the bill (comedy sketches, eccentric dancing, Max Miller, and especially the 'microphoned rendition of "Auf Wiedersehen"') were more to the audience's taste (*Era*, 20 July 1932:19). The *Performer* noted that 'Armstrong is more suited to the specialized audience of hot rhythm fans rather than to patrons of the music hall proper, who will regard his work as a series of musical shrieks' (20 July 1932:10).

Armstrong's Palladium programme consisted mainly of popular songs that he had recorded in the years prior to his visit to London. The first Palladium performance consisted of *Them There Eyes*, *When you're smiling*, *Chinatown my Chinatown*, and *(I'll be Glad when you're Dead) You Rascal You* with *Tiger Rag* and *Confessin'* as encores (*Melody Maker*, August 1932:617) rather than the Hot Five and Hot Seven material that is mainly the subject of modern evaluations of

---

[9] Leonard Feather also described the original band as 'sloppy' and 'makeshift' (1986:10).

Armstrong's abilities.[10] Armstrong had recorded all of these numbers before 1932, and these recordings show that these songs were used as the basis for him to present his instrumental and vocal virtuosity with relatively simple riff-based or sustained harmonies in the band's accompaniment, which was a far cry from the 'sophisticated' symphonic arrangements performed by British dance bands of the time.

Variety audiences and critics could more readily appreciate Ellington's performance, as it conformed more closely to the expectations of a familiar 'band act'. The *Performer* noted admiringly from a variety theatre perspective that 'the work of Ellington's band defies challenge as an artistic instrumental success as well as a commercial money-spinner' (14 June 1933:10). The positive reception of the band was very much secured by the fact that the musical performance was strong and polished, with the band 'playing with the most bewildering precision ever heard from any dance orchestra' (*Rhythm*, July 1933:9). Even the *Times* reviewer appreciated the performance: '[Ellington] does at once and with an apparently easy show of ingenuity what a jazz band commonly does with difficulty or fails to do' (*Times*, 13 June 1933:12). Several reviewers commented on the band's uniform appearance:

> ... a colossal array of coloured musicians in immaculate grey evening dress, playing a mighty collection of glittering gold instruments, not only with all that uncanny musicianship that you might expect, but with showmanship never before seen in this country. (*Rhythm*, July 1933:9)

In addition to the band, the act included vocalist Ivie Anderson, Bessie Dudley 'The Original Snake-Hips Girl' and Bill Bailey and Derby Wilson who tap-danced. (*Melody Maker*, 17 June 1933:2). These features added diversity and visual interest to the band's performance, ensuring that it was compatible with the type of entertainment that was expected at the Palladium. In contrast, the *Performer* noted with some confusion in relation to Armstrong's performance that 'The dancers of the act did not appear' (20 July 1932:10). The combination of well-performed, comprehensible musical material with disciplined and ordered presentation that ensured Ellington's success at the Palladium with the diverse audience:

> Ellington the Amazing. Ellington the Musician. Ellington the Showman. Ellington the Artist ... . The Duke has not only provided a musical thrill for musicians, but a show for the general public ... . (*Rhythm*, July 1933:9)

There is evidence that Ellington's programme had been carefully chosen to appeal to a variety audience: 'A peculiar mixture of playing, torrid in the extreme, to purely melodious' (*Performer*, 14 June 1933:10). The programme performed on

---

[10] *You Rascal You* was used in the Betty Boop cartoon of the same name in which Armstrong was featured partly live action and partly as a cartoon character (see Gabbard, 1996 and O'Meally, 2004 for analysis), and in the film *Rhapsody in Black and Blue* (1932). Neither film was seen in Britain prior to Armstrong's visit, the British Board of Film Classification did not classify the latter, and the cartoon was only classified in January 1933.

the first night at the Palladium consisted of an equal weighting between Ellington's compositions and other popular songs, drawing on material that the band had recorded recently. The first two numbers that the band played, *Ring Dem Bells* and *Three Little Words*, were included in the Amos and Andy film *Check and Double Check* which had been shown in Britain (classified in November 1930), and the programme also included *Black and Tan Fantasy* from the film *Black and Tan* which had been classified on 24 April 1931 for exhibition in Britain.[11] Gabbard has noted that in *Black and Tan* 'Ellington makes the dignified impression that he and at least a few others hoped that he would make' (1996:163), and was thus compatible with the way in which Mills wanted him to be presented in Britain.[12] In addition, three numbers from the film *Bundle of Blues* (*Bugle Call Rag, Rockin' in Rhythm* and *Stormy Weather*) were included. This film, which also featured Anderson and Dudley, was not classified for exhibition in Britain until 10 October 1933. This suggests that the band's European tour acted as useful publicity for their forthcoming projects, which together with the fact that the band may have been familiar to British audiences through their previous film appearances demonstrates the development of a shrewd promotional symbiosis between recordings, film and live appearances.

Comparison with Recordings

Armstrong and Ellington were exotic acts for the Palladium, but aspects of their live performances were surprising even for those with some prior knowledge and expectations of the performers, derived from the relatively limited experience of them in photographs, recordings, film and from preview articles often written by journalists who had little more knowledge than their readers. It is clear that musical details in Armstrong and Ellington's performances were experienced for the first time at the Palladium, illuminating the inadequacy of recordings. Ingman wrote that Armstrong's 'singing is ... like it is on the records, only a thousand times more so!' (*Melody Maker*, August 1932:617) Similarly, Ellington's live performances were a more intense experience for fans of music in comparison with the recordings of his works that they had been able to hear prior to his visit to Britain:

> ... this wonderful orchestra, to which no gramophone record has yet done justice ... . (*Rhythm*, July 1933:9)

> You all know how Ellington's band plays through listening to his records, and I can only say that in the flesh, it is like that, only a thousand times more so. It literally lifts one out of one's seat. (*Melody Maker*, 17 June 1933:2)

---

[11] Classification information is courtesy of the British Board of Film Classification.

[12] Gabbard contrasts Ellington's film persona with the images of Armstrong and Calloway portrayed in the Betty Boop cartoons (African cannibal and singing walrus respectively) (1996:308), which, like Ellington's more positive image, similarly corresponded with the way in which some people viewed their live performances in Britain.

'Mike' could not resist the opportunity to write about Armstrong in his regular 'Hot Record Review' column. He admits that he had been suffering 'a growing indifference to Armstrong's records', which may have been due to the technological inadequacies of recording and, in addition, being unable to experience the visual aspects, as his live performance 'brings to light many points which have hitherto, on the gramophone, been matters for conjecture':

> I had never realised the extreme economy of means by which Armstrong achieves his effect, and the light and shade he uses to build his climaxes ... hearing Armstrong in the flesh has made me revise all my fixed ideas concerning his worth as an artist ... . I cannot reconcile the electric, incessant energetics of the entirely delightful personal Armstrong, both on stage and off, with the lazy and charming person I had conceived in my mind's eye as the Armstrong of the records ... [it is] a matter of what is lost in the way of facial expression and gesture between performance and reproduction ... having rid myself as far as possible of an age-old conception of Armstrong as an elderly gentleman, I am now able by virtue of retaining in my mind's eye all I remember of his personality to enjoy his records a hundred times more. ('Mike', *Melody Maker*, August 1932:665)

No one in Britain, not even the knowledgeable *Melody Maker* critics, had much idea about Armstrong's appearance and personality prior to the Palladium performances. Dan Ingman of *Melody Maker* was astonished when he met Armstrong at Paddington station:

> I nearly collapsed! From his photograph I had been expecting a six-footer, broad in proportion, with a moustache, at least thirty-five years of age. And this boy--! I hardly believed it. That is, until he spoke: there was absolutely no chance of mistaking that voice! (*Melody Maker*, August 1932:616)

As a result, the extra-musical or performative aspects of Armstrong's appearances attracted considerable attention and controversy:

> ... the most amazing thing is his personality. He positively sparkles with showmanship and good humour the whole time ... . He is, in short, a unique phenomenon, and electric personality – easily the greatest America has sent us so far. (*Melody Maker*, August 1932:617)

> I would rather enjoy his records than hear the man in the flesh, however. He is very obviously not the kind of stage personality for this country. His actual presence gave me, in a sense, a shock, and I much regret to have to admit to finding something of the barbaric in this violent stage mannerisms. (Joe Crossman in *Melody Maker*, October 1932:779-80)

Crossman's views were included in a *Melody Maker* feature entitled 'What I Think of Armstrong', which presented views of 'leading London Musicians'. The article demonstrates that there was almost unanimous criticism of Armstrong's stage persona amongst those that had been familiar with his musical performance from recordings.

Race and Performance Style

Armstrong's performance style, together with the perceived extremity of his musical performance, prompted a continuation of the primitivist mode of reception discussed in earlier chapters.[13] This was at the root of both positive and negative reactions depending on the weighting of 'fascination and fear and even envy' (Small, 1987:141) in the psychology of audience members when faced with this latest example of black culture. A combination of these emotions is exemplified in the 'fascination' that led to so many people going to see Armstrong, but the 'fear' that prompted them to leave during his performances:

> The business for Armstrong's first visit to the Palladium was said to be a record for the theatre at that time. So that every performance would be full at Louis' opening, but by the time he had to finish the theatre was half empty. (Gonella, quoted in Jones and Chilton, 1971:161)

> Armstrong … was heartily applauded … although the reception at the conclusion of the act was somewhat mixed, some booing being noticeable. (*Performer*, 20 July 1932:10)

Similarly, particular features of Armstrong's performance could be found to be simultaneously attractive, mystifying and threatening. Many critics simply noted that Armstrong 'puts a tremendous amount of energy into his work' (*Stage*, 21 July 1932:3):

> All the time he is singing he carries a handkerchief in his hand and mops his face – perspiration positively drips off him. He puts enough energy in his half-hour's performance to last the average man several years. (*Melody Maker*, August, 1932:617)

Robert Goffin, who dedicated his book *Aux Frontières du Jazz* to Armstrong and came to London from Belgium to hear Armstrong play in 1933, provides a particularly vivid description:

> In action Armstrong is like a boxer, the bell goes and he attacks at once. His face drips like a heavy-weight's, steam rises from his lips … the whole right side of his neck swells as though it must burst; then, summoning up all the air in his body for another effect, he inflates his throat till it looks like a goitre. (Goffin, trans. Beckett in Cunard, 1934:292)

As Jones and Chilton have suggested, the fact that Armstrong was 'an extremely fervent exponent as well as an unbridled presence on stage' was the main reason for the aforementioned 'exodus' of the Palladium audiences (Jones and Chilton, 1975:162). Descriptions such as Goffin's, although intended to be affirmative, nevertheless suggest that Armstrong would have had the ability to shock and threaten British sensibilities. Armstrong did begin to receive more overt praise by his second week at the Palladium, albeit still vague in detail, suggesting

---

[13] Apparently the Palladium programme 'depicted a monkey wearing a tuxedo and appearing to rise up on two legs to blow a trumpet' (Bergreen, 1997:351).

that after the initial shock audiences and critics had indeed taken him 'to their hearts', or that those that attended the later performances had a better idea of what to expect, although an element of 'stupefaction' may still have remained:

> ... the reception accorded Louis Armstrong is now considerably warmer than it was on the first night ... . (*Stage*, 28 July 1932:3)

> [Armstrong] was a great hit with his admirers, the applause completely holding up the interval. (*Performer*, 27 July 1932:10)

> Louis Armstrong is retained, and the King of the Trumpet too had an enormous reception. There is no doubting the cleverness of Louis' playing, I have never heard anything quite as good. (*Era*, 27 July 1932:19)

According to *Variety News*, Armstrong 'worked a little more piano than last week and was, consequently, more acceptable to English audiences' (*Variety Music, Stage and Film News*, 27 July 1932:4), suggesting the possibility that Armstrong might have responded to the initial criticism of the extreme nature of his performances.

Descriptions of Ellington on stage at the Palladium in 1933 could not have been further removed from the way that Armstrong had appeared to British audiences in the previous year:

> ... the calm, collected Ellington, sitting at the piano, playing and directing his mighty band, without any ostensible effort whatever ... . (*Rhythm*, July 1933:9)

In contrast with Armstrong, whose voice had appeared to Ingman to be out of proportion to his physical appearance, Ellington's personality and appearance was non-threatening to British audiences:

> Tall – over 6ft. – broad, with the shoulders, and build of an athlete, slightly plump in a way that seemed in accord with his obvious good temper. (*Melody Maker*, 17 June 1933:1)

> Ellington was always composed, always the gentleman, even to announcing his own compositions, in which he charmingly alluded as "our own compositions". (*Rhythm*, July 1933:9)

> I met Ellington in his dressing room. All I need say is that his charm is not confined to the stage. (*Era*, 14 June 1933:1)

This encouraged a general response to Ellington of fascination rather than fear, for example the apparently effortless performances of the band prompted the reviewer in *Rhythm* to ponder 'How is it all done?' (*Rhythm*, June 1933:9). Reviews indicate that Ellington was considered to be a showman who was in control of all the aspects of the music and how it was presented, which was reassuring for the audience as it balanced with the undoubted exoticism of the all-black band:

> Duke Ellington is a great showman. He presents his band with all the glamour and effects nature and electricity can give. There are subdued lights and monstrous shadows. His jazz drummer has the flamboyance of a cocktail mixer. His trumpeters abandon themselves in a frenzy. Yet, stripped of all its ornamentation, his band has great technical skill, and under his direction carries jazz to a high degree of syncopation and "hot" rhythm. (*Evening Standard*, 13 June 1933)

It was possible for the trumpeters, and other members of the band, to 'abandon themselves' without appearing threatening to the audience within the controlled framework of Ellington's act. *Rhythm* magazine referred to 'the big showman who makes Louis Armstrong seem insignificant – Fred Jenkins – whose solo work brought such applause that the Duke's piano solo was completely inaudible' (July 1933:9), but yet Jenkins's performances did not provoke any reports of adverse reactions comparable to Armstrong. Armstrong's showmanship was noted in *Melody Maker*, but *Rhythm* clarified that 'in the true sense of the word he is not a showman' as he did not conform to the understood conventions of variety showmanship: 'He shouted exultantly at his audience through the applause, which no showman would have done, and he cannot take a call.' (*Rhythm*, September 1932:11.) The energy of Armstrong's performances led Max Jones to doubt 'if he was in full control of himself' and served to emphasize his incongruous musical performance (Jones and Chilton, 1971:164).

Race and Sexual Implications

It has been shown that the reception of black performers in Britain in the early twentieth century is often closely linked with sexual fascination and fear. Several reviewers of both Armstrong and Ellington in London commented on the sexual implications of their performances. Ellington was more conventionally attractive to women, presenting a 'controlled' image of a charming gentleman:

> A crowd of at least sixty girls and women waited at the stage door in an effort to secure Duke Ellington's autograph. (*Daily Sketch*, quoted in Lawrence, 2001:203)

> There was trouble at the stage door last week. White women were waiting as usual. (*Daily Herald*, quoted in Lawrence, 2001:203)

This allusion to the potential 'trouble' of any liaison shows contemporary problems with inter-racial relationships in parts of London society. The nature of Ellington's sexual appeal, expressed through his music, was even alluded to in the *Times*:

> ... the excitement and exacerbation of nerves which are caused by the performances of his orchestra are the more disquieting by reason of his complete control and precision. It is not an orgy, but a scientific application of a measured and dangerous stimuli. (13 June 1933:12)

For the young Eric Hobsbawm, Ellington's music virtually replaced first love: 'Jazz brought the dimension of worldless, unquestioning physical emotion into a life otherwise almost monopolized by words and the exercises of the intellect.'

(Hobsbawm, 2002:81). Nelson felt the need to defend the criticism that Ellington's music was 'purely physical and sensuous in its appeal' in an article entitled '"Sexophone" and sin' in the *Era* (5 July 1933:15). Rather than denying this aspect of the music, Nelson instead references other composers whose music has a similar effect, notably Wagner. He concluded: 'After all, doesn't Freud attribute every human action primarily to the sexual act?'

In contrast, Armstrong's performances could signify a more overt, wild, 'primitive' and potentially threatening sexuality. Gabbard has noted that 'there was a libidinal energy in Armstrong's solos that could create a kind of foreplay leading up to climaxes' (Gabbard, 1996:143). Whilst it is hard to tell whether the Palladium audiences read his performances in this way, Swaffer noted that Armstrong 'makes love to the instrument as though it were a dusky belle ... he caresses his trumpet like a lover ... making it do things I never heard a trumpet do before' (*Daily Herald*, 25 July 1933:8), anticipating Gabbard's discussions and suggesting that Armstrong's performances could have sexual significance to the Palladium audiences.

Musical Style: Tiger Rag

The personalities that Armstrong and Ellington presented on stage were essentially compatible with the nature of their musical performances. The differing reception of Armstrong and Ellington's performances at the Palladium may usefully be considered with reference to *Tiger Rag*, a number that they both performed. *Tiger Rag* had been introduced to Britain primarily through the performances of the ODJB, who had also performed at the Palladium. It would have been more familiar to the audience than most of the other material that Armstrong and Ellington performed, as it had been widely recorded and performed by many different groups in the intervening period.[14]

Contemporary reviews indicate that Armstrong used *Tiger Rag* as a vehicle for virtuosic extended improvisation, with reports that he improvised eight or ten choruses. (*Melody Maker*, August 1932:617, September 1932: 713). Armstrong had recorded the number as recently as March 1932, in which his spoken introduction describes the piece as a 'trip through the jungle', which would have enhanced the perceived 'primitive' aspects of his performance if he had announced the piece as such at the Palladium. The extremely fast tempo of the performance meant that the number itself was stripped to its bare bones, with a brief rendition of the 'head' followed by an extended trumpet solo, the band indeed relegated to 'mere background'. Ellington's rendition of *Tiger Rag* was reportedly the opposite of Armstrong's extrovert presentation, in that it was 'played with a pianissimo never before achieved' (*Era*, 14 June 1933:1) and known as *The Whispering Tiger* (*Melody Maker*, 17 June 1933:2). The band's unusual rendering of this familiar

---

[14] Comparisons of readers' collections of recordings of this number were the subject of the 'Fermata' column in *Melody Maker* contemporaneously with Ellington's arrival in Britain. This appeared to act as a stimulus for the formation of Rhythm Clubs, where such astounding collections could be shared.

piece was often discussed in contemporary reviews as it most clearly illustrated the difference between Ellington's band and other ensembles to the British public. The number exemplified the controlled discipline of the band: 'Never have I heard men play so perfectly together, with such thorough understanding and so perfectly effortless' (*Rhythm*, July 1933:9). Although improvised solos were included, the fact that these were performed by several different musicians served to establish the holistic excellence of the band, which was more compatible with the audience's expectations than one star musician with inferior colleagues.

The Critics' Reaction

It is notable that the attitude of prominent music critics to Armstrong and Ellington was often at variance with majority opinion, as far as this can be gauged. The distance that had existed between Armstrong and Ellington and their fans prior to their appearances in Britain had contributed to these figures attaining a somewhat mythical status. This was inflamed by the reports that had appeared in the British press, in which, as we have seen, images of Armstrong as an individualistic innovator and Ellington as a great composer had begun to emerge, and such ideas were pursued in subsequent reviews of the Palladium performances in publications such as *Melody Maker* and *Rhythm* in which critics sought to legitimize the music.

Louis Armstrong's reception in Britain was often dependent upon the way in which the aspects of his performance that were understood as 'primitive' were received. Reviewers such as Hannen Swaffer reacted viciously to Armstrong's performances:

> Armstrong is the ugliest man I have ever seen on the music hall stage. He looks, and behaves, like an untrained gorilla. He might have come straight from some African jungle and then, after being taken to a slop tailor's for a ready-made dress-suit, been put on the stage and told to "sing".

> Armstrong's head, while he plays, is a unique as his music. Gradually, it is covered by a thousand beads of perspiration … . He tries in vain to keep dry with a handkerchief. He is a living shower-bath.

> And his neck swells out like a gorged python. (*Daily Herald*, 25 July 1932:8)

It is interesting to note some similarity in the description, but not in meaning or intent, of Armstrong here and in Robert Goffin's account cited above. Primitivist evaluations of Armstrong were not confined to his critics, because for writers such as Goffin, one of Armstrong's most devoted supporters, a performance style that suggested unmediated emotional expression had the effect of confirming Armstrong's artistic originality and creativity, qualities which were perceived to be inherently linked with his race: 'Armstrong is primarily a trumpeter, a stylist and a creator. No white man could have evolved such a style. It is as colourful as he is coloured.' (*Rhythm*, September 1932:11). As Ted Gioia has observed, for Goffin and others jazz was 'an intense experience, and a purely musicological approach to it, they felt, would only confuse matters' and they viewed the jazz musician as 'the inarticulate and unsophisticated practitioner of an art which he himself scarcely understands.' (1988:15).

As the Editorial in *Rhythm* magazine noted, Swaffer's review of Armstrong 'adequately describes the whole show as it must have appeared to anybody who did not understand how perfectly amazing is Armstrong's trumpet work.' (September 1932:9). It is interesting to note that in general those that wished to acclaim Armstrong tended to focus on his trumpet playing, which could be regarded as a more 'artistic' feature of his performances, whilst those that sought to criticize it neglected this aspect in favour of consideration of his singing, which could more easily be regarded as 'primitive' when the criteria of value of Western classical music were applied: 'To the listener oriented to 'classical' singing, Louis's voice, with its rasp and totally unorthodox technique, usually comes as a complete shock' (Schuller, 1968:100). An article in the *Daily Express*, in summarizing the questions being asked by Londoners about Armstrong's performances, contrasted these two modes of performance: 'Louis Armstrong! For or against? Can he play the trumpet or is he a crazy, enraged negro blurting noises at a long suffering public?' (28 July 1932:9). Gabbard has noted the difference between Armstrong's performance style when singing and playing with reference to films of the early 1930s, in that 'when he puts his trumpet to his lips, he becomes a different man' (1996:210). Even Armstrong's singing could be perceived diversely, as noise or art. Whereas Swaffer wrote 'His singing is dreadful, babyish, uncouth ... he makes animal noises into the microphone' (*Daily Herald*, 25 July 1932:8*)*, another critic evaluated Armstrong's singing in a more positive light, still resorting to the jungle metaphor, but emphasizing the artistic nature of primitivism:

> Singing, indeed, is hardly an adequate description of those incoherent, ecstatic, rhythmical jungle noises which none of Armstrong's imitators have yet succeeded in rivaling ... . This savage growling is as far removed from English as we speak or sing it – and as modern – as James Joyce. (*Daily Express*, 20 July 1932:15)

It is ironic that whilst they acknowledged the inadequacies of Armstrong's band, it was the musically knowledgeable critics, such as those of *Rhythm* and *Melody Maker*, that were generally untroubled by it. Max Jones, writing about the performances retrospectively, recalled Armstrong's performance style more clearly than the faults of the band (1971:164). One reason for this was that these critics, unlike variety audiences and reviewers, were primarily interested in Armstrong's performance and they had little interest in the other musicians in the background. But in addition, Gioia has suggested that jazz developed a 'romanticized nineteenth-century sensibility, with a fixation on musical personalities, a growing preoccupation with individual virtuosity, and, above all, a self-seriousness which bordered on pretentiousness.' (1988:15). This recalls Swaffer's pertinent comparison between the reception of Armstrong and Kriesler. Reviewers who attempted to validate Armstrong's performances as art often acclaimed him as a virtuoso soloist with emphasis on quantifiable or technical aspects of his performance and little reference to his presentation:[15]

> [Armstrong said] "This tiger runs very fast, so I expect I'll have to play five choruses to catch him up!" He played *eight* – all different! ... His technique, tone and mastery over his instrument ... is uncanny. Top F's bubble about all over the place, and never once does he miss one. He is enormously fond of the lip-trill, which he accomplished by shaking the instrument wildly with his right hand. (*Melody Maker*, August 1932:617)

The application of similarly romantic ideas about the 'great artist' was influential in the reception of Duke Ellington in Britain. Whereas Swaffer had compared Armstrong to Kreisler, as an effervescent, spontaneous, virtuoso performer, Ellington was consistently portrayed, prior to his arrival in London, in terms that evoke the consummate ease with which a genius is perceived to go about his work, especially by Spike Hughes in *Melody Maker*. Hughes developed these ideas in a positivistic article 'Meet the Duke! Who puts the MUSIC into JAZZ' published in the *Daily Herald* on 13 June 1933. Here Hughes aligns Ellington with 'art' music and composers: 'one of the few real artists America has produced ... the first genuine composer of jazz'. The music is described in absolutist terms: '[it] is not 'about' anything – except the Duke himself' and the band 'is not a "show" band ... it is a band content to play music for its own sake' (13 June 1933:8).

Comparative Evaluation

Following Armstrong and Ellington's visits retrospective comparison was frequent as attempts were made to evaluate their performances in the light of a reappraisal of jazz. Lambert took an extreme view, based on the precedent set by art music of the performer as an interpreter rather than a creator:

> It is the greatest mistake to class Louis Armstrong and Duke Ellington together as similar exponents of Negro music – the one is a trumpet player, the other a genuine composer ... . An artist like Louis Armstrong, who is one of the most remarkable virtuosi of the present day, enthrals us at a first hearing, but after a few records one realizes that all his improvisations are based on the same restricted circle of ideas, and in the end there is no music which more quickly provokes a state of exasperation and ennui. The best records of Duke Ellington, on the other hand, can be listened to again and again because they are not just decorations of a familiar shape but a new arrangement of shapes. Ellington, in fact, is a real composer, the first jazz composer of distinction, and the first Negro composer of distinction. (Lambert, 1934/R1966:187)

---

[15] In an interesting postscript, Louis Armstrong's 'death' was reported in Britain on the front page of the *Daily Express* on 31st March 1933 under the heading '"Man with Iron Lips" killed by his Art: Louis Armstrong Wonder-Master of the Trumpet'. The article describes Armstrong in romantic terms as 'victim to the terrific strain which his art put on him' and recalled the energy of his Palladium performances. *Melody Maker* reported in the May 1933 that Armstrong was not dead and had just been bitten by a dog (396). The following issue announced that Armstrong would be making a return visit to Britain, suggesting that the whole episode may have been an elaborate publicity stunt.

Nelson achieved a balanced evaluation of Armstrong and Ellington in *All About Jazz*, but also had to acknowledge Ellington and his band as 'superior':

> Armstrong, without much doubt, is the world's greatest trumpeter...he is the perfect example of spontaneous "hot" playing. His phrases appear to be constructed on the spur of the moment, and when he is playing one of his inimitable trumpet choruses, or singing in his throaty, negro manner, the rhythms he plays are almost impossible to put down on paper. When he sings, he is often so carried away by the rhythm that he forgets the words, and soars up and down and round the melody in the quaintest way imaginable. (Nelson, 1934:78)

> [Duke Ellington] is halfway between Armstrong and the refined style of the white players. Not that Armstrong is crude; I mean that Ellington himself orchestrates all the numbers for his band, and while their performance has much of the exhuberance of Armstrong, by reason of their orchestrations, it has a more orderly quality. But the players are just as amazing technically as those of Armstrong's band, and the fact that they are not completely subservient to one player (which is the case with Armstrong's orchestra and somewhat detracts from its excellence) gives them, I think, a slight superiority. (Nelson, 1934:78-9)

Having experienced Armstrong and Ellington's live performances in the early 1930s, it would have been clear to critics that the discipline and dignity of Ellington's performances were more readily aligned with notions of high art than Armstrong's exuberance. It is interesting that in appreciation of Armstrong's performances as art, critics in the 1930s adopt the same strategies of separating 'Armstrong the exalted musician from Armstrong the impish stage wag' identified by Giddins, that persist in 'the continuing reluctance to tackle him whole' (Giddins, 1998:87-8). Similarly, Gabbard has noted that in contemporary scholarship Armstrong's films 'are probably ignored to sidestep troubling questions about stage mannerisms that are invisible on the fetishized recordings' (1996:205). Hence, whilst it was possible for Armstrong's performances to be defended as art in the 1930s, these artistic qualities were often regarded as merely performative and negated by the musical material and style of presentation that he adopted as an entertainer, which lacked requisite autonomy.

Ellington's controlled performances of his own compositions represented a way in which jazz could be validated, elevated and developed as an art form:

> ... for the future development of dance music as the art it undoubtedly is, he had certainly not the significance of Ellington ... however, as Armstrong's concern is really only with the executive side of "jazz" ... . (Hughes in *Melody Maker*, October 1932:779)

Goffin noted that 'the orchestra of Duke Ellington ... will bring jazz and Negro music to all those who are in love with the classical tradition, it will satisfy the cultivated aspirations of all those who up till now have been disappointed' (trans. Beckett in Cunard, 1934:293). Hence Hannen Swaffer, noted for his unflattering reviews of black entertainment in the 1920s, was able to appreciate Ellington's performances as 'proof that the much despised Negro is working out a culture all his own. You know you are in the presence of something that will go right across the world', particularly when Ellington had explained to him his plans to write 'a suite in which he will tell in polyphonic form the history of his people' (*People*, 18 June 1933, quoted in Nicholson, 1999:137).[16] Ellington's profile as a jazz composer allowed for the possibility of future developments in jazz that were not subservient to popular song material, regarded as banal and regressive by these writers. Hughes and Nelson respectively wrote optimistically at the time of Ellington's first performances:

> Duke Ellington alone has brought this music out of the semi-twilight of small night-clubs into the broad daylight of the outside world. (*Daily Herald*, 13 June 1933:8)

> What, I thought, would Wagner have thought of it all? Would he have commended or exalted? I am confident he would have hailed this music as one of the most significant phases of modern musical art. (*Era*, 14 June 1933:1)

Problems

The reality of the Palladium performances presented these critics with significant problems in their reliance on Ellington to promote the artistic possibilities of jazz. Negative criticisms of Ellington's performances tended to come from the music critics that had been familiar with his work and were his greatest supporters prior to his arrival in Britain. Together with the overwhelming success of the Palladium performances with the general public, this suggests that these performances were not what Hughes and others had hoped for and expected. Collier has pointed out that 'Hughes's was a minority opinion' (1987:157), but yet he was apparently given free rein to unleash his views prominently in *Melody Maker*, a forum in which he had established a reputation of expertise.

In the review of Ellington at the Palladium in *Melody Maker* (17 June 1933:1-2), a 'Special Representative', probably Hughes, praises the quality of the performers involved in the act, but follows this with two substantial criticisms, which centre on what he perceived to be the more commercial aspects of Ellington's performance. Hughes' first point relates to the programme: 'it seemed to me that it could have been better chosen.' He points out that Ellington had been previewed as a 'a sponsor of a new kind of music' and that the audience would only have been able to hear this in *Mood Indigo* which was played as the second encore. The programme did include other Ellington numbers but Hughes clearly regarded these as inferior within Ellington's output, and the inclusion of more mainstream pieces was interpreted as an obvious attempt to ensure popularity.

Hughes is critical of the 'interpolated acts' which 'seemed to me to be so unnecessary' as they detracted from the performances of the band. Constant

---

[16] Even Adorno, for whom Armstrong was 'castrated' in his performances by his reliance on popular songs, acknowledged the potential of Ellington, 'who is a trained musician and the principal representative of today's "classical" stabilized jazz, has named Debussy and Delius as his favourite composers', although ultimately considered that his compositions are bound by formal constraints (1936, trans. Daniel [1989]:59-60).

Lambert also commented that 'It is a little irritating to see them [Ellington and his band] reduced to a subordinate role for the sake of a cabaret turn' (*Sunday Referee*, 25 June 1933:18). As discussed in Chapter 3, the inclusion of singing was considered to be an indication of commercial motives, and for this reason, Hughes may have felt that he had to include some criticism of Ivie Anderson: 'although she sang her two numbers admirably, seemed to interfere with the band'. Bailey and Derby are similarly criticized for restraining the performance of the band, as they 'tap-danced for four minutes, whilst the band played stop-accompaniment very quietly'. Hughes did acknowledge that Bessie Dudley 'seemed to be more a part of the show, if only because the band was in full blast the whole time'.

Melody Maker may have anticipated the nature of Ellington's performances at the Palladium, as a special concert for musicians, following the precedent of the success of Elizalde's concert in 1929, had been arranged prior to Ellington's arrival. Hughes expressed the hope that the commercial presentation of the band at the Palladium would 'throw into sharp contrast The Melody Maker concert.' (17 June 1933:2). This concert took place on a Sunday afternoon at the New Trocadero Cinema at the Elephant and Castle and had sold out weeks in advance (*Melody Maker*, 3 June 1933:2). The event was reported in *Melody Maker* under the heading 'Four Thousand Delighted Fans: But "Mike" Is Not So Pleased About It' (1 July 1933:2). Although the band received a fantastic reception, and upon leaving the Trocadero were besieged by huge crowds and 'The Duke almost had his clothes torn off his back', Hughes was unhappy about the balance of the programme, providing a long list of Ellington's numbers that he believed should be included rather than popular songs such as *Stormy Weather* and *Minnie the Moocher* and even Ellington's own *Sophisticated Lady*, and asked:

> ... is Duke Ellington losing faith in his own music and turning commercial through lack of appreciation, or does he honestly under-estimate the English musical public ... . Is he afraid to play quiet music which will make an audience listen so that there is a moment's silence at the end, or would he rather play loud and fast so that it is greeted with instantaneous but less discriminate applause?' (*Melody Maker*, 1 July 1933:2)

Hughes's attitude belies a typically British experience of Ellington's music via records (hence his similar objections to the performances that he had heard in the Cotton Club). These could be listened to carefully without any unnecessary visual distractions, rather like the conventional mode of experiencing the 'art' music with which Hughes wished to align Ellington.[17] Some letters to *Melody Maker*

---

[17] Hughes subsequently attempted to influence both Ellington's programming and the audience behaviour. A later concert was more to Hughes' satisfaction: 'there is very little for me to say in the way of criticism ... . Only three pieces played were not actually Duke Ellington's compositions ... . If a couple of thousand people have learned within three weeks that Cootie and Tricky are really expressing something extremely personal and moving, then there is indeed some hope that these same people will realise, by the time the Duke gives another concert, that applause during a performance is not done in the best circles.' (*Melody Maker*, 22 July 1933:3.)

expressed disappointment with the live performances in comparison to the records with which they were familiar:

> I often wonder whether the force of Ellington as a composer and orchestrator is not due to the medium (i.e., the record) by which he mainly gives us his compositions … .

> I came across to England to hear Ellington, and I returned, severely doubting the genius that had been attributed to him. Long after midnight, however, I played over five of his records, of my own choosing, and retired to bed – reassured. (*Melody Maker*, 15 July 1933:14)

The band's normal function when they performed live was to provide music for general entertainment and dancing, either staged or public. The format of Ellington's Palladium shows was clearly commensurate with his normal style of performance at such venues. It is possible that the group could exercise a different attitude to repertoire and performance style in formal concerts and broadcasts or in the recordings with which their British fans were familiar. Indeed, the band performed a different programme for their BBC broadcast on 14 June. This included *Rose Room* and *Creole Rhapsody*, numbers that Hughes had hoped to hear at the Palladium and that Ellington may have considered more suitable for a radio broadcast than a variety show (*Melody Maker*, 24 June 1933:7).

The Legacy of the Visits

Re-evaluation of Jazz

The debates surrounding the relative merits of composer and performer and commercialism in jazz that resulted from critical consideration of the performances of Armstrong and Ellington were taken up by prominent writers such as Nelson, Lambert and Hughes in the national and trade press, and this culminated in the seminal publications from the former two authors in 1934 discussed in Chapter 3. Although disagreements persisted, fundamentally, the importance of African-American musicians in the development of jazz was recognized:

> We are of the opinion that the time is ripe for the advent of another coloured band in this country, as our bands have been in a stereotyped rut and it is time that a certain judicious kick in the pants was administered. (*Rhythm*, June 1933:11)

Nelson recalled the change in attitude, whereas in the past famous Negro bands 'were all very well in their way, in our opinion, but their jazz was a poor thing beside the refined product of the best white bands … . To-day Ellington, Armstrong and the other coloured bands have practically assumed the position of arbitrators of modern rhythmic style' (Nelson, 1934:162). The word 'jazz' was beginning to come back into more regular use in Britain from the mid-1930s, having lost some of its undesirable associations through the more frequent experiences of black music on record, on the radio and on the variety stage where it could be widely experienced by the British population rather than remaining the mysterious accompaniment to scandalous underworld activities.

Modern critics have noted the potential of Armstrong and Ellington to transcend racial stereotypes:

> [Armstrong's] ability to balance the emotional gravity of an artist with the communal entertainer's good cheer helped demolish the Jim Crow/Zip Coon/Ol'Dan Tucker stereotypes prominent in the 1920s. (Giddins, 1998:87)

> [In *Black and Tan*] Ellington's role as a talented composer with dignity and principles also reveals how much Ellington was able to rise above the conventional depictions of African Americans. (Gabbard, 1996:161)

Certainly, significantly less racial prejudice was expressed in contemporary reviews of Armstrong and Ellington in Britain than was the case of the plantation revues ten years earlier, suggesting that transcendence was occurring to some degree in Britain. This was aided by the fact that these performers also presented material that adhered less overtly to the conventions of black entertainment and which did not, therefore, evoke comparisons with minstrelsy. In addition, as we have seen, 'primitivism' itself could be appreciated as a positive quality. Undoubtedly, the appreciation of Armstrong and Ellington as artists in their own right had significant impact, in many cases precipitating the continuing evolution of both positive and negative circumstances for jazz and black musicians in Britain.

Opposition to Jazz

At the same time as African-American jazz was beginning to receive greater recognition it became subject to restriction from powerful institutions, namely the BBC, the Musicians' Union and the government. The BBC broadcasted performances by both Armstrong (in relay from the Palladium) and Ellington (from the studio, for which the band received a substantial fee (Ulanov, 1946:131)). 'Detector', writing in *Melody Maker* at the time of Armstrong's broadcast, accused the BBC of restricting the development of jazz through policies which meant that 'The air is chock full of the banalities and vulgarities of dance bands which aren't, other which can't, and still more which daren't', and accused the *Radio Times* of deciding 'for everyone, without being asked, what merits 'jazz' lacks and what part it takes in the musical thought of the moment.' There was the suggestion that the inevitably negative reactions to Armstrong's broadcast could be used to justify the BBC's standard policies: 'The 'impediments' at the BBC are still in existence, no doubt fortified by the support they received from all sorts of lay press ignoramuses who tried to decry Armstrong's work because it was above their heads.' (*Melody Maker*, September 1932:719). The *Radio Times* presented a typical mixture of listener's comments both for and against Ellington's performance, and the debates on the merits of jazz and dance music continued in the 'Listener's Letters' column in the *Radio Times* throughout this period. The broadcasting of Armstrong and Ellington and the inclusion of articles in support of African-American jazz, discussed in Chapter 3, does suggest that there was some sympathy with jazz within the BBC at this time.

Nevertheless, the Corporation's fundamentalist policy on jazz and dance music continued largely unabated. In 1932 the BBC had replaced Jack Payne with Henry Hall with the intention of creating a 'Paul Whiteman' orchestra (BBCWAC R29/13, 11 March 1932) with 'a *sweet* soft sound for a change' (BBCWAC Contributors 910 Hall, Henry, 13 January 1932, emphasis in original), to perform 'tunes not necessarily in strict dance time, concert arrangements, and special comedy and other orchestrations (in other words light entertainment not confined to pure dance music)' (BBCWAC R29/13, 2 June 1932). The 1932 BBC Handbook had stated hopefully:

> The present style of dance playing is what in the USA, home of dance music, they term "sweet", that is to say, it is quiet, melodious and subtly orchestrated, as opposed to the "hot" style which held sway until recently, and which, in the strident eccentricity of its tone and rhythm, marked a step back to the native "jazz" of the jungle. (1932:204)

Although the formation of new BBC Dance Orchestra under Hall was 'not intended to make impossible thereby the playing of "hot" orchestrations' (BBCWAC R29/13 2 June 1932), the views of prominent members of the BBC such as R.H. Eckersley on hot music remained unequivocal:

> I do not think that the difference between what people call "hot jazz", and quick numbers cleverly orchestrated, is properly understood. I, myself, am entirely against the kind of stuff that Louie [*sic.*] Armstrong plays, and should deprecate the introduction of it into the programmes, but there is nothing harmful, in my opinion, about the clever orchestration of quick music. (BBCWAC Entertainment: Jazz 1933-1946, File 1, 1 December 1933)

> There is practically no really "hot" music broadcast (by which is implied definitely "negroid" music of the Ellington-Armstrong type), though Henry Hall does include from time to time clever arrangements of tunes which cannot, however, be said to fall within the category of "hot" music …. I really think we are trying to meet a variety of tastes in the best possible way, and I can assure you there is no sympathy with what I would again term the "negroid" type of music. (BBCWAC Entertainment: Jazz 1933-1946, File 1, 7 December 1933)

The increasing identification of jazz specifically as African-American music was also undesirable for the Musicians' Union, in that Americans could potentially be shown to provide entertainment that was different to anything that could be experienced in Britain and would be able, theoretically, to continue to obtain work permits. It was unfortunate that it was Duke Ellington that indirectly and unintentionally brought the situation regarding reciprocity of British and American bands and musicians to a head, precipitating a downward spiral that was to culminate in the severe restrictions on the appearances of American musicians in Britain from 1935. Hylton's backing of Ellington's 1933 visit was well-publicized in the national press, and comparison between treatment of Hylton and Ellington by the American and British governments respectively was inevitable:

Ever since Jack Hylton took courage in his hands and backed his belief in the Ellington proposition to the tune of an enormous guarantee, musicians, fans and the general public have gone Ellington mad. (*Melody Maker*, 3 June 1933:2)

... a word of praise and many grateful thanks to Jack Hylton for making this historical visit possible. (*Rhythm*, June 1933:9)

Jack Hylton, under whose guidance the Negro Band is visiting England - and Jack himself is barred from appearing in the States! (*Daily Herald*, 9 June 1933:12)

Hylton had strong reasons for backing Ellington's visit, on one hand he was undoubtedly philanthropic in that he wanted to give British musicians and enthusiasts a chance to experience Ellington, but also it is likely that he considered that his personal role in Ellington's successful visit might allow it to be reciprocated by his own band in the States, where he was evidently in demand. Certainly the *Era* had reported this possibility under the heading 'Hylton for America? Ellington in Exchange' months before Ellington's arrival in Britain (14 December 1932).

Hylton actually protested against a subsequent application for Ellington to appear in Britain 'in view of the refusal of the American Union to allow him (Jack Hylton) to play in America' (TNA: PRO LAB8/1926, Foreign Bands 1934). This further application for Duke Ellington to appear in Britain had been received by the Ministry of Labour in 1934 and initially refused on the basis that it included proposed performances by the band in cinemas and dance halls, as well as in 'cafés of the restaurant type', from which foreign bands had been excluded since 1932, but were becoming increasingly hard to define. Following a deputation from the Agents Association, the Entertainment's Protection Association, Paramount Theatres Ltd and the Association of Ball Rooms and Dance Halls, at which it was argued that cinemas and dance halls should not be treated differently to variety theatres in which foreign bands were allowed to perform, as all these venues essentially presented variety entertainment, the Ministry would be forced to reconsider a new application. The importance of novelty in variety entertainment was noted, and this could be enhanced by reciprocal exchange, which would prevent British acts from becoming too familiar and would allow the introduction of new ideas by Americans. However, the admission of foreign bands into new types of venues would set a precedent and in effect considerably widen the range of performance opportunities available to American visitors, potentially precipitating other applications from similar bands that would be difficult to refuse. Therefore, R.E. Gomme proposed a reconsideration of the whole policy, particularly in the light of the continued exclusion of British bands from America:

It is, I suggest, worth considering whether, in view of the attitude of the American Union, we should not be justified in refusing permits for any American band to come here - even for a Variety performance ... . Alternatively, we might consider whether the threat of the refusal of permits could be used to induce the American Union to change their attitude. (TNA: PRO LAB8/1926, Foreign Bands, 26 September 1934).

There is reference here to the refusal of the American Federation of Musicians to allow British bands to play in America, which was based on unemployment amongst American musicians. The Musicians' Union opposition to these American musicians in Britain was also primarily due to unemployment amongst British musicians. However, British bands could have potentially attracted good fees in America as they presented a contrast to the American ensembles. Similarly, decreasing employment opportunities led American bands to seek engagements in Britain, where they were popular and well-paid as they functioned as novelty entertainment (TNA: PRO LAB8/1926, 24 October 1934, Gomme to Broad). Therefore, had a policy of reciprocity been agreed at this time, both British and American musicians stood to benefit.

An important difference between Britain and America was the relative power of the Unions, as the AFM was perceived by the British government to be responsible for the attitude towards British musicians by threatening all-out strikes if they had been employed, whereas the British MU regularly lobbied government for changes in policy. When initially proposing a refusal to grant permits to American bands, the British government repeatedly emphasized that they realized that the opposition to British musicians was not the policy of the American government, but at the same time had little information about the situation other than through the press or from 'aggrieved musicians' in Britain (TNA: PRO LAB8/1926, 24 October 1934). The Ministry sought advice from Wiggin in the British Embassy in Washington, especially when a report appeared in the *Daily Telegraph* in October 1934 under the heading 'U.S. to keep out Foreign Artists: Stringent Regulations' which was certainly news to the officials concerned. Meanwhile, it was hoped that the refusal of permits for Ellington's band alone might precipitate the AFM into revising its policies. The reasons for the refusal were communicated to the agent Harry Foster, who was attempting to secure the permits, in October 1934, in the hope that he might have some power to influence the AFM (TNA: PRO LAB8/1926, 24 October 1934). It is easy to see why the government felt compelled to act to restore a balance between the treatment of British and American musicians in each other's countries, but the pursuance of a policy of initially uninformed threats rather than direct negotiation seems unwise in retrospect.

Further investigations by British Embassy staff in Washington, including an interview with Colonel MacComack, the Commissioner of Immigration and Naturalization, revealed that new regulations had been drawn up to clarify the Immigration Act of March 1932 particularly in view of what the American government perceived as 'rigid restrictions placed upon the entry of American instrumental musicians into Europe, and particularly into the United Kingdom' which apparently hinged on a misunderstanding about the conditions of Whiteman's previous visit. Although MacCormack acknowledged the strength of the AFM, particularly with respect to the pressure that they could apply upon 'private musical interests', he stated that Federation had not yet been able to 'browbeat the government' into agreeing to ban all foreign performers from America. He suggested that the British Ministry of Labour should apply the same restrictions on Ellington as set out in their own March 1932 Act 'and then await developments' rather than engaging in a 'retaliation race', although in effect this had already begun (TNA: PRO LAB8/1926, 30 November 1934).

Essentially the American 1932 Act did not allow for the employment of alien instrumental musicians if similar American musicians were unemployed, exceptions being 'artists and professional actors', the definition of which was set out in a clause whereby an instrumental musician could only be considered an artist if he was of 'distinguished merit or ability or was a member of an organization of distinguished merit and in either case was coming to the United States to perform engagements requiring superior talent.' Engagements not considered to require 'superior talent' included 'radio broadcasting, cabarets, roof gardens, motion picture houses or productions, vaudeville performances, conventions, dances, fairs or in hotel or theatre orchestras', which effectively excluded most British dance bands who usually performed such functions. It was now clear that the opposition to British bands in America was not solely the result of the actions of the AFM, and this enabled the British government to act decisively (TNA: PRO LAB8/1926, 30 November 1934).

Ray Noble was permitted to conduct in America in January 1935, and this was interpreted by the Ministry as a successful result of the refusal of Ellington's permits. However, in the same month, a new application for permits for Ellington's band to appear at the Palladium was received by the Ministry, but the policy remained that the application should be rejected (TNA: PRO LAB8/1926, 7 February 1935) and subsequently it was decided that applications for all 'USA bands of this type' would also be refused (TNA: PRO LAB8/1926, 28 March 1935). The chief justification for this action was the United States regulations that 'made it more difficult for United Kingdom musicians to obtain engagements in the United States than for United States musicians to obtain them in the United Kingdom' and the attitude of the AFM was used as 'a second line of defence' for the decision (TNA: PRO LAB8/1926, 13 February 1935). A Press Communiqué was issued on 29 March 1935, stating that: 'the Minister does not feel able to continue to grant permits freely to American bands to take engagements of the Variety Hall type. He will, however, be glad to revert to his former policy as soon as he can be assured that no less favourable treatment will be accorded to British Bands seeking engagements in the USA.' Essentially the government policy formulated in 1935 was maintained for the next twenty years.

British Musicians in America

In Britain, these governmental restrictions, introduced alongside the increasing recognition of the importance of American jazz composers and performers, led to the start of a trend for the most serious musicians and enthusiasts to visit America for themselves, such as the critic Leonard Feather who moved to New York in 1935 (1986:12). Even before Ellington's visit to Britain, Spike Hughes had recognized that 'the jazz composer must rely on the improvising soloist to provide something which is not written down' and had recorded several of his compositions and arrangements with a band of black musicians that included Benny Carter, Coleman Hawkins and Luis Russell during his visit to America in

1933 (1951:142). Hughes probably realized that African-American performers could not only authenticate his work symbolically, as had been the case with Leslie Thompson and Joey Shields, but could also add to the musical value of his compositions.

There were loopholes in the regulations and restrictions imposed by both Britain and America at this time that allowed for the continuation of the transatlantic transfer of performers. In October 1935, Hylton did finally sail for the USA, having obtained a permit as he was classed as a conductor rather than an instrumental musician. He was permitted to take singers, comedians and arrangers with him, but in the end the sponsors of his American radio programmes, Standard Oil, paid for the musicians of Hylton's British band not to play, and this allowed them to have a two-week holiday in America. The British band actually were used on two of the shows, as Hylton managed to circumvent American regulations by broadcasting his first programme from London, and subsequently from the boat on which they travelled to New York. Hylton was a great success in New York, negotiated subsequent radio broadcasts beyond his initial contract, and also appeared on the stage (Faint, 1999:38-40). The singer Magda Neeld recalled that Hylton was threatened by Petrillo, at that time president of the Chicago local of the AFM, and had to be escorted from the stage by a bodyguard during a performance in Detroit as he was apparently on the Mafia hit-list (Neeld, n.d.:149-51 in Jack Hylton Archive).

Black Musicians in Britain

American musicians such as Fats Waller, Art Tatum, and Coleman Hawkins appeared in Britain after 1935 in the guise of solo variety performers, and others such as Dizzy Gillespie and Dickie Wells came to Britain as members of bands that accompanied revue shows on the stage rather than in the pit (Rye in Oliver, 1990:55-6). The continued popularity of black entertainers on the British variety stage was important not only for the contributions that these performers made to West End theatre, but indirectly in encouraging the development of jazz performance, especially in the resident black British population and more recent West Indian immigrants who were not affected by the 1935 restrictions. The nightclub scene of Soho continued to be inherently linked with the West End theatres, and as more black performers were being featured in variety, so there were more clubs that catered for their needs. These clubs also provided a meeting place for the resident black population and fuelled the fascination of many white Britons with black people.[18]

Clubs such as the Nest and Jigs attracted numerous visiting black variety performers, particularly as they were situated close to the Palladium, where many of these artists were working. Such clubs often employed black musicians but were also frequented by their white colleagues. Louis Stephenson commented that it was

---

[18] Information in this section was obtained from interviews with Clare Deniz, Frank Deniz, Joe Deniz, and Don Johnson, Louis Stephenson and Leslie Thompson in the Oral History of Jazz in Britain collection at the National Sound Archive.

hard to tell whose band was actually playing, as other musicians would always be 'sitting in'. Musicians recalled seeing George Chisholm, Buck and Bubbles, Adelaide Hall, Gracie Fields (Clare Deniz), Art Tatum, Fats Waller, the Mills Brothers and Bill Johnson (Louis Stephenson) and the Midnight Steppers, Stump and Stumpy and the Blackbirds cast (Joe Deniz) who provided fantastic impromptu cabaret at the Nest. White Britons visited the Nest for the attraction of interacting with black people, and the owner Meyer Cohen would bring black people into the club specifically to talk to the white customers (Stephenson recalls 'working' in this way). This idea was later taken up by the Shim-Sham club, the first club of its kind 'above ground'. Jigs Club seems to have had a more dubious reputation, and was remembered by Clare Deniz as 'a gambling club'. Ellington recalled visiting Jigs and eating rice and peas ('a real West Indian dish' (Nicholson, 1999:144)). Gonella took Armstrong and subsequent American visitors to Jigs, which he described as 'frequented chiefly by coloured folk' (Brown, 1985:65).

By the mid-1930s, some musicians of West Indian origin born in the ethnically diverse Tiger Bay area of Cardiff were beginning to respond to the need for black musicians in the clubs. Joe Deniz was one of the first musicians to come to London to play for a bottle party club on Carnaby Street and then at a basement club in Little Newport Street. When rival gangs destroyed the club, Deniz was forced to return to Cardiff. As the only employment opportunity available for young black men in Tiger Bay was to go to sea, the life of a musician was understandably appealing. Joe Deniz soon returned to London to play at the Nest, and was joined in London by his friend Don Johnson, guitarist and vocalist; Clare, a pianist who was to become his sister-in-law; and later by his brother, Frank, also a guitarist.

In early twentieth century Tiger Bay had a strong tradition of plucked-string instrument performance of calypsos and Portugese music that the community demanded for celebrations. Initially at least, this was probably the material that the musicians performed in London clubs, although they were certainly aware of jazz prior to moving to London. Don Johnson and Joe Deniz encountered jazz on records brought back by sailors in the late 1920s, but had no need to adopt it seriously as there were no opportunities to perform it. Johnson gave a Duke Ellington record away as he thought that it sounded so discordant in comparison with calypsos. Frank Deniz, who was a sailor for several years before becoming a professional musician, went to jazz clubs wherever he could when his ship was in port, and also heard Dixieland and big band jazz on 78s. These experiences meant that the musicians were able to adapt to public expectations of their performances and branch into jazz, and could play standards such as *Honeysuckle Rose* and *Tiger Rag*. Adaptability was often a matter of survival for black musicians, as Thompson recalled: 'There was no work, outside the entertainment and music business, for Black people. Believe me, I tried.' (Green, 1985:57.) It is significant that these musicians were often as reliant on recordings as white Britons to develop what would be perceived as an authentic musical style for their performances.

The vogue for black entertainment in London also led to the importation of West Indian musicians Louis Stephenson, Yorke de Souza, Bertie King and Louis 'Jiver' Hutchinson in November 1935, who performed at the Cuba Club established by brothers Happy and Cyril Blake. Clearly, there were opportunities for black musicians in London at this time, as Frank Deniz identified, being coloured was an asset as you could 'assume the mantle of being American'. However, Joe Deniz pointed out that the better clubs and hotels rarely employed black musicians. He had deputized for the regular guitarist in Ambrose's band at Ciro's, but he 'lasted exactly one night' as the club owner objected to black people on the bandstand. The demand for performances by black musicians which led to the increase in their numbers in London, together with the continuing difficulties of their integration into mainstream dance bands was a situation exploited fully by Leslie Thompson and Ken 'Snakehips' Johnson in the latter half of the 1930s.

The presence of so many talented black musicians in London allowed Thompson to eventually realize his dream of forming an all-black dance band in 1935. This included many of the musicians mentioned above, who recalled being worked very hard by Thompson in the early rehearsals of the group to achieve 'the lift or swing' of Lunceford and Ellington (Green, 1985:90). The band represented prestigious and stable employment for the musicians, and Thompson recalled that as a result of their hard work in rehearsing American arrangements the band sounded quite different from any other dance band in Britain at the time (Green, 1985:90). The band performed from 1936 under various names (The Aristocrats of Jazz, The Emperors of Swing and The (Jamaican) Emperors of Jazz) and achieved great success. The dancer Ken Johnson fronted the group and 'often received top billing', and later controversially took control of the group away from Thompson (Simons, sleeve note to TSCD781:14).

Jazz in Britain and British Jazz

Summarizing the changes that had taken place in the British music scene by the end of the 1930s, Leslie Thompson wrote:

> It was transformed from English jazz to American jazz. The American recordings that had come to England to full effect, and everyone was aiming to be American: and to a degree they succeeded. The polish of the sectional performances of the orchestras increased, and the phrasing became quite Americanised. This was due to records and visits of individuals … most of their British fans were musicians. After their performances to the paying public at a theatre these chaps would go on to parties, which had a musical clientele. Naturally the Americans gravitated to the Nest, Jig's, Bag O'Nails, and such night spots. At those places they met their fans – white musicians. So, in that decade the bands in England became very polished, American style. They captured the heart of rhythmic music – to swing – so the listener would tap his foot to the music. (Green, 1985:99)

The restrictions imposed on American musicians performing in Britain from 1935 would undoubtedly affect the presence of American jazz, but yet circumstances were in place by the 1930s that allowed the evolution of jazz in Britain to continue. As we have seen, the advances in recording technology were matched by the development of jazz criticism in Britain. Although some of the resultant writing, considered above with reference to Armstrong and Ellington, has been shown to be misinformed and misguided, it is clear that critics could often offer insight and support to the growing body of jazz musicians and enthusiasts in Britain. The visits of Armstrong and Ellington and other American musicians in the 1930s allowed critics the possibility of re-evaluation of their ideas about jazz through the formulation of new criteria under which jazz could be appreciated as art. The Palladium performances proved that it was possible for popular music to be artistic, and the importance of the black contribution to jazz was recognized. Comparisons between Armstrong's and Ellington's recordings and their live performances highlighted the importance of improvisation and freedom of expression, albeit the extent of this was surprising and even shocking, as a critical feature of jazz performance in a way that had not been possible for these commentators to fully realize before. This influenced the way in which jazz recordings were evaluated and ensured that jazz criticism could continue to develop in response to innovations in the music in America, which now would arrive in Britain primarily in recorded form.

By the mid-1930s recordings ensured that a specific audience for jazz in Britain had developed which was supported by the Rhythm Clubs that presented a forum for exchange of knowledge and appreciation of jazz through listening and amateur performance. The oppositional stance to jazz by the establishment could not be wholly sustained when young jazz enthusiasts were moving into positions of responsibility; for example, there were changes in the BBC's policies in the late 1930s. The African-American saxophonist Benny Carter arranged for Henry Hall's BBC Dance Orchestra from 1936, and Leslie Perowne states that 'The BBC became jazz-conscious in about 1937, largely through the interest of Harman Grisewood, now Chief Assistant to the Director-General, who, with me (I was in the Gramophone Department), did a series of gramophone programmes called "Kings of Jazz". About this time, our New York representative – Felix Greene – arranged the first series of "America Dances", direct relays from New York.' (BBCWAC R47/416/1 1963.) Jazz enthusiasts provided the core audience for this progressive programming, as well as ensuring the demand for the continued importation of American jazz records into the country. In addition, correspondents' reports in the British trade press kept enthusiasts of informed of the latest developments in American jazz.

The developments in recording and associated criticism were also influential on young musicians who were employed in dance bands of the 1930s. The continuation of some jazz performance in Britain on the variety stage allowed the valuable informal interactions between British and American musicians to continue in London's nightclubs. Dance music had demonstrated the ability to adopt 'jazz-like' features in the 1920s, and now with suitably skilled musicians it was but a short step for these ensembles to develop towards the style of the popular American swing bands that could be heard on recordings. It would seem to be no coincidence that an all-black dance band achieved such success in introducing swing to Britain in the wake of the demand for black jazz created by Armstrong and Ellington, which was largely denied almost immediately by the restrictions on American musicians in Britain. This chapter has shown that although Britain was by no means free from racial discrimination in the 1930s, the performances and reception of black musicians could transcend the stereotypes that were the legacy of blackface entertainment and the music could be appreciated seriously. The Johnson–Thompson band was to contribute to the re-definition of the artistic status of jazz in Britain as entertaining and exhilarating dance music, rather than conventionally in the concert hall in the way that many British critics had intended. The British public were not solely dependant on American bands and musicians to provide them with experiences of jazz, necessarily due to the governmental restrictions, but also since numbers of both white and black Britons were capable of disseminating the music in live performances. These performances now had the potential to be more than just imitations, and enriched with personal contributions of British musicians. Fundamentally, what can be observed by 1935 is not only the presence of jazz in Britain, but also the evolution of British jazz.

Appendix 1

Songs Consulted in Chapter 2

Title	Written / Composed	Date	Publisher (all in London)	BL. Number
I'm Certainly Living a Ragtime Life	Gene Jefferson / Robert S. Roberts	1900	Francis Day and Hunter	h3986.ss(11)
I Love my Little Honey	Ben Harney	1900	Charles Sheard and Co.	h1654.rr(27)
Rag-time Nursery Rhymes	Sam Richards	1901	Francis Day and Hunter	h3986.qq(24)
The Rage of Ragtime	Edward Kent	1903	Hopwood and Crew	h3984.yy(37)
Oysters and Clams or the Rag-time Oyster Man	Jack Drislane, A.J. Mills / Theodore Morse	1906	Francis Day and Hunter	h3651(45)
The Rag-Time Milkman	Alfred Ellerton / Alfred Ellerton Jnr	1910	Shapiro, Von Tilzer Music	h3983.gg(59)
Rag-Time Crazy	R.M. Marks / John Neat	1910	E. Marks and Son	h3995.o(14)
You've Got to Sing in Rag-Time	Worton David and George Arthurs	1911	Francis Day and Hunter	h3990.zz(36)
Don't Drive me Crazy with Your Ragtime Song	J. Sinclair	1912	E. Marks and Son	h3996.e(26)
Hear the Ragtime Band play Dixie	Walter Tewson and Alfred Glover	1912	Paxton	h3991.t(44)
Play that Piccolo Rag-Time Tune	George Arthurs	1913	Reynolds	h3988.uu(39)
The Ragtime Billiard Player	George Arthurs	1913	Star	h3988.uu(40)
Goodbye Mr Ragtime	Lawrence Barclay / Barclay and Alf Glover	1913	Feldman	h3989.d(5)
The Ghost of the Rag-time Coon	Patrick L. Barrow	1913	West and Co	h3989.f(42)
On Your Rag-time Rag Shop Banjo	Frank W. Carter and Gilbert Wells	1913	Francis, Day and Hunter	h3990.i(47)

Title	Written / Composed	Date	Publisher (all in London)	BL Number
The Ragtime Gollywog Man	Elven Hedges and Penyston Miles	1913	Feldman	g1520.kk(50)
Who Killed Ragtime?: A Modern Nursery Rhyme	Robert Innes	1913	Star	g1520.pp(11)
There ain't going to be any Ragtime	Frank Leo	1913	Francis Day and Hunter	h3994.cc(24)
Don't Sing in Ragtime	J.P. Long, Paul Pelham and Billy Merson	1913	Francis Day and Hunter	h3994.hh(10)
I don't want a Ragtime Coon	Lester Barrett / Charles Lucas	1913	Francis, Day and Hunter	h3994.jj(48)
The Rag-time Craze	Jack Hulbert / Alan Murray	1913	Reynolds	h3995.j(46)
That Ragtime Minstrel Band	Pearl and Roth	1913	Francis Day and Hunter	h3995.x(11)
Rag-Time Crazy	George Rapley	1913	Feldman	h3995.jj(30)
Miss Ching-A-Loo: The Ragtime Chinese Wedding	R.P. Weston, F.J. Barnes, Maurice Scott	1913	Star	h3992(35)
That Ragtime Suffragette	Harry Williams and Nat D Ayer	1913	Feldman	h3988.zz(14)
The Rag-Time Villain Man	Patrick L. Barrow	1914	West and Co	h3989.f(43)
Rag-time Postman Bill	F. C. Smith	1914	West	h3996.f(47)
Change that Rag into a March Refrain	Fred E. Cliffe and Jay Whidden	1915	Francis Day and Hunter	h3990.t(34)
Ragtime Kisses	Arthur Charles	1917	Escott and Co.	h3990.o(1)
When I hear that Jazz Band Play	Gene Buck / Dave Stamper	1917	Francis Day and Hunter	h3996.n(22)

Title	Written / Composed	Date	Publisher (all in London)	BL Number
Jazz!	Clifford Grey / Nat. D. Ayer	1918	Feldman	h3988.yy(1)
Strike up that Band: A Military Rag	R.S.B. Ribbands / A.R. Don	1918	West	h3991.j(1)
Stick Around for the New Jazz Band	A.J. Mills / J.A. Tunbridge	1918	Star Music	h3991.ii(5)
Everybody Loves a Jazz Band	Coleman Goetz / Leon Flatlow	1919	Herman Darewski	h3993.e(9)
Heigho! Jazz it with Me	Jack Foley	1919	Herman Darewski	h3993.e(45)
That Mandarin Jazz	Milton Hayes / Ronald Franklin	1919	H. Sharples and Son	g426.d(33)
That Jungle Jazz in Congo Land	Harry and Burton Lester	1919	Francis Day and Hunter	h3994.dd(31)
The Jazz Band Cabaret	Tom Mellor and A.C. Findon	1919	Herman Darewski	h3994.xx(47)
The Jazz Jazz Tinker's Wedding	Tom Mellor and Alf J. Lawrence	1919	Herman Darewski	h3994.xx(48)
That Blue-Eyed Jazz Band	A.T. Courtney / John W. Miller	1919	Whitehall Music Co.	h3995.b(8)
The Wedding Jazz	Clifford Grey / Ivor Novello	1919	Ascherberg, Hopwood and Crew	h3670.a(25)
Oh! That Lancashire Jazz Band	Wynn Stanley and Andrew Allen	1919	The Lawerence Wright Music Co.	h3996.n(62)
Play me a Jazz Band Tune	Clay Smith, R.P. Weston and Bert Lee	1919	Francis Day and Hunter	h3996.u(24)
That Javanese Jazz Band	Enrique Smith	1919	Francis Day and Hunter	h3996.f(43)
Come and Jazz with Me	Clifford Grey / T.C. Sterndale Bennett	1919	Reynolds and Co	h2452(33)

Title	Written / Composed	Date	Publisher (all in London)	BL Number
Johnson's Jazz-time-Band	'Bay' / Reginald Tabbush	1919	West	h3991.q(4)
The Coster Jazz Song	Clifford Harris / Jas W. Tate	1919	Francis, Day and Hunter	h3991.r(24)
Our Big Jazz Band	Clifford Harris / Jas W. Tate	1919	Francis Day and Hunter	h3991.r(31)

Appendix 2

Synopsis of *In Dahomey: A Negro Musical Comedy*

After the alterations made to the show in Britain, *In Dahomey* began with a prologue set in Africa. Then the story begins with two would-be detectives, Shylock Homestead (Bert Williams) and Rareback Pinkerton (George Walker) who become embroiled in a case to find a silver casket, belonging to Hamilton Lightfoot, that eventually leads them to West Africa. They become involved in a scheme to defraud the would-be African colonizers and in particular, their leader Lightfoot. When it turns out that the slow-witted Homestead is actually far wealthier than the old man Pinkerton, he manages to extract enough money to put himself into decent clothes. Dressed as an African king, Pinkerton does a dance that wins the hearts of the Dahomeans. Homestead and Pinkerton are made Caboceers due to their large gifts of rum to the Dahomean King. Meanwhile, the colonists have been captured and Shylock and Pinkerton ply the King with yet more alcohol to get the prisoners freed.

Sources

Cook, M. (Symposium paper in 'Cook' file in IJS:9)
Riis, T. (1989:91-2)
Riis, T. (1996:xxv)
The Stage 21 May 1903 (p. 14)
The Era 23 May 1903 (p. 16)

Appendix 3

Songs Consulted in Chapter 5

Title	Written / Composed	Date	Publisher (all in London)	BL Number
The Negro and His Banjer	Dibdin	1790	The author	g380.e(15)
Ring de Banjo	Stephen Foster	1853	Campbell, Ransford and Co.	h1437(8)
'Tis the banjo softly speaking	Fred Caughan / Louis H. D'Egville	1883	Chappell	h1788 j(41)
Twang the Banjo! Humorous song	Herbert Harraden	1889	Bath	h1260.m(35)
Banjo Mania: A humorous song	Corney Grain	1889	J. Bath	h1260.m(32)
Bobbie's Banjo	Herbert Harraden	1898	Bath	h3980.cc(35)
The Old Banjo	Arthur Wimperis / Christine	1910	Von Tilzer	h3990.q(25)
That Banjo Song	J.W. Hamer / Chas Elbert	1912	Ascherberg, Hopwood and Crew	h3992.hh(6)
The Ghost of the Rag-time Coon	Patrick L. Barrow	1913	West and Co.	h3989 f(42)
On Your Rag-time Rag Shop Banjo	Frank W. Carter and Gilbert Wells	1913	Francis, Day and Hunter	h3990.i(47)
Banjo Moon	Hugh E. Wright / Kennedy Russell	1917	Ascherberg, Hopwood and Crew	h3809.b(25)
The Ghost of the Old Banjo	Medley Barrett	1919	Darewski	h3989.e(9)

Bibliography

General Reference Books

Chilton, J. (1972) *Who's Who of Jazz: Storyville to Swing Street* (Chilton Book Company, Philadelphia).

Chilton, J. (1997) *Who's Who of British Jazz* (London, Cassell).

Cohen-Stratyner (ed.) (1988) *Popular Music, 1900-1919* (Gale Research Inc, Detroit, Michigan).

Hitchcock, H.W. and Sadie, S. (1986) *The New Grove Dictionary of American Music* (London, Macmillan).

Kennington/Read (eds) (1980) *The Literature of Jazz: A Critical Guide* (Chicago, American Library Association).

Kernfeld, B. (ed.) (1994) *The New Grove Dictionary of Jazz* (London, Macmillan).

Meadows, E.S. (1981) *Jazz Reference and Research Materials – A Bibliography* (New York, Garland).

Meeker, D. (1977) *Jazz in the Movies: A Guide to Jazz Musicians 1917-1977* (London, Talisman).

Merriam, A.P. (1954) *A Bibliography of Jazz* (Philadelphia, American Folklore Society).

Sadie, S. (ed.) (1984) *The New Grove Dictionary of Musical Instruments* (London, Macmillan).

Southern, E. (1982) *Biographical Dictionary of Afro-American and African Musicians* (Greenwood Press, Westport, Connecticut).

Discographies

Heier, U. and Lotz, R.E. (1993) *The Banjo on Record – A Bio-Discography* (Connecticut, Greenwood Press).

Jewson, R., Hamilton-Smith, D. and Webb, R. (1978) *Horst H. Lange's The Fabulous Fives* (Middlesex, Storyville and Co. Ltd).

Lord, T. (2000) *The Jazz Discography* (Vancouver, Lord Music Reference).

Rust, B. (1978) *Jazz Records, 1897-1942* (New Rochelle, New York, Arlington House).

Seeley, R. and Bunnett, R. (1989) *London Musical Shows on Record 1889-1989* (Middlesex, General Gramophone Publications Ltd).

Walker, E.S. and Walker, S. (1971) *English Ragtime: A Discography* (Author, England).

Website Databases

Duke University Historic American Sheet Music Online Database
    http://scriptorium.lib.duke.edu/sheetmusic/
London Dance Places
    http://www.mgthomas.co.uk/DanceBands/IndexPages/LondonDancePlaces.htm
Red Hot Jazz Archive
    http://www.redhotjazz.com

Sources

(1919) Programme for The Palladium, week beginning 21 April 1919 (includes ODJB).
(1924) *The Savoy Orpheans* (Privately published at the Savoy, London).
(1933) Programme for 'A Concert of the Music of Duke Ellington presented by The Melody Maker' at the Trocadero, Elephant and Castle, Sunday 25 June 1933.
Cook, W.M. (1903)[1] *In Dahomey: A Negro Musical Comedy* Book by Jesse A Shipp, Lyrics by Paul Lawrence Dunbar and others, Music by Will Marion Cook (London, Keith Prowse and Co.).
Richardson, P.J.S. (ed.) (1919) *The Darewski Jazz Chart: Learn to Jazz at Home* (London, Herman Darewski).

Newspapers

All published in London unless otherwise stated.

General

Daily Graphic 6 April 1923 (The increase in the use of gramophone records for dancing).
Dancing Time 1918, 1919, 1920.
Dancing World 1919.
Era 19 February 1919 (p. 9) ('Alien Musicians'), 12 March 1919 (John Lester's Frisco Five), 9 April 1919 (p. 14) (Debate on Jazz).
Encore 11 October 1917 ('Mr Jazz Arrives'), 7 November 1918 ('The Jazz Boys'), 31 October 1918 (Review of ' The Jazz Boys').
Hot News and Rhythm Record Review 1935.
London Amusement Guide 1919, 1920, 1921.
Melody Maker 1926-1935.
Observer 16 January 1919 (p.14) ('The Origin of Jazz').
Outlook 26 January 1924 (pp. 57-58) ('The Song of the Saxophone' by William Bolitho).
Performer 17 April 1919 (p. 29) (The take-up of jazz), 1 May 1919 (p. 37) (The popularity of K-K-K Katy).
Radio Times September 1923-June 1928, 1932-33.
Rhythm 1927-1935.
Swing Music 1935.
Times 14 January 1919 (p. 11), 15 March 1919 (p. 7), 18 March 1919 (p. 7), 19 March 1919 (p. 12), 29 April 1919 (p. 15).

In Dahomey

Daily Mail 18 May 1903 (p. 3).
Daily News 16 May 1903 (p. 6), 18 May 1903 (p. 12).
Era 23 May 1903 (pp. 14, 16), 20 June 1903 (p. 12), 27 June 1903 (p. 12), 3 October 1903 (p. 15).
Globe 18 May 1903 (p. 8).

---

[1] The date given on the score is 1902. This must be an error, as many of the numbers contained in the score were not included until the show came to London in 1903, and the *Era* confirms that a score was published in London late in May 1903.

New York Times 19 July 1903 (p. 3).
Pall Mall Gazette 18 May 1903 (p. 11).
Standard 18 May 1903 (p. 5).
Star 16 May 1903 (p. 2), 18 May 1903 (p. 1).
St James Gazette 18 May 1903 (p. 15), 24 June 1903 (p. 7).
Sphere 23 May 1903 (p. 162).
Stage 21 May 1903 (p. 14).
Sunday Sun 17 May 1903 (p. 6).
Times 18 May 1903 (p. 12).
Weekly Dispatch 10 May 1903 (p. 8), 24 May 1903 (p. 8), 31 May 1903 (p. 8), 7 June 1903 (p. 8), 28 June 1903 (p. 5).

Dan Kildare/Ciro's Coon Club Orchestra

Daily Telegraph 19 April 1915 (p. 11).
Era 21 April 1915 (p. 17), 25 September 1918 (p. 14), 2 October 1918 (p. 11).
News of the World 27 June 1920 (p. 5).

Joe Jordan

Era 5 May 1915 (p. 14), 12 May 1915 (p. 14).
Newcastle Evening Mail 22 June 1915 (p. 4).
Scotsman 31 May 1915 (p. 1).
Stage 6 May 1915 (p. 17), 13 May 1915 (p. 14), 3 June 1915 (p. 25), 24 June 1915 (p. 7).

Tennessee Students

Referee 7 January 1906 (p. 4).
Stage 7 December 1905.

Louis Mitchell and the Seven Spades

Era 27 September 1916 (p. 7).
Stage 12 October 1916 (p. 15), 28 September 1916 (p. 13).
Encore 9 August 1917 (p. 11), 27 September 1917 (p. 10).

The Versatile Four/Three

Encore 6 September 1917 (p. 3), 13 September 1917 (p. 3), 10 January 1918 (p. 3), 4 April 1918 (p. 3).
Era 26 March 1919 (p. 14).

Murray Pilcer

Sound Wave and Talking Machine Record March 1919 (p. 101), April 1919 (pp. 145, 148, 165).

Original Dixieland Jazz Band

Daily News 4 April 1919 (p. 5).

Encore 17 April 1919 (p. 5), 1 May 1919 (pp. 4, 5).
Era 19 February 1919 (p. 14), 9 April 1919 (p. 14), 16 April 1919 (p. 14), 23 April 1919 (p. 14).
Glasgow Herald 4 April 1919 (p. 9).
Italian American Digest (pub. New Orleans) Spring 1989, vol. 15 (1).
Knights of Columbus News Bulletin 28 June 1919.
Liverpool Echo 1 April 1919.
Pall Mall Gazette 23 April 1919.
People 27 April 1919 (p. 4).
Performer 10 April 1919 (p. 23), 10 April 1919 (p. 25).
Star 19 April 1919 (p. 3).
Times 23 April 1919, 24 April 1919, 25 April 1919.
Town Topics: 'The Joy Rag' 12 April 1919 (p. 2), 19 April 1919 (p. 2).
West London Observer 24 October 1919 (p. 5).

Southern Syncopated Orchestra

Bailie (Glasgow) 7 January 1920 (p. 7).
Bristol Evening News 6 April 1920.
Bristol Times and Mirror 6 April 1920 (p. 5).
Clapham Observer 19 March 1920 (p. 7), 26 March 1920 (p. 7), 2 April 1920 (p. 7).
Daily Graphic 12 November 1919 (p. 6), 9 December 1919 (p. 6).
Daily Herald 2 August 1919, 4 August 1919 (p. 3).
Daily Record and Mail (Glasgow) 26 December 1919 (p. 9).
Dancing World October 1920, 1 No.6 (p. 4).
Dunfermline Press 24 January 1920 (p. 4).
Edinburgh Evening News 21 January 1920 (p. 5).
Evening Argus (Brighton) 29 July 1921 (p. 2), 2 August 1921 (p. 4), 9 August 1921 (p. 2), 16 August 1921 (p. 2), 23 August 1921 (p. 2), 30 August 1921 (p. 2).
Nottinghamshire Guardian 24 April 1920 (p. 2).
People 29 June 1919 (p. 4), 27 July 1919 (p. 4).
Performer 12 August 1920 (p. 27).
Referee 6 July 1919 (p. 4), 14 December 1919 (p. 7), 7 March 1920 (p. 11), 7 November 1920 (p. 3).
Scotsman 21 January 1920 (p. 8).
Sheffield Daily Telegraph 27 April 1920 (p. 4).
Sound Wave October 1920 (p. 698).
South London Press 2 April 1920 (p. 11).
Stage 13 May 1920 (p. 11), 24 June 1920 (p. 10), 8 July 1920 (p. 8), 4 November 1920 (p. 11), 16 December 1920 (p. 12).
Telegraph 11 August 1919 (p. 8), 6 August 1920 (p. 16).
Times 11 August 1919 (p. 13), 9 December 1919 (p. 12), 15 May 1920 (p. 5), 25 September 1919 (p. 13), 29 October 1919 (p. 29), 1 November 1919 (p. 9), 12 November 1919 (p. 17).

Paul Whiteman Band

Era 14 March 1921 (pp. 14, 17), 21 March 1921 (pp. 13, 14), 4 April 1921 (p. 11), 14 May 1921 (p. 13).
Encore 1 March 1921, 22 March 1921 (p. 2), 28 March 1921 (p. 11).
Stage 5 March 1921 (p. 14).

Plantation Revues

Daily Graphic 25 January 1923 (p. 10), 3 March 1923 (p. 4), 5 March 1923 (p. 7), 6 March 1923 (p. 7), 8 March 1923 (p. 10), 10 March 1923 (p. 10), 15 March 1923 (pp. 8, 9, 13), 4 April 1923.
Era 14 March 1923 (pp. 1, 11), 21 March 1923 (pp. 9-10), 11 April 1923 (p. 11), 6 June 1923 (p. 11).
Encore 15 March 1923 (p. 3), 22 March 1923 (p. 3), 5 April 1923 (p. 12), 7 June 1923 (pp. 9-10).
John Bull 28 October 1922.
Performer 7 March 1923 (pp. 5, 6), 14 March 1923 (p. 5), 21 March 1923 (p. 5).
Referee 8 April 1923 (p. 8).
Stage 5 April 1923 (p. 14), 7 June 1923 (p. 17).
Star 1 June 1923 (p. 6), 28 July 1923 (p. 11).
Sunday Times 18 March 1923 (p. 6).

Leon Abbey

Encore 22 December 1923 (p. 10).

Nightclub scene

Daily Express 14 March 1922 (p. 1, 4).
Evening News 13 March 1922 (p. 3), 14 March 1922 (p. 1), 3 May 1922 (p. 3).
John Bull 1 August 1925 (p. 11).

Louis Armstrong

Daily Express 20 July 1932 (p. 15), 31 March 1933 (p. 1).
Daily Herald 12 July 1933.
The Era 20 July 1932 (p. 19), 27 July 1932 (p. 19).
Melody Maker July - October 1932.
Performer 20 July 1932 (p. 10).
The Stage 21 July 1932 (p. 3), 28 July 1932 (p. 3).
Variety Music, Stage and Film News 20 July 1932 (p. 4).

Duke Ellington

Daily Express 13 June 1933 (p. 11).
Daily Herald 10 June 1933, 13 June 1933 (p. 8).
Era 14 June 1933 (p. 1).
Evening Standard 13 June 1933, 14 June 1933.
Melody Maker November 1932, January-May 1933, 17 June 1933, 24 June 1933, 1 July 1933, 8 July 1933, 15 July 1933.
Radio Times 9 June 1933 (pp. 611, 613, 642).
The Stage 15 June 1933, 22 June 1933.
Sunday Referee 18 June 1933 (p. 11), 25 June 1933 (p. 18).

The National Archives: Public Record Office Files

Lattimore Court Cases
L. 175
High Court of Justice, Chancery Division, 1920 between George William Lattimore, (plaintiff) and Albert de Courville, B. E. Peyton, George Smith, Henry Saparo and Fred Coxcito (defendants).

Affidavits (TNA: PRO J4/9220)
79	George William Lattimore
96	Benton Elsworth Peyton
97	Henry Saparo
98	George Mitchell Smith
99	Fred Coxcito
100	George Mitchell Smith

Orders (TNA: PRO J15/ 3550) and (TNA: PRO J15/3551)

L. 542
High Court of Justice, Chancery Division, 1920 between George William Lattimore, (plaintiff) and Ernest C. Rolls (defendant).

Affidavits (TNA: PRO J4/9221)
296	Motion to continue interim injunction
297	Will Marion Cook
298	Ernest Charles Rolls
304	George Lattimore

Orders (TNA: PRO J15/ 3552) and (TNA: PRO J15/3553)

L. 647 High Court of Justice, Chancery Division, 1920 between George William Lattimore, (plaintiff) and Will Marion Cook, Ernest C. Rolls and André C. Charlot (defendant).

Affidavits (TNA: PRO J4/9221)
305	George Lattimore
306	Lawerence Morris
309	Frank Douglas Withers/Anthony Rivera
310	Will Marion Cook
323	Will Marion Cook
327	Fred Coxcito
334	George Lattimore

Orders (TNA: PRO J15/3553)

L. 57 High Court of Justice, Kings Bench Division, 1920, between George William Lattimore, (plaintiff) and A. P. de Courville (defendant).

(TNA: PRO J54/1731)

Plantation Revues

LAB2/1187/EDAR954/1923	Actor's Association Opposition to black performers.
LAB2/1188/EDAR1149/1926	Alien Labour Policy and Procedure.

Nightclubs

MEPO 2/2053	Nightclub irregularities.
MEPO 3/2969	Police supervision of nightclubs.
HO 45/11599	'Cocaine' film.
HO 45/16205	Nightclubs: entertainments, liquor licensing, police supervision etc.

Restrictions on American Musicians

LAB2/1187/EDAR3011/1922/Amended	
LAB2/1188/EDAR3406/1925	Taxation of American Musicians.
LAB2/1188/EDAR278/41/1925	American bands at the Kit Cat.
LAB8/1926	Decision to refuse permits to American musicians.
LAB2/1188/EDAR528/2/1929	Complaint by London Trades Council regarding the employment by the Café de Paris of American musicians.
LAB2/1188/AR3434/1930	Employment and training: aliens restriction department.
LAB2/1189/ETAR9494/1931/(Amended)	Decision to refuse permits to artists of international standing.

Archive Files

Oral History Holdings of the William Ransom Hogan Archive of New Orleans Jazz, Tulane University (referenced as HJA).

Danny Barker	30 June 1959
	Fall 1988
Sidney Bechet	June 1944
	19 November 1945
	1957
	1958
Tom Brown	1956
Eddie Edwards	1 July 1959
Emanuel Sayles	17 January 1959
	29 January 1961
Papa Jack Laine	21 April 1951
	26 March 1957
	25 January 1959
	23 May 1960

Nick LaRocca	21 May 1958
	26 May 1958
	2 June 1958
Johnny St Cyr	27 August 1958
Tony Sbarbaro and Emile Christian	11 February 1959
Harry Shields	28 May 1961

Oral History of Jazz in Britain interviews in the National Sound Archive, London.

Clare Deniz	T9808Y-T9810Y
Frank Deniz	T9910Y-T9912Y
Joe Deniz	T9654-T9656
George Elrick	H6138
Harry Gold	T9657-T9660
Nat Gonella	H6215
Harry Hayes	B1760
Don Johnson	T9661-3
Humphrey Lyttleton	C90/39/01
Gerry Moore	T9651BW-T9653BW
Van Phillips	H6170-H6171
Louis Stephenson	B2444

Information from files in the Institute of Jazz Studies, Rutgers University, Newark, New Jersey (referenced as IJS).

Information from files in the National Jazz Archive, Loughton Public Library, Loughton, Essex (referenced as NJA).

Information from files in the BBC Written Archives Centre, Caversham Park, Reading (referenced as BBCWAC).

Information from files in the Jack Hylton Archive, Rare Book Archive, Lancaster University Library, Lancaster.

General Bibliography

(1919) 'A Negro Explains "Jazz"' in *The Literary Digest*, April 26 1919, pp. 28-29.

(1973) 'The Return of the Banjo' in *Esquire Magazine*, LXXX (5) November 1973, pp. 171-75.

Various authors (1955) ODJB issue of *Second Line*, 6 (9-10), September-October 1955.

Adcock, J. (1926) *Wonderful London: The World's Greatest City Described by its Best Writers and Pictured by its Finest Photographer* (London, Fleetway House).

Adorno, T.W. [1955] trans. Weber, S. and Weber, S. (1967) 'Perennial Fashion – Jazz' in *Prisms* (London, Neville Spearman).

Adorno, T.W. [1936] trans. J. O. Daniel (1989) 'On Jazz' in *Discourse*, 12 (1), pp. 45-69.

Adorno, T.W. ed. Bernstein, J.M. (1991) *The Culture Industry: Selected Essays on Mass Culture* (London, Routledge).

Aldam, J. (n.d.) *Why Jazz is Misunderstood* (in NJA 'Jazz – General' File).

Amstell, B. (with Deal, R.) (1986) *Don't Fuss, Mr Ambrose* (Tunbridge Wells, Spellmount Ltd).

Ansermet, E. (1959) 'Will Marion Cook's Orchestra' in Williams, M. (1959) *The Art of Jazz: Essays on the Nature and Development of Jazz* (New York, Oxford University Press).

Asburnham, G. (1930) *'Syncopation' George Ashburnham's Piano Method* (Teddington).

Asquith, C. (1968) *The Diaries of Lady Cynthia Asquith 1915-1918* (London, Century).

Atkins, E.T. (ed.) (2003) *Jazz Planet* (Jackson, University Press of Mississippi).

Averty, J.- C. (1969) 'Sidney Bechet 1919-1922' in *Jazz Hot* 250, pp. 22-3.

Badger, R.R. (1989) 'James Reese Europe and the Prehistory of Jazz' in *American Music*, 7 (1) Spring 1989, pp. 48-67 (Chicago, University of Illinois).

Banfield, S. (ed) (1995) *The Blackwell History of Music in Britain; Volume VI, The Twentieth Century* (Oxford, Blackwell).

Bailey, P. (1986) *Music Hall: the Business of Pleasure* (Milton Keynes, Open University Press).

Barker, F. (1957) *The House that Stoll Built, The Story of the Coliseum* (London, Frederick Muller).

Barnard, S. (1989) *On the Radio: Music Radio in Britain* (Milton Keynes, Open University Press).

Beaton, J. and Rye, H. (1978) 'Sam Wooding in England and France' in *Storyville*, 74, pp. 47-9.

Bechet, S. (1960) *Treat it Gentle* (London, Cassell).

Berrett, J (1999) *The Louis Armstrong Companion: Eight Decades of Commentary* (New York, Schirmer).

Berendt, J. (1992) *The Jazz Book: From Ragtime to Fusion and Beyond* (New York, Lawrence Hill Books).

Bergmeier, H.J.P. (1978) 'Sam Wooding Recapitulated' in *Storyville*, 74, pp. 44-47.

Bergreen, L. (1997) *Louis Armstrong: An Extravagant Life* (HarperCollins).

Black, G. (1994) *Living Up West: Jewish Life in London's West End* (London, The London Museum of Jewish Life).

Blesh, R. and Janis, H. (1971) *They All Played Ragtime* (New York, Oak Publications).

Bloom, C. (2002) *Bestsellers: Popular Fiction Since 1900* (Basingstoke, Palgrave).

Bohan, E. (1982) *The Incorporated Society of Musicians: The First Hundred Years* (London, ISM).

Born, G. and Hesmondhalgh, D. (eds) (2000) *Western Music and Its Others: Difference, Representation and Appropriation in Music* (California, University of California Press).

Boulton, D. (1959) *Jazz in Britain* (London, The Jazz Book Club).

Bradbury, M. and McFarlane, J. (eds) (1991) *Modernism: A Guide to European Literature 1890-1930* (London, Penguin).

Bradbury, M. (2001) *The Modern British Novel 1878-2001* (London, Penguin Books).

Bradley, J. (1947) *Dancing Through Life* (London, Hollis and Carter).

Bratton, J.S. (1986) *Music Hall: Performance and Style* (Milton Keynes, Open University Press).

Brown, R. and Brown, C. (1985) *Georgia on my Mind: The Nat Gonella Story* (Portsmouth, Milestone Publications).

Brown, S.E. (1986) *James P. Johnson: A Case of Mistaken Identity* (Metuchen, New Jersey, London, Scarecrow Press and the Institute of Jazz Studies).

Briggs, A. (1961) *The History of Broadcasting in the UK* (Oxford, Oxford University Press).

Brunn, H.O. (1963) *The Story of the Original Dixieland Jazz Band* (London, Jazz Book Club).

Burke, T. (1934) *London in My Time* (London, Rich and Cowan).

Burke, T. (1940) *The Streets of London* (London, Batsford).

Cammeyer, A. (1934) *My Adventuresome Banjo* (London, Cammeyer's).

Carnovale, N. (2000) *George Gershwin: A Bio-Bibliography* (Westport, Connecticut, Greenwood Press).

Carr, I. (1973) *Music Outside: Contemporary Jazz in Britain* (London, Latimer).

Carter, M.G. (2000) 'Removing the "Minstrel Mask" in the Musicals of Will Marion Cook' in *The Musical Quarterly*, 84 (2): 206-220.

Carver, F.H. (1952) 'My Minstrel Days' in *International Musician*, January 1952 in 'Minstrel' file in HJA.

Cashmore, E. (1997) *The Black Culture Industry* (London, Routledge).

Castle, V. and I. (1914) *Modern Dancing* (New York, Harper and Brothers).

Chamberlain, C. (2000) 'Searching for "The Gulf Coast Circuit": Mobility and Cultural Diffusion in the Age of Jim Crow, 1900-1930' in *The Jazz Archivist*, 14, pp. 1-18.

Chanan, M. (1995) *Repeated Takes: A Short History of Recording and Its Effects on Music* (London, Verso).

Chanan, M. (1996) *The Dream that Kicks: The Prehistory and Early Years of Cinema in Britain* (London, Routledge and Kegan Paul).

Charters, A. (1970) *Nobody: The Story of Bert Williams* (New York, Macmillan).

Charters, S.B. and Kunstadt, L. (1962/R1981) *Jazz: A History of the New York Scene* (New York, Da Capo).

Chilton, J. (1987) *Sidney Bechet: The Wizard of Jazz* (Hampshire, Macmillan Press).

Chilton, J. (1980) *A Jazz Nursery: The Story of the Jenkins' Orphanage Bands* (London, Bloomsbury Bookshop).

Clarke, D. (1995) *The Rise and Fall of Popular Music* (London, Viking).

Cliffe, P. (1990) *Fascinating Rhythm: Dance Tunes from between the Wars and the Stars Who made them Magical* (Hertfordshire, Egon).

Cochran, C.B. (1932) *I Had Almost Forgotten ...* (London, Hutchinson and Co.).

Colin, S. (1977) *And the Bands Played On: An Informal History of British Dance Bands* (London, Elm Tree).

Collier, J.L. (1983) *Louis Armstrong: a Biography* (London, Michael Joseph).

Collier, J.L. (1987) *Duke Ellington* (London, Michael Joseph).

Collins, G. (1978) 'Herman Darewski Feature' in *Memory Lane*, 11 (41), pp. 25-27.

Cook, D. (1996) *The Culture Industry Revisited: Theodor W. Adorno on Mass Culture* (Maryland, Rowman and Littlefield).

Cook, M. (n.d.) *From Clorindy to the Red Moon and Beyond: A Symposium Paper* (transcript in 'Cook' file in IJS).

Cook, W.M. (1947) 'Clorindy, the origin of the cakewalk' in ed. Gilder, R., Isaacs, H.R., MacGregor, R.M., and Reed, E. (1950) *Theatre Arts Anthology* (New York, Theatre Arts Books).

Cope, P. (2001) *Let Paul Robeson Sing!: a Celebration of the Life of Paul Robeson* (Paul Robeson Cymru Committee/Bevan Foundation/Theatre Museum).

Crowder, H. with Speck, H. (1987) *As Wonderful As All That: Henry Crowder's Memoir of His Affair with Nancy Cunard, 1928-1935* (Introduction and Epilogue by Robert L. Allen) (Navarro California, Wild Trees Press).

Cunard, N. (1934) *Negro: Anthology made by Nancy Cunard 1931-1933* (London, Nancy Cunard at Wishart and Co.).

Cundall, T. (1946) 'The Story of Fred Elizalde' in *Clef*, June 1946, pp.16-18.

Daniel, J.O. (1989) Introduction to 'On Jazz' in *Discourse*, 12 (1), pp. 39-44.

Dankworth, J. (1998) *Jazz in Revolution* (London, Constable).

Davis, L. (1934a) 'The Genesis of Jazz part 1' in *Melody Maker*, June 2 1934, pp. 7-8.

Davis, L. (1934b) 'The Genesis of Jazz part 2 (When the sax was a rarity)' in *Melody Maker*, June 9 1934, p. 6.

Davis, M. (ed.) (1976) *The Diaries of Evelyn Waugh* (London, Weidenfield and Nicolson).

De Courville, A. (1928) *I Tell You* (London, Chapman and Hall).

Demetz, K. (1992) 'Minstrel Dancing in New Orleans' Nineteenth Century Theaters' in *Southern Quarterly*, 20 (2) Winter 1992, pp. 28-40.

Dixon, G. (1992) 'Musical Theatre and the African-American Experience: A Black History Month Remembrance of Will Marion Cook (1869-1944)' in *Allegro*, February 1992, pp. 14-15.

Doctor, J. (1999) *The BBC and Ultra-Modern Music, 1922-1936: Shaping a Nation's Tastes* (Cambridge, Cambridge University Press).

Dodge, Roger Pryor (1995) *Hot Jazz and Jazz Dance: Collected Writings 1929-1964* (New York, Oxford University Press).

Donegall (1944) 'The Marquis of Donegall Reminisces on the ODJB.' in *Jazz Tempo* (17), p. 21.

Driberg, T. (1974) *Swaff: The Life and Times of Hannen Swaffer* (London, Macdonald).

Driggs, Frank and Lewine, H. (1996) *Black beauty, White heat: A Pictorial History of Classic Jazz, 1920-1950* (New York, Da Capo).

Du Bois, W.E.B. (1903) *The Souls of Black Folk* (Chicago, A. McClurg and Co; published online at Bartleby.com, 1999. http://www.bartleby.com/114/).

Duval, L. (1933) 'The Genesis of Jazz' in *Radio Times*, 17 March 1933, p. 658.

Edwards, E. (1947) 'Once Upon a Time' in *Jazz Review*, May 1947, pp. 5-6.

Ehrlich, C. (1976/R1990) *The Piano: A History* (Oxford, Clarendon Press).

Ehrlich, C. (1985) *The Music Profession in Britain since the 18th Century* (Oxford, Clarendon Press).

Ehrlich, C. (1989) *Harmonious Alliance: A History of the Performing Right Society* (Oxford, Oxford University Press).

Elizalde, F. (1929) 'Jazz – What of the Future?' in *Gramophone* February 1929, pp. 392-93.

Ellington, Duke (1974) *Music is my mistress: An Autobiography* (London, W.H. Allen).

England, B. (1973) 'Leon Abbey and His Recordings' in *Storyville*, 49, pp. 7-9.

Englund, B. (1976) 'Chocolate Kiddies: The show that brought jazz to Europe and Russia in 1925' in *Storyville*, 62, pp. 44-50.

Epstein, D.J. (1975) 'The Folk Banjo: A Documentary History' in *Ethnomusicology*, 19 (3) September 1975, pp. 347-371.

Fabian, R. (1954) *London After Dark* (London, Naldrett Press).

Faint, P.J. (1999) *Jack Hylton, His Life in Music* (unpublished MPhil thesis, University of Lancaster).

Feather, L. (1986) *The Jazz Years: Earwitness to an Era* (London, Pan).

Fenton, A. (1969) 'Jazz Research' in *Jazz Monthly*, 173 July 1969, pp. 13-14.

Field, F. and Haikin, P. (1971) *Black Britons* (Oxford, Oxford University Press).

Firman, B. (1984) *Autobiography* (unpublished, also partially available on http://www.jabw.demon.co.uk/firman1.htm).

Fitzgerald, F.S. (1998) *Jazz Age Stories* (edited with an introduction and explanatory notes by Patrick O'Donnel) (London, Penguin).

Fordham, J. (1995) *The Amazing Story of Ronnie Scott and His Club* (London, Kyle Cathie).

Foss, H.J. (1933) *Music in My Time* (London, Rich and Cowan).

Fox, C. (1985) 'Back on the Beat: The Best of British Jazz' in *The Sunday Telegraph Magazine*, 474, November 1985, pp. 43-51.

Fox, R. (1975) *Hollywood, Mayfair and all that Jazz: the Roy Fox Story* (London, Leslie Frewin).

Francis, H. (1974) 'Jazz Development in Britain, 1924-1974' in *Crescendo* Part 1 March 1974, p. 4 and 7; Part 2 April 1974, pp. 18-40 (also at http://www.jazzprofessional.com).

Frith, S. (1996) *Performing Rites: Evaluating Popular Music* (Oxford, Oxford University Press).

Frith, S. (1992) 'The Industrialisation of Music' in *Popular Music and Communication* (London, Sage).

Fryer, P. (1984) *Staying Power: The History of Black People in Britain* (London, Pluto Press).

Gabbard, K. (ed.) (1995) *Jazz Among the Discourses* (Durham, Duke University Press).

Gabbard, K. (1996) *Jammin' at the Margins: Jazz and the American Cinema* (Chicago, University of Chicago Press).

Gaisberg, F.W. (1946) *Music on Record* (London, Robert Hale).

Gale, I. (1990) *Waugh's World: A Guide to the Novels of Evelyn Waugh* (London, Sidgwick and Jackson).

Gendron, B. (2002) *Between Montmartre and the Mudd Club: Popular Music and the Avant-garde* (Chicago, University of Chicago Press).

George, D. (1982) *The Real Duke Ellington* (London, Robson Books).

Gerard, C. (1988) *Jazz in Black and White* (Westport, Connecticut, Praeger).

Giddins, G. (1998) *Visions of Jazz: The First Century* (Oxford, Oxford University Press).

Giddins, G. (1998/R2001) *Satchmo: The Genius of Louis Armstrong* (London, Da Capo).

Gilbert, B.B. (1980) *Britain since 1918* (London, Batsford Academic and Educational).

Gilbert, D. (n.d.) *American Vaudeville: Its Life and Times: Williams and Walker, Comic Character Traits* (in 'Williams' file in IJS).

Gillespie, D. with Fraser A. (1980) *Dizzy* (London, W.H. Allen).

Gilliam, B. (ed.) (1994) *Music and Performance During the Weimar Republic* (Cambridge, Cambridge University Press).

Gilroy, P. (1993/R2002) *The Black Atlantic: Modernity and Double Consciousness* (London, Verso).

Gioia, T. (1988) *The Imperfect Art: Reflections of Jazz and Modern Culture* (Oxford, Oxford University Press).

Godbolt, J. (1986) *A History of Jazz in Britain 1919-1950* (London, Paladin).

Goddard, C. (1979) *Jazz Away from Home* (London, Paddington Press).

Goffin, R. (1946) *Jazz from Congo to Swing* (London, Musicians Press Ltd.).

Goffin, R. (1947) trans. Bezou, J.F. (1977) *Horn of Plenty: The Story of Louis Armstrong* (New York, Da Capo).

Gold, H. and Cotterrell, R. [ed.] (2000) *Gold, Doubloons and Pieces of Eight: The Autobiography of Harry Gold* (London, Northway Publications).

Gonella, N. (1934) *Modern Style Trumpet Playing: A Comprehensive Course* (London, Selmer).

Gottlieb, R. (ed.) (1997) *Reading Jazz* (London, Bloomsbury).

Graves, R. and Hodge, A. (1940) *The Long Weekend: A Social History of Britain 1918-1939* (London, Cardinal).

Green, J. (1983a) '*In Dahomey* in London in 1903' in *Black Perspective in Music*, 11 (1), pp. 23-40.

Green, J. (1983b) 'Jack Hylton: The Beginning of an Orchestral Leader' in *Memory Lane*, 15 (59) Summer 1983, pp. 26-27.

Green, J. (1985) *Leslie Thompson: An Autobiography as told to Jeffrey P. Green* (Crawley, Rabbit Press).

Green, J. (1998) *Black Edwardians: Black People in Britain 1901-1914* (London, Frank Cass).

Green, J. and Lockhart, R. (1986) 'A Brown Alien in a White City: Black Students in London, 1917-1920' in Lotz/Pegg (eds) *Under the Imperial Carpet: Essays in Black History 1780-1950* (Crawley, Sussex, Rabbit Press).

Greenhalgh, P. (1988) *Ephemeral Vistas: The Expositions Universelles, Great Exhibitions and World's Fairs* (Manchester, Manchester University Press).

Gretton, R.H. (1930) *A Modern History of English People 1880-1922* (London, Martin Secker).

Gulliver, R. (1977) 'Leon Abbey' in *Storyville*, 73, pp. 5-28 (with additional research material from Frank Driggs and Bertrand Demeusy).

Gura, P. and Bollam, J. (1999) *America's Instrument: The Banjo in the Nineteenth Century* (University of North Carolina Press).

Guttridge, L. (1956) 'The First Man to Bring Jazz to Britain' in *Melody Maker*, 14 July 1956, p. 6.

Hale, K. (1994) *A Slender Reputation: An Autobiography* (London, Frederick Warne).

Hamm, C. (1979) *Yesterdays: Popular Song in America* (New York, Norton).

Haralambos, M. and Holborn, M. (1990) *Sociology: Themes and Perspectives* (London, Unwin Hyman).

Harris, R. (1957) *Jazz* (Middlesex, Penguin).

Harris, R. (1957) *Jazz Column (for Members of the Jazz Book Club)* 1, January/February 1957 (in NJA 'Jazz Clubs' file).

Hasse, J.E. (1985) *Ragtime: Its History, Composers and Music* (London, Macmillan).

Hayes, C. (1988) *Dance Music at the Savoy Hotel 1920-1927 (Based on the Series about W.F. De Mornys – Entertainments Manager at the Savoy Hotel and titled 'The First Impresario of Jazz' Published in 'Memory Lane' in 1978)* (Isle of Wight, the author).

Hayes, C. (1989) *Signature Tunes* (Isle of Wight, the author).

Heath, T. (1957) *Listen to My Music* (London, Frederick Muller Ltd).

Heier, U. and Lotz, R.E. (1993) *The Banjo on Record – A Bio-Discography* (Connecticut, Greenwood Press).

Heindel, R.H. (1940) *The American Impact on Great Britain 1898-1914* (Philadelphia, University of Pennsylvania Press).

Henery, J. and Garvie, C. (1985) 'Deplorable, Dissolute and Depraved' in *The Wire*, 22, December 1985, pp. 8-11.

Hentoff, N. and McCarthy, A. (eds) (1959) *Jazz: New Perspectives on the History of Jazz by Twelve of the World's Foremost Jazz Critics and Scholars* (London, Cassell).

Hill, D. (1993) *Sylvester Ahola: The Gloucester Gabriel* (Metuchen, New Jersey and London, Scarecrow Press).

Hiller, B. (1983) *The Style of the Century, 1900-1980* (London, The Herbert Press).

Hiller, B. (1968/R1985) *Art Deco of the 20s and 30s: A Design Handbook* (London, The Herbert Press).

Hobsbawm, E. (2002) *Interesting Times: A Twentieth Century Life* (London, Allen Lane).

Hoefer, G. (n.d.) *Portrait of Bert Williams – 'The Jonah Man'* (in 'Williams' file, IJS).

Holbrook, A. (1973) 'Our word JAZZ' in *Storyville*, 50, December 1973-January 1974, pp. 46-58.

Hughes, P. [Spike] (1946) *Opening Bars: Beginning an Autobiography* (London, Pilot Press).

Hughes, P. [Spike] (1951) *Second Movement* (London, Museum Press).

Hustwitt, M. (1983) '"Caught in a whirlpool of aching sound": the production of dance music in Britain in the 1920s' in *Popular Music*, 3 (1) pp. 7-31.

Hynes, S. (1990) *A War Imagined: The First World War and English Culture* (London, Bodley Head).

Jackson, S. (1964) *The Savoy: The Romance of A Great Hotel* (London, Frederick Muller Limited).

Jenkinson, J. (1986) 'The 1919 Race Riots in Britain: A Survey' in Lotz/Pegg (eds) *Under the Imperial Carpet: Essays in Black History 1780-1950* (Crawley, Sussex, Rabbit Press).

Johnson, J. (1991) 'New Orleans's Congo Square: An Urban Setting for Early Afro-American Culture Formation' in *Louisiana History: The Journal of the Louisiana Historical Association*, 32 (2) Spring 1991, pp. 117-57.

Johnson, J. (2000) 'Jim Crow Laws of the 1890s and the origins of New Orleans jazz: correction of an error' in *Popular Music*, 19 (2), pp. 243-51 (Cambridge, Cambridge University Press).

Jones, LeRoi (1969) *Black Music* (London, MacGibbon and Kee).

Jones, M. (1960) Billy Mason in *Melody Maker*, 29 October 1960, pp. 12-13.

Jones, M. Chilton, J. and Feather, L. (1970) *Salute to Satchmo* (Melody Maker Publications, London).

Jones, M. and Chilton, J. (1975) *Louis: The Louis Armstrong Story 1900-1971* (St Albans, Mayflower).

Jones, M. (1987) *Talking Jazz* (Hampshire, Macmillan Press).

Jones, S. (1994) *In Darkest London: Antisocial Behaviour 1900-1939* (Nottingham, Wicked Publications).

Kater, M. (1992) *Different Drummers* (New York, Oxford University Press).

Kennedy, R. (1994) *Jelly Roll, Bix and Hoagy: Gennett Studios and the Birth of Recorded Jazz* (Bloomington and Indianapolis, Indiana University Press).

Kenney, W.H. (1993) *Chicago Jazz, A Cultural History 1904-1930* (New York, Oxford University Press).

Kern, S. (1983) *The Culture of Time and Space 1880-1918* (Cambridge, Harvard).

Kift, D. trans. Kift, R. (1996) *The Victorian Music Hall: Culture, Class and Conflict* (Cambridge, Cambridge University Press).

Kimball, R. and Balcom, W (1972) *Reminiscing with Sissle and Blake* (New York, Viking Press).

Kmen, H.A. (1966) *Music in New Orleans: The Formative Years 1791-1841* (Baton Rouge, Louisiana State University Press).

Kofsky, F. (1998) *Black Music, White Business* (New York, Pathfinder).

Kohn, M. (1992) *Dope Girls: The Birth of the British Drug Underground* (London, Lawrence and Wishart).

Krotzer Laborde, K. (2000) 'A Weird, Wacky Vaudeville for the Millennium in the New Orleans' in *Times-Picayune* (New Orleans), 24 March 2000.

LaRocca, N. (1936a) 'Jazz Stems from Whites Not Blacks, Says La Rocca' in *Metronome*, October 1936.

LaRocca, N. (1936b) 'History of the Original Dixieland Jazz Band' in *Tempo*, October 1936, pp. 4, 11, 12.

LaRocca, N. (various) Scrapbooks held at HJA.

Lambert, C. (1928) 'Jazz' in MacCarthy, D. (ed.) *Life and Letters*, 1 (1) June 1928.

Lambert, C. (1933) 'The Future of Highbrow Jazz' in *Radio Times*, 17 March 1933, p. 659.

Lambert, C. (1934/R1966) *Music Ho!* (London, Faber).

Latrobe, B.H. ed. Wilson Jr. S. (1951) *Impressions Respecting New Orleans: Diary and Sketches 1818-1820* (New York, Columbia University Press).

Lawrence, A.H. (2001) *Duke Ellington and his World: A Biography* (New York and London, Routledge).

Lee, E. (1970) *Music of the People: A Study of Popular Music in Great Britain* (London, Barrie and Jenkins).

Leedman-Green, E. (1996) *A Concise History of the University of Cambridge* (Cambridge, Cambridge University Press).

Leppert, R. (1988) *Music and Image: Domesticity, Ideology and Socio-cultural Formation in Eighteenth-century England* (Cambridge, Cambridge University Press).

Levin, F. (1986) Lou'siana Swing in *Jazz Journal International*, 39 (8) August 1986, pp. 12-13.

Linn, K. (1991) *That Half-Barbaric Twang: The Banjo in American Popular Culture* (Urbana, University of Illinois).

Lipman, V.D. (1990) *A History of the Jews in Britain Since 1858* (Leicester and London, Leicester University Press).

Little, K. (1948) *Negroes in Britain: A Study of Racial Relations in English Society* (London, Kegan Paul).

Lively, A. (1998) *Masks: Blackness, Race and the Imagination* (Chatto and Windus, London).

Lloyd Webb, R. (1993) 'Confidence and Admiration: The Enduring Ringing of the Banjo' in Heier, U. and Lotz, R.E. *The Banjo on Record – A Bio-Discography*, pp. 7-26 (Connecticut, Greenwood Press).

Lorimer, D.A. (1975) 'Bibles, Banjoes and Bones' in Gough, B. (ed.) *In Search of the Visible Past: History Lectures at Wilfred Laurier University 1973-74* (Waterloo, Ontario, Wilfred Laurier University Press).

Lotz, R. (1986) 'Will Garland and His Negro Operetta Company' in Lotz/Pegg (eds) *Under the Imperial Carpet: Essays in Black History 1780-1950* (Crawley, Sussex, Rabbit Press).

Lotz, R. (1997) *Black People – Entertainers of African Descent in Europe and Germany* (Bonn, Birgit Lotz Verlag).

Lucas, J. (1997) *The Radical Twenties: Writing, Politics, Culture* (London, Five Leaves).

Lyttelton, H. (1980) *The Best of Jazz: Basin Street to Harlem* (London, Penguin).

Lyttleton, H. (1975) *Take It from the Top: An Autobiographical Scrapbook* (London, Robson Books).

Mackerness. E.D. (1964) *A Social History of English Music* (London, Routledge and Kegan Paul).

Madge, C. and Harrison, T. (1939) *Britain – by Mass Observation* (London, Penguin).

Mahar, W.J. (1999) *Behind the Burnt Cork Mask: Early Blackface Minstrelsy and Antebellum American Popular Culture* (Urbana and Chicago, University of Illinois).

Maine, B. (1939) *The BBC and Its Audience* (London, Thomas Nelson).

Marsh, J.B.T. (1895/R1902) *The Story of the Jubilee Singers with their Songs (with supplement containing an Account of their Six Years Tour around the World and many New Songs by F.J. Loudin)* (London, Hodder and Stoughton).

Martland, P. (1997) *Since Records Began: EMI the First 100 Years* (London, Batsford).

Matthew, J.M. (1990) *J.B. Souter, 1890-1971* (Exhibition Catalogue) (Perth, Perth Museum and Art Gallery).

Mayerl, B. (1926) *The Billy Mayerl School of Modern Syncopation for the Pianoforte* (London, W. J. Mayerl and G. Clayton).

McCarthy, A. (1971) *The Dance Band Era: The Dancing Decades from Ragtime to Swing: 1910-1950* (London, Studio Vista).

McClary, S. (2000) *Conventional Wisdom: The Content of Musical Form* (Berkeley, University of California Press).

McKibben, R. (1998) *Classes and Cultures: England 1918-1951* (Oxford, Oxford University Press).

Mellers, W. (1964) *Music in a New Found Land* (London, Rockliff).

Melly, G. (2000) *Owing Up: The Trilogy* (London, Penguin).

Mendl, R.W.S. (1927) *The Appeal of Jazz* (Glasgow, Robert Maclehose).

Meyrick, K. (1933) *Secrets of the 43* (London, John Long).

Middleton, R. (1972) *Pop Music and the Blues* (London, Victor Gollancz).

Middleton, R. (1990) *Studying Popular Music* (Milton Keynes, Open University Press).

Mitchell, T. (1992) 'Orientalism and the Exhibitionary Order' in Dirks, N.B. (ed.) (1992) *Colonialism and Culture* (Ann Arbor, University of Michigan Press).

Moody, B. (1993) *The Jazz Exiles* (Reno, University of Nevada Press).

Morgan, K.O. (2000) *Twentieth-Century Britain: A Very Short Introduction* (Oxford, Oxford University Press)

Moseley, S.A. (ed.) (1924) *Brightest Spots in Brighter London: A Comprehensive Guide to London Amusements, Shopping Centres and Features of Interest to the Visitor* (London, Stanley Paul).

Moseley, S.A. (1935) *Broadcasting in My Time* (London, Rich and Cowan).

Nathan, H. (1962) *Dan Emmett and the Rise of Early Negro Minstrelsy* (Norman, Oklahoma Press).

Napoleon, A. (1967) 'A Pioneer Looks Back: Sam Wooding 1967' in *Storyville*, 9, pp. 3-8, 37-39 and 10, pp. 4-8.

Nelson, S.R. (1933) 'The Future of Jazz' in *The Era*, 5 April 1933, p.5.

Nelson, S.R. (1933) 'Ellington and After! Art or Debauchery?' in *The Era*, 21 June 1933, p. 3.

Nelson, S.R. (1933) '"Sexophone" and sin' in *The Era*, 5 July 1933, p. 15.

Nelson, S.R. (1934) *All About Jazz* (London, Heath Cranton Ltd).

Nicholson, S. (1999) *Reminiscing in Tempo: A Portrait of Duke Ellington* (London, Pan Books).

Nicolson, H. (1941) *Half my Days and Nights: Autobiography of a Reporter* (London and Toronto, Heinemann).

Nott, J. (2003) *Music for the people: popular music and dance in inter-war Britain* (Oxford, Oxford University Press).

Odell, J. S. (1984) 'Banjo' in Sadie, S. (ed.) (1984) *New Grove Dictionary of Musical Instruments* (London, Macmillan).

Ogren, K. (1989) *The Jazz Revolution: Twenties America and the Meaning of Jazz* (New York, Oxford University Press).

Oliver, P. (1984) *Songsters and Saints: Vocal Traditions on Race Records* (Cambridge, Cambridge University Press).

Oliver, P. (1990) *Black Music in Britain* (Milton Keynes, Open University Press).

Oliver, P. (1997) *The Story of the Blues* (London, Pimlico).

O'Meally, R. (2004) 'Checking Our Balances: Louis Armstrong, Ralph Ellison and Betty Boop' in *The Source: Challenging Jazz Criticism*, 1, pp. 43-58.

Ord-Hume, A.W.J.G. (1984) *Pianola: The History of the Self-Playing Piano* (London, George Allen and Unwin).

Osgood, H. (1926/R1978) *So This is Jazz!* (Boston, Little, Brown).

Ostransky, L. (1978) *Jazz City: The Impact of Our Cities on the Development of Jazz* (Englewood Cliffs, NJ, Prentice Hall).

Paddinson, M. (1983) *Adorno's Aesthetics of Music* (Cambridge, Cambridge University Press).

Paddinson, M. (1982) 'The critique criticised: Adorno and popular music' in Middleton, R. and Horn, D. (eds) (1982) *Popular Music 2: Theory and Method* (Cambridge, Cambridge University Press).

Panassie, H. (1942) *The Real Jazz* (New York, Smith and Durrell).

Panassie, H. (1947) *Louis Armstrong* (Paris, Editions du Belvedere).

Panayi, P. (ed.) (1993/R1996) *Racial Violence in Britain in the Nineteenth and Twentieth Centuries* (London, Leicester University Press).

Patey, D.L. (1998) *The Life of Evelyn Waugh: A Critical Biography* (Oxford, UK and Cambridge, USA: Blackwell).

Payne, J. (1947) *Signature Tune* (London, Stanley Paul and Co.).

Pearce, R. (1992) *Britain: Domestic Politics 1918-39* (London, Hodder and Stoughton).

Pearsall, R. (1973) *Victorian Popular Music* (Newton Abbot, David and Charles).

Pearsall, R. (1975) *Edwardian Popular Music* (London, David and Charles).

Pearsall, R. (1976) *Popular Music of the Twenties* (Newton Abbot, David and Charles).

Pegg, M. (1983) *Broadcasting and Society* (London, Croom Helm).

Pernet, R. and Rye, H. (n.d.) Visiting Firemen 18: Louis Mitchell in *Storyville* (1998-99 volume), pp. 221-48.

Perry, G. (1993) 'Primitivism and the "Modern"' in Perry, G., Frascina, F. and Harrison, C. (1993) *Primitivism, Cubism, Abstraction: The Early Twentieth Century* (New Haven, Yale University Press).

Petters, J. (1984) 'Jazz Drumming from New Orleans to Bebop' in *Jazz Journal International*, 37 (11) November 1984, pp. 6-8.

Pickering, M. (1986) 'White Skin, Black Masks: "Nigger" minstrelsy in Victorian Britain' in Bratton, J.S. (ed.) *Music Hall: Performance and Style* (Milton Keynes, Open University Press).

Pickering, M. (1997) 'John Bull in Blackface' in *Popular Music* 16 (2), pp. 181-202.

Pickering, M. (2001) *Stereotyping: The Politics of Representation* (Hampshire and New York, Palgrave).

Pleasants, H. (1961) *Death of a Music?* (London, Victor Gollancz).

Pleasants, H. (1969) *Serious Music – And All That Jazz* (London, Victor Gollancz).

Potter, P. (1998) *Most German of the Arts: Musicology and Society from the Weimar Republic to the End of Hitler's Reich* (New Haven, Yale University Press).

Porter, L. and Ullman, M. (1988) Sidney Bechet and his Long Song in *The Black Perspective in Music*, Fall 1988, pp. 135-50.

Powell, R. J. (1998) *Black Art and Culture in the 20th Century* (London, Thames and Hudson).

Radano, R. and Bohlman, P. (eds) (2000) *Music and the Racial Imagination* (Chicago, University of Chicago Press).

Raeburn, B.B. (1991) 'Jazz and the Italian Connection' in *The Jazz Archivist*, 6 (1) May 1991, pp. 1-5 (Hogan Jazz Archive).

Raeburn, B.B. (1997) 'Celebrating Sidney Bechet' in *Gambit Weekly*, 18 February 1997, pp. 15-17.

Ramsey, F. and Smith, C.E. (1939) *Jazzmen: The Story of Hot Jazz Told in the Lives of the Men Who Created It* (New York, Harcourt Brace Jovanovich).

Rayno, D. (2003) *Paul Whiteman: Pioneer in American Music Volume 1:1890-1930 (Studies in Jazz No. 43)* (Maryland and Oxford, Scarecrow).

Read, D. (1979) *The Age of Urban Democracy: England 1868-1914* (London, Longman).

Read, O. and Welch, W. (1994) *From Tin Foil to Stereo: Evolution of the Phonograph* (New York, Sams).

Reith, J.C.W. (1924) *Broadcast over Britain* (London, Hodder and Stoughton).

Reynolds, H. (1927) *Minstrel Memories: The Story of Burnt Cork Minstrels in Great Britain 1836-1927* (London, Alston Rivers).

Rhodes, Chip (1998) *Structures of the Jazz Age: Mass Culture, Progressive Education and Racial Disclosures in American Modernism* (London, Verso).

Rhodes, Colin (1994) *Primitivism and Modern Art* (London, Thames and Hudson).

Riis, T. (1989) *Just before Jazz: Black Musical Theater in New York, 1890-1915* (Washington, Smithsonian Institution).

Riis, T. (1996) *The Music and Scripts of 'In Dahomey'* (Recent Researches in American Music: vol. 25/ Music of the United States of America: vol. 5) (Madison, AR Editions).

Robinson, J.B. (1994) 'Jazz reception in Weimar Germany: in search of a shimmy figure' in Gilliam, B. (ed.) (1994) *Music and performance during the Weimar Republic* (Cambridge, Cambridge University Press).

Rollini, A. (1987) *Thirty Years with the Big Bands* (Hampshire and London, Macmillan).

Rose, A. (1981) *Notes on Sam Wooding* in 'Wooding' file in HJA.

Ross, L. (2003) *African-American Jazz Musicians in the Diaspora* (Lewiston, the Edwin Mellen Press).

Rouse, D. (1989) 'Musicians from D.C.: the Bohee Brothers' in *Tailgate Ramblings*, 19 (12) December 1989.

Russell, D. (1987) *Popular Music in England 1840-1915: A Social History* (Manchester, Manchester University Press).

Rust, B. (1967) Grateful for the Warning in *Storyville*, 9, pp. 24-28.

Rust, B. (1972) *The Dance Bands* (London, Ian Allen).

Rye, H. (trans.) (1978) 'The Bertin Depestre Salnave Musical Story' as told to Bertrand Demeusy in *Storyville*, 78, pp. 207-19.

Rye, H. (1980a) 'Visiting Firemen 1: Duke Ellington' in *Storyville*, 88, pp. 128-30.

Rye, H. (1980b) 'Visiting Firemen 2: Louis Armstrong' in *Storyville*, 89, pp. 184-7.

Rye, H. (1980c) 'Visiting Firemen 3: Cab Calloway and his Cotton Club Orchestra' in *Storyville*, 90, pp. 30-31.

Rye, H. (1983a) 'Visiting Firemen 7: Noble Sissle and Eubie Blake' in *Storyville*, 105, pp. 88-105.

Rye, H. (1983b) 'Visiting Firemen 8: Leon Abbey and his orchestra' in *Storyville*, 108, pp. 207-12.

Rye, H. (1984a) 'Visiting Firemen 9: The Blackbirds and their Orchestras' in *Storyville*, 112, pp. 133-47.

Rye, H. (1984b) 'Additional information to Previous Visiting Firemen Installments' in *Storyville*, 114, pp. 216-17.

Rye, H. (1986) 'The Southern Syncopated Orchestra' in Lotz/Pegg (eds) *Under the Imperial Carpet: Essays in Black History 1780-1950* (Crawley, Sussex, Rabbit Press).

Rye, H. (1988a) 'Visiting Fireboys: The Jenkins Orphanage Bands in Britain' in *Storyville*, 130, pp. 137-43.

Rye, H. (1988b) 'Visiting Firemen 13: The Plantation Revues' in *Storyville*, 133, pp. 4-15.

Rye, H. (1988c) 'Visiting Firemen 14: Joe Jordan 1915' in *Storyville*, 134, pp. 55-8.

Rye, H. (1990a) 'Fearsome Means of Discord: Early Encounters with Black Jazz' in Oliver, P. (ed.) (1990) *Black Music in Britain* (Milton Keynes, Open University Press).

Rye, H. (1990b) 'The Southern Syncopated Orchestra' in *Storyville*, 142, pp. 137-46; 143, pp. 165-78; 144, pp. 227-34.

Rye, H. (1997) 'Visiting Firemen: Additional Information to Previous Installments' in *Storyville*, (1996-97 volume), pp. 28-29.

Rye, H. and Brooks, T. (1997) 'Visiting Firemen 16: Dan Kildare' in *Storyville*, (1996-97 volume), pp. 30-57.

Rye, H. (1999) 'Visiting Fireman: Additional Information to Previous Installments' in *Storyville*, (1998-99 volume), pp. 127-28.

Sanjek, R. (1988) *American Popular Music and Its Business* (New York, Oxford University Press).

Said, E. (1978/R1991) *Orientalism: Western Conceptions of the Orient* (London, Penguin).

Salter, I. (1973) 'The Strange Career of Fred Elizalde' in *Memory Lane* 5 (4), pp. 11-13.

Sampson, H.T. (1980) *Blacks in Blackface: A Source Book on Early Black Musical Shows* (Metuchen, Scarecrow Press).

Seroff, D. (1986) 'The Fisk Jubilee Singers' in Lotz/Pegg (eds) *Under the Imperial Carpet: Essays in Black History 1780-1950* (Crawley, Sussex, Rabbit Press).

Schafer, W.J. (1976) 'The Transition: Ragtime into Jazz' in *The Mississippi Rag*, 3 (10) August 1976.

Schiff, D. (1997) *Gershwin: Rhapsody in Blue* (Cambridge, Cambridge University Press).

Schönherr, U. (1991) 'Adorno and Jazz: Reflections on a Failed Encounter' in *Telos*, 87, pp. 85-97.

Schreyer, L.H. (1985) 'The Banjo in Ragtime' in Hasse, J.H. (ed.) (1985) *Ragtime: Its History, Composers and Music* (London, Macmillan).

Schreyer, L.H. (1993) 'The Banjo in Phonograph Recording History' in Heier, U and Lotz, R.E. (1993) *The Banjo on Record- A Bio-Discography* (Connecticut, Greenwood Press).

Schuller, G. (1968, R1986) *Early Jazz: Its Roots and Musical Development* (New York, Oxford University Press).

Schuller, G. (1989) *The Swing Era: The Development of Jazz 1930-1945* (New York, Oxford University Press).

Schuller, V. (1944) 'From Dixieland to Reisenweber's' in *Jazz Tempo*, 17, p. 20.

Scholes, P. (1947) *The Mirror of Music* (1844-1944) (London, Novello & Co. & Oxford University Press).

Scott, D.B. (2003) *From the Erotic to the Demonic: On Critical Musicology* (Oxford, Oxford University Press).

Scott, D.B. (1998) 'Orientalism and Musical Style' in *Musical Quarterly*, 82 (2), pp. 309-35.

Scott, D.B. (1989/R2001) *The Singing Bourgeois: Songs of the Victorian Drawing Room and Parlour* (Aldershot, Ashgate).

Shapiro, N. and Hentoff, N. (1955) *Hear Me Talkin' To Ya: The Story of Jazz Told By the Men Who Made It* (New York, Dover).

Sherwood, M. (2003) 'White Myths, Black Omissions: the Historical Origins of Racism in Britain' in *International Journal of Historical Learning, Teaching and Research*, 3 (1) (http://www.ex.ac.uk/historyresource/journal5/journalstart.htm).

Sidran, B. (1981) *Black Talk* (New York, Da Capo).

Small, C. (1987) *Music of the Common Tongue: Survival and Celebration in Afro-American Music* (London, Calder).

Southern, E. (1971) *The Music of the Black Americans: A History* (New York, Norton).

Southern, E. (ed.) (1978) 'In Retrospect: Black-Music Concerts in Carnegie Hall, 1912-1915' in *Black Perspective in Music*, 6 (1) Spring 1978, pp. 71-88.

Southern, E. (ed.) (1983) *Readings in Black American Music* (New York, Norton).

Spencer, N. (1921) 'Tales of the Syncopated Orchestra' in *Dancing Times*, February 1921, pp. 409-11.

Squibb, F. (1963) 'Review of The ODJB in England' in *Jazz*, 2 (3) March 1963, pp.16-17.

Stowe, D.W. (1994) *Swing Changes: Big Band Jazz in New-Deal America* (Cambridge, Harvard).

Stanbridge, A. (2004) 'Burns, Baby, Burns: Jazz History as a Contested Cultural Site' in *The Source: Challenging Jazz Criticism*, 1, pp. 81-99.

Stannard, M. (1986) *Evelyn Waugh: The Early Years 1903-1939* (London, J.M. Dent and Sons).

Stearns, M.W. (1956) *The Story of Jazz* (New York, Oxford University Press).

Stearns, M. and J. (1966) 'Williams and Walker and the Beginnings of Vernacular Dance on Broadway' in *Keystone Folklore Quarterly*, Spring 1966, pp. 3-12.

Stearns, M. and J. (1968) *Jazz Dance: the Story of American Vernacular Dance* (New York, Schirmer).

Steele, V. (1985) *Fashion and Eroticism: Ideals of Feminine Beauty from the Victorian Era to the Jazz Age* (New York, Oxford University Press).

Stevenson, J. (1984) *British Society 1914-45* (London, Penguin).

Sudhalter, R.M. (1999) *Lost Chords: White Musicians and their Contribution to Jazz, 1915-1945* (New York, Oxford University Press).

Tanner, P. (1971a) 'Stompin' at the Savoy with Fred Elizalde' in *Jazz Monthly*, 191, pp. 26-30.

Tanner, P. (1971b) 'In Defence of Elizalde' in *Storyville*, 36, pp. 216-18.

Tanner, P (1981) 'Spike: A Study of Spike Hughes's Excursion into Jazz, 1930-33' in *Memory Lane*, 13 (50), pp. 11-15; Part Two 13 (51), pp. 9-11; Final Installment, 13 (52), pp. 28-30.

Terry, R. (1934) *Voodooism in Music* (London, Burns Oates and Washbourne).

Thompson, K.C. (1954) 'Notes on the Banjo: Jazz's No. 1 Instrument' in *Second Line*, 5 (3-4) March-April, pp. 3-6.

Titterton, W.R. (1912) *From Theatre to Music Hall* (London, Stephen Swift).

Tipping, B. (1930) 'Looking Back' in *Rhythm*, April 1930, pp. 18-20; May 1930, pp. 26-28; June 1930, pp. 16-18; November 1930, p. 57.

Toll, R. C. (1974) *Blacking up: the Minstrel Show in Nineteenth Century America* (New York, Oxford University Press).

Tonks, E. (1944) Makers of Jazz in *Jazz Tempo*, 17, pp. 22-3.

Tracy, S. (1995) *Bands, Booze and Broads* (Edinburgh, Mainstream).

Tracy, S. (1997) *Talking Swing: The British Big Bands* (Edinburgh, Mainstream).

Tucker, Mark (ed.) (1993) *The Duke Ellington Reader* (New York, Oxford University Press).

Ulanov, B. (1946) *Duke Ellington* (London, Musicians Press).

Van Der Merwe, P. (1989) *Origins of the Popular Style: The Antecedents of Twentieth-Century Popular Music* (Oxford, Clarendon Press).

Vincent, J. (1997) The Banjo in *Jazz* Journal, 30 (3), p. 20.

Vincent, T. (1995) *Keep Cool – The Black Activists Who Built the Jazz Age* (London, Pluto Press).

Virgets, R. (1989) 'Nick LaRocca: The Forgotten Legend of Jazz' in *Gambit*, 25 April 1989, pp. 15-17.

Walker, E.S. (1971) 'Fred Elizalde' in *Storyville*, 33, pp. 92-6.

Walker, E.S. (1972) 'The Southern Syncopated Orchestra' in *Storyville*, 42, pp. 204-08.

Walker, E.S. (1977) 'The Red Devils and Sidney Bechet in England' in *Storyville*, 76, pp. 136-8.

Walker, E.S. (1978) *Don't Jazz, it's Music: Some Notes on Popular Syncopated Music in England during the Twentieth Century* (Walsall, the author).

Walker, E.S. (1980) 'The Spread of Ragtime in England' in *Storyville*, 88, pp. 123-27.

Walker, S. and Walker, C. (1984) *Light Blue Rhythm: The Story of the Cambridge University Dance Bands* (no publisher, contained in NJA).

Walsh, J. (1950) 'Favorite Pioneer Recording Artists: Bert Williams, A Thwarted Genius' in *Hobbies*, September 1950, pp. 23-25, 36; November 1950, p. 21.

Walvin, J. (1973) *Black and White: the Negro in English Society 1855-1945* (London, Allen Lane).

Ward, M. and N. (1978) *Home in the Twenties and Thirties* (London, Ian Allen).

Warner, R. (1977) 'On Banjos and Guitars' in *Storyville*, 73, p. 31.

Waugh, E. (1928/R2003) *Decline and Fall* (London, Penguin).

Waugh, E. (1930/R2003) *Vile Bodies* (London, Penguin).

Way, C. (1991) *The Big Bands go to War* (Edinburgh, Mainstream).

Weightman, J. (1973) *The Concept of the Avant Garde* (London, Alcove Press).

Whitcomb, I. (1972) *After the Ball: Pop Music from Rag to Rock* (London, Allan Lane).

White, M. (1958) 'How Come You Do Me Like You Do? (Jazz in Britain – the Beginnings)' in Gammond, P. (ed.) *The Decca Book of Jazz* (London, Fredrick Muller).

Whiteman, P. (1948) *Memories in Wax: Records for the Millions*, (http://www.shellac.org/wams/wpaulw1.html).

Wilcock, E. (1996) 'Adorno, Jazz and Racism: "Uber Jazz" and the 1934-37 British Jazz Debate' in *Telos: A Quarterly Journal of Critical* Thought, 107, Spring 1996, pp. 63-80.

Wilcox, B. (1987) 'Way up West Again: A Trip through the Nostalgic Years and Places' in *Memory Lane*, 75, Summer 1987, pp. 31-5; 76, Autumn 1987, pp. 36-9; 77, Winter 1987-88, pp. 22-4; 79, Summer 1988, pp. 36-8.

Wilford, C. (c. 1945) *What is Ragtime/Presenting Billy Jones* (in NJA 'Jones' file).

Witkin, R. (1998/R2000) *Adorno on Music* (London, Routledge).

Wooding, S. (1939) 'Eight Years Abroad with a Jazz Band' in *The Etude*, April 1939, pp. 233-4.

Woolf, V. (1977) *The Diary of Virginia Woolf* (London, Hogarth Press).

Zammarchi, F. (1997) 'The Triumph of a New Orleans Artist in Europe' in *Louisiana Endowment for the Humanities*, Spring 1997, pp. 34-43.

Discography

Emile Berliner's Gramophone: The Earliest Discs 1888-1901 Symposium 1058.

Black British Swing: the African Diaspora's Contribution to England's Own Jazz of the 1930s and 1940s Topic Records TSCD781.

Cylinder Jazz: Early Jazz and Ragtime Recordings from 1897-1928 Saydisc SDL 112.

The Earliest Black String Bands Volume 1: Dan Kildare Document Records, Austria DOCD5622 (sleeve notes by Rainer Lotz).

The Earliest Black String Bands Volume 2: The Versatile Four Document Records, Austria DOCD5623 (sleeve notes by Rainer Lotz).

The Earliest Black String Bands Volume 3: The Versatile Three/Four, 1919-20 Document Records, Austria DOCD5624 (sleeve notes by Rainer Lotz).

Fred Elizalde and His Anglo American Band Retrieval RTR 79011.

Duke Ellington and His Orchestra 1933 Classics 637.

Bert Firman and His Orchestra: Swing High Swing Low CD AJA 5407.

The Bert Firman Bands 1926-27 MELLO 0006.

The Goofus Five Timeless CBC 1-017 JAZZ.

The Greatest British Dance Bands Pulse/Castle Communications PBX CD 422.

Spike Hughes and His All American Orchestra Ace of Clubs ACL 1153.

Jack Hylton and his Orchestra 'Hot Hylton' 1926-1930 Retrieval RTR 79024.

Jazz in Britain: the 1920s Parlophone PMC 7075.

Jazz Century 5: The First Recording Bands Off-air recording of Radio 3 broadcast, 1999.

Light Music at the Savoy: the 1920s Flapper, Past 701.

Murray Pilcer and His Jazz Band: Wild, Wild Women and *K-K-K- Katy* [National Sound Archive NP5915W].

The ODJB in England 1919 Columbia 33S 1087 (sleeve notes by Brian Rust).

The ODJB in England 1919/20 Columbia 33S 1133 (sleeve notes by Brian Rust).

Oh What a Lovely War! World Record Club SH130.

The Piccadilly Players 1928 (Vol. 1) MELLO 010.

Ragtime, Cakewalks and Stomps Vol. 2: 1898-1917 'I'll Dance Till the Sun Breaks Through' Saydisc SDL 210.

Ragtime, Cakewalks and Stomps Vol. 4: 1900-1917 'Rusty Rags' Saydisc SDL 253.

The Rhythmic Eight 1927-28 Vol. 1 MELLO 0004.
Paul Whiteman 'The King of Jazz': His Greatest Recordings 1920-1936 ASV CD AJA
  5170.
The Young Nat Gonella 1930-1936 Retrieval RTR 79022.

Index